Understanding Growth and Poverty

Understanding Growth and Poverty

Theory, Policy, and Empirics

Raj Nallari and Breda Griffith

THE WORLD BANK
Washington, D.C.

ISBN: 978-0-8213-6953-1
eISBN: 978-0-8213-6954-8
DOI: 10.1596/978-0-8213-6953-1

Library of Congress Cataloging-in-Publication Data

Nallari, Raj, 1955-
  Understanding growth and poverty : theory, policy, and empirics / Raj Nallari, Breda Griffith.
    p. cm.
  Includes bibliographical references and index.
  ISBN 978-0-8213-6953-1 — ISBN 978-0-8213-6954-8 (electronic)
  1. Poverty. 2. Economic development. 3. Development economics. I. Griffith, Breda.
II. World Bank. III. Title.
  HC79.P6N35 2011
  339.4'6—dc22

                                                                                    2010044914

Cover photograph: Michael Foley/The World Bank
Cover design: Naylor Design

Contents

Tables

Preface

This volume is an introduction to the theories and policies that affect economic growth and poverty. It is a compilation of lecture notes used in face-to-face and e-learning courses presented by the World Bank Institute's (WBI) Poverty Program during 2004–08. The Poverty Program is one of WBI's core learning programs. The discussion is less technical than others, and the intended audience includes policy makers, policy analysts, and representatives of donor agencies and civil society organizations.

The volume is divided into three parts. Part I discusses basic concepts and measurement issues pertaining to poverty, national income, and economic growth. Part II deals with the macroeconomic policies that are critical for economic growth in the short term. It covers government-enforced fiscal and exchange-rate policies and the roles of financial institutions, development assistance (or aid), debt relief, and trade policies. Part III covers the structural and sectoral policies that affect longer-term economic growth and poverty reduction. To underscore the impact of good governance and effective service delivery in growth and poverty reduction, separate chapters are devoted to institutional and technological development, education, health, labor, and land. Newer growth issues—urbanization, regulation, infrastructure, the informal economy, the political economy of policy making, volatility, and the globalization of financial flows—are also discussed. So-called natural capital and climate change are introduced and linked to growth.

The volume ends with a chapter that summarizes our knowledge of growth theory, reviews the process of growth in 13 successful countries, and draws out implications for other developing countries. We hope that this chapter may be of help to policy makers in identifying the constraints to economic growth and development that may be unique to each country.

Throughout, attempts have been made to bring together theoretical discussions with empirical evidence to give readers a clearer picture of the impact of economic policies on growth and poverty reduction.

The lecture notes that underpin this volume were prepared under the guidance of Roumeen Islam. Research assistance from Indira Iyer and Oliver Rajakaruna and the financial support of the government of Japan are greatly appreciated.

Abbreviations

ADF	African Development Fund
AE	adult equivalent
AfDB	African Development Bank
AfDF	African Development Fund
AIDS	acquired immune deficiency syndrome
BMGF	Bill and Melinda Gates Foundation
C	consumption
CarDB	Caribbean Development Bank
CAMELS	capital adequacy, asset quality, management soundness, earnings and profitability, liquidity, and sensitivity to market risk
CAB	current-account balance
CBN	cost-of-basic-needs
CE	Council of Europe
CEPR	Centre for Economic Policy Research
CIS	Commonwealth of Independent States
CMH	Commission on Macroeconomics and Health
CPI	consumer price index
DAC	Development Assistance Committee
DAH	development assistance for health

EBRD	European Bank for Reconstruction and Development
EC	European Commission
ECA	export credit agency
EFA	Education for All
ESAF	Enhanced Structural Adjustment Facility, IMF
EU	European Union
FDI	foreign direct investment
FEI	food-energy intake
FTI	Fast-Track Initiative
G-3	Group of Three
G-7	Group of Seven
G-8	Group of Eight
GAVI	The Global Alliance for Vaccines and Immunisations
GDP	gross domestic product
GEF	Global Environment Facility
GEM	Global Entrepreneurship Monitor
GER	gross enrollment rate
GF	Global Fund
GFATM	Global Fund for AIDS, TB, and Malaria
GHG	greenhouse gas
GNDI	gross national disposable income
GNI	gross national income
GNP	gross national product
HBS	household budget survey
HDI	Human Development Index
HIPC	Heavily Indebted Poor Countries (Initiative)
HIV	human immunodeficiency virus
I	investment
IAEA	International Atomic Energy Agency
IBRD	International Bank for Reconstruction and Development
ICT	information and communication technology
IDA	International Development Association
IDB	Inter-American Development Bank
IDP	internally displaced persons
IFAD	International Fund for Agricultural Development
IFC	International Finance Corporation

IFI	international financial institution
IFMC	International Monetary and Financial Committee
ILO	International Labour Organization
IMF	International Monetary Fund
LSMS	Living Standards Measurement Study
M	imports
MDGs	Millennium Development Goals
MDRI	Multilateral Debt Relief Initiative
MFI	microfinance institution
NDP	net domestic product
NER	net primary enrollment rate
NGO	nongovernmental organization
NPV	net present value
ODA	official development assistance
OECD	Organisation for Economic Co-operation and Development
OLS	ordinary least squares
PCR	primary completion rate
PEPFAR/ Emergency Plan	President's Emergency Plan for AIDS Relief
PFM	public financial management (system)
PIU	project implementation unit
PPP	purchasing power parity
PRGF	Poverty Reduction and Growth Facility, IMF
PRSP	Poverty Reduction Strategy Paper
R&D	research and development
SAF	Structural Adjustment Facility, IMF
SAR	Special Administrative Region
SEEA	System of Integrated Environmental and Economic Accounting
TB	tuberculosis
TFP	total factor productivity
TI	Transparency International
UN	United Nations
UNAIDS	Joint United Nations Programme on HIV/AIDS
UNDP	United Nations Development Programme
UNECE	United Nations Economic Commission for Europe
UNESCO	United Nations Education, Scientific and Cultural Organization

UNFCCC	United Nations Framework Convention on Climate Change
UNFPA	United Nations Population Fund
UNHCR	United Nations Refugee Agency
UNICEF	United Nations Children's Fund
UNRWA	United Nations Relief and Works Agency for Palestine Refugees in the Near East
UNTA	United Nations Transitional Authority
UPE	universal primary education
VA	value added
VAT	value added tax
VSL	value of a statistical life
WBI	World Bank Institute
WDI	World Development Indicators
WEF	World Economic Forum
WFP	United Nations World Food Programme
WHO	World Health Organization
WPI	wholesale price index
X	exports

All dollar amounts are U.S. dollars unless otherwise indicated.

Introduction

The story of growth and poverty reduction in our changing world is much debated. A half-century ago, the challenge was to lift low-income countries from the trap of self-perpetuating low growth to a path of higher growth. Today, many economies in the developing world are growing quickly, but more than 100 countries remain mired in conditions of low growth and high poverty.

Between 1960 and 2008, three major shifts affected our thinking about growth and poverty. These big shifts were (a) from the "commanding heights" of state-directed development to market-driven approaches; (b) from structural concerns with deregulation, liberalization, and privatization to a new view of the sectoral sources of growth, particularly agriculture and financial services; and (c) from macroeconomic approaches to growth to microeconomic (and now macro–micro) ones. Somewhere along the way, the recognition grew that poverty reduction was a goal in itself and need not depend on how fast or slow a country was growing. It was also recognized that, by riding the wave of globalization that swept the world beginning two decades ago, countries could grow very quickly indeed and lift millions out of poverty—China is the prime example. But the global economic crisis that reached a crescendo in 2008 threatens now to undo those gains. More shifts in thinking may be required.

In the 1960s, the conventional wisdom in economics was that investment in physical capital would lead to growth and that, as long as there was growth, the benefits would trickle down to the poor. Import substitution policies were in vogue at the time. The importance of the private sector was acknowledged, and the International Finance Corporation (IFC)—the private sector arm of the World Bank—was set up in 1956. In the early 1970s, when the trickle had failed to materialize, a new mantra emerged. "Redistribution with growth" emphasized the basic needs of the bottom 40 percent of the population. Pro-poor policies for managing education, health, water, and demographics were deemed important. But the oil shocks of 1973 and 1979–80, as well as the accompanying commodity price shocks (for example, in sugar and copper), riveted the attention of economists and policy makers on ways to achieve macroeconomic stability by reducing domestic demand, curbing inflation, and improving the balance between the internal and external economies. Moreover, lending under the International Monetary Fund's (IMF) structural adjustment facility, introduced in 1986, required loan recipients to agree to a macroeconomic program, underscoring the importance of a country's macropolicy environment. Concerns about getting prices right led to the deregulation of prices, the liberalization of trade and agriculture, and the privatization of public enterprises, along with a paring down of the role of the state. As the East Asian economies grew rapidly in the 1980s, with a spectacular record of exports, and as growth reduced poverty in those countries, export-led growth became the new rallying cry. China's rapid growth and its success in lifting millions of Chinese out of poverty appeared to confirm the benefits of open economies and free trade. But with the collapse of the Soviet bloc and its command economies, the key role of institutions that support the functioning of markets became plainly apparent, as policy makers in the Russian Federation, Central and Eastern Europe, and Central Asia struggled to make the transition from centrally planned economies to market-based ones. Economists developed a new appreciation for the role of property rights, the rule of law, and other institutions in sustaining growth and ensuring equity.

A surge in the globalization of goods, services, capital, and labor after the East Asian crisis of 1997–98 ushered in a period of remarkable growth in the developing world, but that long run ended abruptly with the arrival of the global crisis of 2007–09, which now threatens the gains made since the 1990s.

How that crisis will shape our view of the road to growth is not yet clear. But it is our hope that the half-century of accumulated experience reported in this volume will influence economists and policy makers, enabling them to make choices that are well informed by the knowledge of what has gone before.

Our overarching aim is to give the reader a broad understanding of the impact of economic policies on growth and poverty reduction in developing countries. After describing basic economic relationships that summarize the workings and the measurement of the macroeconomy—and after confirming that growth is the most critical factor in alleviating poverty—we turn to individual policy areas. These include the various roles of government, among them setting fiscal policy and maintaining an environment conducive to the effective operation of a market economy. Policies governing money supply, exchange rates, and the financial sector are also covered.

After assessing several decades of experience with development assistance, the aim of which has been to place poor countries on a path of sustainable long-run growth, our study turns to a discussion of external debt. In the 1980s and 1990s, debt contracted by low-income countries from commercial and official sources became unsustainable, crippling their growth, keeping millions in poverty, and forcing an international reappraisal of lending policies, the centerpiece of which was a set of debt-forgiveness policies that was put forward with the launch of the Jubilee 2000 debt relief campaign. The remainder of the volume examines problems that can keep the poor from moving out of poverty. Trade, institutional development, regulation, education, health, labor markets, land and agriculture, natural resources, urbanization, technology, and politics—all are core components of public policy and need to be handled correctly if poverty is to be addressed effectively. Because many developing countries lack the capacity to mobilize resources—administrative and financial— to move the poor out of poverty, the international community must be actively involved.

The first step in understanding the policies needed to reduce poverty in developing countries is to analyze poverty data. This requires an aggregate measure of poverty, a difficult task and the subject of chapter 1. While nonmonetary aspects of poverty (such as access to services) are critical, monetary aspects lend themselves more easily to measurement. Fairly narrow indicators of welfare based on individual household consumption are generally used. These are then compared with a minimum standard of those indicators, known as the poverty line. From that comparison, summary statistics are computed to provide an overall measure of poverty in a given country.

The second step is understanding the key relationships among the various economic agents in an economy. Macroeconomics is the branch of economics that studies those relationships in the context of the national economy. Three approaches, described in depth in chapter 2, are used to measure aggregate economic activity: production, expenditure, and income. With the tools of the first two chapters, we are equipped to analyze the important questions of how various policies influence poverty in developing countries.

Turning from theory to real-world findings in chapter 3, we find that sustained economic growth is the most critical factor in alleviating poverty. That said, there are differences across countries in how poverty responds to growth. The initial level of income inequality and changes in inequality over time play an important role here, as do growth patterns and stages of economic development. These differences have led to a focus on pro-poor growth, defined as the variants of the growth process that are most effective in raising the incomes of the poor. As discussed in the chapter, assessing whether growth is pro-poor requires detailed information on changes in income and its distribution—and the extent to which those changes improve the welfare of the poor.

Focusing next on specific areas of public policy, we describe the roles that governments can play in an economy. Chapter 4 explores how governments can create conditions that are conducive to the effective operation of a market economy. These include establishing a sound legal and social framework, providing public goods (such as roads), regulating economic activity, redistributing wealth, and stabilizing the economy. The chapter then examines fiscal policies, treating expenditure and taxation policies in turn, before looking at the impact of fiscal policy on the business cycle, private investment, and inflation. The chapter concludes by investigating the ways fiscal policy can benefit the poor, primarily through government expenditure.

Monetary and exchange-rate policies also play an important role in the economy. After examining the nuts and bolts of monetary policy, chapter 5 explores the different forms, causes, and measures of inflation. We show that although a loose monetary policy can help the economy in the short run, it usually results in high and volatile inflation, the costs of which are typically borne most heavily by the poor. We also show that low inflation is good for long-term growth and for poverty reduction. Various exchange-rate policies are then examined, ranging from formal dollarization to free-floating exchange-rate regimes. The choice of regime depends on a country's characteristics, including its inflation performance, monetary credibility, trading patterns, and vulnerability to external shocks.

The causal link between a well-functioning financial system and economic growth, as described in chapter 6, has been firmly established. The converse also holds: poor macroeconomic fundamentals, including imbalanced growth and high inflation, can hinder development of the financial system. While the link between financial development and income inequality remains less clear, recent empirical studies have found that financial development tends to reduce income inequality. Where financial markets remain underdeveloped, policy measures are needed to widen access of the poor to financial services—by strengthening institutional infrastructures, liberalizing markets, and fostering greater competition. We describe how developing countries have progressively liberalized their financial systems in recent decades, freeing interest rates, improving legal and supervisory frameworks, and increasing transparency. The increasingly important role played by microfinance and emigrants' remittances is the final topic of the chapter.

Is development assistance effective in spurring growth and reducing poverty? Because the record is mixed, the scaling up of aid poses a daunting policy challenge for both developing countries and donors. For an understanding of how future aid flows might best be used, chapter 7 examines the international aid record from the 1950s to the present, comparing trends in both official and private capital flows to developing countries. Private flows have swelled in recent decades, while official aid dipped in the mid-1990s and began to recover only in 2005 before being imperiled again by the global economic crisis.

If the Millennium Development Goals (MDGs) promulgated by the United Nations in 2000 are to come close to being met, it is important not only that aid be increased but also that it be made more effective. While the vast literature on the efficacy of aid is inconclusive, a key finding, one picked up by policy makers, is that aid works best in good policy environments. Recent literature also suggests that the type of aid matters—that is, not all aid should be aimed at achieving higher growth. Chapter 7 also includes a discussion of the so-called Dutch disease, which can affect a country's competitiveness by causing its currency to appreciate as aid is scaled up. Recent research suggests that, generally, aid should be spent by the government over the long run, with the liquidity impact managed by the sale of foreign exchange by the central bank. This, of course, requires good coordination of fiscal and monetary policies.

In parallel with increases in development assistance, developing countries' debts have been forgiven to free up funds for high-priority purposes and to avoid the negative outcomes associated with chronic debt "overhangs." According to the debt-overhang theory, which appears to be borne out by the empirical evidence discussed in chapter 8, debt lowers growth by curtailing investment and social spending, thereby reducing the potential for poverty reduction. We then turn to a discussion of the unsustainable debt burden experienced by low-income countries beginning in the 1980s and the response of the international financial community. The chapter describes debt-relief programs, beginning with the first nonconcessional arrangements of the 1980s and continuing through to the Heavily Indebted Poor Countries (HIPC) Initiative and the most recent Multilateral Debt Relief Initiative (MDRI) under which the debt burdens of the poorest developing countries have been written off in their entirety. The chapter ends with a discussion of the relative merits of development assistance and debt relief in the context of growth for developing countries.

In chapter 9, we investigate how developing countries (except those in Sub-Saharan Africa) have opened their economies to trade in recent decades. During the same period, flows of foreign direct investment to developing countries have intensified. Although the relationship between openness and inequality is inconclusive, the evidence suggests that trade is good for growth and that growth, in turn, is good for the poor. But to work best, the policies that a country uses to open itself to trade must be properly sequenced and coordinated. Domestic policies aside, advanced countries have the power to greatly increase the benefits of agricultural trade to the developing world. They could do so by reducing the subsidies they provide to their farmers, which make it nearly impossible for developing-country producers to compete in important global agricultural markets. The monetary value of such subsidies dwarfs the aid provided to poor countries.

The role of institutions and technology in promoting or discouraging growth is examined in chapter 10. Institutions are much more than buildings and organizations. They include the informal rules and norms that govern personal and social behavior, as well as the formal rules and norms that provide the predictability needed for societies to function. We focus on institutional quality, property rights, and governance. Governance is a multifaceted concept that encompasses citizens' voices and government accountability, political stability, government effectiveness, regulatory quality, the rule of law, and corruption. The empirical literature clearly shows that institutions matter greatly for economic growth. Far less is known about how to develop high-quality institutions that are appropriate for a given country's stage of development.

Likewise, technological development has been shown to increase economic growth, but debate abounds on whether it is endogenous (internal) or exogenous (external) technological change that drives the growth process. It is well documented, however, that latecomers can leapfrog across several stages of development and that the channels of technology diffusion are many.

Turning in chapter 11 to public policy in developing countries, we first examine the role of education in the lives of the poor and its implications for economic growth and poverty reduction. The chapter begins by noting the positive impact of education in stimulating economic growth and combating poverty, a benefit emphatically confirmed in empirical literature. Although major progress has been made in recent decades to improve access to education in developing countries, a proper education remains out of reach for many of the world's poor, particularly in Africa. Gender inequality is also a particularly severe problem in education, with girls receiving less education than boys. A number of global initiatives have accorded high priority to improving education in developing countries. One of the MDGs, for example, is to achieve universal primary completion by 2015. While some poorer regions appear on track to achieve that goal, this is not true for most countries in Africa, the Middle East, and South Asia. Many countries in these regions are not in a position to mobilize the resources needed to provide even universal primary education. We conclude the chapter by noting that, although the amount of aid devoted to education has increased in recent years, it still falls far short of what is needed.

Basic health care is also critical for economic progress, yet for many of the world's poor this basic right remains out of reach. The disparity in health indicators across countries is still very wide. Developing countries' health records—and the responses of the international donor community—are the subject of chapter 12. Corruption, mismanagement, weak administrations, and a shallow pool of financial resources make it difficult to stop diseases that are easily prevented in better environments. At the same time, the widely acknowledged human and economic costs of poor health care in the developing world are being tackled at the international level. Health reforms adopted under national poverty-reduction strategies are being supported by donors, even as other forms of development assistance are scaled back. But even greater financial assistance is needed.

The labor market is one of the main conduits through which economic growth can reduce poverty. Chapter 13 examines labor markets in developing countries. Countries in which the labor force is large or growing quickly often choose a pattern of economic growth that provides jobs. This is understandable, as employment is the surest way out of poverty. But the cost of labor-friendly economic growth often results in low labor productivity; thus, labor-friendly growth can become self-limiting. That said, because the labor force is growing quickly in many developing countries, often accompanied by a shift away from agricultural employment, some form of labor-friendly growth may be called for if an increase in unemployment or an increase in so-called informal employment is to be avoided. Other labor concerns highlighted in the chapter are unequal wages and marked differences in access between men and women to the labor market.

Access to and ownership of land are particularly important for helping the poor move out of poverty. Owners of land have a greater incentive than nonowners to make their land more productive, and land can be used as collateral to raise funds for investment in greater productivity. Chapter 14 examines constraints on access to and ownership of land in developing countries. It starts by examining how the history of land tenure in many developing countries prevented much of the population, particularly women, from gaining secure title to land. We go on to show how inequality in the distribution of land seriously affects three key aspects of economic development: institutional development, education, and financial development. Governments can play an important role in redressing problems in this area—for example, by establishing institutions to facilitate the transfer and exchange of land rights (and property rights more generally). A further legitimate role for government is the implementation of second-generation reforms that address insecurity of land rights through registration and titling. The chapter ends on a cautionary note, indicating that, although such reforms have been successful in certain regions, including Latin America, it is not clear that they would be effective (or are needed) in every region, given the hold of traditional systems of informal tenure.

Increasing productivity is a sure way to spur economic growth. Productivity is defined as output growth (the sum) that is greater than the growth in inputs (the parts). Chapter 15 focuses on innovation and technological absorption as critical for improving productivity. Although most developing countries have policies designed to encourage the adoption of technologies generated by advanced economies, our knowledge about the particular policies that will directly enhance technological success, and thus raise productivity, remains inadequate. Entrepreneurship appears to be a key factor in promoting technological innovation and the commercialization of new technologies. Small and medium-size firms, not large companies, are still the center of technological innovation and adoption.

Urbanization signals modernization and industrialization and is viewed as a natural part of an economy's transition from low-productivity agriculture to higher-productivity industry and services. At the same time, rapid urbanization puts stress on the provision of basic infrastructure services—water, sanitation, electricity, and roads. With the world's urban population projected to double by 2050, chapter 16 discusses the progress of urban growth across countries and lays out emerging issues in urbanization. These include unemployment, poverty, slums, megacities, land management, and housing. To meet the MDGs, countries must address these issues. Once optional, urban planning is now a necessity.

Corruption, the topic of chapter 17, undermines growth and poverty reduction. The private sector and public employees share the blame. We focus on institutional and governance issues associated with the growth—and control—of corruption. Those factors include the rule of law, crime and violence, voice and accountability, and transparency.

The right amount of regulation of products, labor markets, businesses, and financial institutions is important for economic performance, as noted in chapter 18. Over- and underregulation are equally likely to strangle markets, depriving governments of tax revenues. In almost all developing countries, the failure to find the right level of regulation has driven economic activity underground, swelling the so-called informal sector. Bureaucratic harassment, corruption, and poor provision of essential infrastructure contribute to this unhealthy phenomenon.

Managing growth in the face of externally induced economic shocks is a continuous challenge for governments in the developing world. Middle East oil producers and many African countries that export primary commodities face a special challenge in responding to unpredictable dips and spikes in prices that make it difficult to maintain a consistent level of consumption at home and a steady pace of growth. Chapter 19 traces the channels through which shocks travel around the world. Through the effect of shocks on commodity prices, interest rates, and exchange rates, policies in the industrial world often hit developing countries in a manner similar to natural disasters such as tsunamis, floods, and earthquakes. Despite prodigious expansion in recent decades, the world's trade and financial systems are still ill prepared to deal with large-scale, highly contagious financial crashes, such as those observed during the 1980s, the late 1990s, and 2007–09. During global crises, we still must expect that policy responses will be largely improvised and institutional arrangements ad hoc. Policy makers will face domestic pressure to resort to short-term fixes and policies, such as protectionism, that have been proven to be self-defeating. The maintenance of sound economic policies makes more sense, even during periods of crisis, and provides much greater opportunities for growth.

Only 13 developing countries have been able to sustain high growth for 25 or more consecutive years. The economic policies common to those countries are discussed in chapter 19. The essence of those policies is the maintenance of macroeconomic stability, which involves keeping inflation in check, fiscal deficits and debt ratios low, and savings and investment rates high. Other policies and practices common to the successful 13 were engagement with the global economy, reliance on markets, free movement of labor and capital, and strong political leadership. At the firm level, efficiency was promoted by improving the investment climate to stimulate economic activity and sustain growth. For successful low-income countries, agricultural growth was also vital for reducing poverty and protecting overall growth.

Economies rarely thrive in the throes of political instability, but that does not mean that stability will ignite or sustain growth. If the political system is stable but inequitable and stultifying, the economy will function only within narrow limits. Chapter 20 provides a glimpse into systems where elites benefit at the expense of the poor, where collusion among large firms, politicians, and the bureaucracy perpetuates traditional power structures. In such systems, a small group of elites monopolizes economic rewards—including public services—to the detriment of the poor and the middle class. Only sustained pressure from domestic advocacy groups and the international community can move elites in such countries to implement the reforms necessary to increase equity and growth.

Too often, growth has been based on the depletion of nonrenewable natural capital. Chapter 21 focuses on the problems of deforestation, high carbon emissions, and climate change. In such circumstances, it can be said that markets have failed in both a narrow sense, because those who reap benefits from actions that result in deforestation and pollution do not incur the costs of those actions, and a broad sense, because sooner or later growth based on the exploitation of natural resources will sputter, as stocks of those resources dwindle. Ultimately, the problem affects everyone on the planet. Global problems call for global solutions, with advanced and developing countries taking coordinated actions to dramatically reduce carbon emissions, combat deforestation, and encourage effective market mechanisms that recognize the full costs of economic transactions.

The literature on growth and poverty is voluminous and still evolving. In the short chapter that concludes this volume, we attempt to distill the most important lessons from our experience with growth and poverty. We observe that poverty and inequality in income and assets are more persistent over time than is growth. Especially in Latin America, those conditions can be traced to historical factors, inherited economic structures, and particular resource endowments. Yet even under such circumstances, targeting policies and programs toward the poor can help reduce social inequities while simultaneously enhancing growth. Moving toward a virtuous circle of growth and poverty reduction requires complementary policies in several areas. For instance, the poor have access only to substandard schools and receive public services of low quality. Poor regions are less likely than more prosperous regions to attract investments in infrastructure, which keeps them poor. Because poor people can expect lower returns on their investments in education and training, they are less likely to make those investments. Social safety nets that reduce the risks of unemployment in poorer regions might induce more poor people to invest in education.

There is ample evidence that history, in the form of initial conditions, shapes long-term growth, while short-term fluctuations in output growth are driven primarily by shocks, especially commodity booms and busts. To weather the shocks, savings rates should be increased during booms, but it is unclear how best to accomplish that goal. To avoid the worst effects of downturns, expansionary fiscal policies that focus on essential infrastructure construction and on protecting the poor through social safety nets are appropriate. In some countries, high levels of remittances from migrant workers have acted as private safety nets during downturns and helped to smooth consumption in the short term. In the long term, resilience depends on political stability and market-supporting institutions that protect property rights, ensure the rule of law, process financial transactions efficiently, invest in robust infrastructure, and encourage the formation of human capital through education. With such institutions in place, openness to free flows of goods, capital, and skilled labor will enhance growth by promoting global competition, spreading new technologies, and encouraging urbanization. Although economic development is associated with dynamic manufacturing and service sectors (where innovation and technological adoption flourish), agricultural employment will remain important as a source of jobs in low-income countries as they make the transition to higher growth.

Looking ahead, rates of growth and poverty will be determined by the way nations use knowledge, technology, and energy in firms and households and by the effects of the warming climate on economic activities. Above all, the distribution of political and economic power within and among countries will determine the direction and dynamics of growth and development. The challenge today remains essentially that of the 1960s: how to lift people out of the trap of low growth and high poverty. We have traveled the world only to return home.

PART I

Poverty, National Income, and Economic Growth

CHAPTER 1

Poverty and How We Measure It

To design effective policies and strategies to reduce poverty, it is critical to understand its characteristics in a given country or region. The techniques of poverty measurement can shed light on whether poverty is increasing or decreasing and on whether economic growth is benefiting the poor. Poverty profiles of countries and regions can help governments identify the poor by region, level of education, ethnicity, gender, or form of employment. Figure 1.1, for example, depicts the distribution of the poor in Thailand in 1988, 1994, and 2002—the incidence of poverty decreased significantly between 1988 and 2002. With good poverty data, the effects of government policies on the poor can be evaluated, and the forms of growth that have a better chance of benefiting the poor can be identified and promoted.

Poverty and Well-Being

Measuring the characteristics and extent of poverty requires a definition of well-being, a concept that can be approached from many angles. Well-being can be defined as command over commodities or resources, as access to assets, or as the ability to function in society. Poverty, then, would be defined as a condition involving critical shortages of those

Figure 1.1   Distribution of the Poor in Thailand

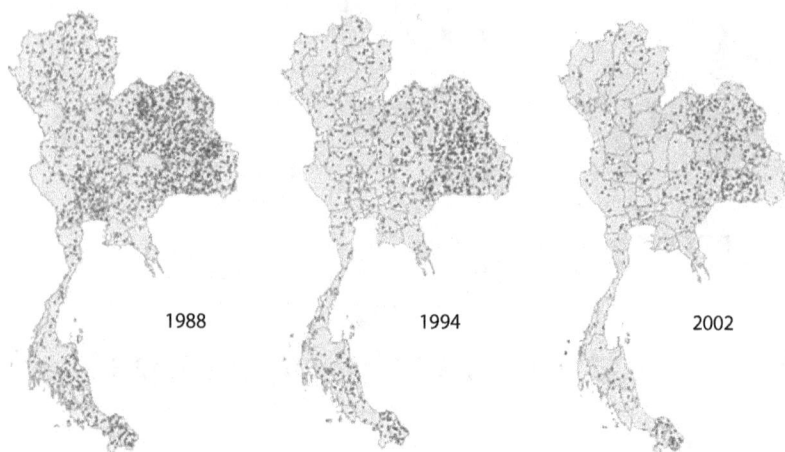

Source: Jitsuchon and Richter 2007, 244.
Note: Each dot represents 10,000 people who are poor, measured by the Poverty Headcount Ratio.

elements. As a practical matter, the measurement of poverty focuses on assessing whether individuals and households have enough resources to meet their basic needs.

Although commonly used techniques for measuring poverty focus on the monetary aspects of poverty, nonmonetary dimensions are important and should not be forgotten. The poor are seldom poor only in income. In addition to having little money, they are more likely than the nonpoor to be cold, hungry, malnourished, illiterate, sick, unemployed, alcoholic, depressed, or excluded from society. Thus, poverty is not just a shortage of quantifiable resources but a more general state of *vulnerability* marked by a lack of access to health services and education, low self-confidence, and a sense of powerlessness. Generally defined as the risk associated with being poor or of falling deeper into poverty, vulnerability is a key component of well-being. It is only because these important concepts are difficult to measure that they are excluded from most poverty measures.

Most often, well-being is measured through *inputs*—the number of calories consumed in a day, or food consumption as a fraction of total spending. But it is also possible to measure outcomes, such as rates of malnutrition. At the community level, welfare can be evaluated by looking at life expectancy, infant mortality rates, or school enrollment. Properly viewed as complements to, rather than replacements for, the more commonly used measures of per capita consumption, these measures provide a more complete and multidimensional view of the well-being of a population.

In sum, there is no perfect measure of well-being or poverty. But that does not mean poverty should not be measured; rather, it argues for a degree of caution in our approach to poverty measures and for care in analyzing how the measures are constructed.

Measuring Poverty

Measuring poverty requires three basic steps:

- An indicator of welfare must be defined.
- A minimum acceptable standard of that indicator must be established to separate the poor from the nonpoor. That standard is often known as the poverty line.
- A summary statistic must be devised to aggregate the information obtained from the distribution of the chosen welfare indicator. The position of that summary statistic relative to minimum acceptable standards must be determined.

As noted, the broad concept of well-being forms the basis of our overall approach to poverty, but the most common way of measuring poverty focuses on economic welfare—in other words, the monetary aspects of poverty, as in figure 1.2.

Figure 1.2 shows the proportion of people living on less than $1.25 a day. Approximately one-quarter of the developing world's population, or 1.4 billion people, lived on less than $1.25 a day in 2005. This was an improvement on the 1981 figure of 1.9 billion people, or one-half of the developing world's population, but the progress across regions was uneven.

Consumption- and Income-Based Measures of Welfare

It is possible to measure household welfare by looking at *household income* (as opposed to household expenditures), but several complications often make it a second choice for poverty analysts. For one thing, households may be reluctant to report income if they have engaged in tax evasion or have illegal earnings; generally, they are more willing to report what they have spent than what they have earned. In addition, some types of income are not always easy to measure, such as farm income or changes in the value of assets (for example, farm inventories or

Figure 1.2   Proportion of the Developing World's Population Living on Less than $1.25 a Day

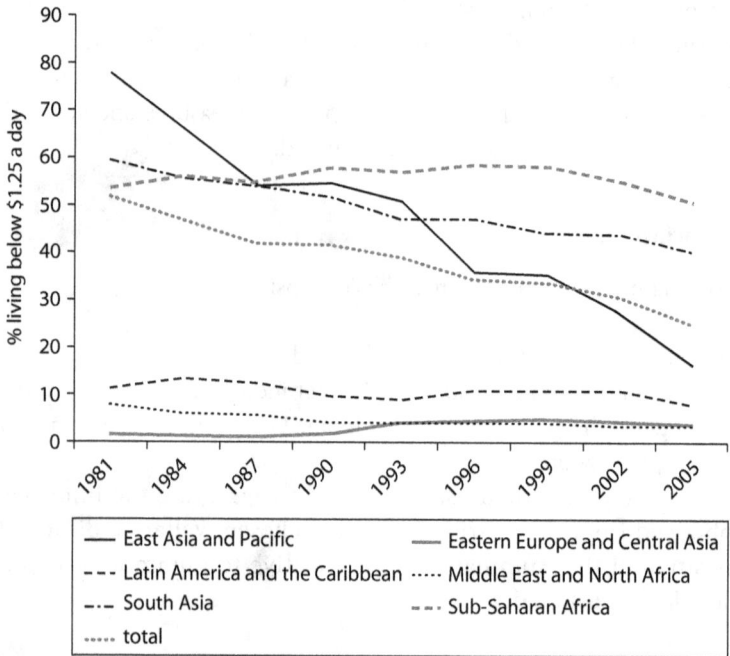

Source: Compiled from data in Chen and Ravallion (2008, 42).

housing). In addition, the incomes of the poor often vary considerably over time, as, for example, in rural areas dependent on rain-fed agriculture.

For these reasons, *consumption-based* measures of living standards are generally preferred to *income-based* measures. Consumption is likely to be more stable than income, and consumption-based measures minimize the reporting problems noted above. Consumption includes both purchased goods and services and those that are provided from one's own production ("in-kind" sources).

Consumption as a measure of well-being is not free of complications, however. In order to make comparisons across households using consumption measures of poverty, it is necessary to calculate the value of durable goods owned by the household in the year of measurement, including both the depreciation of the item during the year and the interest cost of having money locked up in the item, as opposed to having that money in an interest-bearing account. It is important to measure durable goods because we know that even some households that cannot afford adequate quantities of food spend some of their money on other items (such as clothing). Those items, too, represent very basic needs of the household and should be included in our poverty measures. The potential for error in computing the value and depreciation of each durable good that the household owns can be quite large. Housing must also be included in consumption; generally, its cost is estimated by calculating actual rent payments or, as in the case of owner-occupied houses, imputed rent payments (what the household would have to pay in rent if it did not own its home).

If poverty is assessed based on household consumption or expenditure per capita, as discussed above, the analysis can include an "expenditure function." In simple terms, an expenditure function shows the minimum expenditure required to meet a given level of need—or, in economic terms, to derive a given level of utility. The level of utility is derived from a list of goods at given prices. If one takes into account those prices and certain household characteristics (such as the number of adults and young children in the household), the expenditure function will compute the amount of spending that is needed to reach a certain level of utility.

Accounting for Differences in Household Consumption

Since households differ in size and composition, a simple comparison of aggregate welfare can mislead us about the well-being of the individuals in a given household. The most straightforward way of dealing with this problem is to convert from a measure of household consumption to a measure of individual consumption by dividing household expenditures by the number of people in the household. This easy procedure does not take into consideration the fact that different individuals have different needs (a young child typically needs less food than an adult, for example) or that there are economies of scale in the consumption of nonfood items. We deal with this problem by assigning a system of weights, using an equivalence scale that measures the number of adult males to which the household is equivalent. In this way, each member of the household counts as a fraction of an adult male. There is no consensus on an appropriate scale of equivalence, however, or on its usefulness in practice. Two methods are commonly used to deal with the problem. One is to choose a scale that is already being used; for example, the Organisation for Economic Co-operation and Development (OECD) scale assigns a two-adult household an "adult equivalent" of 1.7. Another is to estimate an equivalence scale for the population by looking at the aggregate household consumption of various goods during a given survey period.

The amount of a household's consumption is measured against the *poverty line* to determine whether that household is in poverty. The poverty line is obtained by specifying a bundle of goods and services considered adequate for basic consumption needs and then estimating the cost of meeting those needs. The poverty line represents a minimum standard required by an individual to fulfill his or her basic food and non-food needs. In practice, it makes sense to define more than one poverty line, because there are many ways to evaluate whether or not an individual or household is poor. A poverty line can be generated for all households in a given group and adjusted from household to household, taking into consideration the differences in prices that they face, as well as differences in their demographic composition. For example, a small household in a rural area may face low housing costs and relatively modest food prices. Thus, its poverty line (defined in money terms) may be low compared to that of a large household living in a city, where housing tends to be more expensive and food prices may also be higher.

A poverty profile undertaken in Cambodia in 1999 used an approach along the lines described above, constructing one poverty line for each of the three major regions in the country based on the prices prevailing in those regions. Whether a household in a given region was poor was determined by comparing its expenditure per capita with the regional poverty line.

Nominal poverty lines (as opposed to relative ones) can change over time, owing to changes in prices (typically from inflation) or revisions of the real poverty threshold. This raises the question of whether relative or absolute poverty lines should be used.

Relative poverty lines. Focusing on the poorest segment of a given population at a given time enables the design of targeted programs geared toward that segment rather than toward those who are relatively better off. Relative poverty lines need to be tailored to the overall level of development of a country; they tend to be revised upward with increases in per capita consumption. As relative poverty lines are defined in relation to the overall income distribution within a country, comparison of relative poverty across countries may not be of any relevance. For instance, while the poverty line for a family of four in the United States in 2006 was $20,650,[1] the incomes of those living in relative poverty in the United States cannot be compared to those living in relative poverty in Vietnam because living standards and prices in the two countries differ significantly.

Absolute poverty lines. An absolute poverty line is fixed over time, enabling poverty analysts to judge the impact of antipoverty policies over a period of years and to compare poverty rates across countries (provided the same poverty line is used in all). The World Bank commonly uses two absolute poverty lines—per capita consumption of less than $1.25 a day (formerly $1 a day) and per capita consumption of less than $2 per day in 2005 purchasing power parity terms. Using improved price data from the latest (2005) round of the International Comparison Program at the World Bank, poverty estimates released in August 2008 show that about 1.4 billion people in the developing world (one in four) were living on less than $1.25 a day in 2005, down from 1.9 billion (one in two) in 1981.

Table 1.1 reports some historical figures on the incidence of absolute poverty around the world.

Table 1.1   Percentage of People in the Developing World Living on Less than $1.08 and $2.15 per Day

	1981	1984	1987	1990	1993	1996	1999	2002	2004
$1.08 per day at 1993 PPP									
East Asia and Pacific	57.73	39.02	28.23	29.84	25.23	16.14	15.46	12.33	9.05
China	63.76	41.02	28.64	32.98	28.36	17.37	17.77	13.79	9.90
Europe and Central Asia	0.70	0.51	0.35	0.46	3.60	4.42	3.78	1.27	0.94
Latin America and the									
Caribbean	10.77	13.07	12.09	10.19	8.42	8.87	9.66	9.09	8.64
Middle East and North									
Africa	5.08	3.82	3.09	2.33	1.87	1.69	2.08	1.69	1.47
South Asia	49.57	45.43	45.11	43.04	36.87	36.06	34.92	33.56	30.84
India	51.75	47.94	46.15	44.31	41.82	39.94	37.66	36.03	34.33
Sub-Saharan Africa	42.26	46.20	47.22	46.73	45.47	47.72	45.77	42.63	41.10
Total	40.14	32.72	28.72	28.66	25.56	22.66	22.10	20.13	18.09
Total excluding China	31.35	29.69	28.75	27.14	24.58	24.45	23.54	22.19	20.70
$2.15 per day at 1993 PPP									
East Asia and Pacific	84.80	77.17	68.53	69.73	65.04	52.49	49.34	41.68	36.58
China	88.12	79.00	68.64	72.16	68.13	53.34	50.05	40.94	34.89
Europe and Central Asia	4.60	3.93	3.08	4.31	16.53	17.97	18.57	12.88	9.79
Latin America and the									
Caribbean	28.45	32.25	29.57	26.25	24.09	25.24	25.31	24.76	22.17
Middle East and									
North Africa	29.16	25.59	24.24	21.69	21.41	21.40	23.62	21.09	19.70
South Asia	88.53	87.01	86.57	85.62	82.22	82.12	80.41	79.73	77.12
India	88.92	87.89	86.98	86.30	85.33	84.12	82.67	81.37	80.36
Sub-Saharan Africa	74.52	76.98	77.36	77.05	76.09	76.42	75.85	73.81	71.97
Total	66.96	64.25	60.73	60.79	59.44	55.52	54.24	50.69	47.55
Total excluding China	59.08	58.87	57.89	56.78	56.43	56.26	55.63	53.85	51.58

Source: World Bank 2007.
Note: PPP = purchasing power parity.

Several important conceptual problems come up when working with absolute poverty lines. First, it is often difficult to agree on a standard of living to be measured by the poverty line. In practice, almost all poverty lines are set in terms of the cost of buying a basket of goods (a commodity-based poverty line), but one can argue that individual standards of living, or "utilities," are independent—that is, a household of four with an income of $12,000 per year would not be considered poor in Indonesia, but when that household compares its position with that of a household with an average income in the United States, it may feel very poor. This implies that the commodity-based poverty line should rise as a country becomes more affluent, both in nominal terms and in terms of purchasing power, because the minimum level of resources needed to participate fully in society probably rises simultaneously. In addition, it may be difficult to define the correct commodity value of the poverty line because both the size and demographic composition of households vary.

One way to determine the poverty line is to set "objective" standards—that is, to set the poverty line at a level that enables individuals to achieve certain capabilities, such as leading a healthy and active life and participating fully in society. A common way of approaching this is to begin with nutritional requirements. Two common methods are the food-energy intake (FEI) method and the cost-of-basic-needs approach.

The goal of the FEI is to find the level of consumption expenditure (or income) that allows the household to obtain enough food to meet its energy requirements. To do this, one must first determine the amount of food that is deemed adequate. Vietnam, for example, sets this value at 2,100 calories per day, while recognizing that different individuals may need more or less food. After the calorie level is set, food expenditure lines can be estimated by figuring the cost of obtaining the 2,100 calories each day. There are important weaknesses to this approach. For example, the cost and availability of food differ from urban to rural areas, influencing the type of calories that people consume and making comparisons difficult.

The cost-of-basic-needs approach uses a consumption bundle that is deemed adequate, including both food and nonfood components, and estimates the cost of the bundle for various subgroups, such as urban and rural residents or the populations of different regions. The key difference in this approach is that the poverty line is measured in money, so it does not insist (as with the FEI) that each basic need must be met, only that it *could* be met. But this approach poses challenges of its own, among them how to measure the nonfood components of the poverty line, such as home heating needs (countries in colder climates will put more emphasis on the cost of energy needed for home heating than will countries in warmer climates).

Measures of Poverty—Summary Statistics

Armed with information on per capita consumption and a poverty line, several aggregate measures of poverty can be computed:

Headcount index. By far the most widely used aggregate measure of poverty is the headcount index, which simply measures the proportion of the population that is counted as poor. The headcount index is simple to construct and easy to understand—both important qualities. But it has several weaknesses. For one, it does not capture the degree or *depth* of poverty. Thus, if a somewhat poor household were to give part of its wealth to a very poor household, the headcount index would remain unchanged, even though poverty as a whole would have dropped. The easiest way to reduce poverty as measured by the headcount index would be to target benefits to people living just below the poverty line, because they are the ones who can be moved across the poverty line most cheaply, even though they are not the neediest people in the population. In addition, the headcount index expresses the percentage of *individuals* who are poor, and not the percentage of households. When we use it, we make the critical assumption that all household members enjoy the same level of well-being, which may not be true.

Poverty gap index. Another measure of poverty is the poverty gap index, which adds up the distances that poor people fall from the poverty line and expresses the sum as a percentage of the poverty line. The poverty gap index is thought of as a way to measure the total cost of bringing each poor member of a society up to the poverty line, but it depends for accuracy on exact information on each poor member of society—information that very few governments have. The main drawback of the poverty gap index, however, is that, because it is a measure of the average gap between poor people's standard of living and the poverty line, it is not capable of capturing inequality among the poor. For example, the poverty gap index may be the same for two countries, but the poor population in one of those countries may be composed of very poor people and others who are close to the poverty line, whereas in the other country the poor population may show very little variation in the degree of poverty. Despite these important differences, the poverty gap index of the two countries would be similar. The main advantages of the poverty gap index are (a) that it gives policy makers an idea of the minimum amount of financial resources that would be needed to tackle poverty and (b) that it highlights the importance of identifying the characteristics of the poor, as it demonstrates the potential savings of well-targeted programs to alleviate poverty.

Squared poverty gap. This is often described as a measure of the *severity* of poverty. While the poverty gap takes into account the distance separating the poor from the poverty line, the squared poverty gap uses the square of that distance. Thus, the poverty gap is weighted by itself, giving more weight to the very poor.

Poverty profiles. A poverty profile is a comprehensive poverty comparison that demonstrates how poverty varies across subgroups of society. After setting out the major facts on poverty and inequality, the poverty profile examines the pattern of poverty by geography (region, urban/rural, mountain/plain, and so on), by community characteristics (for example, communities with or without a school), and by household characteristics (for example, by education of household head or by size of household). A well-presented poverty profile can be immensely informative and useful in assessing how economic changes in a specific sector or region are likely to affect aggregate poverty, even if it uses relatively simple graphs and tables. Regional poverty comparisons are particularly important for targeting development programs to poorer areas.

The 1999 poverty study for Cambodia, for example, showed that headcount poverty rates were highest in the rural sector and lowest in Phnom Penh in 1997. Approximately 40 percent of the rural population, 11 percent of Phnom Penh's population, and 30 percent of other urban residents lived in households that were below the poverty line (table 1.2). Poverty profiles can also show access to services by households in different regions and shed light on the relationship between education levels in a household and the likelihood that a household will be poor.

The following are just some of the questions that can be included in a poverty profile:

- Which are the most important goods in the consumption basket of the poor?
- To what public services do the poor have access?
- What is the quality of those services?
- What are the main sources of income for the poor?

Table 1.2   Cambodia: Poverty Measures

percent

	Head count index		Poverty gap index		Poverty severity index	
	1993/94	*1997*	*1993/94*	*1997*	*1993/94*	*1997*
Food Poverty Line						
Phnom Penh	6.2	3.4	1.3	0.5	0.4	0.1
Other urban	19.6	15.4	4.4	3.3	1.4	1.1
Rural	21.9	20.0	4.0	3.9	1.1	1.2
Total	20.0	17.9	3.7	3.5	1.1	1.1
Poverty Line						
Phnom Penh	11.4	11.1	3.1	2.2	1.2	0.6
Other urban	36.6	29.9	9.6	7.5	3.6	2.7
Rural	43.1	40.1	10.0	9.7	3.3	3.4
Total	39.0	36.1	9.2	8.7	3.1	3.1

Source: World Bank, *Describing Poverty Profiles*; available at http://info.worldbank.org/etools/docs/library/103073/ch7.pdf.

- Do the poor have access to credit?
- Are certain population groups in society at a higher risk of being poor than others?

Vulnerability

While poverty is being reduced in many countries, detailed analysis of household data indicates that in most countries, many households live with incomes barely above the national poverty line. When a household is near the poverty line, that household is said to be vulnerable. A natural disaster, economic shock, or change in policy may affect its consumption level and cause it to fall below the poverty line. Poor delivery of public services increases the chance that the near-poor will fall into poverty.

Collecting Data

The main instruments for collecting data to support poverty analyses are *household surveys*. It is important to understand the issues associated with setting up such surveys and interpreting the data they generate.

Measures of poverty and inequality are always based on data that have been collected using *samples* of households. This has two important implications. First, it means, obviously, that measures of poverty and inequality are generated from a sample and not from the entire population. For that reason, they estimate the true state of the population with at least some degree of error, which should be acknowledged in a statement of the "confidence interval" (the probability that a statistic is accurate within a certain range). Survey data may also need to be weighted to get the right estimates of certain measures, such as mean income and poverty rates. This requirement implies that information about the sample frame (essentially the design of the sample selected) must be clearly documented.

Coverage of goods and income sources in the survey should be comprehensive, extending over food and nonfood goods and encompassing all income sources. Consumption should cover monetary expenditures on goods and services, plus the monetary value of all consumption from income in kind, such as food produced on the family farm and the rental value of owner-occupied housing. Similarly, the definition of *income* should include income in kind. Valuation of nonmarket (untraded) goods can be quite complicated. None of the available techniques is widely preferred.

A second issue is how to compare households at similar consumption levels. Households' size and demographic composition vary, as do the wages households receive and the prices they must pay. The general approach to measuring across households is to examine demand patterns to reveal consumer preferences for various market goods, and then to study the minimum total expenditure that would be required for a consumer to achieve his or her actual utility level, but at predetermined (and arbitrary) reference prices and with demographics fixed over all the households. This would give a monetary measure of utility, which could be deflated by a suitable price index and an equivalence scale.

Ideally, one should not rely solely on a household-level survey in making interpersonal comparisons of welfare. A separate *community* survey (done at the same time as the household interviews, and possibly by the same interviewers) can provide useful supplementary data on the local prices of a range of goods and local public services. By matching these to the household data, one can greatly improve the accuracy and coverage of household welfare assessments. This has become common practice in the World Bank's Living Standards Measurement Study (LSMS) surveys.

The LSMS surveys ask respondents about a wide variety of topics, not just demographic characteristics or other narrow issues. These surveys also include a household questionnaire that often runs to 100 pages or more and that can be adapted to the needs of each country. A related community questionnaire asks community leaders (teachers, health workers, village officials) for information about the whole community, such as the number of clinics, access to schools, tax collection, demographic data, and agricultural patterns. Another part of the LSMS is a price question-naire, which collects information about a large number of commodity prices in each community where the survey is undertaken. This is useful because it allows analysts to correct for differences in prices by region and over time.

Household Surveys and National Accounts

What is the best way of measuring whether or not economic growth is benefiting the poor? In recent years, that question has generated lively debate. The central issue is how to assess whether a unit of growth increases the income or consumption of the poor by at least as much as it does for the economy as a whole. Studies from the 1990s showed that in many cases, economic growth did not reduce poverty as much as expected, although there was no evidence that it increased inequality either. The main poverty-measurement issues revolve around the use of data from the household budget survey (HBS) versus data from national accounts (the topic of the next chapter) in assessing consumption levels, and how to deal with biases that may occur in the HBS data. There is strong evidence that rich households are less likely to comply with HBS reporting, for a variety of reasons, perhaps to conceal income or consump-tion. The result is that upper incomes are underrepresented in the HBS. By contrast, national accounts will pick up the transactions of upper-income households through key economic aggregates. Thus, average consumption as measured by national accounts tends to be higher than average consump-tion as revealed in the HBS data. But because the HBS instruments are bet-ter at capturing consumption that takes place in the informal sector, many argue that the HBS data more accurately reflect the consumption of the poor, even if national accounts provide a more accurate measure of the consumption of the population as a whole. This debate is particularly important for countries undergoing high rates of economic growth, but the issues are relevant for other countries as well.

Conclusion

Aggregate poverty measures are a prerequisite for any study of how eco-nomic policies affect the poor. Arriving at accurate measures is difficult, however, because poverty is multifaceted. While the nonmonetary aspects of poverty (such as political voice, access to health and education, and so on) are critical, the monetary aspects lend themselves more easily to measurement and to comparisons across countries, regions, and time periods. To that end, fairly narrow indicators of welfare based on individual household consumption are generally used to measure poverty. These are compared with a minimum standard of that indicator, often known as the poverty line. By comparing the indicators with the standard, economists generate simple summary statistics—such as the headcount index, poverty gap index, and squared poverty index—to provide a broad overall measure of poverty. Macroeconomic growth and household (microeconomic) perspectives are both important for poverty reduction. The developing countries of East Asia have been more successful in reducing poverty than most other regions because of policies that promoted widespread education, trade, and infrastructure investment.

Note

1. U.S. Department of Health and Human Services, *The 2007 HHS Poverty Guidelines*; available at http://www.hhs.gov.

Bibliography

Chen, S., and M. Ravallion. 2008. "The Developing World Is Poorer Than We Thought, but No Less Successful in the Fight against Poverty." Policy Research Working Paper 4703, World Bank, Washington DC.

Jitsuchon, S., and K. Richter. 2007. "More Than a Pretty Picture; Using Poverty Maps to Design Better Policies and Interventions." World Bank: Washington DC.

Ravallion, M., and S. Chen. 2004. "How Have the World's Poor Fared Since the Early 1980s?" Policy Research Working Paper 3341, World Bank, Washington, DC.

World Bank. 1990. *World Development Report 1990: Poverty*. Washington, DC: World Bank.

———. 2002a. *World Development Report 2000/01: Attacking Poverty*. Oxford: Oxford University Press.

———. 2002b. *PRSP Source Book*. Washington, DC: World Bank.

———. 2003a. *Poverty Reduction Strategy Papers—Progress in Implementation*. Washington, DC: World Bank.

———. 2003b. *World Development Report 2003: Sustainable Development in a Dynamic Economy: Transforming Institutions, Growth and the Quality of Life*. Oxford: Oxford University Press.

———. 2004. *World Development Report 2004: Making Services Work for Poor People*. Oxford: Oxford University Press.

———. 2007. *World Development Indicators*. Washington, DC: World Bank.

———. 2008. *Global Monitoring Report*. Washington, DC: World Bank.

———. "Describing Poverty: Poverty Profiles." http://info.worldbank.org/etools/docs/library/103073/ch7.pdf.

CHAPTER 2

National Income and How We Measure It

Measuring poverty is only the first step toward creating pro-poor economic policies. The second step—understanding how an economy works—requires some knowledge of macroeconomics, the branch of economics that studies the economy as a whole with reference to key variables—among them the economy's output, inflation, unemployment, balance of payments, and exchange rate. Macroeconomics explains changes in these variables and guides policy makers in their pursuit of economic objectives such as economic growth and smooth business cycles, the central concerns of macroeconomics. The system of *national accounts* provides a framework in which macroeconomic data can be compiled and used for economic analysis.

This chapter examines how economic growth is measured by identifying the components of growth and examining how these components relate to one another within the national accounts framework. It also introduces the *external sector* (the world beyond the nation's borders) to clarify key relationships between a country's national accounts and its balance of payments. Extensions to the national accounts in the form of environmental accounts, informal sector accounts, happiness, and national well-being are also briefly discussed.

Macroeconomic Sectors

In macroeconomics, the economy is divided into five sectors—households, enterprises, the financial sector, the government, and the rest of the world.

- *Households* supply land, labor, and capital; they demand goods and services. They may also work as producers by forming unincorporated enterprises. They make decisions on how much to consume, how much to save, and how much to invest in financial markets.
- *Enterprises* employ factors of production (such as land, labor, and capital) to produce goods and services for the market. They make decisions about production and investment.
- The *financial sector* provides financial services to households, government, and enterprises. It includes the banking system and other financial institutions such as mutual funds, credit unions, pension funds, and insurance companies.
- The *government* creates a regulatory and legal framework for economic activity; provides public goods such as education, health, infrastructure, and a social safety net; oversees the tax system; and manages government spending on the finished products of enterprises and direct purchases of resources, including labor. Government spending excludes transfers of government receipts to households.
- The *rest of the world* refers to an economy's transactions with nonresidents. This category includes nonresidents' spending on local products and services and residents' spending abroad on products and services.

The circular flow of income, expenditure, and financing captures the important relationships among the five economic sectors and the factor markets for labor, land, and capital (figure 2.1).

Macroeconomic Concepts

Arising from the interaction and behavior of the economic sectors are certain key macroeconomic concepts that play a central role in macroeconomic analysis. These are defined as follows in the framework of the system of national accounts.

- *Gross output* is the value of all goods and services produced in the economy. This measure suffers, however, from double counting, as when the value of wheat is counted first in the production of bread

Figure 2.1   Circular Flow of Income in National Accounts

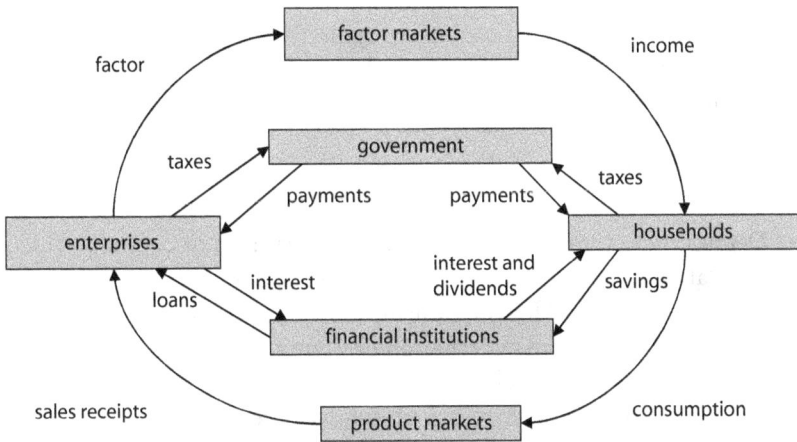

Source: Mankiw 2002.

and second in the sales of bread. The concept of value added provides a way around this problem.

- *Value added* is the value of gross output less that of intermediate goods. A microchip bought by a computer company and used in the production of its computers is an intermediate good because the chip is ultimately purchased as part of a final good, the computer. Value added also distinguishes between market output and nonmarket output, which includes subsistence farming and owner-occupied housing.

- *Consumption* takes two forms. *Intermediate* consumption refers to inputs into production. *Final* consumption refers to goods and services—both imported and domestically produced—used by households and the government. To return to the computer example: a microchip purchase by a computer maker is intermediate consumption; a computer purchase by a household is final consumption. The same computer, purchased by an enterprise, is investment; purchased by a government, it is government expenditure.

- *Gross domestic product (GDP)* is the sum of value added across all sectors in the economy. It measures the value of the final goods and services in an economy. To ensure that total output is measured accurately, goods and services produced in a specific year must be counted only once. Most products go through several production stages before reaching the market and, thus, may be bought and sold several times. To avoid multiple counting of goods, which would exaggerate the value of the GDP, only the market value of the final goods is included, not that of intermediate or secondhand goods.

- *Gross investment* (gross capital formation) refers to additions to the physical stock of capital. This includes
    - ○ final purchases of machinery, equipment, and tools by business enterprises;
    - ○ construction; and
    - ○ changes in inventories.[1]
- *Depreciation*, sometimes called the consumption of capital, reflects natural wear and tear over time. It is used to differentiate net from gross investment. The relationship between gross investment and depreciation indicates whether an economy's production capacity is expanding, static, or declining.
- *Net investment* is gross investment minus depreciation.
- *Net exports* are the value of exports of goods and services minus the value of imports of goods and services. The difference measures the impact of foreign trade on aggregate demand (the total demand for goods and services in an economy) and on GDP (total output).
- *Absorption*, or domestic aggregate demand, is total final consumption by the sectors (including government) plus gross investment.

Determining Gross Domestic Product

GDP and "real GDP" (GDP adjusted for inflation) are key measures of the amount of economic activity in a country. If real GDP rises for a given year, more products and services were produced during that year. Higher production usually, but not always, means higher living standards. There are cases in which higher real GDP does not lead to a better standard of living—for example, where growth creates problems of environmental degradation, imbalances between work and other aspects of life, and income inequality. But, as we will see in later chapters, a large change in real GDP, or, simply, greater economic growth, is the best measure of poverty alleviation in developing countries.

Three Approaches to GDP

GDP is obtained by calculating the total final value of all goods and services produced by a country's factors of production in a given time period, usually a year. Since output cannot be produced without inputs, the expenditures that make up GDP are closely linked to the employment of labor, capital, and other factors of production. Thus, GDP can be defined using three basic approaches—production, expenditure, and income. They yield equivalent results, once statistical discrepancies are resolved.

The production approach. In the production approach, GDP is the sum of gross value added (VA) in the economy, or, as defined above, the difference between the value of production (output) and the value of all goods and services used in the production process (intermediate consumption):

$$GDP = \Sigma VA \qquad (2.1)$$

where

ΣVA = the sum of value added across all sectors in the economy.

The expenditure approach. Earlier we identified five economic sectors: households, enterprises, the financial sector, the government, and the rest of the world. The expenditure approach to GDP measures the spending by households, enterprises, government, and the rest of the world on final goods and services. The aggregates are defined as consumption (C) by government and households, investment (I) or gross private domestic spending by enterprises, and net exports or exports (X) minus imports (M). A hypothetical example of the expenditure approach to GDP is depicted in table 2.1.

$$GDP = C + I + (X–M) \qquad (2.2)$$

Table 2.1   Hypothetical Example of the Expenditure Approach to GDP
US$ billions

	Year 1	Year 2	Year 3
Consumption	65.5	69.4	73.2
Public	5.9	7.2	7.2
Private	59.6	62.2	66.0
Investment	20.0	28.3	26.1
Public	6.8	7.2	7.0
Private	13.2	21.1	19.1
Changes in inventories	–0.9	1.5	–2.9
Exports of goods and services	14.5	17.3	20.1
Imports of goods and services	16.2	20.0	24.0
Statistical discrepancy	0.3	0.8	1.1
Gross domestic product	83.2	97.3	93.6

Source: Authors.

where

C = final consumption of durable and nondurable goods
by government and households ($Cg+Cp$),
I = gross investment (fixed capital formation and changes in
inventories) both by government and enterprises ($Ig+Ip$),
X = exports of goods and nonfactor services,
M = imports of goods and nonfactor services.

The income approach. GDP also can be measured as the sum of the incomes generated by resident producers. The following components are included:

- *Compensation of employees.* This is the largest income category, comprising primarily wages and salaries paid by businesses and government to suppliers of labor. It also includes wages and salary supplements such as social insurance, pension fund contributions, and health care paid by employers on behalf of their workers.
- *Rents.* Rents consist of income payments received by households and businesses that own and therefore supply property resources. The rental income is what remains after depreciation is subtracted from gross rental revenues.
- *Interest.* Interest is the money paid by private businesses to suppliers of capital. It includes interest on savings deposits.
- *Profits.* What is generally termed "profit" can be broken down in national income accounts into *proprietors' income* and *corporate profits.*
  - Proprietors' income is the net income of sole proprietorships and partnerships.
  - Corporate profits may be collected by government as tax on corporate income, distributed to stockholders (households or enterprises) as dividends, or retained as undistributed corporate profits that are invested in new plants and equipment, thus increasing the assets of the business.
- *Business taxes* are taxes on production. Firms treat these as costs of production. They are added to the prices of products sold.
- *Subsidies.* Subsidies received by the firm are subtracted from the prices of products sold.

Therefore:

$$GDP = W + OS + (T\text{--}SP) \qquad (2.3)$$

where

W = compensation of employees as defined above
OS = the gross operating surplus of enterprises, including profits, rents, interest, and depreciation as defined above
T–SP = taxes less subsidies on products.

Nominal and Real GDP

Because GDP measures the total value of a nation's output in a given year, it captures both the changes in output and the changes in the prices of that output over time. To isolate changes in physical output over time, we differentiate between nominal and real GDP and deflate nominal GDP by an overall price index called the implicit GDP deflator.

Nominal GDP measures the value of output of the economy at current prices.

Real GDP, or *GDP at constant prices*, measures the value of a country's output using the prices of a single base year. Although not an ideal measure of living standards or real income, real GDP is the most widely used measure of real income growth. It is useful in capturing real output growth.

Implicit GDP is an index that measures the average price level of an economy's output relative to the base year. The index has a value of 100 in the base year. Thus, the percentage change in the GDP deflator measures the rate of price increases for all goods and services in the economy.

The following relationships are found:

- *Nominal GDP = real GDP × GDP deflator/100*
- *Real GDP = nominal GDP/GDP deflator × 100*
- *GDP deflator = nominal GDP/real GDP × 100*

In terms of the rate of growth:

$$(1 + v) = (1 + g) \times (1 + p) \tag{2.4}$$

where

v = rate of growth of nominal GDP (percent),
g = rate of growth of real GDP (percent),
p = rate of inflation as measured by the GDP deflator (percent).

Other Standard Aggregates

Two things must be noted about GDP as a measure of total output. First, GDP refers to production that takes place *within* an economy. It includes the output of domestically owned corporations in the country (but not abroad) and of foreign-owned corporations operating in the economy. Second, GDP includes depreciation.

Because GDP is a domestic concept—one that refers to the production of, and income arising from, goods and services by firms based in the country and by foreign firms operating in the country—it does not cover the economy's overall income from all sources. To get at the rest of the economy's income, we must investigate gross national income (GNI) and gross national product (GNP).

GNI *and gross national disposable income.* GNI includes income generated abroad and paid to residents but excludes income generated domestically and paid to nonresidents. The difference between the two is termed "net factor income" (Y_f). Examples of factor incomes are (a) capital income, which includes dividends on direct investment and interest on external borrowing or lending; (b) labor income of migrant and seasonal workers; and (c) service income on land, building rentals, and royalties.

$$GNI = GDP + Y_f \qquad (2.5)$$

where Y_f refers to net factor income from abroad.

But net income from abroad need not be related to factors of production. Private transfers of income may arise from workers' remittances; public transfers may arise from government grants. Allowing for net current transfers—the difference between transfers received by the residents of a country and transfers made to nonresidents—we arrive at the concept of gross national disposable income (GNDI):

$$GNDI = GNI + TR_f \qquad (2.6)$$

where TR_f is net current transfers received from abroad.

Savings. The total income available to residents for use in final consumption or savings is GNDI, as noted above:

$$GNDI = C + S \qquad (2.7)$$

where

C = spending on final goods and services by government and households,
S = gross national savings.

When final consumption is subtracted from GNDI, we are left with gross national savings:

$$GNDI - C = S. \tag{2.8}$$

Gross national product. GNI deals with income, GDP with production and income. Neither allows us to differentiate between the nationality of producers and the location of production. To do so, we need the concept of GNP. GNP refers to the goods and services produced by national corporations in the country, plus goods and services produced by national corporations in other countries. GNI at market prices is the same as GNP.

GDP is a "gross concept" and therefore includes depreciation. The corresponding net concept is that of net domestic product (NDP), which strips out depreciation, and is given as

$$NDP = GDP - D \tag{2.9}$$

where D = depreciation or consumption of fixed capital.

In practice, depreciation at the level of the entire economy is difficult to measure precisely and is measured with some lag. Thus, GDP is the preferred aggregate for measuring total output, even though it may overestimate production.

How GDP Is Used

The macroeconomic aggregates outlined above are used in economic modeling and analysis. GDP allows the comparison of economic data across countries. For meaningful comparisons, the GDP of each country must be expressed in terms of a common unit, such as the U.S. dollar. The unit may be nominal or constant (real). Adjusting GDP and GDP per capita to arrive at purchasing power parity (PPP) also facilitates comparison across countries, as the typical consumption bundle tends to be more expensive in richer countries, rendering comparison with poorer countries less meaningful. PPP measures are designed to overcome this shortcoming by using the "ratio of the prices in national currencies of the same good or service in different countries" to measure PPP-adjusted GDP (OECD 2008, 435). Countries can be compared and ranked using PPP-adjusted GDP per capita (table 2.2).

Governments, research organizations, universities, and international organizations such as Eurostat, the International Monetary Fund (IMF), the World Bank, the Organisation for Economic Co-operation and

Table 2.2   PPP-Adjusted GDP per Capita in the European Union, 1999

EU-15 = 100	Index	Rank
High income		
Luxembourg	186	1
Denmark	121	2
Upper middle income		
Netherlands	114	3
Ireland	112	4
Austria	111	5
Belgium	107	6
Germany	106	7
Italy	103	8
Sweden	101	9
Finland	101	9
United Kingdom	101	9
France	100	12
Lower middle income		
Spain	82	13
Portugal	74	14
Greece	68	15

Source: Compiled from data in OECD 2006.

Development (OECD), and the United Nations (UN) all use GDP as a measure of economic performance in their research and policy analysis.

The Business Cycle

The economic system traditionally cycles through booms and busts, a movement known as the business cycle. The purpose of macroeconomic policy is to smooth out the business cycle by balancing growth, unemployment, and inflation. Policies that reduce unemployment might lead to a rise in inflation, whereas restraining inflation may prevent growth in jobs, at least in the short run. Thus, there is often a political struggle over inflation and unemployment levels. The black line in figure 2.2 represents a typical pattern of economic booms and busts, as measured by GDP growth.

When we look at the GDP growth rate, we notice that it reaches maximum and minimum points (peaks and troughs) with some degree of regularity. Individual business cycles vary substantially in duration and intensity, but they all display common phases:

• *Peak.* The peak is the point at which business activity has reached a temporary maximum (point A in figure 2.2). The economy is at full

Figure 2.2   The Business Cycle

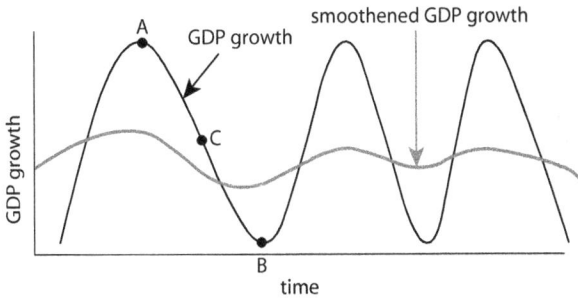

Source: Authors.
Note: A = peak, B = trough, C = recession.

employment, and the level of real output is at or very close to its capacity. Prices may rise during this phase.

- *Recession.* The peak may be followed by a period of decline in total output, income, employment, and trade lasting at least six months. This is known as a recession (point C in figure 2.2). During the recession, activity in many sectors of the economy contracts, but prices are unlikely to fall unless the recession is severe and prolonged, as in a depression.

- *Trough.* The trough of the slowdown is the phase in which output and employment reach their lowest levels (point B in figure 2.2). The trough may be short or long.

- *Recovery.* In the phase of recovery, or expansion, output and employment increase toward full employment. As recovery intensifies, prices may begin to rise before full employment is reached and before production has risen to full capacity.

Economic developments are typically described in terms of movements of variables that are related in some way to output, such as GDP, GNP, growth, employment, unemployment, prices, job creation, interest rates, housing, and consumption. Some variables, such as consumption and imports, follow a cycle similar to that of GDP—when GDP is growing faster, these variables also grow faster, and vice versa. These variables are said to be *procyclical.* Other variables move in the opposite direction and are said to be *countercyclical.* Examples are net exports and the unemployment rate. Still other variables are *acyclical,* meaning that they move in a way that is not linked systematically to GDP.

Other Changes in Business Activity

Not all changes in business activity result from business cycles. Some examples include:

- *Seasonal variations.* At certain times of the year, buying surges, causing considerable change in the tempo of business activity. The holiday season at the end of the year is an example.
- *Secular trends.* Business activity may expand or contract over a long period of years, a phenomenon known as a secular trend.

All economic actors are affected by business cycles but in various ways and to different degrees. With regard to production and employment, service industries and industries producing nondurable consumer goods are typically most insulated from the most severe effects of any recession. By contrast, firms and industries producing capital goods and consumer durables are usually hard hit by recessions. Two factors explain this:

- *Ability to postpone.* Within limits, purchases of durable goods can be postponed. During recessions, producers frequently delay the purchase of more modern production facilities and the construction of new plants, whereas in good times, capital goods are often replaced even before they depreciate fully. Similarly, during recessions, households often delay the purchase of big-ticket items—automobiles, washing machines, refrigerators, dishwashers, and so on.

- *Monopoly power.* Many industries that produce capital goods and consumer durables are highly concentrated—that is, a small number of large firms dominate the market. These firms can set above competitive prices to increase their profit. When recession hits, they are reluctant to lower prices for fear of upsetting the industry price structure and possibly sparking a price war. Their reluctance to lower prices means that the initial effects of a drop in demand are a decline in production and an increase in unemployment.

Volatility

Another important concept is that of *volatility*—the amplitude of deviations from the mean in a given series (usually measured using standard deviation). A variable is more volatile if it swings greatly from peak to trough. GDP is relatively volatile: by looking at the variables that constitute it, their shares in the aggregate, and their relative volatility, we can gauge what factors influence GDP the most. For example, consumption of nondurables and services may account for roughly 60 percent of our measure of GDP, with broad investment and government consumption accounting for 20 percent each. Thus, large and unpredictable swings in consumption (perhaps because of drought or famine) will bring about volatility in GDP.

The complex relationship between economic growth and macroeconomic volatility, usually measured by the standard deviation of per capita output growth, has become clearer in recent decades. During the 1980s, it was thought that macroeconomic volatility had a minor impact on economic growth, but research conducted in the 1990s (reported in Kose, Prasad, and Terrones 2004) suggested that macroeconomic volatility could reduce long-term economic growth in many developing economies. The same research found, however, that volatility and growth had a slightly positive relationship in industrialized and emerging market economies.[2]

The Balance of Payments

The previous sections examined how we assess and measure a country's domestic economic activity, as represented by GDP. The *balance of payments* allows us to assess and measure a country's international economic transactions. The balance of payments refers to exports and imports of goods and services and financial flows between a country and the rest of the world for a given period, keeping an account of payments to and receipts from nonresidents.

Based on the double-entry accounting system, whereby each recorded transaction is represented by two entries with equal values but opposite signs—a credit and a debit—the sum of all credits should be equal to the sum of all debits. In other words, payments should always be in balance. Some examples of items recorded as credits and debits are shown in table 2.3.

In reality, of course, accounts tend not to balance, and thus all balance-of-payments accounts include an item known as "net errors and omissions." That item is recorded as a net item because of the possibility that credit errors might offset debit errors—that is, that an underestimation of exports might be offset by an overestimation of imports. Because it is a net item, the magnitude of net errors and omissions cannot be taken as an indicator of the relative accuracy of the balance of payments.

Table 2.3   Examples of Credit and Debit Items in the Balance of Payments

Exports of goods and services	Credit
Imports of goods and services	Debit
Increase in financial liabilities	Credit
Decrease in liabilities	Debit
Increase in financial assets	Debit
Decrease in assets	Credit

Source: Authors.

Main Components of the Balance of Payments

The balance of payments has three main components—the current account, the capital account, and net errors and omissions (discussed above).

Current account. The current account is subdivided into four smaller accounts—merchandise trade, services, investment income, and transfer payments. The current-account balance is the difference between the credits and debits in these subaccounts.

- The *merchandise trade* account includes imports and exports of tangible goods, such as cars, computers, and clothes. If a country imports more than it exports in this category, it is said to have a trade deficit.
- The *services* account includes payments in exchange for services, such as transportation, construction, insurance, banking, education, and tourism.
- The *investment income* account reflects domestic residents' investment earnings from foreign stocks, bonds, real estate, and other assets, minus foreigners' investment earnings from domestic assets.
- The *transfer payments* account includes gifts from and payments by private citizens or the government to people living abroad, and vice versa.

Capital account. The capital account includes a variety of subaccounts, all dealing with purchases and sales of financial assets or real estate—stocks, bonds, land, buildings, businesses, and so on. The balance on the capital account is the sum of the changes in these subaccounts. Added to changes in the central bank's reserves during the period, it should equal the balance on the current account. If it does not, there is a statistical discrepancy. Given the magnitude of money flows and the difficulty of measuring and recording millions of international trade transactions, the discrepancy is sometimes substantial.

Analyzing the Nation's External Position

Under the double-entry accounting system, the sum of credits equals the sum of debits, producing a zero balance. But it is possible to have imbalances—surpluses and deficits—in the external account. A surplus arises in the trade account when a country exports more than it imports; a deficit arises if the converse holds. The merchandise-trade balance is often a timely indicator of trends in the current account as a whole (because data on trade in goods are often easier to collect and more readily available than data on trade in services). The current-account balance is one of the most useful indicators of an external imbalance. Persistent large deficits in the current account call for policy adjustments, since a country cannot continue to finance deficits indefinitely by borrowing abroad or drawing down its reserves.

The overall balance of payments equals the current-account balance plus the capital-account balance, plus any errors and omissions. The overall balance is the leading indicator of the country's external payments position. Deficits are usually financed by a decline in net foreign assets or reserves. Changes in reserve holdings are commonly viewed as an indicator of the extent to which the central bank has been financing payments imbalances.

Some Basic Accounting Relationships

This section links four of the five macroeconomic sectors—households, enterprises, the financial sector, and the rest of the world—with the key macroeconomic concept of GDP. The government sector is examined in further detail in chapter 5. We introduce two sets of links between a country's national accounts and its balance of payments. These links, too, are basic accounting relationships that lie at the heart of macroeconomic analysis. The first set comprises the links between aggregate income and demand (or aggregate savings and investment) and the external current-account balance. The second set deals with the resource gap of the non-government (private) sector and its financing.

Aggregate Income, Absorption, and the Current Account

GDP, or the value of goods and services produced by the domestic economy, can be derived from a basic macroeconomic axiom stating that the value of domestic production must be equal to the value of incomes that are domestically generated. Thus:

$$GDP = C + I + (X - M). \tag{2.10}$$

Given that absorption (A) or domestic demand equals $C + I$, then:

$$GDP = A + (X - M). \tag{2.11}$$

In other words, total income equals absorption plus net exports. And given that $GNI = GDP + Y_f$, then:

$$GNI = A + (X - M + Y_f). \tag{2.12}$$

And given that $GNDI = GNI + TR_f$, then:

$$GNDI = A + X - M + Y_f + TR_f \tag{2.13}$$

and so:

$$GNDI - A = X - M + Y_f + TR_f. \tag{2.14}$$

$$X - M + Y_f + TR_f \tag{2.15}$$

equals the current-account balance (CAB).

The identity $GNDI - A = CAB$ is the absorption approach to the balance of payments. Basically, the identity states that a current-account deficit arises whenever an economy spends beyond its means or absorbs more than it produces. Thus, to reduce a current-account deficit, a country must increase its income or reduce absorption. In the short term, increasing income requires the presence of unused production capacity; in the medium and long term, structural policies to help boost capacity are required. Domestic absorption can be reduced by shrinking either private or government consumption of goods and services.

We can go one step further by remembering that $GNDI - C = S$. Thus:

$$GNDI = S + C. \tag{2.16}$$

Substituting for $GNDI$ gives us:

$$S + C - A = X - M + Y_f + TR_f \tag{2.17}$$

Given that $A = C + I$, then:

$$S - I = X - M + Y_f + TR_f \tag{2.18}$$

or:

$$S - I = CAB. \tag{2.19}$$

Thus, the current account of the balance of payments is equal to the gap between savings and investment in an economy. Accordingly, the current-account balance may be viewed as a country's use of foreign savings. In a closed economy, savings must equal investment, but in an open economy any excess of investment over savings is met by recourse to foreign savings, creating a deficit that must eventually be covered by increased savings or reduced investment. The identity says nothing about the theory that underlies current-account behavior. Other factors such as the influence of exchange rates, interest rates, and exogenous shocks need to be considered when explaining current-account developments.

The Resource Gap of the Private Sector and Its Financing

The private sector, also known as the real or nongovernment sector, is defined as the sum of the household and enterprise sectors. Any gap between the income and expenditures of the private sector must be financed. The relationship can be expressed in accounting terms. Savings by the private sector are equal to the difference between the private sector's disposable income and its consumption. The private sector is denoted by the subscript p in the following identities.

$$S_p = GNDI_p - C_p. \tag{2.20}$$

The private sector's absorption, or aggregate demand, can be expressed as

$$A_p = C_p + I_p \tag{2.21}$$

where I_p is gross investment by the private sector.

It therefore follows that:

$$A_p = GNDI_p - S_p + I_p$$
$$A_p - GNDI_p = -(S_p - I_p)$$
$$F_p = -(S_p - I_p)$$

where F_p = the private sector's financing gap.

Thus, the gap between the private sector's savings and investment reflects an excess of absorption over income. To maintain balance, the gap must be financed from elsewhere in the economy, including the sector known as the "rest of the world." Examples of such financing include foreign direct investment from abroad (FDI_p), net borrowing by the private sector from abroad (NFB_p), and private sector borrowing from the banking system—the latter being identical to net credit from the banking system to the private sector (ΔNDC_p). These financial inflows are offset by financial outflows from the private sector, such as lending to the banking system in the form of increased currency holdings and deposits ($\Delta M2$) and lending to the government, or nonbank borrowing by the government from the private sector (NB).[3] Therefore:

$$F_p = FDI_p + NFB_p + \Delta NDC_p - \Delta M2 - NB. \qquad (2.22)$$

It follows that

$$S_p - I_p + FDI_p + NFB_p + \Delta NDC_p - \Delta M2 - NB = 0. \qquad (2.23)$$

Environmental Accounts

GDP as measured in the national accounts of countries does not consider depreciation, depletion, or degradation of natural capital or wealth (water, soil or land, air, forests, and other natural endowments) in the course of production of goods and services. Cleanup and abatement costs incurred to restore environmental wealth are also not considered in the present scheme of national-income accounting. Therefore, until the system of national accounts is revised to include environmental accounts that will encourage policy makers to consider natural resource management in their decision making, GDP will not be an accurate measure of *sustainable* income.

In the System of Integrated Environmental and Economic Accounting, environmental costs, benefits, and natural resource assets, as well as expenditures for environmental protection, were presented as satellite accounts in a manner consistent with the accounting framework of the UN system of national accounts. In 2003, the *Integrated Environmental and Economic Accounting Handbook* (UN 2003)—presented jointly by the UN, European Commission (EC), IMF, OECD, and World Bank— provided methods for estimating environmental and natural resource–related expenditures that were not effectively captured in the system of national accounts. These included accounts to track natural resource assets and stock depletions, the use of energy and fuel materials, and the generation of pollutants and wastes, as well as expenditures for environmental protection and resource management.

The World Bank (2006) takes into account the GDP from national accounts and separately calculates "green data." If one uses Bolivia as an example, gross savings as revealed in the national accounts is about 20 percent of GNI. But when environmental accounts are considered, net savings falls to –20 percent of GNI, where:

Adjusted net savings = gross savings – consumption of fixed capital + education expenditures – [energy depletion, mineral depletion, net forest depletion, and emissions of carbon dioxide].

As shown in a schematic representation in figure 2.3, Bolivia, for example, consumes a great deal of "environmental wealth" to generate its GDP.

It is possible to convert GDP from national accounts into environmental accounts using data from the World Bank's Wealth of Nations database. According to the Bank's system, the difference between a nation's wealth in a given year and its wealth the year before reflects its environment-adjusted GDP.

Informal Sector Activities

In recent years, the informal sector has been expanding in most developing countries, representing about 30 to 50 percent of their economies by most accounts. The informal economy, casually referred to as the black market, is known also as the hidden, shadow, parallel, unreported, or cash economy—with some distinctions among the terms. Following the definitions of Feige (1987), an *illegal economy* consists of the income generated from economic activities pursued in violation of the legal statutes that define the scope of legitimate forms of commerce. An *unreported economy* consists of those legal and illegal economic activities that evade fiscal rules and tax laws. The *informal economy* comprises economic activities that circumvent the costs of—and are excluded from the benefits and rights conferred by—the nation's laws and administrative rules governing property relationships, commercial licensing, labor contracts, torts, financial credit, and social systems. An estimate of the informal economy is the income generated by economic agents who operate informally.

Figure 2.3   GNI and Resource Use

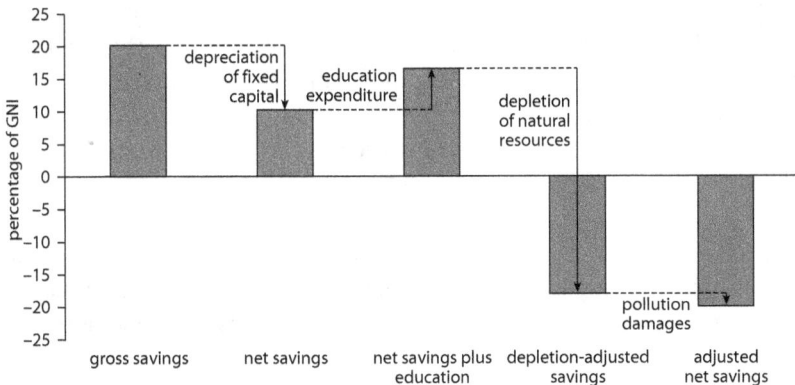

Source: Hamilton 2006, 40, based on *World Development Indicators.*

There is a large body of literature on the factors that shape the informal sector. Three broad factors are distinguished:

- *The burden of direct and indirect taxation, both actual and perceived.* A rising burden of taxation provides a strong incentive to work in the informal economy.
- *The burden of regulation* (as an indicator of the burden of all other government activities). Increases in the burden of regulation are a strong incentive to enter the informal economy.
- *Citizens' attitudes toward the state.* Attitudes toward the state are an indicator of individuals' readiness to leave their formal occupations and enter the informal sector.

Although by definition the informal economy is not directly tracked by the government, its growth and contraction can be gauged by several indicators. If activities in the informal economy rise, for example, demand for currency is likely to increase. If the number of workers in the hidden sector increases, one should see a decrease in participation in the formal economy, expressed either as fewer workers or a contraction in hours worked. As inputs (especially labor) move out of the official economy and into the growing informal economy, the displacement can be expected to depress the economy's official growth rate.

Happiness and National Well-Being Accounts

Since the 1950s, measures of economic performance have expanded to include nonmonetary aspects—such as indicators of human development, gender equity, freedom and empowerment, poverty reduction, equal opportunity, sustainability, and even happiness.

The "economics of happiness" is an approach to assessing subjective welfare that combines techniques used by economists and psychologists. Up to a certain threshold, increases in incomes result in increases in happiness, but beyond a certain level, further increases in incomes do not lead to higher levels of happiness. Among the specific findings from statistical "happiness" research are the following:

- *Money does buy a reasonable amount of happiness.* But it is useful to keep this in perspective. Very loosely, for the typical individual, a doubling of salary affects happiness much less than marriage and other life events.

- *At the national level, the picture changes.* Whole countries—at least in the West, where almost all the research has been done—do not seem to get happier as they get richer. Sixty-four percent of Danes say they are happy, compared with only 16 percent of the French. What accounts for these large differences in happiness among countries? Across nations, women report greater well-being than men. Why?

- *There are twists and turns in the path.* Unemployment and divorce clearly bring unhappiness. Education is associated with high reported levels of happiness, even after controlling for income. But good and bad life events wear off—at least partially—as people get used to them. For example, lottery winners are happy for a short period of time, but after a time, they revert to their old level of happiness.

- *Happiness often hinges on one's position relative to others.* Experiments have shown that people care about how they are treated compared with peers. In the laboratory, they will even pay to hurt others to restore what they see as fairness. From large statistical studies, it appears that one's reported well-being depends on one's earnings relative to an average or "comparison" wage. Wage inequality depresses reported happiness in a region or nation (controlling for many variables), but the effect is not large.

Overall, happiness is strongly correlated with good health and weakly correlated with income. Newer measures of well-being have been constructed in some countries using survey questions on happiness, family satisfaction, job satisfaction, work stress, and tiredness.

Conclusion

After measuring poverty, the second step in assessing how economic policies can affect the poor is understanding the key relationships among the various agents in an economy—households, firms, the financial sector, government, and the rest of the world. Those relationships are the subject matter of macroeconomics, the branch of economics that studies the national economy as a whole. The central concern of macroeconomics is the measurement of economic activity and growth, captured by GDP and its movements. An economy's position relative to other countries is measured by the balance of payments. The links between the domestic economy and the rest of the world can be expressed in the accounting relationships presented in this chapter. With the tools of the first two chapters, we are now equipped to analyze the important questions of how various policies influence poverty in developing countries.

Notes

1. Inventory changes are considered a part of investment for the year as long as they cover products made but not sold in that year. GDP includes as part of current production the market value of any additions to (or withdrawals from) inventories during that year, along with the value of goods that were manufactured and sold during the year.
2. Emerging market economies are also known as transitional economies, meaning that they are in the process of moving from a closed to an open market economy while building accountability within the system. Examples include the countries of the former Soviet Union and the nations that were once Soviet allies in Central and Eastern Europe.
3. The nonbank private sector consists of people, companies, building societies, and the rest of the private sector (except for banks). If the government's expenditure is greater than its revenue (tax and nontax), then the government has to borrow to cover this deficit. It does so by selling government securities to the nonbank private sector.

Bibliography

Acemoglu, D., S. Johnson, J. Robinson, and Y. Thaicharoen. 2003. "Institutional Causes, Macroeconomic Symptoms: Volatility, Crises, and Growth." *Journal of Monetary Economics* 50: 49–123.

Agenor, P. R. 2003. *Development Macroeconomics*. Washington, DC: World Bank.

Blanchard, Olivier, and Stanley Fischer. 1989. *Lectures in Macroeconomics*. Cambridge, MA: MIT Press.

Bryant, Ralph, David Currie, Jacob Frenkel, Paul Masson, and Richard Portes, eds. 1989. *Macroeconomic Policies in an Interdependent World*. Washington, DC: The Brookings Institution.

Bryant, Ralph, Dale Henderson, Gerald Holtham, Peter Hooper, and Steven Symansky, eds. 1988. *Empirical Macroeconomics for Interdependent Economies*. Washington, DC: The Brookings Institution.

Feige, E. L. 1987. "The Anatomy of the Underground Economy." In *The Unofficial Economy*. S. Alessandrini and B. Dallago, eds. Aldershot, UK: Gower Publishing Company Ltd.

Hamilton, K. 2006. *Where Is the Wealth of Nations? Measuring Capital for the 21st Century*. Washington, DC: World Bank.

Kahneman, Daniel, Alan Kreuger, David Schkade, Norbert Schwarz, and Arthur Stone. 2004. *American Economic Review* 94 (May): 429–34.

Keynes, John Maynard. 1936. *The General Theory of Employment, Interest, and Money*. London: Macmillan.

Kose, M. A., E. S. Prasad, and M. E. Terrones. 2004. "Taking the Plunge without Getting Hurt." *Finance and Development* (December): 44–47.

Maddison, Angus. 2002. *The World Economy: Historical Statistics*. Paris: OECD.

Mankiw, N. 2002. *Macroeconomics*. 5th ed. New York: Worth.

OECD (Organisation of Economic Co-operation and Development). 2006. *Eurostat-OECD Methodological Manual on Purchasing Power Parities*. Paris: OECD.

———. 2008. *OECD Glossary of Statistical Terms*. Paris: OECD.

Phelps, Edmund S. 1990. *Seven Schools of Thought in Macroeconomics*. Oxford: Oxford University Press.

UN (United Nations). 2003. *Handbook of National Accounting: Integrated Environmental and Economic Accounting—An Operational Manual*. New York: United Nations.

World Bank. 2006. *World Development Report 2006: Equity and Development*. Washington, DC: World Bank.

CHAPTER 3

Growth, Poverty, and Inequality: An Overview

Economists since Adam Smith have used growth models and related tools to answer a key question: Why have some countries grown rapidly over the past few centuries while others have not? Although a great swath of the economic literature over the past 50 years has focused on growth factors—primarily macroeconomic policies and institutions—our understanding of the root causes of growth remains incomplete. This chapter examines the strategies adopted by some successful countries, and the tools and techniques that economists use to understand and measure the growth process.

Growth Theory, Then and Now

The influential model of Robert Solow (1956) holds that growth in output is determined by inputs of capital and labor. Remarkably, the inventions and innovations that contribute to the increased productivity of all factors of production and that drive the entrepreneurial spirit of capitalism are not part of the model. Instead, technical progress is exogenous—that is, it is assumed to come from outside. In Solow's scheme, domestic economic policies cannot affect the steady-state, long-run growth rate. But structural policy reforms in trade, finance, and privatization—as well as sectoral policy changes, especially in agriculture—have some, albeit minimal, impact on gross domestic product (GDP).

Against this backdrop, the growth theory of Romer (1986) introduces the idea that incentives can affect technical progress and, therefore, that national policies can alter a country's long-run growth rate. But Romer's and related theories focus on expanding the technological frontier—thus, their relevance to policy making in developing countries is minimal.

A decade later, institutions and government policies—called *social infrastructure* (Hall and Jones 1999)—came to be seen as important to the growth process because they affected both the level and the distribution of output across various groups and individuals in a country. Such theories form the basis for the current consensus view of growth in the developing world, a view supported by data from more than five decades of economic performance.

Countries may start with similar endowments (land, natural resources, labor, and so on), but, because of differences in institutional structures (political, legal, and so on), they implement different macroeconomic and sectoral policies and follow different development paths. Structures that lead to success in one country may not, and often cannot, be replicated in others. But political leadership that favors market-oriented policies and private economic activity can trigger growth spurts, which may be short lived, as in several Latin American countries during the 1970s and 1980s. Turning points, or major policy changes, occur at different times in different countries.

Patterns of economic performance vary across countries. There are high-growth and low-growth countries, as well as those that have grown at a consistently rapid pace and those that have experienced short-term spurts. Growth in the high-income countries averaged 2.7 percent from 1960 to 2000 (figure 3.1) and was accompanied by significant improvements in social indicators such as literacy, infant mortality, life expectancy, and so on. Regions such as East and Southeast Asia experienced an average growth rate of 4.4 percent during the same period. But the gap between the per capita GDP of advanced and developing countries remains large.

Rates of economic growth across countries do not appear to be closely related to initial levels of per capita income. By the 1960s, most developing countries had gained independence from colonial powers and were roughly at the same level of income and development; 50 years later, some had increased their GDP many times, while others were even worse off than at their independence (Rodrik 2004). On the other hand, rates

Figure 3.1   Per Capita GDP Growth Rates by Country Groupings
1995 US$

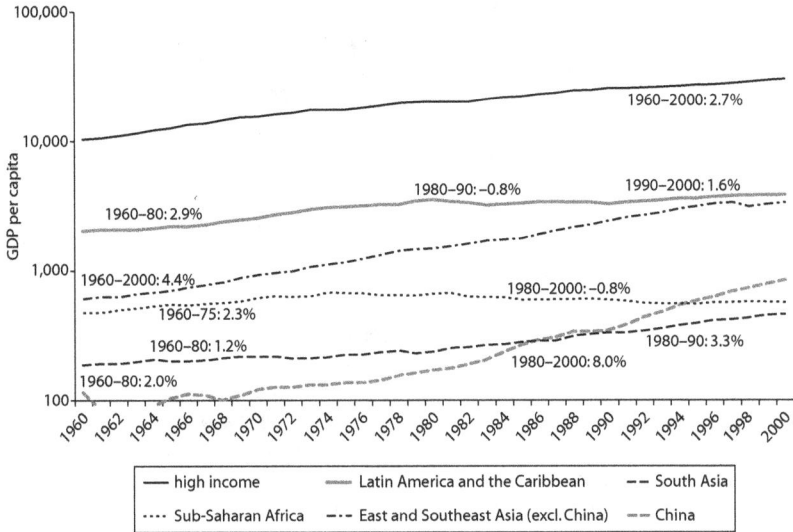

Source: Rodrik 2004.

of population growth are negatively related to both per capita income and per capita GDP growth across countries.

Growth in physical capital, human capital, and research and development spending explains only about half of the variation in output within or across countries. Other factors, such as savings rates, factor productivity, proclivity to trade, the generation and exploitation of knowledge, sound macroeconomic policy, and the extent and quality of government regulation, explain the rest (table 3.1). Countries that have high savings and investment rates, for example, tend toward higher GDP growth rates—and the opposite is true for countries with low savings and investment rates.

Total factor productivity (defined as output produced per worker for a given cost or over a certain period) is more important than capital accumulation. But to understand total factor productivity, we need to know what drives knowledge accumulation and the use of new technologies. We also need to understand the incentives for knowledge creation. (These questions, and their answers, lie at the heart of a new field known as knowledge for development.)

Having a high volume of trade with other countries (also called trade openness) is positively correlated with knowledge sharing, learning by

Table 3.1   Economic Policies and Growth—A Review of the Evidence

Policy area	Indicator category	Econometric results
I. Structural policies and institutions		
Education	Enrollment rates, years of education	[+]: Barro (1991, 2001); Mankiw, Romer, and Weil (1992); Loayza, Fajnzylber, and Calderón (2005)
	Quality of education	[+]: Barro and Lee (2001)
	Allocation of talents	[+]: Murphy, Shleifer, and Vishny (1991)
	R&D investment	[+]: Coe and Helpman (1995)
Financial development	Private domestic credit (% GDP)	[+]: Levine, Loayza, and Beck (2000); Loayza, Fajnzylber, and Calderón (2005)
	Liquid liabilities (% GDP)	[+] via total factor productivity growth: Beck, Levine, and Loayza (2000)
		[+] only for countries with well-developed financial systems: Rioja and Valev (2004)
Government burden	Distortionary taxation	[–]: Kneller, Bleaney, and Gemmell (1999) for OECD, Gupta and others (2005) for developed countries
	Corporate taxes	[–]: Lee and Gordon (2005)
	Labor income tax, marginal tax rates	[0]: Lee and Gordon (2005)
	Government consumption	[–]: Loayza, Fajnzylber, and Calderón (2005)
Infrastructure	Infrastructure stocks	[+]: Sanchez-Robles (1998); Bougheas, Demetriades, and Mamuneas (2000); Easterly (2001b); Esfahani and Ramirez (2003); Calderón and Servén (2004)
	Infrastructure, quality	[+]: Calderón and Servén (2004)
Governance	Institutional quality (Business Environment Risk Intelligence; International Country Risk Guide)	[+]: Knack and Keefer (1995)
	Absence of corruption	[+]: Mauro (1995)
	Kaufmann et al. indicators	[+]: Dollar and Kraay (2003); Acemoglu, Johnson, and Robinson (2001, 2002); Hall and Jones (1999)
Trade openness	Exports and imports (% GDP)	[+]: Ben-David (1993); Edwards (1998); Dollar and Kraay (2003)
	Index of outward orientation/openness	[+]: Dollar (1992); Sachs and Warner (1995); Wacziarg and Welch (2003)
	Openness adjusted by geography	[+]: Frankel and Romer (1999); Loayza, Fajnzylber, and Calderón (2005)
II. Stabilization policies		
Macroeconomic stabilization	CPI inflation rate	[–]: Fischer (1993); Loayza, Fajnzylber, and Calderón (2005)

(continued next page)

Table 3.1   Economic Policies and Growth—A Review of the Evidence

Policy area	Indicator category	Econometric results
		[–] for high-inflation periods: Bruno and Easterly (1998); Fischer, Sahay, and Végh (2002)
External imbalances	Real exchange rate overvaluation	[–]: Dollar (1992); Easterly (2001b); Loayza, Fajnzylber, and Calderón (2005)
		[–] the larger the impact, the higher the overvaluation: Collins and Razin (1999); Aguirre and Calderón (2005)
Financial turmoil	Systemic banking crises	[–]: Kaminsky and Reinhart (1999); Dell'Arriccia, Detragiache, and Rajan (2005); Loayza, Fajnzylber, and Calderón (2005)

Source: Lopez 2006, 77.
Note: CPI = consumer price index; R & D = research and development. [+] implies a positive and significant relationship between growth and the corresponding economic policy. [–] reflects a negative and significant relationship, and [0] denotes no statistical relationship between the variables.

doing, and higher GDP growth rates. But questions about the relationship between trade and growth remain. A growing economy needs both more imports and lower tariffs. But is reducing tariffs and nontariff barriers enough to spur growth? The connection between financial liberalization and growth is similarly unclear.

In the short to medium term, GDP growth is negatively related to large fiscal deficits, high inflation, high corporate taxes, excessive and unpredictable regulation, high interest rates, scarcity of credit, low rates of investment, and the misalignment of domestic currency. The Washington Consensus of the 1980s (a set of macroeconomic policies that sought to reduce distortions in prices and markets to spur growth) emphasized the need for fiscal discipline, competitive exchange rates, trade and financial liberalization, privatization, and deregulation. Economic policies adopted under this agenda came to be known as "first-generation reforms." The main criticism of these reforms was that they were adjustments without a human face, expressions of trickle-down economics and insensitivity to the social disruption and human suffering they caused.

In the 1990s, "second-generation reforms" were introduced that focused on upgrading public financial management, reducing corruption, improving corporate governance, providing social safety nets, and fighting poverty through well-targeted programs. Also, in the 1990s, it became evident that although finance was important for growth, the direction of financial flows was observed to be from developing to developed countries. This phenomenon, which has persisted, contrasted sharply with economic theory, which suggests that resources should flow toward countries that yield higher marginal rates of return—in other words, developing countries.

Institutions and Modern Growth Theory

Institutions are important because they determine how and to what extent public policies designed to encourage or discourage knowledge creation, technological adoption, and capital accumulation will be carried out. The right institutions, functioning properly, can provide incentives to accumulate physical and human capital, innovate, develop and adapt to new technologies, and reorganize the production and distribution of goods and services. Growth appears to occur in countries where private property rights are protected from infringement by individuals and government, and where the legal system facilitates private transactions (for example, by providing for the enforcement of contracts).

Also needed are institutions that provide incentives to adopt modern technology. Because technology forces the constant reorganization of productive units, it tends to generate forces opposed to further change. Technologies and institutions must change in tandem, but it appears that institutions evolve more slowly than technologies—and this mismatch creates problems. A country's ability to accommodate changes over decades depends on its political and economic institutions. But institutions that are good for one period in time may not be good for the next. This explains why, over the centuries, civilizations such as those of Egypt, Greece, Rome, and Persia declined. Economic, political, legal, and social institutions do not evolve independent of one another. But they develop at different speeds, complicating the tasks of economic management and forecasting.

Although it is known that the rate of growth is shaped by property rights, the rule of law, and constraints on executive power, the exact way these factors affect national wealth and per capita income is not well understood. Even less well understood is how labor relations and the behavior of interest groups affect growth. Thinkers differ on whether presidential systems perform better than parliamentary ones, whether democracies perform better than autocracies, and whether income growth drives autocracies toward democratic systems. The studies conducted to date are inconclusive.

Modern growth theory, as formulated by Acemoglu and Johnson (2007), deals with these unresolved questions and provides some measure of the factors necessary to generate and sustain growth over the long run. It links the proximate causes of economic phenomena to fundamental causes, in particular institutions. The central question of why some countries grow and others do not is tackled directly and formulated with greater breadth and precision than before. Acemoglu and Johnson go back in time, showing that intercountry growth differences began to show up as early as 1800. Those nascent differences were amplified during the Industrial Revolution, during which new organizational forms and technologies were adopted.

At the dawn of the nineteenth century, some countries such as the United Kingdom, and, later, the United States and Canada, began a process of rapid industrialization based on the adoption of new technologies. As industrialization took off, it produced a shift from agriculture to manufacturing—a structural transformation. Now, as then, some societies may fail to take off because they fail to adopt new production technologies, often because they lack the right type of institutions or firms. They may lack appropriate financial markets, labor skills, managers, and professionals. Often, the presence or absence of facilitating institutions can be traced to social choices—political and economic. Behind those choices are individuals and groups that stand to win or lose from a given change.

The reward structures faced by firms and individuals play a central role in shaping whether they undertake the investments in new technology and human capital necessary for takeoff, industrialization, and economic growth. These reward structures are determined by policies and institutions, and politics plays a major role in shaping institutions, which, in turn, decide whether a society can embark upon modern economic growth. When no way can be found to compensate influential parties that are likely to lose from change, or when likely winners have insufficient political power, we may expect policies and institutions that are not growth enhancing. In such circumstances, distortionary policies may be adopted to block growth, usually to protect politically powerful incumbent producers or to stabilize the established political regime. As technology, market structures, and factor endowments interact with those policies—at any given moment, myriad transactions are occurring among firms, consumers, and government agencies—the path of the nation's economic growth is shaped.

Democracies and dictatorships are likely to make different policy choices and to create different types of reward structures. Although there are no perfect political institutions, and each political arrangement is likely to favor some groups at the expense of others, authoritarian political systems (such as absolute monarchies, dictatorships, autocracies, and oligarchies) concentrate power in the hands of a small minority and pursue economic policies that are favorable to the interests of this minority. Authoritarian systems also usually rely on some amount of repression to maintain the unequal distribution of political power and economic benefit. They also adopt economic institutions and policies that protect incumbents and create benefits, known as "rents," for those who hold political power.

Participatory regimes—systems in which people have a say in governance—place constraints on rulers and politicians (thus preventing the most absolutist tendencies in political systems) and give voice to new economic interests, so that a strict decoupling of political and economic power is avoided. Such regimes include constitutional monarchies, where broader sections of the society take part in economic and political decision making, and democracies, where political participation is greater than in nondemocratic regimes.

The distinguishing feature of participatory regimes is that they give voice and security (both economic and political) to a broader cross section of society than do authoritarian regimes. As a result, they are more open to the creation of new businesses and provide a more level playing field and more secure property rights to a larger portion of society. Thus, in some ways, the contrast between authoritarian political systems and participatory regimes can be expressed as a contrast between the growth-promoting cluster of institutions and growth-blocking, extractive institutions.

Returning to the earlier question of what factors matter most for growth, it now appears that although increases in capital, labor, and land contribute to (and may even be essential for) growth, technology adoption is more important than any of these over a longer period of time. There is no longer any doubt that technology is a prime driver of economic growth over the long term and a major factor in cross-country differences in economic performance—quite a change from a half-century ago, when Solow (1956) introduced his seminal theory. Using cross-country data, economists have made considerable progress in understanding the relationship of physical and human capital to investments by firms in technology and by individuals, families, and governments in education. Because investment decisions depend on the rewards that individuals, firms, and governments can expect from their investments, understanding differences in investment levels is intimately linked to understanding how reward structures differ across societies and how individuals respond to those differences.

There are marked differences across societies in the institutions that influence technology adoption and diffusion. Most developing economies do not invent their own technologies, but adopt them from the world's technology leaders or adapt them from technologies in use elsewhere. The difference lies in how quickly and effectively new technologies are adapted and absorbed. Among the important questions that remain unanswered by modern growth theory are the role of contracts (broadly conceived) in the spread of innovation and the origin of structural transformations that affect rates of economic growth.

The world comprises millions of implicit or explicit contracts. Suppliers enter into agreements with downstream customers; industrial firms have agreements with financial firms (such as banks); employers and employees enter into contracts; governments agree to protect inventors' property rights in return for disclosure of their inventions. These understandings are all subject to ambiguities and other pitfalls and sticking points known to economists and lawyers as moral hazard, adverse selection, holdups, and principal-agent complications. How important are contracts to the process of economic growth?

We are still far from understanding the contractual foundations of economic growth and their role in determining the pace of technology diffusion. It is not inconceivable that more secure contracts (better worded, better enforced) could stimulate innovation and technological upgrading in industrialized economies. Or that they could facilitate technology transfer to the developing world. These are basic, but—as yet—unanswered questions.

Some structural changes in economies and societies can be viewed as by-products of economic growth. The increase in services relative to agriculture is a prime example. But other structural changes—including developments in financial markets, changes in legal regimes, growing urbanization, and the commitment of individuals and societies to education—are not simple by-products of economic growth, although they are intimately linked to economic development. To understand how structural transformations might delay or prevent economic growth, we require models with stronger theoretical foundations, a unified approach to these related issues, and a greater effort to link models of economic development to the wealth of research on economic behavior in less-developed economies.

Economic Growth and Poverty Reduction

Sustained growth reduces poverty. The economic literature is firm on this point. Numerous cross-country studies have concluded that the main determinant of poverty reduction is the pace of economic growth.

Kraay (2004) found that approximately "half of the variation in short-run changes in poverty can be explained by growth in average incomes. In the medium to long run, between 66 and 90 percent of the variation in changes in poverty can be accounted for by the growth in average incomes." A report from the Operationalizing Pro-Poor Growth Research Program (AFD and others 2005) revealed that in countries that experienced economic growth between 1990 and 2003 (11 of 14 studied), a 1 percent increase in GDP per capita reduced poverty (as measured by the annual change in poverty headcount) by 1.7 percent. For some countries, such as Vietnam, the reduction was spectacular—a halving of the poverty rate from 58 percent to 29 percent (or almost 8 percent a year). Poverty declined by rates of between 3 and 6 percent per year in El Salvador, Ghana, India, Tunisia, and Uganda (figure 3.2).

Consistent with the positive relationship between growth and poverty reduction, it has also been found that incomes of the poor appear to rise proportionately with average incomes (Dollar and Kraay 2002). Plotting per capita incomes of the poor against average per capita income for 137

Figure 3.2   Economic Growth and Poverty Reduction in Select Countries, 1990–2003

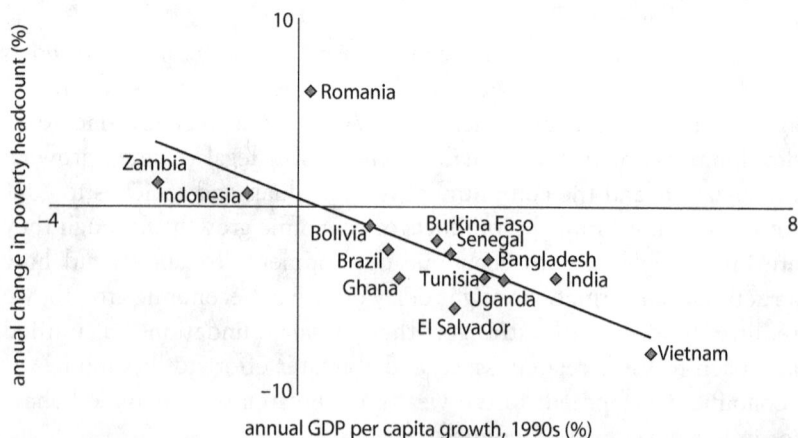

annual GDP per capita growth, 1990s (%)

Source: AFD and others 2005.

countries, Dollar and Kraay found a strong, positive linear relationship between the two variables (with a slope of 1.07) (figure 3.3, panel a). Moreover, plotting the annual average growth in incomes of the poor against average annual growth in average incomes for 92 countries also

Figure 3.3   Average Per Capita Incomes and Growth

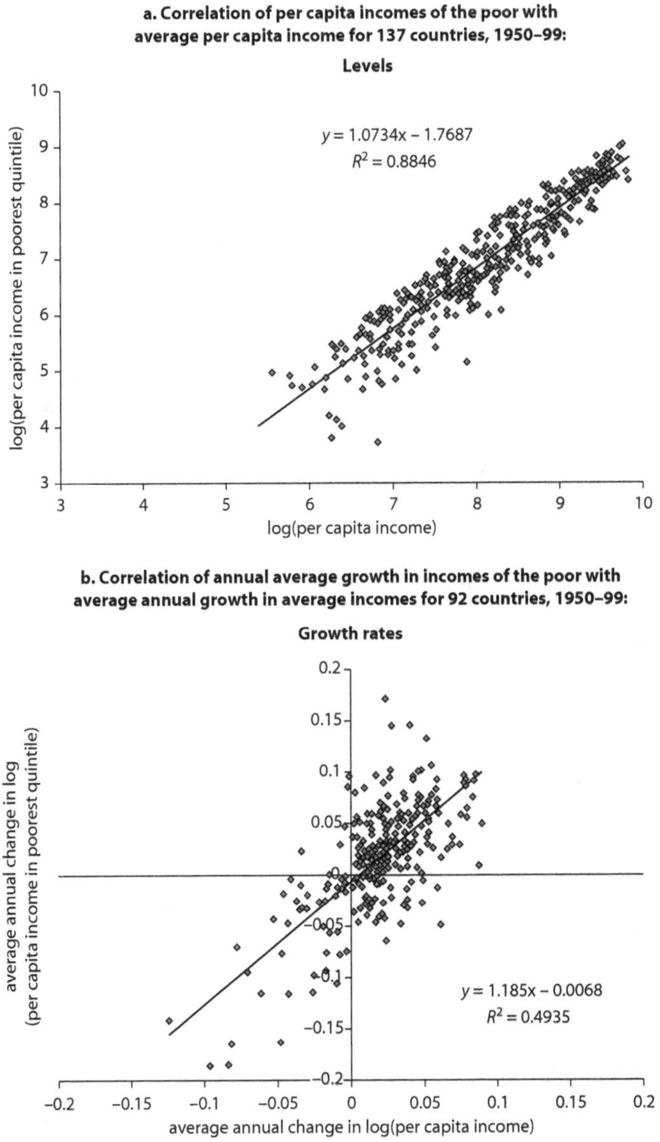

a. Correlation of per capita incomes of the poor with average per capita income for 137 countries, 1950–99:

Levels

$y = 1.0734x - 1.7687$
$R^2 = 0.8846$

b. Correlation of annual average growth in incomes of the poor with average annual growth in average incomes for 92 countries, 1950–99:

Growth rates

$y = 1.185x - 0.0068$
$R^2 = 0.4935$

Source: Dollar and Kraay 2002.

yielded a strong positive, linear relationship between the variables, with a slope of 1.19 (figure 3.3, panel b). Other researchers, too, have found that poverty trends tracked growth trends very closely in the 1980s and 1990s. For example, according to Chen and Ravallion (2000), on average, growth in the consumption of the poorest fifth of the population tracked economic growth one for one over this period.

Unsurprisingly, the converse also holds: low or declining economic growth leads to increases in the incidence of poverty. Thus, in the vast majority of countries studied by Chen and Ravallion (2000), economic decline led to falling consumption. In a more recent study, López (2004) found that economic decline in per capita income in Argentina (1993–2002) and Zambia (1991–98) led to increases in the incidence of poverty (table 3.2). Similarly, three of the countries in the Operationalizing Pro-Poor Growth study—Zambia, Indonesia, and Romania—that exhibited little or no economic growth over the study period (1990–2003) experienced increases in poverty.

Few economists doubt that economic growth is necessary for the long-term reduction of poverty. But how close is the link between the two? In their 2002 study, Dollar and Kraay gathered information on the per capita income of the poor (defined as the bottom quintile of the income distribution) and on overall per capita income. Using data from 137 countries in panel a of figure 3.3 and 92 countries in panel b of figure 3.3 over five decades, Dollar and Kraay pieced together 418 sample periods (some countries had more than one observation) during which it was possible to measure changes in the income of the poor and of the country overall. Noting that the per capita income of the poorest quintile grew in line with overall per capita GDP for the 80 countries covered over the four decades, the authors drew the following conclusions:

- Growth matters—and the poor generally are not left behind in the growth process.

Table 3.2   Examples of the Link between Economic Growth and Poverty

Country	Period	Annual change in income per capita (%)	Change in poverty headcount (%)
China	1981–2000	+8.5	50 > 8
Vietnam	1993–2002	+6	58 > 29
Argentina	1993–2002	−0.18	21 > 55
Zambia	1991–98	−2.4	69 > 75

Source: López 2004.

- The incomes of the poor do not fall disproportionately during economic crises.
- Greater economic openness, the rule of law, fiscal discipline, and low inflation all contribute to (or are at least associated with) faster economic growth and, thus, help the poor.
- Democracy and greater public spending on health and education do not have a measurable effect, one way or another, on the incomes of the poor.

The relationship between economic growth and poverty reduction appears to hold for both *absolute* and *relative* measures of poverty (López 2004). As demonstrated in chapter 1, an absolute measure is expressed as an income below a prespecified threshold, such as an adjusted purchasing power parity (PPP) of $1.25 per person per day, or a country-specific poverty line based on subsistence needs. A relative measure is expressed as a prespecified proportion of the population, usually the lowest quintile of the population.

Variations in Poverty Responses to Growth

Poverty responds to economic growth differently across countries. Key factors in determining the country's response are the presence (or absence) of productivity gains, the sector composition of growth (and its labor intensiveness), and the extent of inequality in the society. Understanding these factors enables us to view growth in a pro-poor context, a topic developed in more detail in the following section.

Growth derives from economic inputs—capital and labor—and from the efficiency of their use. Because simply adding inputs typically becomes less effective in generating growth over time—a phenomenon referred to as diminishing marginal returns—it is usually necessary to make factors more productive to sustain growth. This is done through technological advances, improved management know-how, and increases in skills through education. Viewed through this prism, the robust growth experience of Uganda (more than 6 percent a year on average since the mid-1980s) and the country's consequent success in lowering poverty is not as impressive as commonly thought. Pattillo, Gupta, and Carey (2005) found that Uganda's growth achievements were predominantly due to capital accumulation (investment) and had very little to do with productivity gains. "Because increasingly higher investment rates (and consequently, rising national or external saving) are not feasible," noted the authors, slow growth in the productivity of the factors of production threatened Uganda's gains. The country would have to improve productivity to sustain its growth and consolidate its achievements in reducing poverty.

The composition of economic growth also has implications for poverty reduction. The sectoral composition of economic growth can explain why given rates of economic growth can lead to different rates of poverty reduction. Growth that derives from the intensive use of unskilled labor will have a greater immediate impact on reducing the incidence of poverty than will growth built on skilled labor, given that the poor are more likely to be unskilled. Loayza and Raddatz (2006) showed not only that the incidence of poverty falls in the face of aggregate economic growth, but also that poverty reduction is stronger when growth has a labor-intensive inclination. The Operationalizing Pro-Poor Growth group (AFD and others 2005) found that most of the absolute reduction in poverty in countries experiencing economic growth occurred in rural areas, where the majority of the poor live and earn their livelihoods from agriculture. Land and labor policies affect the participation of the rural poor in the economy, with consequent implications for economic growth and poverty reduction. These points are discussed in later chapters.

The level of inequality in a society and how inequality changes over time are other important determinants of how the incidence and severity of poverty will be affected by economic growth. Senegal and Burkina Faso had similar levels of economic growth—2.2 percent per capita per year—over a similar time frame (López 2004). But poverty declined by 2.5 percent annually in Senegal and just 1.8 percent in Burkina Faso. According to López, Senegal made more progress because it was a less unequal society.

Is unequal distribution of income good or bad for a country's development? Opinions differ about the pattern of distribution that is most likely to produce growth—about whether, for example, the Gini coefficient, a measure of income inequality (see glossary), should be closer to 25 percent (as in Sweden) or to 40 percent (as in the United States) and whether the optimal distribution changes as national income changes. An excessively equal income distribution can be bad for economic efficiency. Take, for example, the experience of communist countries, where deliberately low levels of inequality (with no private profits and minimal differences in wages and salaries) deprived people of incentives to participate in economic activities through diligent work and vigorous entrepreneurship. Among the consequences of attempts to equalize incomes were poor discipline and low initiative among workers, poor quality and limited selection of goods and services, slow technical progress, and, eventually, slower economic growth and more poverty. But, beyond this extreme, some studies suggest that countries with more equal distribution of certain assets (public goods, land, and so on) tend to grow faster (figure 3.4).

Using a comprehensive cross-country data set, Deininger and Squire (1996) found that *inequality* generally tends to favor economic growth. They also found that inequality in the distribution of assets has a greater impact on growth than does income inequality, although the two are closely related. Despite this, Deininger and Squire suggest that certain redistributive policies, in particular those that improve access to credit for the poor, can help boost growth. Governments have, of course, tried redistributive policies in the past—for example, through land redistribution, employment programs, and subsidies, and by improving access to credit, public goods, infrastructure, health, and education—but with varying degrees of success. Further research on the impact of public spending on equality is urgently needed.

Figure 3.4   Land Distribution and the Pace of Growth

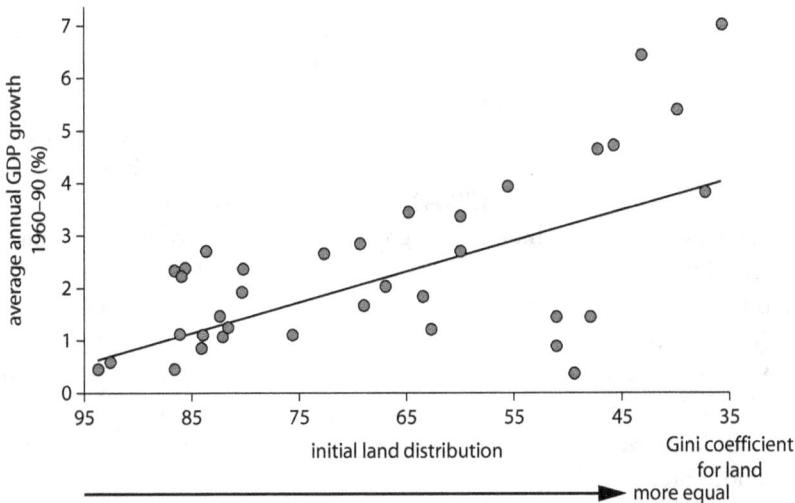

Source: Deininger and Squire 1996.

Pro-Poor Growth

From the previous section, we know that the incidence of poverty drops with economic growth. We also know that the precise effect of growth on poverty depends on the initial level of income inequality in the country and how it changes with economic growth. The concept of pro-poor growth was introduced in the 1990s to provide greater insight into the relationship of economic growth, poverty, and income inequality. It captures the way in which national economic growth improves the welfare of the poor through changes in income inequality.

At its simplest, pro-poor growth is growth that raises the incomes of the poor. More formally, the literature suggests two definitions. The first focuses on whether the distributional shifts accompanying growth favor the poor—that is, whether poverty falls in response to growth by more than it would have if all incomes had grown at the same rate. The second focuses on whether economic growth benefits poor people in absolute terms, as reflected by changes in an appropriate measure of poverty. The measures of poverty generally used are the headcount index and the poverty gap. The concepts of relative and absolute poverty are used to detect underlying levels of inequality.

Assessing whether growth is pro-poor requires knowledge of distributional changes in income and the extent to which those changes have improved the welfare of the poor. To measure the extent to which growth is pro-poor, we break down poverty (as measured by the headcount index, for example) into a component attributable to economic growth and a component attributable to the change in income distribution. This method, developed originally by Datt and Ravallion (1992) and more recently by Kraay (2004), has proved informative about the reasons behind variations in the rate of poverty reduction across countries. According to Kraay (2004), the potential sources of pro-poor growth are three: (a) a high rate of growth of average incomes, (b) a high sensitivity of poverty (poverty elasticity) to growth in average incomes, and (c) a poverty-reducing pattern of growth in relative incomes.

The outcome from the large sample of developing countries considered by Kraay during the 1980s and 1990s is that more than 90 percent of the variation in poverty over the medium to long term is due to the growth in *average* incomes, suggesting that policies and institutions that promote broad-based growth should be central to the pro-poor growth agenda. The remainder of the variation comes from changes in relative income (or inequality). Kraay himself has acknowledged that although the evidence from these cross-country comparisons suggests trends, it provides little guidance about what policies and institutions will promote pro-poor growth.

The distributional effect of growth on the rate of poverty reduction has also been explored. Using a log normal distribution (most studies use a linear model), Bourguignon (2003) showed that distributional changes in income were responsible for variations in the response of poverty to growth over time. He suggested as well that redistribution contributes to a permanent increase in the elasticity of poverty and thereby accelerates the rate of poverty reduction for a given rate of growth. Distributional changes have been important in explaining differing rates of poverty reduction in specific countries. Ravallion (2001) suggested that the median rate of decline in the $1/day headcount index was 10 percent per year among countries that combined growth with falling inequality, but only 1 percent per year for those countries for which growth came with rising inequality.

Undeniably, extreme income inequality hampers the ability of growth to reduce poverty—in fact, it is a barrier. Ravallion (2001) found that for countries where inequality was very high, a 1 percent increase in average household income levels had a much lower impact on poverty (0.6 percent reduction) than it did in countries where inequality was low (4.3 percent). Rising inequality also reduced the impact of future economic growth on poverty reduction. Bourguignon (2003) found that a fall in the Gini coefficient from 0.55 to 0.45 (0.45 still indicating relatively high inequality) would cause poverty to drop by more than 15 percentage points in 10 years. It would take 30 years to achieve the same reduction in poverty if inequality remained unchanged.

While the literature is largely united on the point that growth tends to be neutral in its effect on income distribution (as discussed earlier in this chapter), it would seem that faster economic growth is necessary to reduce poverty in countries with high inequality. India provides a good example (box 3.1).

Three important points emerge from this discussion. First, growth is the fundamental factor for poverty reduction. Second, progressive change in income distribution will accentuate the poverty-reducing power of growth. And third, high initial inequality reduces the impact of growth on poverty reduction. The economic literature suggests that the relative importance of growth rates and inequality in determining how growth will affect the poor depends on country conditions, notably the initial levels of income and inequality. In low-income countries, the need to accelerate pro-poor growth to reduce poverty has emerged as critical,

Box 3.1

How to Achieve Pro-Poor Growth—The Case of India

Economic growth tends to reduce poverty. That does not mean, however, that every policy that promotes growth will reduce poverty. Economic policies often have distributional implications that cannot be ignored if one is interested in how those policies affect poverty.

The case of India is instructive. The incidence of poverty in India has been falling at a rate of about one percentage point per year since about 1970, with an interruption owing to macroeconomic difficulties in the early 1990s. But some states have done far better than others, both historically and in the wake of the economic reforms of the past 10 years. And the growth rate needed to achieve a constant reduction in poverty has been rising over time. In other words, the responsiveness of poverty rates to increases in nonagricultural output and, to a lesser extent, agricultural yields has been declining.

Here the geographic composition of India's growth has played an important role: widening regional disparities and limited growth in lagging areas have made the overall growth process less pro-poor. By and large, economic growth has not occurred in the states where it would have the most impact on poverty. These differences are compounded by differences in access to infrastructure and social services (health care and education) that make it harder for poor people to take up the opportunities afforded by aggregate economic growth (Ravallion and Datt 2002).

Heterogeneity in the impact of growth on poverty holds important clues about what else governments need to do to reduce poverty, in addition to promoting economic growth. Some observers believe that growth alone is sufficient (Bhalla 2002b). Others believe that combining growth-promoting economic reforms with policies to help the poor participate fully in the opportunities unleashed by growth will reduce poverty more quickly than relying on growth alone.

Source: Authors.

particularly in the context of poverty reduction strategies and the efforts to accelerate progress toward the Millennium Development Goals.

Economists agree that growth reduces poverty. But it also appears that the relationship is reciprocal—poverty reduction is good for growth. This is true because relief from poverty unleashes the productive power of the poor. The poor have limited access to financial services, infrastructure (roads, water, power, and telecommunications), education, and health services. Alleviation of poverty generally brings improvements in access to such services through both direct and indirect channels. When people have more money to spend, service providers of all stripes—water sellers, telecommunications companies, transport operators, and banks—have a greater incentive to extend their offer of services. The poor make use of those services to develop their productive potential—by carrying goods to market, communicating with potential employers or customers, investing in education, or protecting their health. Being able to afford food, medicine, and clothing also allows the poor to derive greater benefit from the services to which they already have access. Healthy people are more productive and more likely to prosper in their employment. Properly nourished children get more out of school. Workers with a little extra cash can use public transportation to reach better jobs. Free of the constant threat of hunger and ruin, they may be more likely to take advantage of a wide range of investment opportunities, from specialized agriculture to more education to microbusinesses.

The task of crafting policies to assist lagging regions is complicated by the interconnectedness of the many factors that make for growth[1]— including customers with money to spend, workers with skills to sell, and infrastructure that allows goods to be produced and transported at a competitive price. Enterprises naturally seek out areas that are already rich in such factors. The result is a self-reinforcing cycle: concentrations (agglomerations) of economic activity tend, because of their dynamism and generally higher returns to capital and labor, to attract more such activity, while areas poor in productive factors languish. This means that efforts to stimulate growth in poor areas must be coordinated to make incremental advances on multiple fronts. In the absence of coordinated policies, the investment of public funds to facilitate growth and labor mobility in regions with a legacy of poor access to markets, education, and infrastructure may have the perverse effect of lowering overall aggregate growth (by drawing resources away from more immediately productive uses), thus presenting governments with the dilemma of favoring either growth or equity. In many cases, however, coordinated policies—generally including conditional cash transfers for the poor—can enhance both poverty reduction and long-term growth.

The challenge of making simultaneous progress on multiple fronts is central to the fate of the large group of countries where the world's poorest billion people live. Located mostly in Africa, the Caribbean, and the Pacific, these mostly small nations have not shared in the benefits of globalization that have accrued to most people in the developed and developing worlds (Collier 2007). The average per capita GDP growth of the economies of the bottom billion was 0.5 percent in the 1970s, 0.4 percent in the 1980s, and –0.5 percent in the 1990s. In comparison, per capita GDP growth in other developing countries increased from 2.5 percent in the 1970s to 4.0 percent in the 1980s and 1990s.

These countries and their populations have not benefited from globalization for reasons too complex to present here. Trade policy is partly to blame. For example, Africa has failed to develop jobs in export manufactures, such as garments and textiles, because European countries impose tariffs and other restrictions on imports of garments from Africa. The subsidies that the United States and European Union pay to domestic agricultural producers prevent many smaller countries from competing in export markets for the protected products. (We return to this point in the chapter on trade.) Corruption and poor governance prevent poor countries from making the most of cyclical booms in commodity markets. Instead of being invested, windfall profits from high oil and mineral prices are siphoned off by elites. Conflicts over control of natural resources and between ethnic groups have also stunted the growth of many countries and prevented them from participating, except as suppliers of raw materials, in the global system.

Again, a coordinated set of changes will be required if the bottom billion are to share in the benefits of global growth. The industrialized economies have a major role to play—through trade reform, the provision of security commitments in areas beset by conflict, and more generous aid (for example, to improve governance).

Conclusion

This chapter offered a quick survey of theories of economic growth. Along the way, we identified points on which economists have reached consensus, as well as several important questions still to be answered. The core finding of the chapter, one firmly supported by the evidence, is that sustained economic growth is the most critical factor in alleviating poverty. The poor usually are not left behind in the growth process but share in the gains that result from growth. That said, the rate at which poverty shrinks as growth accelerates differs from country to country. The initial level of income inequality in the country and changes in inequality over time play important roles here, as does the pattern of economic growth—and especially whether growth is concentrated in areas where poor people live. The links among economic growth, poverty, and inequality have led to a focus on what is termed pro-poor growth, that is, growth that raises the incomes of the poor. In a virtuous circle of causation, poverty reduction is also good for growth.

Note

1. Returns on assets such as education depend to a large extent on the presence of complementary public assets, such as roads, communications systems, and credit markets. In the same way, a pro-growth policy of building roads in a region may have little immediate impact unless the local population has the skills to create or attract new enterprises.

Bibliography

Acemoglu, D., and S. Johnson. 2007. "Disease and Development: The Effect of Life Expectancy on Economic Growth." *Journal of Political Economy* 115: 925–85.

Acemoglu, D., S. Johnson, and J. Robinson. 2001. "The Colonial Origins of Comparative Development: An Empirical Investigation." *American Economic Review* 91: 1369–1401.

———. 2002. "Reversal of Fortune: Geography and Institutions in the Making of the Modern World Income Distribution." *The Quarterly Journal of Economics* 117 (4): 1231–94.

AFD (Agence Française de Développement), BWZE (Bundesministerium für Wirtschaftliche Zusammenarbeit und Entwicklung), DFID (U.K. Department for International Development), and the World Bank. 2005. "Pro-Poor Growth in the 90s." Operationalizing Pro-Poor Growth Research Program.

Aguirre, A., and C. Calderón. 2005. "Real Exchange Rate Misalignment and Economic Performance." Working Paper 315, Central Bank of Chile, Santiago, April.

Alesina, A., and R. Perotti. 1996. "Income Distribution, Political Instability, and Investment." *European Economic Review* 40: 1203–28.

Barro, R. 1991. "Economic Growth in a Cross-Section of Countries." *Quarterly Journal of Economics* 106: 407–43.

Barro, R. 2000. "Inequality and Growth in a Panel of Countries." *Journal of Economic Growth* 5: 5–32.

———. 2001. "Human Capital and Growth." *American Economic Review* 91: 12–17.

Barro, R., and J. Lee. 2001. "Schooling Quality in a Cross-Section of Countries." *Economica* 68 (272): 465–88.

Barro, R., and X. Sala-i-Martin. 2003. *Economic Growth.* 2d ed. Cambridge, MA: MIT Press.

Beck, T., R. Levine, and N. Loayza. 2000. "Finance and Sources of Growth." *Journal of Financial Economics,* 261–300.

Ben-David, D. 1993. "Equalizing Exchange: Trade Liberalization and Income Convergence." *Quarterly Journal of Economics* 108: 653–79.

Bhalla, S. 2002a. "Recounting the Poor." *Economic and Political Weekly* 38 (4): 338–50.

———. 2002b. *Imagine There Is No Country: Poverty, Inequality, and Growth in the Era of Globalization.* Washington, DC: Institute for International Economics.

———. 2002c. "Trade, Growth and Poverty: Re-examining the Linkages." Presented at the Fourth Asia Development Forum, Seoul, Republic of Korea, November 3–5.

———. 2002d. "Poor Results and Poorer Policy: A Comparative Analysis of Estimates of Global Inequality and Poverty." Presented at a conference on Globalization, Inequality, and Well-being, Munich, November 8–9.

Bougheas, S., P. Demetriades, and T. Mamuneas. 2000. "Infrastructure, Specialization, and Economic Growth." *Canadian Journal of Economics* 33: 506–22.

Bourguignon, François. 2003. "The Growth Elasticity of Poverty Reduction: Explaining Heterogeneity Across Countries and Time Periods." In *Growth and Inequality,* ed. T. Eichler and S. Turnovsky. Cambridge, MA: MIT Press.

———. 2004. "The Poverty-Growth-Inequality Triangle." This paper was presented at the Indian Council for Research on International Economic Relations February 4.

Bruno, M., and W. Easterly. 1998. "Inflation Crises and Long-Run Growth." *Journal of Monetary Economics* 41: 3–26.

Bruno, M., L. Squire, and M. Ravallion. 1998. "Equity and Growth in Developing Countries: Old and New Perspectives on the Policy Issues." In *Income Distribution and High-Quality Growth,* ed. V. Tanzi and K. Chu. Cambridge, MA: MIT Press.

Calderón, C., and L. Servén. 2004. "The Effects of Infrastructure Development on Growth and Income Distribution." Policy Research Working Paper 3400, World Bank, Washington, DC.

Cashin, Paul, Paolo Mauro, and Ratna Sahay. 2001. "Macroeconomic Policies and Poverty Reduction: Some Cross Country Evidence." *Finance and Development* 38 (2): 46–49.

Chen, S., and M. Ravallion. 2000. "How Did the World's Poorest Fare in the 1990s?" *Global Poverty Monitoring Database*. World Bank, Washington, DC. http://www.worldbank.org/research/povmonitor/method.htm.

———. 2004. "Household Welfare Impacts of China's Accession to the WTO." In *China's WTO Accession*, ed. W. Martin. Washington, DC: World Bank.

Christiaensen, L., L. Demery, and S. Paternostro. 2002. *Reforms, Economic Growth, and Poverty Reduction in Africa: Messages from the 1990s*. Washington, DC: World Bank.

Coe, D., and E. Helpman. 1995. "International R&D Spillovers." *European Economic Review* 39: 859–87.

Collins, S., and O. Razin. 1999. "Real-Exchange-Rate Misalignments and Growth." In *The Economics of Globalization: Policy Perspectives from Public Economics*, 59–81. Cambridge: Cambridge University Press.

Collier, P. 2007. *The Bottom Billion: Why the Poorest Countries Are Failing and What Can Be Done About It?* Oxford, U.K.: Oxford University Press.

Cord, L., J. Lopez, and J. Page. 2003. "When I Use a Word . . . Pro-Poor Growth and Poverty Reduction." In *Attacking Poverty: What Makes Growth Pro-Poor?* ed. M. Krakowski. Baden-Baden, Germany: Nomos Verlagsgesellschaft.

Datt, G., and M. Ravallion. 1992. "Growth and Redistribution Components of Change in Poverty Measures: A Decomposition with Application to Brazil and India in the 1980s." *Journal of Development Economics* 38 (2): 275–95.

———. 2002. "Is India's Economic Growth Leaving the Poor Behind?" *Journal of Economic Perspectives* 16 (3): 89–108.

Deininger, K., and L. Squire. 1996. "A New Data Set Measuring Income Inequality." *World Bank Economic Review* 10 (3): 565–91.

Dell'Ariccia, G., E. Detragiache, and R. Rajan. 2005. "The Real Effect of Banking Crises." IMF Working Paper WP/05/63, International Monetary Fund, Washington, DC.

Department for International Development. 2004. "What Is Pro-Poor Growth and Why Do We Need to Know?" Briefing, U.K. Department for International Development, London.

Dollar, D. 1992. "Outward-Oriented Developing Economies Really Do Grow More Rapidly: Evidence from 95 LDCs, 1976–85." *Economic Development and Cultural Change* 40: 523–44.

Dollar, D., and A. Kraay. 2002. "Growth Is Good for the Poor." *Journal of Economic Growth* 7: 195–225.

———. 2003. "Institutions, Trade, and Growth." *Journal of Monetary Economics* 50: 133–62.

Easterly, W. 2001a. *The Elusive Quest for Growth: Economists' Adventures and Misadventures in the Tropics*. Cambridge, MA: MIT Press.

————. 2001b. "The Lost Decades: Developing Countries' Stagnation in Spite of Policy Reform 1980–1998." *Journal of Economic Growth* 6 (2): 135–57.

Edwards, S. 1998. "Openness, Productivity and Growth: What Do We Really Know?" *Economic Journal* 108: 383–98.

Esfahani, H., and M. Ramírez. 2003. "Institutions, Infrastructure and Economic Growth." *Journal of Development Economics* 70: 443–77.

Fischer, S. 1993. "The Role of Macroeconomic Factors in Growth." *Journal of Monetary Economics* 32: 485–511.

Fischer, S., R. Sahay, and C. Végh. 2002. "Modern Hyper- and High Inflations." *Journal of Economic Literature* 60: 837–80.

Frankel, J., and D. Romer. 1999. "Does Trade Cause Growth?" *American Economic Review* 89: 379–99.

Gupta, S., B. Clements, E. Baldacci, and C. Mulas-Granados. 2005. "Fiscal Policy, Expenditure Composition, and Growth in Low-Income Countries." *Journal of International Money and Finance* 24: 441–63.

Hall, E., and Charles I. Jones. 1999. "Why Do Some Countries Produce So Much More Output Per Worker Than Others?" *Quarterly Journal of Economics* 114 (1): 83–116.

Kaminsky, G., and C. Reinhart. 1999. "The Twin Crises: The Causes of Banking and Balance of Payments Problems." *American Economic Review* 89: 473–500.

Knack, S., and P. Keefer. 1995. "Institutions and Economic Performance: Cross-Country Tests Using Alternative Institutional Measures." *Economics and Politics* 7: 207–27.

Kneller, R., M. Bleaney, and N. Gemmell. 1999. "Fiscal Policy and Growth: Evidence from OECD Countries." *Journal of Public Economics* 74 (2): 171–90.

Kraay, A. 2004. "When Is Growth Pro-Poor? Cross-Country Evidence." Policy Research Working Paper 3225, World Bank, Washington, DC.

Lee, Y., and R. Gordon. 2005. "Tax Structure and Economic Growth." *Journal of Public Economics* 89 (5–6): 1027–43.

Levine, R., N. Loayza, and T. Beck. 2000. "Financial Intermediation and Growth: Causality and Causes." *Journal of Monetary Economics* 46 (1): 31–77.

Loayza, N., P. Fajnzylber, and C. Calderon. 2005. *Economic Growth in Latin America and the Caribbean*. Washington, DC: World Bank.

Loayza, N., and Claudio Raddatz. 2006. "The Composition of Growth Matters for Poverty Alleviation." Policy Research Working Paper 4077, World Bank, Washington, DC.

López, J. H. 2004. "Pro-Growth, Pro-Poor: Is There a Tradeoff?" Policy Research Working Paper 3378, World Bank, Washington, DC.

———. 2006. "Pro-Poor Growth in Latin America." In *Poverty Reduction and Growth: Virtuous and Vicious Circles*, ed. G. E. Perry, O. S. Arias, J. H. López, W. F. Maloney, and L. Servén. Washington, DC: World Bank.

López, Ramon E., 2008. "Sustainable Economic Growth: The Ominous Potency of Structural Change." Working Paper 46592, University of Maryland, Department of Agricultural and Resource Economics.

Mankiw, N., D. Romer, and D. Weil. 1992. "A Contribution to the Empirics of Economic Growth." *Quarterly Journal of Economics* 107 (2): 407–37.

Mauro, P. 1995. "Corruption and Growth." *Quarterly Journal of Economics* 110 (3): 681–712.

Murphy, K., A. Shleifer, and R. Vishny. 1991. "The Allocation of Talent: Implications for Growth." *Quarterly Journal of Economics* 106 (2): 503–30.

Pattillo, C. A., S. Gupta, and K. J. Carey. 2005. "Sustaining and Accelerating Pro-poor Growth in Africa." International Monetary Fund, Washington, DC.

Ravallion, M., 2001. "Growth, Inequality, and Poverty: Looking Beyond Averages." *World Development* 29: 1803–15.

———. 2004. "Pro-Poor Growth: A Primer." Policy Research Working Paper 3242, World Bank, Washington, DC.

Ravallion, M., and S. Chen. 1997. "What Can New Survey Data Tell Us about Recent Changes in Distribution and Poverty?" *World Bank Economic Review* 11 (2): 357–82.

Ravallion, M., and G. Datt. 2002. "Why Has Economic Growth Been More Pro-Poor in Some States of India Than Others?" *Journal of Development Economics* 68: 381–400.

Rioja, F., and N. Valev. 2004. "Does One Size Fit All? A Reexamination of the Finance and Growth Relationship." *Journal of Development Economics* 74 (2): 429–47.

Rodrik, D. 2004. "Industrial Policy for the Twenty-First Century." Center for Economic Policy Research, London.

Romer, Paul M. 1986. "Increasing Returns and Long Run Growth." *Journal of Political Economy* 94: 1002–37.

Sachs, J., and A. Warner. 1995. "Economic Reform and the Process of Global Integration." *Brookings Papers on Economic Activity 1995* (1): 1–118.

Sala-i-Martin, Xavier. 2002. "The Disturbing 'Rise' of Global Income Inequality." Working Paper 8904, National Bureau of Economic Research, Cambridge, MA.

Sanchez-Robles, B. 1998. "Infrastructure Investment and Growth: Some Empirical Evidence." *Contemporary Economic Policy* 16 (1): 98–108.

Solow, Robert M. 1956. "A Contribution to the Theory of Economic Growth." *Quarterly Journal of Economics* 70: 65–94.

Wacziarg, R., and K. Welch. 2003. "Trade Liberalization and Growth: New Evidence." NBER Working Paper 10152, National Bureau of Economic Research, Cambridge, MA, December.

World Bank. 2004. *Beyond Economic Growth*. 2d ed. Washington, DC: World Bank.

———. 2005. *Pro-Poor Growth in the 1990s: Lessons and Insights from 14 Countries*. Washington, DC: World Bank.

PART II

Government Policy, Growth, and the Poor

CHAPTER 4

Government and the Economy— Focus on Fiscal Policy

Perfect markets operating under ideal circumstances will allocate resources efficiently. Markets are not perfect, however, and circumstances are rarely ideal, a state of affairs that suggests a role for government. For example, government can tax or regulate the undesirable (if unintended) consequences of business activity, such as pollution. It can produce public goods (such as roads and military defenses), redistribute income, and define and enforce property rights. Government may also have a role to play in stabilizing the economy using monetary and fiscal policies. Fiscal policy, which deals with the various uses of taxes and public expenditures, is the focus of this chapter, with special attention devoted to its effect on the poor. Monetary policy—which deals with money supply, interest rates, inflation, and exchange rates—is discussed in the next chapter.

The Role of Government in the Economy

The government provides the legal framework and services needed for the effective operation of a market economy. In the context of economic development, that mission has five primary parts: providing a legal and social framework for economic activity; providing public goods; regulating economic activity; reallocating resources; and stabilizing the economy. We will deal with each in turn.

The existence of a problem in the market (or market failure) does not necessarily imply that government intervention can allocate resources more efficiently. A substantial amount of information is required to find the optimal allocation of resources, meaning that "government failure" may end up being worse than the original market failure that government action was meant to address. Even where enough information exists to solve a problem in the market, governments might not act efficiently. Interest groups will always become involved in public policy issues that affect them directly, and their interests may not be consistent with the interests of the general public.

At times, there will be conflicts among a government's many goals. If a government pursues redistributive goals—for example, by transferring income from one group of people to another through higher taxes—it may reduce the efficiency of resource allocation. Thus, there can be an explicit trade-off between efficiency and equity.

Setting the Legal and Social Framework for Economic Activity

By creating a sound legal framework, government establishes the legal status of business enterprises and ensures the right and protection of private ownership, a key factor in encouraging entrepreneurship within a country's borders. By establishing the rules of the game, government directs the relationships among businesses, resource suppliers, and consumers, thus improving resource allocation (which, in turn, supports efforts to alleviate poverty).

The protection of individuals' rights to the goods and services they exchange in a market system is almost everywhere provided by government, although private sector protection often complements government protection. Three basic institutions protect individual rights in a market economy: police forces, national defense forces, and the court and criminal justice systems. By protecting individual rights, government creates a system that allows individuals to interact with one another through voluntary agreement, reserving the legitimate use of force for government. Another important function of government is the enforcement of contracts, so that citizens can make agreements with the confidence that legal recourse is available should a party fail to fulfill its commitments.

The protection of rights and the enforcement of contracts are necessary for a functioning economy, and their enactment makes up a sizable portion of the public budget. Countries with well-developed laws and regulations enjoy a higher level of economic activity than those that provide few safeguards. The democratic model of checks and balances uses one branch of government to constrain the others, while the democratic election of officials circumscribes the overall power of government.

Providing Public Goods and Ensuring Positive Externalities

Public goods and externalities provide the main theoretical justifications for government production.

Public goods are those that can be enjoyed by all citizens without exclusion. Some examples include lighthouses, national defense, the legal system, and parks. Public goods are also indivisible; they must be produced in such large units that they cannot ordinarily be sold to individual buyers. Because of these characteristics, it is not feasible to charge for their consumption, and private suppliers lack the incentive to supply them.

Externalities, or spillovers, occur when some of the costs or benefits of an economic activity are passed on (or spill over) to parties other than the immediate seller or buyer. Some externalities have a beneficial effect on others and are referred to as positive externalities; those that have a detrimental effect are referred to as negative externalities. Pollution is an example of a negative externality, whereas training, education, and investment in research and development have positive effects and, thus, are positive externalities. The market, left on its own, will tend to produce too many goods and services that carry negative externalities (indicating a need to tax those externalities or impose restrictions on their emergence) and too few goods and services involving positive externalities (indicating a need for government provision or subsidization).

Regulating Economic Activity

Regulation is called for when the private sector allocates resources inefficiently and when the imposition of rules can provide incentives for more efficient private production, thus avoiding the need for direct government intervention.

The market does not regulate property rights, financial markets, or trade relations. It does not provide a judicial system for the enforcement of contracts. It does not enact or enforce standards to promote human health, ensure public safety, or protect the environment. The state must provide these services directly—or regulate their providers. Similarly, monopolies have no incentive to produce efficiently or to charge appropriate prices, so the state must regulate them. It does so either by regulating prices or by setting service standards under antimonopoly laws.

In cases where monopolies cannot be avoided and may have particularly detrimental effects, it may be best for the public sector to provide the good or service in question.

Good regulations allow markets to operate efficiently; bad ones interfere with market operations. Developing countries tend to have too few of the good kind (property rights, a well-functioning judiciary, effective environmental and financial regulations) and too many of the bad kind (too many obstacles to obtaining business licenses, overregulation of trade, tight price controls, and so on).

The stability of regulation is also important: one of the most damaging effects of ill-considered state action is uncertainty. Economic actors need to be assured that the rules and regulations of an economy, the protection of property rights, and the provision of public goods are not subject to continuous change. Only in this way can a society function optimally and attract investment.

Reallocating Resources

There are a few closely related reasons why a government may redistribute income. One is to improve the well-being of those members of society who are least fortunate, thus providing a safety net for people who have fallen on hard times (perhaps in the course of economic fluctuation) and ensuring that everyone has access to a minimal standard of living. Another is to provide greater equality, where that is a desired social goal. Although these two goals seem interrelated, they are different and may require different public policies. Helping the poor is not necessarily the same thing as promoting greater equality.

At the extreme, the goal of equality could be achieved by confiscating the wealth of those who hold above-average amounts and giving it to those with below-average amounts until everyone has the same amount. This would destroy the incentive to be productive, however, and thus create an inefficient society for everyone.

Although a market economy benefits society as a whole, it does not benefit everyone all the time. There are always winners and losers. But whatever the origin of unequal income distribution, each society must decide how much state intervention to allow, and to what end. The features shared by the most egalitarian societies are a public education system, a health-care system, unemployment insurance, and a public pension system.

Public education is redistributive in that it provides everyone with equal opportunity. The tax system (the subject of the second part of this chapter) is another way of redistributing income, usually for the purpose of achieving greater equality (although not all policies will have this effect). Higher taxes on upper-income individuals are often intended to further the goal of equality, but they may reduce the incentives of those affected to earn income, thereby reducing total tax revenue and limiting the options available to the state to reduce poverty. Likewise, taxation of investment income may further the goal of equality, but it also can discourage savings and investment, making the economy less productive, reducing economic growth, and leaving those at the lower end of the income scale worse off. The design of the tax structure will depend on whether the goal of redistribution is to achieve greater equality or to provide direct help to the poor and vulnerable.

As individuals know how best to allocate funds to meet competing demands and so maximize their well-being, cash transfers targeted to the poor and destitute—those who cannot help themselves—are usually the best form of redistribution. But evidence has also shown that cash payments may be misused by the poor, in particular, men, who may spend them on alcohol, cigarettes, and entertainment. Also, targeted transfers may "leak" to the nonpoor; if it is impossible to control such leaks, cash transfers may not be the best policy. Community- and region-targeted programs are other vehicles of redistribution. In the long term, the best ways of reducing poverty are to ensure greater access to credit, land, schooling, and health care; to better enforce property rights; and to provide food in return for work. Work requirements are seen as a means of preventing welfare dependency, a situation thought to emerge when benefits (especially cash) are not based on quid pro quo.

Recently, countries such as Brazil have been successful in introducing conditional cash transfer programs that encourage parents to keep their children in school (or take some other desired action) in return for cash compensation. The Employment Generation Scheme in Mumbai, India, employs unskilled manual laborers in public infrastructure projects; anyone who wants a job is hired. Workers are paid in basic supplies, suggesting that the poor are assumed to have limited ability to manage their own finances.

Poor people can become trapped in poverty. The reasons are many: lack of education, credit, land, jobs, or roads to get to work or to bring goods to market. Perversely, dependency on social safety nets and welfare programs (even those that provide access to education and health care) can become part of the problem. Thus, it is important to anticipate the consequences of redistributive policies and to act quickly to correct those that are undesirable—because they induce dependency or have some other side effect that may outweigh the benefits achieved by the redistribution. Decades of empirical evidence from both developed and developing countries suggests that optimal redistributive policy should comprise the following features:

- Welfare payments are made in cash rather than in kind to allow recipients to exercise their judgment and discretion.
- A relatively high level of guaranteed income is combined with a phasing out of benefits.
- Benefit programs are not financed by overtaxing those with the highest marginal incomes.

Stabilizing the Economy

Stabilization policies are designed to address acute fluctuations in economic activity that may be caused by demand-side shocks (such as an abrupt drop in demand for a country's exports) or supply-side shocks (such as the quadrupling of oil prices in the 1970s). These fluctuations are addressed using the instruments of fiscal policy (discussed in the next section of this chapter) and monetary policy (the subject of the next chapter).

Some stabilizers are automatic—that is, they are activated by movements in certain related indicators. A prime example is unemployment compensation: if the economy falls into recession, unemployment compensation payments increase as people become unemployed. Tax payments also typically decline as economic activity decreases. Such stabilizers provide channels through which the volatility of economic activity is automatically suppressed as it moves through the business cycle.

Other stabilizers require a conscious policy choice. So-called active stabilization policies were very popular in the period immediately following World War II, influenced by the conventional wisdom that one of the key reasons for the Great Depression was the failure of the U.S. Federal Reserve and the American government to cut interest rates and increase spending after the crash of 1929. This view was popular at least until the 1970s, when many governments found that expansionary policies would not work if the problem impeding growth lay not in demand but rather in supply. If a government attempted to use monetary or fiscal policy to create more demand when the supply side of the economy was either at full employment or could not expand because of another bottleneck or rigidity, the result would be inflation and, in an open economy, a balance of payments deficit (as imports increased). The "stagflation" of the 1970s was an example of this phenomenon. Since the 1980s, skepticism has grown about the effectiveness of active, countercyclical macroeconomic policy, especially fiscal policy, which is typically harder than monetary policy to activate and fine-tune. Although monetary policy is seen to have some role in stabilizing economic activity, it is now widely believed that the primary goal of monetary policy should be to restrain inflation. That said, in exceptional circumstances such as the ongoing financial crisis, monetary policy has an important role to play in helping to stabilize demand.

Fiscal Policy: Taxing and Spending

Simply stated, fiscal policy consists of taxing and spending, with the first needed to finance the second. This section reviews the purposes of public spending, how it is financed, and the role (and financing) of budget deficits and government borrowing.

The Purposes of Public Expenditure

Public expenditure, a measure of the value of goods and services bought by the state, plays five principal roles in the economy: it (a) contributes to demand for the economy's products and services; (b) stabilizes the economy; (c) increases the public endowment of goods; (d) redistributes wealth; and (e) creates positive externalities for the economy and society, especially through capital investments.

Public expenditure can be classified according to the types of goods and services purchased (capital goods, consumption goods, personnel), the official body that finances the expenditure (central government ministry, regional or local authority), and the macroeconomic purpose the expenditure is designed to serve (justice and public order, education, health).

No single level of government spending can be said to fit all circumstances. But the aggregate level of spending must be consistent with a country's macroeconomic framework. If it is not, persistently high or rising budget deficits can result in various forms of macroeconomic imbalances. For example, as we discuss later, excessive budgets can give rise to inflation and crowd out private investment.

Financing Public Expenditure

Government finances its expenditure through taxation, fees, revenues from state-owned enterprises, borrowing, grants (such as foreign aid), and the creation of new money. In developed countries, most government revenue is raised through taxation. In countries where the tax system is not well developed, nontax revenue may be the primary source of government finance. Nontax revenue comprises fees levied by government (such as customs and excise duties) as well as profits and dividends from state-owned enterprises.

Taxes are commonly divided into the following categories:

- *Income tax*, levied on the income of households and businesses
- *Corporate income tax*, levied on firms' profits
- *Sales and excise taxes*, levied on commodities.

It is important to maintain a balance between direct and indirect taxation. Direct taxation is generally a better tool for improving income distribution: those who earn more pay more. By contrast, indirect taxation—such as through international trade duties or through sales or value added tax (VAT)—although it tends to generate revenues more easily and is thus conducive to macroeconomic stability, is considered regressive because all purchasers pay the same tax on a given transaction, regardless of their income or ability to pay. That is, indirect taxes impose a disproportionate burden on the poor. This inequity is often addressed by exempting certain basic goods, such as food, from taxation.

Government revenue may also come in the form of foreign grants, as discussed in chapter 7 of this book. Grants may be either transfers of cash or provisions of goods and services from bilateral or multilateral donors. Grants have obvious benefits: they do not detract from private sector incomes in the recipient country and they rarely affect interest rates and inflation. But the costs can be high: grants tend to create a dependency on international aid that may impede development of the domestic market and other institutions. In addition, they often come with conditions that compromise government autonomy and may be costly to fulfill or may distract from other goals important to citizens' well-being.

The ideal tax system generates a stable and assured source of revenue at a low cost (relative to the revenue it generates). Its simple structure makes compliance easy. It is understood by both taxpayers and administrators. It is broad based in its application and does not distort production, consumption, or trade. It distributes the tax burden in a manner that is perceived to be fair and equitable (box 4.1).

Box 4.1

Five Characteristics of an Efficient Tax System

1. *Economic efficiency.* The tax system should not interfere with the efficient allocation of resources.
2. *Administrative simplicity.* The tax system ought to be easy and relatively inexpensive to administer.
3. *Flexibility.* The tax system should be able to respond easily (in some cases, automatically) to changed economic circumstances.
4. *Political responsibility.* The tax system should be designed so that individuals know or can learn what they are paying for and so that there is no disconnect between the preferences of individuals and the actions of the state.
5. *Fairness.* The tax system ought to be fair in the way it treats all individuals.

Source: Stiglitz 1984.

Raising revenues by a few taxes with simple rate structures helps to contain administrative and compliance costs and avoids resentment of excessive taxation. By a broadening of the tax base and providing of limited exemptions, it is possible to raise revenues at lower rates and to make the revenue stream more predictable. For example, a VAT or a single-stage sales tax, when levied at a low and uniform rate on a broad base, is more efficient than the cumulative taxation of goods as they move along successive stages of production (a phenomenon known as cascading). By contrast, preferential tax rates and other fiscal incentives for investment are usually found to be ineffective in most developing countries.

Government revenue collection depends not only on the structure of the tax system but also on its efficient administration, something that is often missing in developing economies. Perhaps for this reason, recent studies have shown that a country's government revenue, measured as a percentage of gross domestic product (GDP), correlates positively with its per capita income (figure 4.1).

Deficits and Borrowing

When a government spends more than it collects in revenue and grants, it is said to be running a budget deficit. Common wisdom holds that if a

Figure 4.1   Central Government Revenue and Log Per Capita GDP in 105 Developing Countries

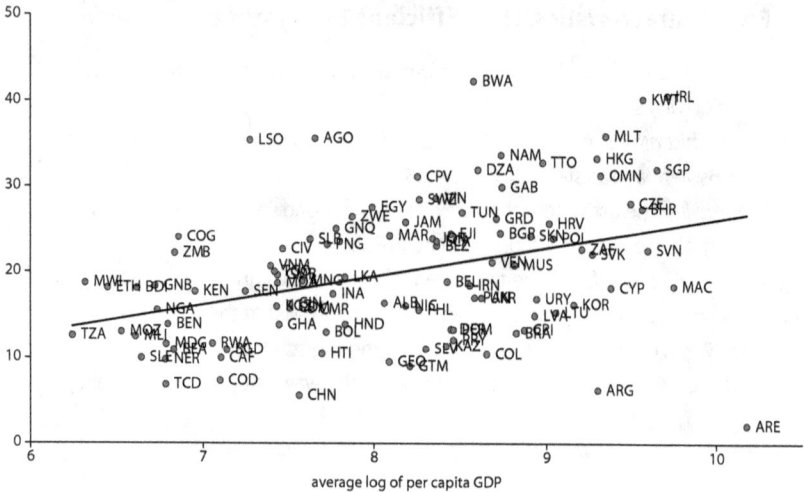

average log of per capita GDP

Source: Gupta 2007.

government cuts taxes and runs a budget deficit, then the private sector, including households, will respond to the increase in disposable income by saving and consuming more (according to each household's marginal propensity to consume, a concept introduced in chapter 2 of this book). But since household savings, for example, rise by only a fraction of the budget deficit, national savings (both private and public) must decline under deficit conditions. In a closed economy with no inflow of foreign savings, national savings are equal to domestic investment. In such an economy, a decline in national savings will push up real interest rates and reduce investment demand, increasing private savings—a cycle known as the crowding out of investment.

A growing budget deficit leads to a buildup of public debt. Unless a government's budget deficit is covered by private savings minus invest-ment, it will create (in an open economy) a current-account deficit with the rest of the world, obliging the country to increase its net foreign debts to cover the deficit.[1] If the government cannot finance the deficit by bor-rowing, pressure will build to finance it through depreciation of the national currency. Depreciation will lead to greater exports and, hence, reduce the current-account deficit. But depreciation leads to inflation, which cuts purchasing power—usually with serious political consequences.

Depreciation also increases the cost of servicing debts denominated in foreign currency.

Financing Public Deficits

Several options exist for financing public deficits, but not all of them are available or appropriate across contexts. The options include the following:

- *Issuing or selling debt instruments or obtaining domestic bank loans.* Issuing debt or borrowing from local banks means that the government is borrowing from its citizens. This may be appealing, since costs are deferred while the government preserves its autonomy relative to the outside world. In addition, there is no risk of inflation in the short run. But selling debt competes for private savings at home, channeling money away from investment and raising the cost of borrowing for the private sector.

- *Borrowing from abroad.* In recent years, some wealthier developing countries have gained access to international capital markets by obtaining a favorable credit rating from one of the large international rating firms. For most low-income countries, however, multilateral development banks (such as the World Bank, the Asian Development Bank, and the African Development Bank) and bilateral donors remain the only source of international finance. Regardless of its source, foreign borrowing defers the costs of government programs without crowding out domestic investment or causing inflation, but it carries risks if loans must be repaid in foreign currency. Foreign borrowing also obliges the borrower to comply with the lender's conditions.

- *Asset sales.* The sale of government property to the private sector (privatization) is another way of financing public deficits. Its appeal lies in the fact that the government need not make plans for repayment, since assets are being exchanged for revenue. But assets can be sold only once, so privatization cannot continue indefinitely.

- *Printing money.* Printing money has the obvious appeal of immediately increasing the supply of ready cash, but its pernicious consequences last much longer—making this the last resort for most governments. Printing money has the perverse effect of lowering the amount of credit available to the private sector; investors, sensing risk, prefer to purchase safer government securities. Even if more money is available overall, it is a harbinger of inflation, which distorts prices and erodes the value of household savings.

The Uses of Fiscal Policy

The government may attempt to use fiscal policy to smooth business cycles and redistribute income. While these are good goals, overreaching can crowd out private investment and trigger inflation. This section discusses these important issues.

Fiscal Policy and the Business Cycle

Governments often have tried to smooth the business cycle through expansionary or contractionary fiscal policy. Under expansionary policy, the government spends money (or forgoes tax revenue) to stimulate aggregate demand in the economy, thereby boosting economic activity. The initial response of aggregate demand is typically greater than the government expenditure (or loss of tax revenue) employed to induce it because of the multiplier effect. When the government raises spending or lowers taxes to increase aggregate demand, businesses respond to the increased demand by increasing investment. As businesses invest more, they hire more workers, increasing employment. There are now more workers with a paycheck, and their spending creates a further increase in demand for goods and services. Businesses respond to that increase by investing more. As they do so, they hire more workers and increase employment—the multiplier effect. With contractionary fiscal policy, the opposite happens.

The fiscal policy the country chooses will depend on its economic situation and the time frame envisaged by policy makers. Short-run fiscal policy may aim at smoothing the business cycle or reducing poverty, but over the long run the aim should be to keep the deficit at a low and stable level to help underpin economic growth. As we will see, high and sustained deficits can discourage investment, ignite inflation, and cause balance of payment problems.

Investment, Inflation, and the Effects of Deficits

We have seen that unchecked government spending and expansionary fiscal policies harm the economy by causing inflation and crowding out private investment. Under expansionary fiscal conditions, inflation is likely to rise as aggregate demand (spending) outstrips the aggregate supply of goods and services. Under such conditions, businesses have difficulty keeping up with orders and respond to the excess demand by raising prices. Under tight labor-market conditions, employers may also be forced to raise wages to attract new workers and retain existing ones.

Consider the same problem from the financing side. High and sustained fiscal deficits, if financed by printing money, set the stage for higher inflation. If the government finances its deficits by borrowing in the bond market or from private banks, rather than from the central bank, interest rates will increase or the terms on private bank loans will become more stringent. Either way, private investment is likely to be crowded out as investors and lenders prefer the sovereign borrower because it poses lower risk.

By contrast, low and stable fiscal deficits send a positive message about a government's ability to service its debt. Such a stance may thus prevent the probability of economic crisis. Macroeconomic stability yields further benefits as well—higher rates of investment, growth, and educational attainment; greater distributional equity; and reduced poverty.

Fiscal Policy and the Poor

In a developing economy, taxation is generally less effective than spending in promoting growth and improving the lot of the poor. The rich generally have ways of avoiding high taxes on their income. Even exempting some staple items from consumption taxes (sales tax or VAT) may not benefit the poor, because the rich can afford to spend a larger absolute amount on the exempted good, so they derive the largest benefit. In such cases, repealing the exemption could yield revenue that could be spent in a more pro-poor way.

On the other hand, there is evidence that increased spending on physical and human capital formation can promote economic growth and reduce poverty. Even during times of fiscal consolidation, protecting investment in physical and human capital does more to ensure long-term economic health than the alternatives (increasing public sector wages, for example). Government spending on health and education contributes to the well-being of a population and increases worker productivity. Reducing communicable disease also increases worker productivity and helps to promote tourism and attract foreign direct investment (FDI).

Governments regulate and prioritize public expenditure through the national budget. By ensuring participation of the poor in allocating resources, tracking expenditures, and monitoring service delivery, the budget can be made more demand driven and pro-poor. Participatory budgeting has been used in many Brazilian municipalities since the mid-1980s. It involves, first, checking that the previous year's budget was executed in line with stated policies and, second, bringing together people from different geographical areas and interest groups to set spending priorities for the next budget. Participatory budgeting has allowed public expenditure to more closely reflect citizens' preferences. In Brazil, for example, participatory budgeting is predominant at the local government level. It has resulted in a large shift toward investment in water and sanitation, the top priorities noted by its citizens (Goldfrank 2007).

Conclusion

In this chapter—the first describing facets of public policy—we discussed the many roles that government can play in an economy, whether through fiscal policy or other means. The chapter first analyzed the primary functions of government in providing the legal framework and services needed for the effective operation of a market economy. These include providing public goods, regulating economic activity, stabilizing the economy, and redistributing income—the most fundamental roles of government. We then looked at fiscal policy, including expenditure and taxation policies, before turning to the impact of fiscal policy on the business cycle and other economic phenomena, including inflation and the crowding out of private sector investment. We concluded by examining the ways in which fiscal policy can benefit the poor—primarily through government expenditure.

Note

1. This was examined in the discussion of absorption, savings, and the current-account deficit in chapter 2 of this book.

Bibliography

Flug, K., A. Spilimbergo, and E. Wachtenheim. 1998. "Investment in Education: Do Economic Volatility and Credit Constraints Matter?" *Journal of Development Economics* 55 (2): 465–81.

Goldfrank, Benjamin. 2007. "Lessons from Latin America's Experience with Participatory Budgeting." In *Participatory Budgeting. Public Sector Governance and Accountability Series*, ed. Anwar Shah. Washington, DC: World Bank.

Gupta, Abhijit. 2007. "Determinants of Tax Revenue Effort in Developing Countries." IMF Working Paper WP/07/184, International Monetary Fund, Washington, DC.

Ray, D. 1998. *Development Economics*. Princeton, NJ: Princeton University Press.

Rebelo, S., and W. Easterly. 1992. "Marginal Income Tax Rates and Economic Growth in Developing Countries." Policy Research Working Paper Series 1050, World Bank, Washington, DC.

Stigler, George J. 1970. "The Case, If Any, for Economic Literacy." *Journal of Economic Education* 1 (2): 77–84.

Stiglitz, Joseph E. 1984. "Price Rigidities and Market Structure." *American Economic Review* 74 (2): 350–55.

CHAPTER 5

Monetary Policy, Inflation, and Exchange Rates

As discussed in previous chapters, poverty can be reduced by increasing economic growth and by raising the poor's share in that growth. Economic growth can be fostered by a set of policies aimed at achieving and maintaining macroeconomic stability: low budget deficits, a low and stable rate of inflation, and sustainable external debt. Of central importance to the rate of inflation in the economy are fiscal and monetary policies. Chapter 4 focused on fiscal policy; here, we offer an introduction to monetary policy and its main instruments. We continue with a description of inflation, its causes, and its impact on economic growth and poverty. We then discuss exchange-rate policies and fixed versus flexible exchange rates.

Definitions and Concepts

Monetary policy may be loosely defined as a central bank's decisions concerning money supply, inflation, and exchange rates. Monetary policy works through changes in money supply and interest rates. For example, in the face of a recession and high unemployment, the central bank may use expansionary monetary policy to stimulate demand. In such a case, with reference to figure 5.1, the central bank would expand the money

Figure 5.1   Money Demand and Money Supply

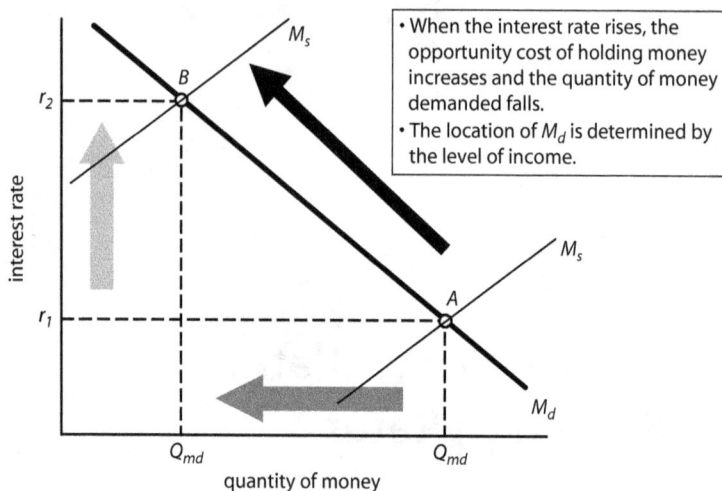

- When the interest rate rises, the opportunity cost of holding money increases and the quantity of money demanded falls.
- The location of M_d is determined by the level of income.

Source: Authors.
Note: When the prevailing interest rate is r_1, the money demand M_d and money supply M_s intersect at point A; the money market is in equilibrium at r_1 and the quantity of money demanded is Q_{md}. When the interest rate increases to r_2, the money supply curve shifts back, and the new equilibrium at point B corresponds to the new interest rate r_2 and a lower quantity of money demanded, Q_{md}.

supply (M_s) and bring down interest rates (from r_2 to r_1), spurring demand for money to rise. We can think of the interest rate as the price of money. If the supply of money increases relative to demand, the price (the interest rate) falls. Lower interest rates mean that it is cheaper to borrow money, which stimulates business investment and induces consumers to spend more. As businesses invest, they hire more workers, increasing employment. Workers' spending creates an increase in aggregate demand for goods and services. Businesses respond to the increase by further increasing investment and employment, and so on.

In managing the money supply, the central bank uses two types of monetary instruments: direct and indirect.

Direct Monetary Instruments
The central bank exerts direct control over the money supply in three ways: (a) through credit ceilings on individual banks, (b) through control of interest rates, and (c) through discriminatory capital-to-asset ratios. All of these instruments have fallen out of favor in industrialized countries, but most developing countries still use them.

Once a national *credit ceiling* has been established, individual ceilings are then established for each major financial institution, based on past market shares. Credit ceilings are reasonably effective in preventing excessive credit expansion in the short term but lose their effectiveness over time because they tend to reduce competition among banks—once a bank reaches its credit ceiling, it has no incentive to attract additional deposits. Banks may concentrate on their established clients and be unwilling to finance new projects that might have proven more profitable. Thus, the flow of capital in the economy is restricted. Furthermore, when credit is disbursed based on administrative criteria rather than profitability, corruption tends to increase. Disaffected depositors and borrowers create incentives for financial dealings outside the control of the central bank. As credit operations are conducted outside the banking system, the central bank loses control of monetary policy.

Interest rate controls are often introduced along with credit ceilings. Over time, these may be ineffective, as it is generally not possible to control both the cost and quantity of credit. Fees on the credit extended may be imposed, thus raising the cost of credit and defeating the original purpose. Moreover, excessive fees and other restrictions on loans reduce the transparency of the price system in providing correct signals for the allocation of resources.

The central bank may impose a minimum *capital-to-asset ratio* to force branches of foreign-owned banks to increase their capital.

Indirect Monetary Instruments

The central bank's indirect instruments of monetary policy include (a) reserve requirements, (b) lending facilities, (c) open-market operations, and (d) deposit management.

Reserve requirements specify the amount of cash that banks must hold in their vaults or on deposit with the central bank. The requirements affect the money supply through the "money multiplier." An increase in reserve requirements typically raises banking system costs—because interest rates paid to banks for reserve holdings are typically less than the rates banks pay to depositors. Those costs tend to be passed on in the form of higher interest rates on loans. Frequent changes in reserve requirements can confuse market participants and lead to excess holdings of reserves. This, in turn, can hamper the effectiveness of monetary policy.

By expanding or restricting access to its *credit and refinancing* (or *rediscounting*) *facilities*, the central bank can influence credit expansion in the economy. But those facilities should provide only *short-term* or *emergency* financing to the banking system. In some developing countries, political pressures have led to the use of this instrument to extend credit to commercial banks with inadequate reserves (such as state-owned banks) or to provide support to troubled financial firms. Reducing access to central bank rediscount facilities and credit is very effective in controlling the money supply, because it curtails credit to the private sector through the banking system, thereby reducing the money supply and controlling inflation. The discount rate—the interest rate that a bank must pay the central bank when it borrows money from it—is generally high to discourage borrowing by commercial banks, which could offset the impact of open-market operations, as discussed below. The central bank also operates as the lender of last resort in emergency circumstances. In doing so, it generally provides credit at high interest rates and only when borrowing banks are in a position to supply high-quality collateral. This encourages banks to first seek funds from the public or from the interbank market.

Open-market operations are purchases and sales (or borrowing and lending) of securities by the central bank to increase or reduce liquidity in the economy. Open-market operations offer several advantages, including development of the money market and the flexibility such operations give the central bank in conducting monetary policy.

The central bank *manages government deposits*. Transferring government deposits between banks and the central bank affects reserve levels. In so doing, the central bank performs its essential role as the government's fiscal agent; however, deposit management, viewed narrowly, is not the most transparent instrument of monetary control. It does nothing, for example, to encourage market development and competition.

Inflation

Inflation is a sustained rise in general price levels combined with a fall in the purchasing power of money. It is measured by weighting the prices of goods and services in order of importance and combining them to produce one of several indexes:

- The *consumer price index* (CPI) measures the price of a selection of goods and services purchased by the average consumer. CPIs are often used in wage and salary negotiations because employees seek pay raises that equal or exceed the increase in the cost of living, for which the best proxy is the rate of increase of the CPI.

- The *wholesale price index* (also known as the producer price index) reflects changes in the prices paid for goods at various stages of distribution, among them prices of raw materials for intermediate and final consumption, prices of unfinished goods, and prices of finished goods.[1]
- The *commodity price index* measures the change in price of a selection of commodities.
- The *gross domestic product (GDP) deflator* is a measure of the changes in prices of *all* goods and services produced in an economy. Although this measure has the advantage of being comprehensive, it typically is available only quarterly, with a long lag, and is subject to revision.

When inflation is zero or very low, the economy enjoys price stability. Under conditions of price stability, inflation has no material impact on individual economic decision making. Moreover, a low, but positive, inflation rate (say, 2 percent a year or less) can have positive effects on the economy, because it allows relative prices and wages to adjust more easily, keeping unemployment lower than it otherwise would be. But once inflation rises above a certain level, it can distort decision making and have negative effects on the economy and growth.

Types of Inflation
Economists distinguish between two types of inflation:

- *Demand-pull inflation* occurs when too much money is chasing too few goods—that is, when the demand for goods and services by consumers, investors, and the government exceeds available supply. Because resources are fully employed, the business sector cannot respond to additional demand by expanding output, so firms typically react by pushing up prices instead.
- *Supply-side (or cost-push) inflation* occurs when a firm passes on an increase in production costs to the consumer in the form of higher prices. The inflationary effect of increased costs may be the result of wage increases that lead to a wage-price spiral (when price increases spark a series of wage demands that lead to further price increases, and so on) or a wage-wage spiral (when one group of workers receives a wage increase that sparks a series of wage demands from other workers). Cost-push inflation may also be stimulated by increased import prices following a rise in world prices for imported raw materials or a depreciation of the local currency.

Central banks can affect inflation by adjusting interest rates and manipulating the other instruments of monetary policy. But they differ in their approach to fighting inflation. High interest rates are perhaps the most common method. The decline in production and rise in unemployment that follow hikes in interest rates prevent price increases. Another school of thought advocates fighting inflation by fixing (or "pegging") the rate of exchange between the national currency and a stable reference, such as the U.S. dollar. This method has had varying success: in spite of efforts to curb inflation, some nations have experienced double- or triple-digit annual rates of inflation in recent years.

Causes of Inflation

As we have seen, inflation is typically caused by excess demand or by producers passing on higher costs in the form of higher prices. The central bank plays a role in creating and quelling both conditions. If the central bank pursues a tight monetary policy—by increasing interest rates or restricting the money supply—excess demand will be wrung out of the system, and producers will not be in a position to pass on all their costs in the form of higher prices. On the other hand, an accommodative monetary policy—low interest rates or rapid expansion of the money supply—will allow price increases to continue or even accelerate (figure 5.2).

Fiscal policy (as discussed in chapter 4) can support or hinder monetary policy operations. Prudent fiscal policy allows government to operate with little or no borrowing by the central bank, thereby lowering the risk of creating excess money. By contrast, profligate fiscal policy and high levels of borrowing can force a central bank into an unsustainable monetary stance.

Inflation and Economic Growth

While inflationary policies can stimulate economic growth in the short term, the economic literature suggests that, over the medium and long term, high rates of inflation are bad for economic growth. Cross-country studies show that countries with consistent positive growth records have, on average, much lower rates of inflation than other countries.

Why might this be? The basic reason is that prices perform a critical signaling mechanism in any market economy, where resources are allocated based on prevailing relative prices. When inflation is high, these price signals become distorted—it becomes difficult to distinguish between relative and secular price changes—and resources are not allocated

Figure 5.2   Path from Expansionary Monetary Policy to Inflation

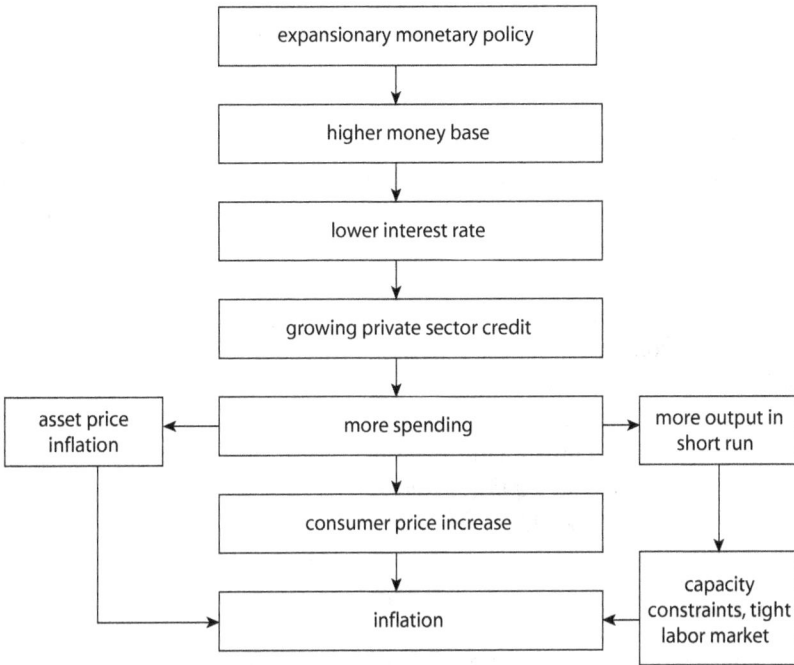

Source: Authors.

efficiently. Moreover, high inflation encourages consumption instead of saving. Higher prices induce people to purchase more products now (before they become more expensive) and discourage people from saving, because money saved for future use will have less value. Savings are needed for investments in capital goods and technology, the real engines of wealth. When investment is curtailed and productivity growth stunted, overall growth is impeded.

In a seminal article, Fischer (1993), while noting a positive relationship between growth and low levels of inflation, showed that economic growth was negatively associated with high levels of inflation (and with large budget deficits and distorted foreign exchange markets). Subsequent studies confirm a nonlinear relationship between inflation and economic growth that is negative once a certain threshold level of inflation is reached. The threshold effect differs according to country conditions. The threshold above which inflation acts as a brake on economic growth is estimated at 1 to 3 percent for industrialized countries and between 7 and 11 percent for developing countries (Khan and Senhadji 2000). Above these levels, the negative relationship between economic growth and inflation holds true regardless of the estimation method (that is, regardless of the level of the threshold, the exclusion of high-inflation observations, data frequency, and other model specifications).

More generally, high rates of inflation are associated with poor macro-economic performance. The typical goal of macroeconomic policy is a high and sustained growth of output, alongside low and stable inflation. As noted by Fischer (1993), inflation serves as "an indicator of the over-all ability of the government to manage the economy." Because it is essential for macroeconomic stability, inflation control is a central component of the macroeconomic policy of most governments and of the structural adjustment programs advocated by the International Monetary Fund. In recent years, African countries have succeeded in bringing down inflation, with average annual inflation on the continent dropping from 17 percent in 1990 to 10 percent in 2003 (in Sub-Saharan Africa, from 20 percent to 12 percent) (Rogoff 2003).

Inflation and the Poor

In the previous section, we noted the negative relationship between economic growth and inflation. Given the positive impact of economic growth on poverty reduction, it is unsurprising that many studies find that the costs of inflation are borne most heavily by the poor. A poll by Easterly and Fischer (2001) showed that inflation was more likely to be rated a top national concern by the poor than the rich. The survey showed that improvements in the share of per capita income retained by the poor were negatively correlated with the rate of inflation, as was the percentage decline in poverty and the percentage change in the real minimum wage. Lower rates of inflation are associated with improvements in the Human Development Index (HDI), regardless of the country's starting point on the index (table 5.1).[2]

On a more practical level, the poor suffer disproportionately from inflation, particularly in rural areas. They lack the resources that enable the wealthy to diversify into inflation-proof assets. Furthermore, they have less access to the financial system and tend to hold their balances in cash, the value of which falls with inflation. The poor also depend heavily on wage labor. Given that wages and prices are sticky—that is, that they do not respond to changed market conditions in the short run—the poor suffer disproportionately when inflation rises rapidly. High inflation

Table 5.1   Growth, Inflation, and the Human Development Index

	Growth in real GDP per capita	Inflation (percent change)	Variability of inflation (standard deviation)
Low HDI (0–0.5)			
Slow change in HDI[a]	–0.22	91.50	259.83
Rapid change in HDI[b]	1.42	13.60	10.81
Medium HDI (0.51–0.70)			
Slow change in HDI[c]	0.63	151.85	311.03
Rapid change in HDI[d]	1.85	54.81	179.01
High HDI (0.71–0.80)			
Slow change in HDI[e]	0.34	82.07	114.53
Rapid change in HDI[f]	5.34	14.77	22.82

Sources: Cashin, Mauro, and Sahay (2001, table 3); United Nations (2000); World Bank, *World Development Indicators,* various years; International Monetary Fund, *International Financial Statistics,* various years.

Notes: a. Botswana, Burkina Faso, Burundi, Cameroon, the Central African Republic, the Democratic Republic of Congo, the Republic of Congo, Côte d'Ivoire, Ghana, Guinea-Bissau, Kenya, Lesotho, Madagascar, Malawi, Mauritania, Niger, Papua New Guinea, Senegal, and Togo.
b. Bangladesh, Benin, Chad, the Arab Republic of Egypt, The Gambia, India, Indonesia, Mali, Morocco, Nepal, Nigeria, Pakistan, and Sudan.
c. Brazil, Colombia, Dominican Republic, Ecuador, El Salvador, Fiji, Guyana, Jamaica, Mauritius, Mexico, Nicaragua, Paraguay, Peru, the Philippines, South Africa, Sri Lanka, and Zimbabwe.
d. Algeria, Bolivia, China, Guatemala, Honduras, the Islamic Republic of Iran, the Republic of Korea, Malaysia, Saudi Arabia, Swaziland, the Syrian Arab Republic, Thailand, Tunisia, and Turkey.
e. Argentina, Costa Rica, Hungary, Panama, Romania, Trinidad and Tobago, the United Arab Emirates, Uruguay, and República Bolivariana de Venezuela.
f. Chile; Hong Kong SAR; China; Israel; Malta; and Singapore.

tends to lower the real minimum wage and the share of national income commanded by the bottom quintile of the population.

Exchange-Rate Policy

Although this chapter is mainly concerned with inflation and its relationship to economic growth and poverty, we conclude with a brief analysis of exchange-rate policy.

Flexible and Fixed Exchange Rates

Flexible rates. Countries with flexible exchange rates allow their currency to rise or fall in value against other currencies, depending on the demand for and supply of the currency relative to other currencies. For example, if the U.S. government supplies many more dollars than the French government supplies euros to the world economy—for example, through a more expansionary monetary policy—then there will be an increase in the relative world supply of dollars and a decrease in the relative supply of euros. Consequently, barring other changes in demand, the price (value) of the dollar relative to the euro will fall (or depreciate), and the price of the euro relative to the dollar will rise (appreciate).

An increase in relative demand can also cause the currency to fluctuate. If one assumes other variables do not change, an increase in demand for U.S. dollars relative to the euro (for example, because of an increase in demand for American goods or financial assets) will increase the price (value) of the American dollar and decrease the price of the euro. The advantage of fluctuating exchange rates is that the rates are more likely to reflect the true underlying value of the currency, thereby minimizing economic distortions.

Fixed rates. Some countries prefer to keep the value of their currency fixed (or pegged) relative to other currencies, regardless of prevailing demand and supply. Advantages of this system include more predictability for businesses engaged in international trade. Fixed exchange rates also can perform a useful role in anchoring inflation expectations in a country that is determined to break from high inflation. The disadvantage is that countries often find it difficult to exit from a pegged exchange rate, even when the exchange rate clearly has become overvalued. In such a situation, central banks often intervene to defend the currency by selling foreign reserves. When central banks' reserves become depleted, however, countries are often forced to devalue their currency. This can lead to higher inflation and import prices—hurting the poor—and can damage the balance sheets of the government (by raising the burden of servicing foreign debt), of banks (if they have more foreign liabilities than assets), and of corporations (again, if they have foreign liabilities unmatched by foreign income streams).

More and more developing countries have adopted floating or flexible exchange-rate arrangements during the past 15 years. Maintaining fixed exchange rates can cause a gradual erosion of competitiveness if domestic inflation is higher than that of trading partners (which is often the case for developing countries). China is a singular example; even as it has maintained a fixed exchange rate, its exports have remained very competitive because its currency has been grossly undervalued.[3] For the most part, however, for developing countries that are heavily dependent on exports of a few commodities, flexible exchange rates often play a useful buffer role.

Other Exchange-Rate Options

Full dollarization. Under this option, followed by Panama and Ecuador among others, the local currency is abolished and a foreign currency (in this case, the U.S. dollar) is adopted as the sole legal tender. Although this has the advantage of providing stability, certainty, and low inflation rates (essentially, U.S. inflation rates), it also has several disadvantages. If a country's trade is not heavily weighted in favor of the adopted currency—for example, if most of its trade was with countries that use the euro—full dollarization might not be a satisfactory option. More generally, unless the country has very close ties with the parent country, adopting the parent's monetary regime may not make much sense. Another disadvantage is that by abolishing its domestic currency, countries give up seignorage—the profits derived from issuing currency at very little cost.

Currency board. Under currency board arrangements, a country retains its own currency but promises to exchange the domestic currency for a foreign currency at a fixed given rate. To back up this promise, the central bank holds reserves at least equal to the domestic base money supply (so that the exchange promise can be fulfilled) and allows the money supply to be determined solely by inflows and outflows of foreign exchange. Domestic credit expansion is prohibited under such a system, even for lenders of last resort. By providing a stronger exchange-rate commitment than regular exchange-rate regimes, a well-run currency board, such as that of Hong Kong SAR, China or that of Lithuania, can provide credibility and anchor expectations—substantial advantages. At the same time, the exit problem is intensified and can result in terrible economic consequences, as in Argentina's forced exit from the currency board in 2001.

Other. Most countries adopt neither of the solutions identified above. Few countries' currencies float freely (that is, free of intervention), and fixed rates rarely last long without some form of exit. Many countries practice "dirty" or managed floating exchange-rate regimes, normally refraining from intervention but resorting on occasion to foreign-exchange transactions when the market is thought to have strayed too far from equilibrium.

Conclusion

This chapter examined the role of monetary and exchange-rate policy. These policies can have a large impact on economic performance, especially in the short term. Badly handled, they can impede economic growth and hurt the poor. The chapter began by examining the nuts and bolts of monetary policy operations and instruments. It described how developing countries still use direct instruments of monetary control, including credit ceilings and interest rate controls. Such policies can be highly distortionary and have been largely abandoned by industrialized countries in recent decades in favor of indirect monetary instruments. Indirect instruments, also used by developing countries, include reserve requirements, central bank lending facilities, and open-market operations. Next, we discussed different inflation measures, different types of inflation, and the various causes of inflation. We saw that while loose (or expansionary) monetary policy can stimulate the economy in the short run, it can cause high and volatile inflation, the costs of which are borne disproportionately by the poor. We concluded with a brief analysis of exchange-rate policy and the various exchange-rate options open to policy makers, ranging from formal dollarization to free-floating exchange-rate regimes. The choice of an exchange-rate regime depends on a country's characteristics, including its inflation performance, monetary credibility, trading patterns, and vulnerability to external shocks.

Notes

1. The prices are the amounts paid by the purchaser, excluding any deductible value added tax or similar deductible tax, but including transport charges paid separately by the producer to deliver goods at the required time and place.

2. The HDI is a measure of well-being that includes three basic dimensions of human development: longevity (life expectancy at birth); educational attainment (literacy and enrollment rates in education); and living standards (GDP per capita at purchasing power parity). The HDI ranges between 0 (low human development) and 1 (high human development).

3. For over a decade, the Chinese government has pegged the value of China's currency—the renminbi—to an artificially low level relative to the U.S. dollar. Most economists believe that if China's currency were allowed to trade freely, it would be worth more. No one can know for sure how much more, but leading economists have estimated that its value would be 10 to 40 percent higher than it is now. With its currency undervalued, China is discounting its own exports, so that exports from China are cheaper than they otherwise would be, helping China's economy grow. Low export prices are good news for consumers in other countries who pay less for the same good. But manufacturing industries outside China suffer because they cannot compete with low Chinese prices.

Bibliography

Anderson, Theodore W. 1971. *The Statistical Analysis of Time Series*. New York: Wiley.

Ball, Lawrence. 1990. "Credible Disinflation with Staggered Price Setting." National Bureau of Economic Research Working Paper 3555. Cambridge, MA.

Brayton, Flint, and Jaime Marquez. 1990. "The Behavior of Monetary Sectors and Monetary Policy: Evidence from Multicountry Models." In *Financial Sectors in Open Economies: Empirical Analysis and Policy Issues*, ed. Peter Hooper, Karen H. Johnson, Donald L. Kohn, David E. Lindsey, Richard D. Porter, and Ralph Tryon. Washington, DC: Board of Governors of the Federal Reserve System.

Bryant, Ralph, Gerald Holtham, and Peter Hooper, eds. 1988. *External Deficits and the Dollar*. Washington, DC: Brookings Institution.

Bryant, Ralph, Peter Hooper, and Catherine Mann, eds. 1992. *Evaluating Policy Regimes: New Research in Empirical Macroeconomics*. Washington, DC: Brookings Institution.

Calvo, Guillermo. 1978. "On the Time Consistency of Optimal Policy in a Monetary Economy." *Econometrica* 46 (6): 1411–28.

Cashin, P., P. Mauro, and R. Sahay. 2001. "Macroeconomic Policies and Poverty Reduction: Some Cross-Country Evidence." *Finance and Development* 38 (2): 46–49.

Dornbusch, Rudiger. 1976. "Expectations and Exchange Rate Dynamics." *Journal of Political Economy* 84 (December): 1161–71.

Easterly, W., and S. Fischer. 2001. "Inflation and the Poor." *Journal of Money, Credit and Banking* 33 (2): 160–78.

Fischer, Stanley. 1990. "Rules versus Discretion in Monetary Policy." In *Handbook of Monetary Economics*, ed. B. Friedman and F. Hahn. Amsterdam: North-Holland.

———. 1993. "The Role of Macroeconomic Factors in Growth." *Journal of Monetary Economics* 32 (3): 485–512.

———. 1996. "Maintaining Price Stability." *Finance and Development* 33 (December): 34–37.

IMF (International Monetary Fund). Various years. *International Financial Statistics*. Washington, DC.

Khan, Mohsin S., and Abdelhak S. Senhadji. 2000. "Threshold Effects in the Relationship between Inflation and Growth." IMF Working Paper WP/00/110, International Monetary Fund, Washington, DC.

McKinnon, Ronald. 1988. "Monetary and Exchange Rate Policies for International Financial Stability." *Journal of Economic Perspectives* 2 (1): 83–103.

Rogoff, K. 2003. "Straight Talk: Unlocking Growth in Africa." *Finance and Development* 40 (December): 54–5.

UN (United Nations). 2000. *A Better World for All*. New York: UN.

World Bank. 2005. *World Development Indicators*. CD-ROM. Washington, DC: World Bank.

CHAPTER 6

Financial Development

A large body of theoretical and empirical literature supports a positive causal link between a well-functioning financial system and economic growth. In particular, the economic growth studies of the past decade show that financial sector depth provokes and sustains economic growth. In fact, it is one of the few robust determinants of the growth path of countries. An important related question is whether macroeconomic developments can stimulate the financial sector. They can, as we demonstrate below.

Although the link between financial sector development and growth is well established, the relationship between financial development and the income of the poor remains unclear. Competing theories predict the impact of financial development on changes in income distribution and poverty alleviation. Recent empirical studies have, however, found that financial development reduces income inequality by disproportionately boosting the incomes of the poor. In particular, studies have found that countries with better-developed financial intermediaries experience faster reductions in poverty and income inequality.

While financial development can be very beneficial, the data show that usage of financial services is far from universal in many developing countries. Fortunately, countries can increase access to financial services by strengthening their institutional infrastructures, liberalizing markets, fostering greater competition, and encouraging innovative uses of know-how and technology.

This chapter analyzes each of these issues in turn. It concludes by discussing other topics relevant to the general theme of financial development and poverty: the history of financial sector reform in developing countries in recent decades, the role of microfinance in providing credit to the poor, and the importance of emigrants' remittances for many developing countries.

Financial Development and Economic Growth

The proposition that financial sector development supports economic growth is fairly well established in the literature. Almost a century ago, Schumpeter (1911) argued that financial intermediation through the banking system played a key role in economic growth by improving productivity and technical change. The specific channels through which financial development can help economic growth include: (a) raising and pooling funds (allowing riskier investments to be undertaken); (b) allocating resources to their most productive use; (c) allowing effective monitoring of the use of funds; (d) providing instruments for risk mitigation; (e) supporting firms' growth opportunities, especially for small and medium enterprises; and (f) reducing inequality.

Turning to the empirical evidence, Jalilian and Kirkpatrick (2005) and Levine (2005) review the current state of play. Recent cross-country econometric analysis provides evidence that financial development is robustly related to economic growth (King and Levine 1993; Arestis and Demetriades 1997; Levine 1997; Rajan and Zingales 1998; Caprio and Honohan 2001). The link seems to work mainly through greater accumulation of physical capital and improvements in economic efficiency under well-developed financial systems.

Recent econometric techniques that use the pooling of cross-country and time-series data make it possible to test the direction of causality between financial development and growth. Studies that employ these techniques—including those of Levine, Loayza, and Beck (2000) and Beck, Levine, and Loayza (2000)—also find a positive link between financial development and growth. The causal factors include the contribution of financial development to private savings, capital accumulation, and productivity, with the last playing the most important role.

In terms of the magnitude of this impact, Caprio and Honohan (2001) have found that a doubling of private sector credit as a share of gross domestic product (GDP)—a common measure of financial depth—is associated with a 2 percentage point increase in the rate of GDP growth.[1] But the literature also finds substantial cross-country heterogeneity in the relationship between financial development and economic growth— unsurprising, given structural, institutional, and policy differences in the economies included in the sample (Jalilian and Kirkpatrick 2005). That topic is covered later in the chapter.

The development of a financial system will necessarily be affected by endogenous and exogenous factors and by the sociopolitical development of individual countries. Endogenous factors refer to indicators of the soundness of individual financial institutions. Commonly used to assess that soundness is the CAMELS framework. The acronym stands for capital adequacy, asset quality, management soundness, earnings and profitability, liquidity, and sensitivity to market risk. Exogenous factors refer to macroeconomic developments that can affect financial system depth.

Imbalances in economic growth rates may have a negative impact on the financial system of a country in at least two respects. First, low or declining aggregate growth rates often weaken the debt-servicing capacity of domestic borrowers and raise credit risk. Second, if an economy is overly dependent on one or two sectors for its economic growth, and if financial institutions are overly exposed in those sectors, an adverse real sector shock may have an immediate impact on the financial system. The system is even more vulnerable if those sectors are subject to exogenous forces, such as climatic conditions. The pattern and trend of inflation has a direct bearing on the stability and health of the financial system. High and volatile inflation complicates the task of accurately assessing credit and market risk in a financial institution's portfolio and its ability to manage and plan for the future. The relationship between financial system development and a country's external position, exchange rates, and international interest rates is complex (table 6.1).

Four Decades of Financial Sector Reform in Developing Countries

The early stage of financial sector reform in developing countries—from the mid-1970s up to the late 1980s—concentrated on liberalizing interest rates, moving to indirect instruments of monetary control (such as

Table 6.1   Possible Effects of Various Policies on the Financial System

Indicator	Pattern/movement	Comment
Current-account deficit as share of GDP	Increasing	May signal vulnerability to currency crisis if foreign investors judge the deficit as unsustainable, causing them to withdraw their investments, with negative implications for the liquidity of the financial system.
External capital inflows	Increasing	May lead to asset price and credit booms.
Ratio of international reserves to short-term liabilities	Low	Seen by investors as a major indicator of vulnerability.
Terms of trade	Fluctuating	Poor terms of trade or a sharp decline in a small country with high export concentrations may precipitate a banking crisis. Terms that are too high or that increase sharply may lead to inflation and asset price bubbles.
Composition, maturity of capital flows	Low investment ratios	Current-account deficits and low investment ratios may signal potential vulnerability of the financial system.
Exchange rate and interest rates	Volatile pattern	The higher the volatility, the higher the foreign-exchange and interest risks for financial institutions, especially if the external debt burden is high or if foreign portfolio investments represent a high share of total foreign investment.
Exchange rate	Volatile	Currency mismatches between bank assets and liabilities.
Exchange-rate guarantees	—	Considered major contributors to volatility in capital flows and excessive foreign currency exposures.
Interest rates	Increasing international rates	Capital outflows. Adverse impact on emerging market borrowers.
Interest rates	Declining	May promote capital inflows that could lead to risky lending.

Source: Authors.
Note: — = not available.

interest rates on reserves and open-market operations), dismantling directed credit, and opening the capital account. For these reforms to take hold and stimulate a broader liberalization of the financial sector, it was necessary to remove impediments to competition.[2] That was done by privatizing banks, introducing new legislation governing the entry and exit of banks from the market (including foreign banks), revising laws and regulations on the taxation of banks and other financial intermediaries, and amending legislation on foreign ownership.

But as world financial markets became more volatile in the 1990s and inflationary pressures in developing countries increased, financial sector reform came to mean something else. The middle stage of the reform movement concentrated on strengthening financial sector infrastructure and individual institutions. Macroeconomic stability and real sector reform were crucial to these requirements.

In practical terms, financial sector reform expanded to include

- the legal framework governing the operations of the central bank, with the establishment of independent central banks enshrined in legislation;
- the legal framework for banks, through the establishment of prudential regulations and banking law;
- the regulatory framework for the nonbanking sector, through the establishment of rules governing the ratio of nonbank assets to financial sector assets and the number of listed companies on the stock exchange; and
- identification of rights and obligations of financial agents, through the establishment of liquidation and bankruptcy laws, payment systems, and accounting and auditing standards.

Strengthening individual financial institutions required the establishment and enforcement of guidelines for supervision, restructuring, and institutional reform, a process that can be summarized as follows:

- *Better bank supervision*—guidelines for the capacity and authority needed to provide effective supervision, licensing criteria, and supervision systems
- *Bank restructuring*—guidelines for capital replenishment, asset liquidation, and privatization
- *Institutional reforms*—management information systems and human resource development programs.

The need for the latest stage of financial sector reform became apparent in the wake of the Asian financial crisis of 1997–98. The crisis demonstrated the links between the corporate and financial sectors and the problems that can arise when these sectors are at different stages of reform. The crisis also highlighted the need for greater transparency and accountability, especially where owners of financial institutions have close connections with those in political power.

Improving transparency and accountability requires improved disclosure of macroeconomic information, stricter disclosure requirements for participants in securities markets, more aggressive investor education, the establishment of rating agencies and credit bureaus, and the adoption of global accounting and auditing standards. Reforms will be successful only when requisite conditions are in place. For example, interest rates should be deregulated only if the regulatory framework is sound, bank supervision is effective, accounting and auditing systems are adequate, financial markets are competitive, and banks have positive net worth and capable management and staff. To use another example, banks should be recapitalized only after systemic problems that allowed them to lose their capital in the first place have been addressed by ceasing lending to defaulters, establishing strong bank supervision and monitoring, and putting in place adequate information systems. At that time, management of insolvent banks should be replaced and state-owned banks should be made part of a privatization plan.

Financial Development and Poverty Reduction

Although the relationship between financial development and growth is well established, the same cannot be said for the direct link between financial development and income inequality, beyond the growth relationship itself. Beck, Demirguc-Kunt, and Levine (2004) provide a comprehensive analysis of this important question. As the authors note, economic theory is ambiguous when it comes to the relationship between financial development and changes in poverty and income distribution. Some models imply that financial development enhances growth and reduces inequality. According to these models, financial market imperfections—such as information problems, transaction costs, and contract enforcement costs—may be especially binding on poor entrepreneurs who lack collateral, credit histories, and connections. These credit constraints will impede the flow of capital to poor individuals pursuing high-return projects, thereby reducing the efficiency of capital allocation and worsening income inequality. Viewed from this angle, financial development reduces poverty by (a) disproportionately relaxing credit constraints on the poor and reducing income inequality, and (b) improving the allocation of capital and accelerating growth.

Other theories, however, question whether financial development reduces poverty. Some research suggests that the poor primarily rely on informal, family connections for capital, so that improvements in the formal financial sector tend to help the rich rather than the poor. For instance, Greenwood and Jovanovic (1990) developed a model that predicts a nonlinear relationship between financial development and income inequality during the process of economic development. At the early stages of development, only the rich can afford to access and profit from financial markets—so financial development *intensifies* income inequality. At higher levels of economic development, financial development helps an increasing proportion of society. Other models imply that if financial development reduces income inequality, the reduction could slow aggregate growth and increase poverty. If the rich save more than the poor, the argument goes, a reduction in income inequality could reduce aggregate savings and slow growth, with adverse implications for poverty. A great deal more empirical evidence is needed before any of the competing theoretical predictions can be declared the winner.

Beck, Demirguc-Kunt, and Levine (2004) attempt to settle the issue by assessing the relationships among financial development, poverty alleviation, and changes in the distribution of income. Employing broad cross-country comparisons, they find that financial development alleviates poverty and reduces income inequality. Their findings also indicate that financial development exerts a disproportionately positive influence on the poor. Their research yields three key findings:

- Even when controlling for real per capita GDP growth, financial development reduces income inequality beyond the growth effects themselves.
- Financial development induces a drop in the Gini coefficient, the leading measure of income inequality.
- Financial development reduces the fraction of the population living on less than $1 or $2 a day and shrinks the poverty gap.

Jalilian and Kirkpatrick (2005) also find that financial development reduces income inequality, but only beyond certain income levels, in line with Greenwood and Jovanovic's (1990) prediction of an inverted-U relationship.

Widening Access to Financial Services

Although financial services can have very beneficial effects, their use in developing countries is far from universal, as Claessens (2005) has noted. Instead of helping the poor, financial systems cater mainly to large enterprises and wealthier individuals. Finance is often allocated on the basis of connections and other nonmarket criteria. Often, many segments of the enterprise and household sectors suffer from lack of access to finance at reasonable costs, hindering growth. Claessens (2005) finds that for most developing countries, basic bank account usage does not exceed 30 percent of households; in the lowest-income countries, usage is less than 10 percent.

Although low usage may reflect lack of demand rather than lack of access, Claessens (2005) argues that this is unlikely in many developing countries, precisely *because* usage is so low. The supply of financial services in such countries is clearly limited, but why? Is it because banks are unwilling to supply financial services to the poor because they believe them to be unprofitable customers? Or are there barriers to supply? If so, can those barriers be removed, for example, through microfinance or through savings and payments services provided by postal and saving banks? Or is there some form of market failure that government intervention can address?

Demand may be slack if financial services are too costly and not well tailored to customer needs. If this is the case, households and firms may rely instead on informal forms of finance. But there are some grounds for hope here. For instance, in 2004 in South Africa, the country's major banks launched a low-cost bank account aimed at extending banking services to low-income households. Initial take-up was reportedly very high. A sharp drop in the costs of international remittances also suggests that banking services are being extended at a more reasonable cost to wider segments of the population.

For a sample of more than 90 countries, Beck, Demirguc-Kunt, and Martinez-Peria (2005) showed that those countries with better-developed financial systems have services that are more evenly distributed among banking clients. This suggests that the overall institutional environment can play a role in the supply of banking services. Furthermore, the institutional environment—a sound legal system, secure property rights, and reliable sources of information—is especially important for the supply of credit to small firms. Banking-system regulations can also affect the rate of usage of financial services. For instance, restrictions on interest rates and other limits on lending can make it difficult for providers of financial services to offer profitable saving or lending instruments.

Against this backdrop, it appears that many developing countries need to improve their legal and regulatory systems as these bear on financial services. Better infrastructure and systems related to information and payments appear to be needed as well. These are all difficult and time-consuming reforms. To complement them, Honohan (2004) suggests that an important way to enhance access—one often easier than improving the institutional environment—is to improve competition in banking systems. For instance, small nonbank financial institutions (including department stores) might be allowed greater use of existing financial networks. Liberalizing entry by foreign banks can further enhance competition and access to banking services by the population at large. Claessens (2005) cites the example of Mongolia, where the failed government-owned Agricultural Bank was sold to a Japanese investor and quickly became a successful bank that provides far greater access to the population at large. Foreign ownership can also induce greater financial stability and improve the overall efficiency of financial intermediation.

Whether universal usage should be a public policy goal is, however, an open question. The fact that the poor do not use financial services may be a problem of poverty more than one of access. Also, our knowledge of the benefits and impact of finance remains insufficient at the micro level. For example, access to credit may be a problem when it leads to overindebtedness, as the poor can be uninformed and overborrow, often on unfavorable terms. Public interventions may be useful in some cases, but they will need to be carefully introduced and tracked. Governments might try to make social security, tax, and other payments in a manner that encourages more bank access, notably by making them electronic when feasible. Authorities could also mandate that banks provide minimum banking services for otherwise excluded segments of the market.

Microfinance and the Poor

There is a growing awareness that building financial systems for the poor means building sound domestic financial intermediaries that can mobilize and recycle domestic savings for this segment of the population. Microfinance institutions (MFIs) have emerged over the past three decades to provide financial services to low-income clients, who for centuries had to rely on a wide range of informal credit providers, such as money lenders.[3]

Early microcredit agencies operated on a nonprofit basis and did not require collateral. They reduced risk through group guarantees, appraisal of household cash flow, and small initial loans to test clients. It soon became apparent that the poor were reliable in repaying uncollateralized loans and were willing to pay a somewhat higher cost for receiving services that would not otherwise be provided by the mainstream banking sector.

Although their usage of financial services is not as great as that of wealthier segments of the population, as noted in the previous section, the poor need and use a broad range of financial services, including deposit accounts, insurance, and facilities to transfer money to relatives living elsewhere. Experience has shown that they can be served profitably, on a long-term basis, and, in some cases, on a large scale. Well-run MFIs can outperform mainstream commercial banks in portfolio quality and function in turbulent times. During Indonesia's 1997 crisis, for example, commercial bank portfolios deteriorated, but loan repayment among Bank Rakyat Indonesia's 26 million microclients barely declined. And, during the recent Bolivian banking crisis, MFIs' portfolios suffered but remained substantially healthier than those of commercial banks.

Other studies illustrate the social function of microfinance. Microfinance has been credited with improving a large range of welfare measures, such as income stability and growth, nutritional needs, health, and school attendance. It also has been widely credited with empowering women by increasing their contribution to household income and assets.

Moreover, examples of financially sound, professional MFIs suggest that microfinance can be made available for the long term, well beyond the duration of donor government subsidies. There is little doubt that microfinance is highly valued by the poor, as shown by their strong demand for such services, their willingness to pay the full cost of those services, and a high loan-repayment rate motivated by a desire to have access to future loans.

On the policy level, microfinance has been embraced by politicians and the development community, with the predictable result that some of its merits have been oversold. To achieve the full potential of microfinance to serve poor households, MFIs will need to become fully integrated with the mainstream financial system in the countries in which they operate. This will require financially sound, professional organizations capable of competing, accessing commercial loans, becoming licensed to collect deposits, and growing to reach significant scale and impact. The majority of MFIs do not yet fit into this category—most are weak, heavily donor dependent, and unlikely to ever reach scale or independence.

But the commercial success of some MFIs is an encouraging sign. The form of their eventual integration into the financial mainstream will depend on the country context and the requirements of customers. The options being pursued include the following:

- Partnership with a commercial bank
- Adoption of microfinance methodologies by retailers, consumer finance groups, building societies, and other institutions that often are better placed than banks to provide the smaller account and transaction sizes required by customers with lower incomes
- Licenses for MFIs
- Allowing MFIs to tap into mainstream credit bureaus to increase their productivity and portfolio quality and to reduce the spreads between their borrowing and saving rates.

Partnerships enable MFIs to cut costs and extend their reach, while banks can benefit from the opportunity to reach new markets, diversify assets, and increase revenues. Partnerships vary in their degree of engagement and risk sharing. In some cases, partnership refers to sharing or renting front offices; in others, to banks making actual portfolio and direct equity investments in MFIs (figure 6.1).

More MFIs are now obtaining their own licenses as banks or specialized financial institutions. This allows them to secure financing by accessing capital markets and by attracting deposits from large institutional investors as well as poor clients. Several MFIs, especially in Latin America, have accessed local debt markets by issuing private placements that have been purchased by local financial institutions. Other countries are considering legislation to create new types of financial licenses, usually with lower minimum capital requirements, specifically designed for MFIs.

MFIs are beginning to tap into mainstream credit bureaus, which allows their clients to build a public credit history, making them more attractive to mainstream banks and retailers. More than 80 MFIs in Peru are registered to use Infocorp, a private credit bureau. Similarly, in Turkey, Maya Enterprise for Microfinance negotiated with a leading bank, Garanti Bankasi, to gain access to the national credit bureau. The central bank in Rwanda requires that MFIs communicate information about their borrowers to a credit bureau.

Figure 6.1   New Links between Microfinance Institutions and Commercial Banks

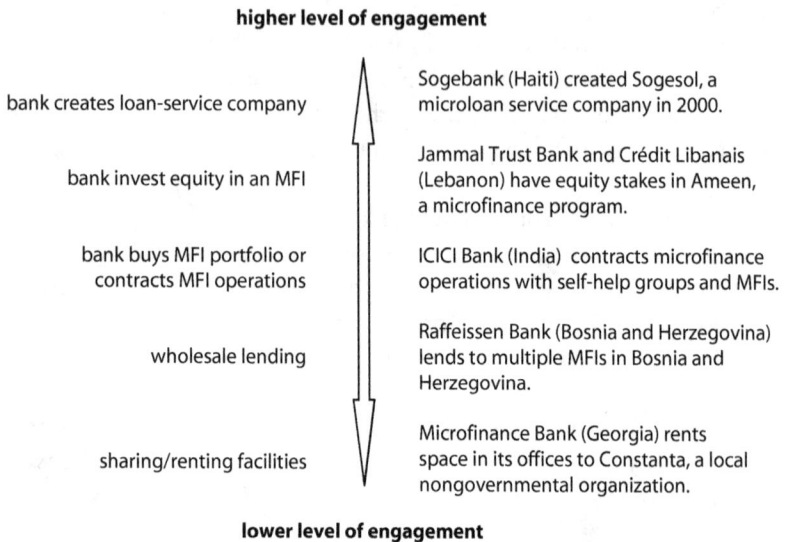

higher level of engagement

bank creates loan-service company	Sogebank (Haiti) created Sogesol, a microloan service company in 2000.
bank invest equity in an MFI	Jammal Trust Bank and Crédit Libanais (Lebanon) have equity stakes in Ameen, a microfinance program.
bank buys MFI portfolio or contracts MFI operations	ICICI Bank (India) contracts microfinance operations with self-help groups and MFIs.
wholesale lending	Raffeissen Bank (Bosnia and Herzegovina) lends to multiple MFIs in Bosnia and Herzegovina.
sharing/renting facilities	Microfinance Bank (Georgia) rents space in its offices to Constanta, a local nongovernmental organization.

lower level of engagement

Source: Consultative Group to Assist the Poor (CGAP), reproduced in Littlefield and Rosenberg (2004).

In general, improvements in information technology help to create new delivery channels for the provision of microfinance. To a large extent, the conduits are already in place—retail shops, Internet kiosks, post offices, lottery outlets; the challenge is to make it possible to provide financial services more cost-effectively in poorer and more sparsely populated areas.

While welcome, such a trend poses a risk of taxing the capacity of supervisory authorities as they assume responsibility for other parts of the financial sector. Moreover, creating the infrastructure for specialized MFIs could also divert mainstream commercial banks and others from becoming involved in microfinance.

Emigrant Remittances

Emigrant remittances have come to represent an increasingly important source of financial flows between developed and developing countries in recent decades. Officially recorded remittances—comprising all unrequited transfers from migrant workers to family and friends in their countries of origin—climbed steeply in the decades between 1970 and 2000, declining only in the late 1990s. They then grew sharply after 2002 ($115.5 billion), peaking at $305 billion in 2008 before dipping in response to the global financial crisis (table 6.2).[4] Future flows are bound to be affected by the simultaneous economic slowdown in the high-income countries—including the United States and Western Europe, which account for almost two-thirds of the remittances that migrants send home to developing countries—and in the developing countries that account for 10–30 percent of the rest. The fact remains that workers' remittances dwarf official aid (the subject of the next chapter) as a source of funds for the developing world.

Improvements in banking technology that reduce the costs of formal remittance services and increase the geographical range over which remittances can be sent have steered unofficial remittances into the formal sector, enabling them to be recorded (Chami, Fullenkamp, and Jahjah 2005). That trend is expected to continue.

Nevertheless, a significant proportion of estimated remittance flows—estimated at between 35 and 70 percent of official remittances—remain unrecorded. Unrecorded remittances are channeled through the informal sector and are not captured in official balance of payment statistics. While remittances that move outside the formal sector may be used for legitimate reasons, they also may be channeled to unproductive and illegal

Table 6.2   Remittance Flows to Developing Countries

US$ billion	2002	2003	2004	2005	2006	2007	2008e
All developing countries	115.5	144.3	164.4	194.8	228.7	280.8	305.4
As % of GDP	1.9	2.1	2.0	2.0	2.0	2.1	1.9
By region:							
East Asia and Pacific	29.5	35.4	39.2	46.7	53.0	65.3	69.6
Europe and Central Asia	13.7	15.5	22.2	31.2	38.3	50.4	53.1
Latin America and the Caribbean	27.9	36.6	43.3	50.1	59.2	63.1	63.3
Middle East and North Africa	15.2	20.4	23.0	24.3	25.7	31.3	33.7
South Asia	24.1	30.4	28.7	33.1	39.6	52.1	66.0
Sub-Saharan Africa	5.0	6.0	8.0	9.4	12.9	18.6	19.8

Source: World Bank 2009.
Note: Remittances are defined as the sum of workers' remittances, compensation of employees, and migrant transfers. See http://www.worldbank.org/prospects/migrationandremittances for data definitions and the entire data set; 2008e = estimate.

activities, such as money laundering, drug money flows, and the financing of terrorism.

Examples of remittance channels, formal and informal, include

- Interbank transfers
- Formal nonbank money-transfer operators
- Post office transfers
- Cash and commodities carriers
- Informal money-transfer operators (Kireyev 2006).

Other channels are specific to a region or country, such as *fei-ch'ien* (China), *padala* (the Philippines), *hundi* (India), *hui kuan* (Hong Kong SAR, China), and *phei kwan* (Thailand). The *hawala* system, historically associated with South Asia and the Middle East, refers to an informal channel for transferring funds from one location to another through service providers—known as *hawaladars*—regardless of the nature of the transaction or the countries involved (El-Qorchi, Maimbo, and Wilson 2002).

While some studies suggest that self-interest is the prime motive for remittance arrangements, most agree that the practice is primarily altruistic (Stark and Lucas 1988; Chami, Fullenkamp, and Jahjah 2005) and mainly confined to transfers between family members. The concentration on the household has formed the basis of studies of the microeconomic impact of emigrant remittances. Those studies have shown that remittances raise household consumption, stimulate investment (notably in real property), and result in better education and health care (Kireyev 2006). Thus, from a microeconomic perspective, remittances should have a positive impact on growth.

But the literature, most of it recent, is not definitive on the macroeconomic impact of remittances. For example, Chami, Fullenkamp, and Jahjah (2005) suggest that remittances have a negative impact on economic growth, whereas Aggarwal and Spatafora (2005) find no effect, and Giuliano and Ruiz-Arranz (2005) argue that remittances promote growth in countries with shallow financial systems but have no impact in countries with well-developed financial systems. The lack of a clear relationship is not surprising. First, the impact on growth will depend on whether the remittances are spent on consumption or investment. To this end, the research suggests that remittances have primarily been used for consumption purposes, with little impact on long-run growth. Second, the research shows that remittance inflows are countercyclical, increasing during periods of weak economic growth in the receiving countries. This countercyclical nature makes it difficult to establish the true impact of remittances on economic growth. It does suggest, however, that remittances can play a large part in maintaining macroeconomic stability and mitigating the impact of adverse shocks. A number of papers (quoted in Spatafora 2005) have attested to this.

The distributive effect of remittances has been the subject of a large part of the evolving literature. Not only have remittances been shown to mitigate the impact of adverse shocks on an economy, but they have also been linked with helping to reduce poverty (Aggarwal and Spatafora 2005). Kireyev (2006) suggests that the decline in the poverty rate in Tajikistan from 81 percent to 60 percent from 2000 to 2003 was helped by the significant level of remittances to that country (where flows of remittances had reached 50 percent of GDP). Moreover, children in households receiving remittances are more likely to receive better education and health care.

But the distributive effects of remittances can also be negative. Kireyev (2006) outlines a number of negative effects of remittances for Tajikistan that also figure in studies of other countries. Remittance inflows may have any of the following negative effects:

- They may impede monetary management and rekindle inflationary pressures, as the unpredictability and seasonal nature of foreign currency inflows create uncertainties for monetary management.
- They may lead to an appreciation of the national currency, hampering competitiveness.
- They may contribute to the expansion of the trade deficit. In Tajikistan, most remittances are used to finance imports.
- They may create a strong disincentive for domestic savings. Declining savings can deplete the resource base for investment and may even turn it negative.
- They may pose a serious moral hazard (see glossary) by reducing the pressure for reforms. Remittances enable households and private businesses to support their own consumption or investment independent of the national government, thus reducing pressure on the authorities to create a better business environment and to deal with the problems that forced emigrant workers to leave the country in the first place.

A related negative associated with migration is brain drain. Although migrants may learn skills that may be useful to their country of origin when and if they return, the loss of human capital that comes with emigration hampers a country's development prospects. Mishra (2006) shows, for example, that the Caribbean countries—which have lost in excess of 70 percent of their best-educated labor force (those with more than 12 years of schooling)—are not fully compensated for brain drain by the significant inflow of remittances.

Some research has focused on the policies and regulations that determine the flow of remittances, but further research is needed on how to create a sustainable development path for the source country.[5] In summary, remittances represent a short-term fix for long-term problems.

Conclusion

The chapter began by demonstrating the well-established causal link between a well-functioning financial system and economic growth. It then identified the impact of macroeconomic fundamentals on the financial system, showing, for example, that imbalanced growth and high inflation harm the financial system. While the link between financial development and income inequality remains unclear, recent empirical studies have found that financial development tends to reduce income inequality. From a brief history of financial sector reform in developing countries, we saw that reforms, which began in the mid-1970s, started by liberalizing interest rates. Later reform efforts concentrated on indirect instruments of monetary control and the dismantling of directed credit before moving on to strengthen the overall financial sector infrastructure, including legal, regulatory, and supervisory frameworks. The most recent reforms have included moves toward greater transparency and better auditing and accounting standards. The chapter then discussed policy measures that can be used to increase access to financial services by strengthening institutional infrastructures, liberalizing markets, and fostering greater competition. The chapter concluded with a discussion of microfinance and emigrants' remittances, both increasingly important channels of financial flows to the poor in developing countries.

Notes

1. Debate persists. Aghion, Howitt, and Mayer-Foulkes (2005) raise serious questions about whether financial development affects steady-state growth or instead influences the rate of convergence with higher-income countries. Either way, however, financial development is positive for economic growth.

2. Assessing the outcome of reforms requires an examination of the following variables: real positive interest rates, the term structure of interest rates, the ratio of M2 to GDP, banking system financial ratios, and the spread between lending and deposit rates. (M2 refers to money and close substitutes for money, i.e., the amount of money in circulation. M2 is a key economic indicator used to forecast inflation.)

3. This section draws on Littlefield and Rosenberg (2004).

4. Recorded flows to Latin America and the Caribbean began to stagnate in 2007 as the U.S. recession, especially in the construction sector, reduced the employment and income of Latin American (especially Mexican) migrants.

5. Multiple exchange rates, restrictions on holding foreign-exchange deposits, large black market premiums, high transaction costs in the form of money-transfer fees, and dual exchange rates all reduce remittance inflows.

Bibliography

Aggarwal, R., and N. Spatafora. 2005. "Remittances, determinants and impact." Mimeo. International Monetary Fund, Washington, DC.

Aghion, P., P. Howitt, and D. Mayer-Foulkes. 2005. "The Effect of Financial Development on Convergence: Theory and Evidence." *Quarterly Journal of Economics* 120 (February): 173–222.

Arestis, P., and P. O. Demetriades. 1997. "Financial Development and Economic Growth, Assessing the Evidence." *Economic Journal* 107 (442): 783–99.

Aslanbeigui, Nahid, and Gale Summerfield. 2000. "The Asian Crisis, Gender, and the International Financial Architecture." *Feminist Economics* 6 (3): 81–104.

Beck, Thorsten, Asli Demirguc-Kunt, and Ross Levine. 2004. "Finance, Inequality, and Poverty: Cross-Country Evidence." NBER Working Paper 10979, National Bureau of Economic Research, Cambridge, MA.

Beck, Thorsten, Asli Demirguc-Kunt, and M. S. Martinez-Peria. 2005. "Reaching Out: Access To and Use of Banking Services Across Countries." Policy Research Working Paper WPS3754, World Bank, Washington, DC.

Beck, T., R. Levine, and N. Loayza. 2000. "Finance and the Sources of Growth." *Journal of Financial Economics* 58 (1): 261–300.

Caprio, G., and P. Honohan. 1999. "Restoring Banking Stability: Beyond Supervised Capital Requirements." *Journal of Economic Perspectives* 13 (4): 43–64.

———. 2001. "Finance for Growth: Policy Choices in a Volatile World." World Bank Policy Research Report, Washington DC, World Bank.

Carlozzi, Nicholas, and John B. Taylor. 1985. "International Capital Mobility and the Coordination of Monetary Rules." In *Exchange Rate Dynamics under*

Uncertainty, ed. J. Bhandari, 186–210. Cambridge, MA: Massachusetts Institute of Technology Press.

Chami, Ralph, Connell Fullenkamp, and Samir Jahjah. 2005. "Are Immigrant Remittance Flows a Source of Capital for Development?" *International Monetary Fund Staff Papers* 52 (1): 55–81.

Claessens, Stijn. 2005. "Access to Financial Service: A Review of the Issues and Public Policy Objectives." Paper presented at the Fifth Services Experts Meeting on Universal Access, organized by the Organisation for Economic Co-operation and Development and the World Bank, Paris, February 3–5.

El-Qorchi, Mohammed, Samuel M. Maimbo, and John F. Wilson. 2002. "Hawala: How Does This Informal Funds Transfer System Work, and Should It Be Regulated?" *Finance and Development* 39 (4): 31–33.

Elson, Diane. 1994. "People, Development, and International Financial Systems." *Review of African Political Economy* 62: 511–24.

Giuliano, Paola, and Marta Ruiz-Arranz. 2005. "Remittances, Financial Development, and Growth." IMF Working Paper WP/05/234, International Monetary Fund, Washington, DC.

Greenwood, J., and B. Jovanovic. 1990. "Financial Development, Growth and the Distribution of Income." Working Paper, University of Western Ontario, London, Ontario.

Gupta, Poonam. 2005. "Macroeconomic Determinants of Remittances: Evidence from India." IMF Working Paper WP/05/224, International Monetary Fund, Washington, DC.

Honohan, Patrick. 2004. "Financial Development, Growth, and Poverty: How Close Are the Links?" Policy Research Working Paper 3203, World Bank, Washington, DC.

Jalilian, Hossein, and Colin Kirkpatrick. 2005. "Does Financial Development Contribute to Poverty Reduction?" *Journal of Development Studies* 41 (4): 636–56.

Khandker, Shahidur R. 2003. "Microfinance and Poverty—Evidence Using Panel Data from Bangladesh." Policy Research Working Paper 2945, World Bank, Washington, DC.

King, R. G., and R. Levine. 1993. "Finance and Growth: Schumpeter Might Be Right." *Quarterly Journal of Economics* 108 (3): 717–38.

———. 1993. "Finance, Entrepreneurship and Growth: Theory and Evidence." *Journal of Monetary Economics* 32 (3): 513–42.

Kireyev, Alexei. 2006. "The Macroeconomics of Remittances: The Case of Tajikistan." IMF Working Paper WP/06/2, International Monetary Fund, Washington, DC.

Levine, R. 1997. "Financial Development and Economic Growth: Views and Agenda." *Journal of Economic Literature* 35 (June): 688–726.

———. 2004. "Finance and Growth: Theory and Evidence." NBER Working Paper 10766, National Bureau of Economic Research, Cambridge, MA.

———. 2005. "Finance and Growth: Theory, Evidence and Mechanisms." In *Handbook of Economic Growth,* ed. Philippe Aghion and Steven Durlauf. Amsterdam: North-Holland.

Levine, Ross, Norman Loayza, and Thorsten Beck. 2000. "Financial Intermediation and Growth: Causality and Causes." *Journal of Monetary Economics* 46 (1): 31–77.

Littlefield, Elizabeth, and Richard Rosenberg. 2004. "Microfinance and the Poor." *Finance and Development* 41 (June): 38–40.

Martinez-Peria, M. S., A. Demirguc-Kunt, and R. Aggarwal. 2006. "Do Workers' Remittances Promote Financial Development?" Policy Research Working Paper 3957, World Bank, Washington, DC.

Mishra, Prachi. 2006. "Emigration and Brain Drain: Evidence from the Caribbean." IMF Working Paper WP/06/5, International Monetary Fund, Washington, DC.

Pattillo, Catherine, Sanjeev Gupta, and Kevin Carey. 2005. "Sustaining Growth Accelerations and Pro-Poor Growth in Africa." IMF Working Paper WP/05/195, International Monetary Fund, Washington, DC.

Rajan, R. G., and L. Zingales. 1998. "Financial Dependence and Growth." *American Economic Review* 88 (3): 559–86.

Ratha, D. 2003. "Workers' Remittances: An Important and Stable Source of External Development Finance." In *Global Development Finance 2003: Striving for Stability in Development Finance,* 157–75. Washington, DC: World Bank.

Schumpeter, J. 1911. *The Theory of Economic Development: An Inquiry into Profits, Capital, Credit, Interest and Business Cycle.* Cambridge, MA: Harvard University Press.

Spatafora, Nikola. 2005. "Workers' Remittances." *IMF Research Bulletin* 6 (4).

Stark, O., and R. E. B. Lucas. 1988. "Migration, Remittances, and the Family." *Economic Development and Cultural Change* 36 (3): 465–81.

World Bank. 2009. *Global Development Finance 2009.* Washington, DC: World Bank.

CHAPTER 7

Development Assistance

Foreign aid—often referred to as official development assistance (ODA)—can contribute to growth and development. The aim of making aid more effective is at the core of all development assistance and encompasses numerous issues, from the predictability of aid flows to the use of country systems to the measurement of development results. Today, as governments face financial uncertainty and challenges such as the threat of climate change, it is more important than ever that aid be channeled to produce sustainable results.

The effort to make aid more effective brings together development stakeholders, donor governments, multilateral donors, recipient country governments, civil society organizations, global programs, and many others. All must coordinate to align with every country's specific priorities, as well as with the development goals identified by partners. The next section focuses on aid sources and trends and the efficacy of aid to developing countries, in particular through poverty reduction.

Aid Sources and Trends

The phenomenon of richer countries helping poorer ones through bilateral grants and loans at low rates of interest (known as concessional loans) began after World War II. The prime motivation for early aid efforts, however, was not to promote growth or reduce poverty, the leading goals today, but rather to enlist allies in the geopolitical realignment that immediately followed the war. Until the 1960s, the bulk of aid was given for large infrastructure projects such as power generation and transportation networks. The 1970s saw a new focus on antipoverty programs. This trend continued into the 1980s and early 1990s, when another shift occurred. During the 1990s, a large portion of aid (approximately 40 percent) was allocated to infrastructure and productive sectors such as agriculture, industry, and trade. Since then, the trend has shifted toward supporting social services—health, education, and water supply and sanitation—and strengthening institutions and civil society. In 2003, social services were targeted by roughly one-third of aid flows—up from one-fifth in 1990. More recently, we have begun to see a reprise of investment in infrastructure. Overall, aid today is viewed as a tool for providing budgetary support to developing nations, thereby helping to improve governance and institutions while also fighting hunger and poverty.

ODA is provided by 22 member countries of the Organisation for Economic Co-operation and Development (OECD) plus the European Commission (EC) through the Development Assistance Committee (DAC),[1] and by 14 other donor countries (many in the Middle East, plus Turkey) that are not DAC members but report their aid activities to it. In addition, countries such as Brazil, China, India, and the Russian Federation—themselves developing countries—have recently emerged as donors, although they still receive development assistance.

ODA is provided for developmental purposes[2] by governments or public funds as grants or as soft loans. ODA loans bear a grant element of at least 25 percent that is calculated at a rate of 10 percent, significantly less onerous than commercial transactions. ODA is provided to specifically defined low- and middle-income countries that are not Group of Eight (G-8) members or European Union (EU) members or countries with accession dates to the EU. Eligible countries are reviewed every three years by the DAC, and countries may graduate from the list or change income groups (Smith 2008).

For the more prosperous developing countries, ODA augments other financial resources available to meet long-term development needs. Those sources include loans and equity investments from private sources, direct investments by foreign firms (for example, firms operating natural resource concessions), and income sent home by migrant workers. Taking the developing world as a whole, all of those sources are greater in volume than ODA. But for many of the world's poorest countries, ODA is the largest and most stable source of development finance.

ODA disbursements by DAC members[3] rose to $114 billion in 2008, up $10.5 billion (10.2 percent) from 2007 (figure 7.1). Allowing for debt relief aid, total net ODA from members of the DAC rose by 11.7 percent in real terms to $121.5 billion, representing 0.31 percent of the members' combined gross national income (GNI) (OECD-DAC 2010). ODA increased by nearly 30 percent in real terms between 2004 and 2008, an unprecedented increase boosted by enormous debt-relief efforts in the earlier part of the period. Also contributing was a 91 percent increase in ODA to Afghanistan and an 84 percent increase to Iraq. While aid commitments to Africa have failed to increase by $25 billion[4]—a pledge made at the Gleneagles G-8 Summit in 2005—aid[5] to Africa increased by 37 percent over 2004–08. The proportion for Sub-Saharan Africa was 41 percent.

At the Monterrey Financing for Development Conference in 2002, specific commitments to increase aid were made. These were further endorsed at the Gleneagles G-8 Summit in 2005 and reaffirmed at the UN Millennium +5 Summit in New York in 2005. In practical terms, these commitments led to an increase in aid from $80 billion in 2004 to $130 billion in 2010 (at constant 2004 prices). This would have represented 0.36 percent of estimated GNI in 2010. Following the financial

Figure 7.1   Net ODA Disbursements Made by DAC Donors

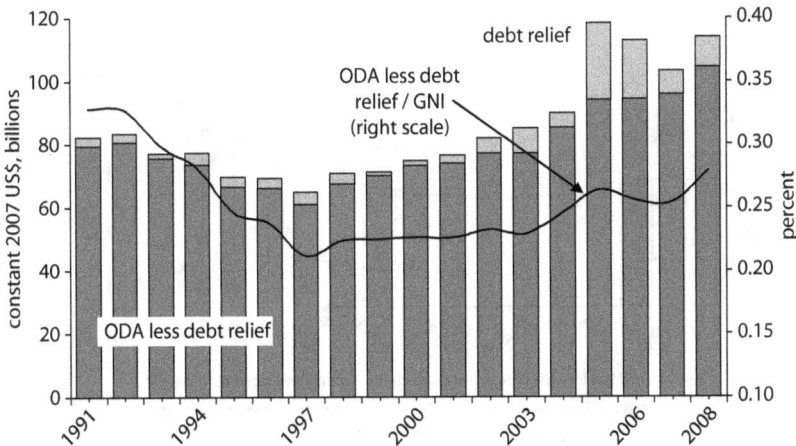

Source: World Bank 2009, 88.
Note: GNI = gross national income.

crisis of 2007 and the ongoing economic downturn, the dollar value of these commitments fell to $124 billion by 2010.

According to the DAC (OECD-DAC 2010), most countries have maintained their commitments for 2010, although some large donors have reduced or postponed their pledges, as illustrated in figure 7.2. In sum:

- expected ODA for 2010 is estimated at $107 billion, a $27 billion increase over the 2004 baseline, with ODA/GNI increasing from 0.26 percent to 0.33 percent; and
- the shortfall ($17 billion) impacts Africa in particular (OECD-DAC 2010, 100).

ODA reaches recipients through individual governments (bilateral donors), through multilateral agencies funded largely by wealthy nations, and through nongovernmental organizations (NGOs) funded by official and private sources. Until the 1960s, more than 90 percent of aid was provided through bilateral channels. By the 1990s, however, only about two-thirds of ODA was direct bilateral financing, with the remainder provided in the form of multilateral financing and grants by NGOs. NGO grants now account for about 11 percent of total global aid.[6]

Figure 7.2   DAC Members' Net ODA, 1990–2008, and Simulations of Net ODA, 2009–10

2004 US$, billions

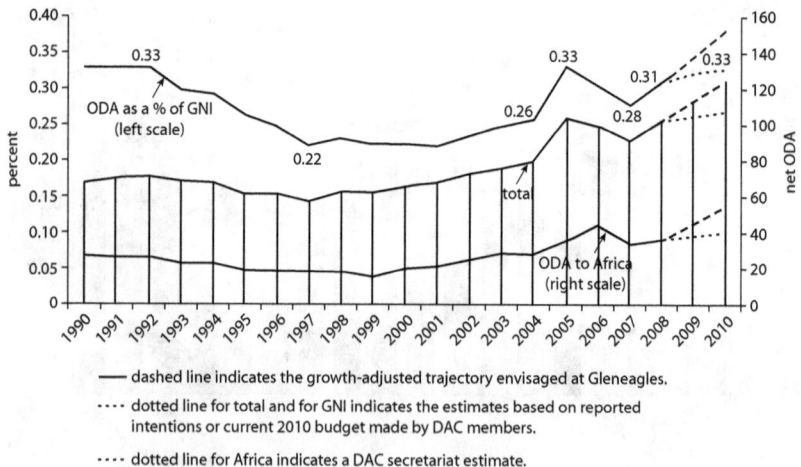

——— dashed line indicates the growth-adjusted trajectory envisaged at Gleneagles.

···· dotted line for total and for GNI indicates the estimates based on reported intentions or current 2010 budget made by DAC members.

···· dotted line for Africa indicates a DAC secretariat estimate.

Source: OECD-DAC 2010, 98. Used by permission.

During the 2000s, the DAC members increased their share of ODA, reaching a high of 76 percent of total net disbursements in 2005 or $95.3 billion. By 2008, net disbursements from DAC members were valued at $87 billion, almost 68 percent of the total (table 7.1). Net disbursements from the multilaterals[7] have averaged around one-quarter of the total since 2003; in 2008, they accounted for $33.9 billion, or 26.3 percent. Net disbursements of ODA from non-DAC countries[8] are small, averaging around $3 to $4 billion in recent years, or 4 percent, although they reached $7.8 billion, or 6 percent of the total, in 2008 (table 7.1).

Policies and guidelines for allocating ODA are recommended at the annual meetings of the Group of Eight industrial economies and the DAC. Multilateral donors—the World Bank, the International Monetary Fund (IMF), regional development banks, and specialized UN agencies—get advice on aid levels from the International Monetary and Financial Committee (IMFC), which meets twice a year.[9]

Since 1996, total net flows of ODA have accounted for around 1 percent[10] of gross domestic product (GDP) in the average recipient country, having declined from a high of 2 percent in 1991 (World Bank 2006a)—a reflection more of growth in the developing world than of a decline in aid. Roughly half (50.8 percent) of ODA goes to least-developed and low-income countries, that is, those with a GNI less than $935 per capita in 2007 (see figure 7.3). Roughly one-third goes to lower-middle-income countries—those with a GNI per capita between $936 and $3,705 in 2007—whose populations include a substantial number of poor people (for example, Algeria, China, and Thailand). Just 6 percent of aid flows in 2008 went to upper-middle-income countries, or those defined with a per capita GNI between $3,706 and $11,455 in 2007 (examples are Argentina and Chile). Aid to countries in or recovering from conflict has risen substantially over the past few years. Iraq accounted for one-third of the aid to the top 10 recipients in 2008 (figure 7.3).

In general, large, populous countries such as China and India tend to receive more aid in absolute terms, although in per capita terms, they receive less than small island economies such as São Tomé and Príncipe (figure 7.4). Exceptions include Mozambique (high absolute and per capita amounts) and Turkmenistan (low absolute and per capita amounts).

Aid in the Context of Overall Capital Flows

ODA accounts for just a portion of the capital that flows into the developing world. Net international flows of private capital dwarf the amount

Table 7.1 Net Disbursements of ODA by Donor Type
Constant 2008 US$, billions

	2001		2002		2003		2004		2005		2006		2007		2008	
	$bn	%	$bn	%	$bn	%	$bn	%	$bn	%	$bn	%	$bn	%	$bn	%
Multilaterals	26.9	32.9	27.8	30.3	24.2	26.2	27.0	28.3	27.0	21.6	29.2	24.0	31.4	27.7	33.9	26.3
DAC members	53.6	65.6	60.1	65.5	64.5	69.6	64.9	68.0	95.3	76.0	87.3	72.0	77.2	68.3	87.0	67.6
Non-DAC members	1.2	1.5	3.8	4.1	3.9	4.2	3.6	3.8	3.1	2.5	4.8	4.0	4.5	4.0	7.8	6.0
Total	81.7	100	91.7	100	92.6	100	95.4	100	125.5	100	121.3	100	113.1	100	128.6	100

Source: Compiled from OECD statistics extracts.

TOTAL DAC COUNTRIES

Net ODA	2007	2008	Change 2007/08
Current (US$, millions)	103,485	121,483	17.4%
Constant (2007 US$, millions)	103,485	115,632	11.7%
ODA/GNI	0.28%	0.31%	
Bilateral share	70%	71%	

Top ten recipients of gross ODA (US$, millions)

1	Iraq	9,462
2	Afghanistan	3,475
3	China	2,601
4	Indonesia	2,543
5	India	2,263
6	Vietnam	1,745
7	Sudan	1,743
8	Tanzania	1,603
9	Ethiopia	1,551
10	Cameroon	1,396

Memo: Share of gross bilateral ODA

Top 5 recipients	22%
Top 10 recipients	31%
Top 20 recipients	43%

Gross bilateral ODA, 2007–08 average, unless otherwise shown

Clockwise from top

By income group (US$, millions)

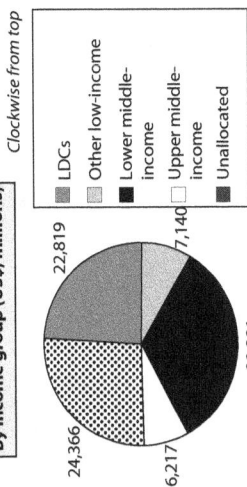

- LDCs
- Other low-income
- Lower middle-income
- Upper middle-income
- Unallocated

22,819 · 27,140 · 32,291 · 6,217 · 24,366

By region (US$, millions)

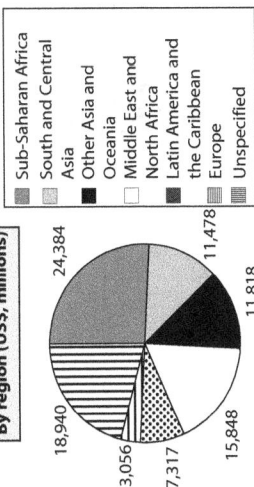

- Sub-Saharan Africa
- South and Central Asia
- Other Asia and Oceania
- Middle East and North Africa
- Latin America and the Caribbean
- Europe
- Unspecified

24,384 · 11,478 · 11,818 · 15,848 · 7,317 · 3,056 · 18,940

By sector

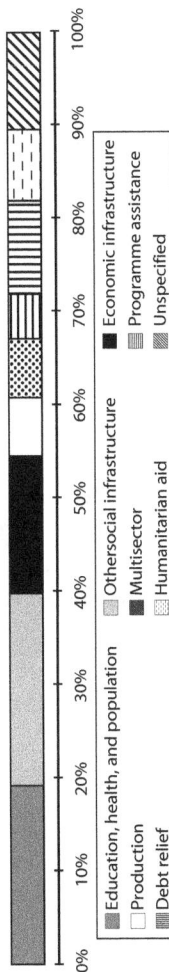

- Education, health, and population
- Other social infrastructure
- Economic infrastructure
- Production
- Multisector
- Programme assistance
- Debt relief
- Humanitarian aid
- Unspecified

StatLink http://dx.doi.org/10.1787/788147304272

Source: OECD-DAC 2010, 103. Used by permission.

Figure 7.4   Recipient Countries' Share of Total Aid

a. Larger countries receive more aid in dollar terms . . .

(billion dollars, 2000–03 average, 2002 prices)[a]

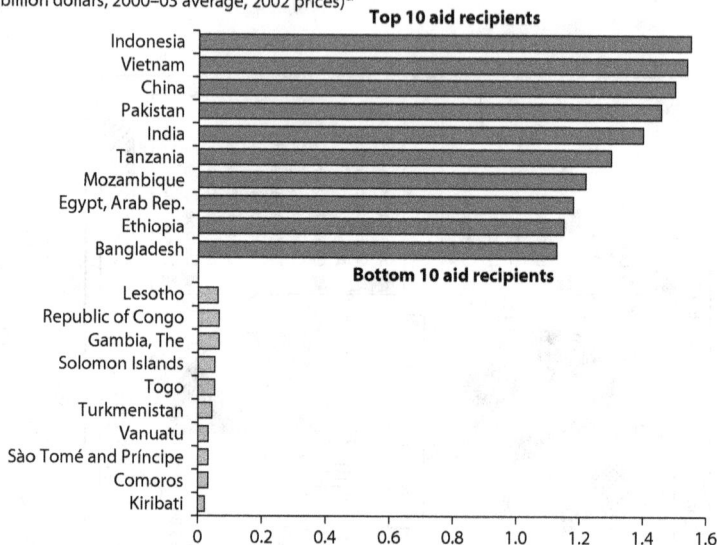

Top 10 aid recipients

Indonesia
Vietnam
China
Pakistan
India
Tanzania
Mozambique
Egypt, Arab Rep.
Ethiopia
Bangladesh

Bottom 10 aid recipients

Lesotho
Republic of Congo
Gambia, The
Solomon Islands
Togo
Turkmenistan
Vanuatu
Sào Tomé and Príncipe
Comoros
Kiribati

0   0.2   0.4   0.6   0.8   1.0   1.2   1.4   1.6

b. . . . but not in proportion to their populations.

(aid per capita, 2000–03 average, 2002 prices)[a]

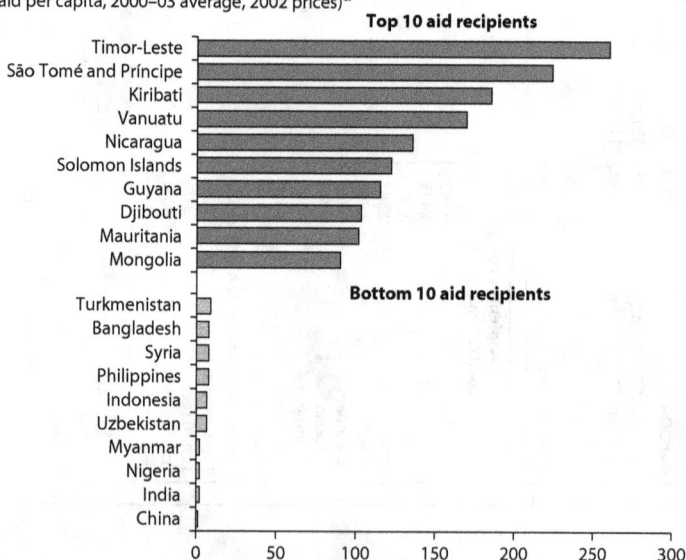

Top 10 aid recipients

Timor-Leste
São Tomé and Príncipe
Kiribati
Vanuatu
Nicaragua
Solomon Islands
Guyana
Djibouti
Mauritania
Mongolia

Bottom 10 aid recipients

Turkmenistan
Bangladesh
Syria
Philippines
Indonesia
Uzbekistan
Myanmar
Nigeria
India
China

0   50   100   150   200   250   300

Source: Siddiqi 2005, 14. Used by permission.

a. Based on countries that recorded a 2004 GNI per capita of $1,575 or less, in accordance with the World Bank's operational category II: International Development Association eligibility or 20–year International Bank for Reconstruction and Development terms excludes the Democratic Republic of the Congo, since its data for 2003 reflect a major debt deal.

flowing as ODA. Since the 1990s, the role of private flows has become increasingly important, driven by market reforms, the lowering of global trade and investment barriers, and a fall in communications and transport costs. The increase continued in the first seven years of the new century (see table 7.2), thanks to improvements in developing regions' investment climates, high corporate earnings, the liberalization of foreign ownership rules, and a strong global recovery from the crises of the late 1990s and the bursting of the dot-com bubble in 2000–01. Investment was particularly strong in East Asia and Pacific and in Europe and Central Asia. The pace of private investment slowed in 2007, however, as the subprime-lending crisis emerged in the United States. It dropped off starkly with the collapse of Lehman Brothers in October 2008. Prior to the ongoing financial slowdown, net private flows to the developing world were on an upward trajectory, reaching a record of $1.2 trillion in 2007, or 8.6 percent of the developing world's GDP (see figure 7.5).

As can be seen from figure 7.6, the global financial crisis affected private capital flows to developing countries severely. In 2008, total net international flows of private capital to the developing world fell to $707 billion or 4.4 percent of average developing country GDP.

Examining the three components of private capital inflows shows that net portfolio equity flows suffered the most, falling by almost 90 percent—from $139 billion in 2007 to just $16 billion in 2008. Short-term debt flows fell from $202 billion in 2007 to –$16.3 billion in 2008 and accounted disproportionately for the fall in private debt flows from $499 billion in 2007 to $108 billion in 2008. Also contributing to the reduction in short-term debt flows was the decline in bond financing (from $85 billion in 2007 to just $11 billion in 2008) and the 40 percent fall in net medium- and long-term bank flows (table 7.2). While foreign direct investment (FDI) fared better (approximately $60 billion more in 2008), its rate of increase slowed compared with previous years. In fact, the developing world increased its share of global FDI[11] in 2008 to a record of 40 percent from an average of 25 percent over the previous decade. This was due to the sharp deterioration of FDI in the developed world (World Bank 2009, 41). Most of the increase ($63 billion) in FDI went to East Asia and Pacific and to South Asia, reflecting economic reforms and the opening up of additional sectors for foreign investment (World Bank 2009, 41).

Across the Regions, Europe and Central Asia were the hardest hit, with net capital inflows falling by almost half—from $472 billion in 2007 to $251 billion in 2008 (see figure 7.6 and table 7.3). Although the amounts are lower for other Regions, the magnitude of decline was large—for

Table 7.2 Net Capital Inflows to Developing Countries
US$, billions

	2001	2002	2003	2004	2005	2006	2007	2008e
Current account balance	15.5	68.6	118.4	171.2	306.6	438.2	406.1	377.9
Financial flows								
Net private and official flows	224.2	162.4	258.6	370.7	498.7	668.3	1,157.7	727.3
Net private inflows	197.3	156.8	269.1	396.5	569.7	739.2	1,157.5	706.9
Net equity inflows	172.3	161.5	181.0	254.7	347.2	462.7	658.6	599.0
Net FDI inflows	166.0	152.5	155.5	216.0	279.1	358.4	520.0	583.0
Net portfolio equity inflows	6.3	9.0	25.5	38.7	68.1	104.3	138.6	15.7
Net debt flows	51.9	0.9	77.6	116.0	151.5	205.6	499.1	128.3
Official creditors	26.9	5.6	-10.5	-25.8	-71.0	-70.9	0.2	20.4
World Bank	7.5	-0.3	-0.5	1.6	2.8	-0.4	4.9	7.1
IMF	19.5	14.1	2.5	-14.7	-40.1	-26.7	-5.1	10.9
Other ODA	-0.1	-8.2	-12.5	-12.7	-33.7	-43.8	0.4	2.4
Private creditors	25.0	-4.7	88.1	141.8	222.5	276.5	498.9	107.9
Net medium- to long-term debt flows	2.1	0.7	26.6	73.3	135.9	166.4	296.4	124.2
Bonds	10.2	10.1	20.4	36.0	56.2	26.6	85.4	10.5
Banks	-1.9	-3.2	10.4	41.3	84.2	144.6	214.5	123.0
Other private	-6.2	-6.2	-4.2	-4.0	-4.5	-4.8	-3.5	-9.3
Net short-term debt flows[a]	22.9	-5.4	61.5	68.5	86.6	110.1	202.5	-16.3
Balancing item	-159.1	-69.9	-90.7	-144.9	-419.5	-476.6	-486.3	-657.5
Change in reserves (-= increase)	-80.4	-160.6	-285.5	-396.2	-385.5	-629.9	-1,077.3	-447.3
Memorandum items								
Private inflows excluding short-term debt	174.4	170.7	203.9	340.7	483.3	629.1	955.0	723.2
Net FDI outflows	12.7	16.8	22.4	44.5	59.2	125.2	138.8	164.0
Net portfolio equity outflows	10.8	6.0	8.2	7.2	11.6	21.5	50.6	80.0
Workers' remittances	95.6	115.9	143.6	161.3	191.2	229.0	265.0	305.0

Source: World Bank 2009, 40.

Note: e = estimate.

a. Combination of errors and omissions and transfers to and capital outflows from developing countries.

142

Figure 7.5   Net Private Capital Inflows to Developing Countries

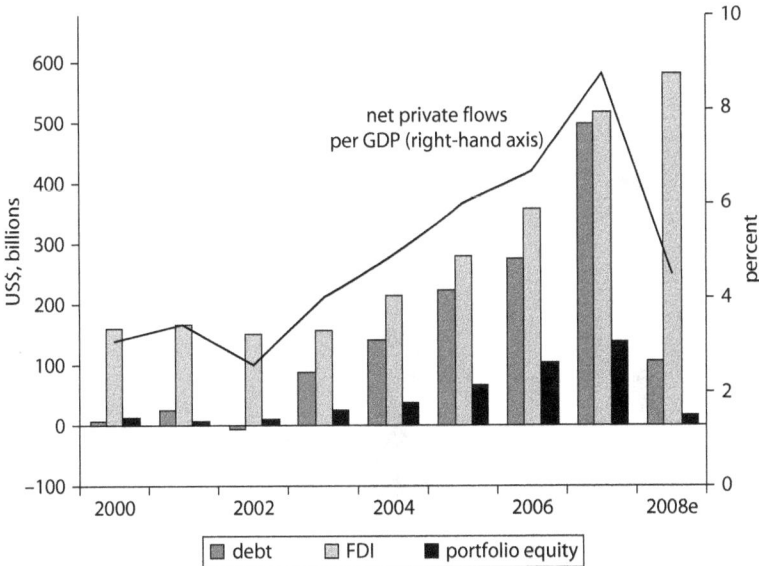

Source: World Bank 2009, 39.
Note: FDI = foreign direct investment. 2008 figures are estimated.

example, a 41 percent decline for Latin America and the Caribbean and Sub-Saharan Africa. Private capital inflows increased by 11 percent between 2007 and 2008 for Middle East and North Africa.

The decline in private capital flows across the Regions was concentrated in short-term debt flows. Short-term debt flows fell by 47 percent for all Regions between 2007 and 2008. The decline was particularly severe in East Asia and Pacific (a decline of 67 percent), South Asia (a decline of 56 percent), and Europe and Central Asia (45 percent). Portfolio equity flows declined by 26 percent for all developing regions between 2007 and 2008, with the decline felt most strongly in Sub-Saharan Africa (66 percent) (World Bank 2009).

The global financial crisis has placed considerable strain on the external financing needs of developing countries,[12] and official creditors have stepped up to the challenge (see table 7.4). Net official lending increased to $20.4 billion in 2008. As can be seen from table 7.4, net lending by official creditors was negative in the previous five years owing to favorable economic conditions in developing countries, which led to reduced demand for multilateral lending, and significant repayments and prepayments to the

Figure 7.6   Net Private Capital Inflows to Developing Regions

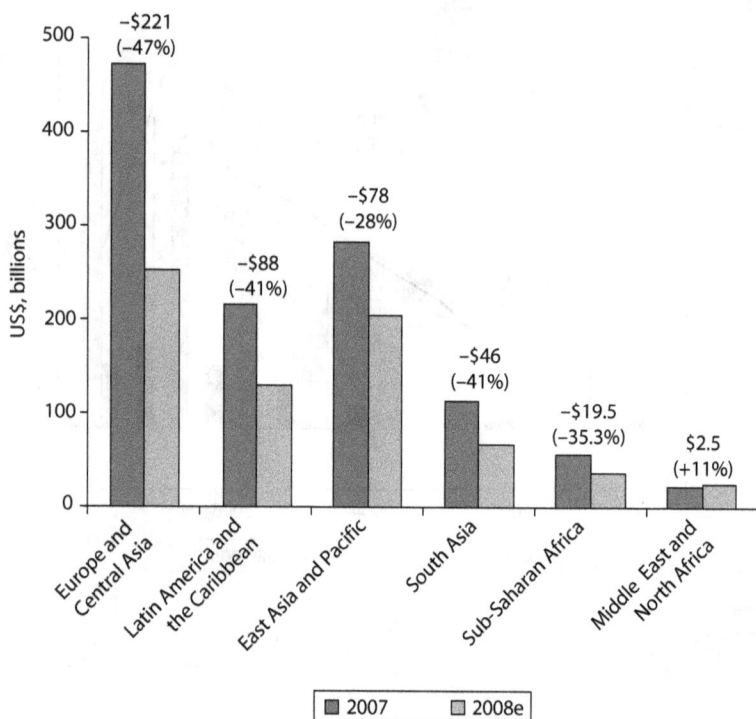

Source: World Bank 2009, 40.
Note: e = estimate.

Table 7.3   Net Capital Inflows to Developing Regions
US$, billions

	2005	2006	2007	2008e
Total	570	739	1,158	707
Region				
East Asia and Pacific	187	206	281	203
Europe and Central Asia	192	311	472	251
Latin America and the Caribbean	113	85	216	128
Middle East and North Africa	19	25	21	23
South Asia	25	72	113	66
Sub-Saharan Africa	33	40	55	36

Source: World Bank 2009, 40
Note: e = estimate.

Table 7.4   Net Official Flows to Developing Countries

	2002	2003	2004	2005	2006	2007	2008e
World Bank	−0.3	−0.5	1.6	2.8	−0.4	4.9	7.1
IMF	14.1	2.5	−14.7	−40.1	−26.7	−5.1	10.9
Other ODA	−8.7	−13.3	−12.8	−34.0	−43.8	0.2	2.4
Total	5.1	−11.3	−25.9	−71.3	−70.9	0.0	20.4

Source: World Bank 2009, 84.
Note: e = estimate; ODA = official development assistance.

Paris Club. Contributing to the drop in lending between 2002 and 2007 was the increasing importance of grants from the International Development Association (IDA), which were not included in the net lending data (World Bank 2009, 85).

Does Aid Spur Economic Growth?

Many studies have examined the relationship between aid and growth. Some have found that aid has no effect on growth and may actually undermine it (for example, Easterly 2001, 2006); others have suggested that, on average, aid has a positive relationship to growth, although not in every country and with diminishing returns. Still others find that aid has a conditional relationship to growth, accelerating it only under certain circumstances (Radelet, Clemens, and Bhavnani 2005). Rajan and Subramanian (2005) find no clear effect at all, positive or negative. Their finding holds across time periods, regardless of the donor or type of aid, and regardless of the characteristics of the recipient country.

"No, Aid Hobbles Growth"

The critics of aid assert that it is often misappropriated or spent unproductively—on limousines and presidential palaces, for example. Some empirical evidence suggests that aid may distort or weaken private sector incentives. Large amounts of aid may also cause currency to appreciate, thus making a country's traded goods less competitive—an effect known as Dutch disease. It has also been asserted that food aid can reduce agricultural prices in the recipient country and adversely affect farmers' income if not effectively managed. There is also evidence that revenue collections are lower in highly aided countries.

Aid can stunt growth in three ways. First, by stimulating demand, it pushes up the price of goods and services and inflates the salaries of professionals such as aid managers, the engineers who work on roads and power connectivity, doctors and nurses, and building contractors. As wages rise, the nontradable sector will increase prices to maintain profitability. The tradable sector lacks this flexibility, however, because it faces external competition that limits the prices it can charge. Producers of tradable goods face a choice between forgoing profits and losing their competitive edge. By pushing up wages of certain goods and services, aid puts pressure on all other sectors to increase wages, leading to a generalized rise in wages throughout a given country.

Second, in a flexible exchange-rate regime, aid inflows will push up the nominal exchange rate of the recipient nation's currency, further reducing the tradable sector's competitiveness. To counter this, aid inflows should be spent in ways that benefit the tradable sector (imported capital and machinery, intermediate goods, and so on).

Third, aid inflows weaken incentives for a country to improve tax collection and administration and to operate efficiently and transparently. With free money flowing in, the government may be better able to avoid accounting for what it spends.

"Yes, Aid Promotes Growth"

Other studies point to a positive relationship between aid and growth. Most do not conclude that more aid leads to more growth but suggest instead that "higher aid flows have been associated with higher growth" (Radelet, Clemens, and Bhavnani 2005).

Some investigators have found that although a scaling up of aid promotes the transfer of real resources from rich to poor countries, beyond a certain threshold (about 5 percent of GDP per year), a surge in aid poses macroeconomic problems and can have a negative impact on growth in the long term, particularly if most of the aid is channeled toward consumption rather than investment. During the 1990s, economists began to ask whether returns on aid flows would diminish as the share of aid in GDP rose. Working along these lines, Clemens, Radelet, and Bhavnani (2004) find diminishing returns once total aid reaches about 17 percent of GDP (or once the subset of aid aimed directly at growth reaches 8 percent of GDP).

Burnside and Dollar (2000) argue that aid positively influences long-term growth in countries that maintain good policies. This makes sense. Building schools, hospitals, roads, and power plants seems like a good idea. But a new school will do little good unless it is filled with teachers who are paid well enough to show up regularly to teach and students who are fed well enough to learn. Hospitals cannot improve health care without trained personnel, adequate supplies, reliable power, and clean water.

"Aid Stimulates Growth under Certain Circumstances"

The conditional view of development assistance suggests a positive impact on economic growth depending on certain variables—for example, the characteristics of aid recipients or the efficacy of donor practices.

World Bank research conducted in the mid-1990s showed higher returns from aid in countries with stronger civil liberties (Isham, Kaufmann, and Pritchett 1995), good policies (Burnside and Dollar 2000), and effective institutions. Further, recipient-country characteristics—such as vulnerability to trade shocks, climate, institutional quality, political conflict, and geography—have all been studied as conditional variables affecting the aid-growth relationship, although Radelet, Clemens, and Bhavnani (2005) raise doubts about the statistical robustness of such findings. Nevertheless, the view that aid works best in countries with sound policies and institutions is widely accepted among donors, including multilateral development banks. (That view is the rationale behind the U.S. Millennium Challenge Account.)

Reflecting the acknowledged importance of host-country conditions, recipient countries have had a greater say in recent years in setting priorities and designing programs in cooperation with donors and civil society. Greater "country ownership" of aid goals and broader participation in the formulation of those goals and in the implementation of aid projects are believed to increase the efficacy of aid.

The effect on growth of various donor practices has received very little systematic research, although many opinions can be found on the matter. Multilateral aid is generally considered more effective than bilateral aid, for example (because it is less likely to be politically motivated or to have burdensome conditions), and aid that is not earmarked for specific purposes is widely believed to generate higher returns than aid limited to prescribed uses.

Recent research into the connection between growth and aid also suggests that the type of aid—in substance and timing—matters. The pioneering work of Clemens, Radelet, and Bhavnani (2004) focuses on aid aimed primarily at economic growth. They reveal that most studies on aid and growth have examined the relationship of total development assistance to growth, even though only a portion of assistance is designed to stimulate growth. Humanitarian and food aid, for example, are not aimed at spurring growth; neither are educational materials or judicial reform. The same authors also note that most studies used cross-sectional data at intervals of four years—too short a period to capture the impact of aid on growth. (On the other hand, the authors acknowledge that problems of causality arise if the time period is too long.)

Based on their hypothesis that "not all aid is alike," Clemens, Radelet, and Bhavnani (2004) examine the effects of (a) humanitarian aid, (b) early-impact aid, and (c) late-impact aid on economic growth. Their results show that (a) and (c) have very little or no effect on growth (figure 7.7). On the other hand, early-impact aid—aid to build infrastructure and support productive sectors and budgets, which accounts for about half of total aid—has a positive relationship to growth over a four-year period.

Figure 7.7   Economic Growth and the Type and Timing of Aid

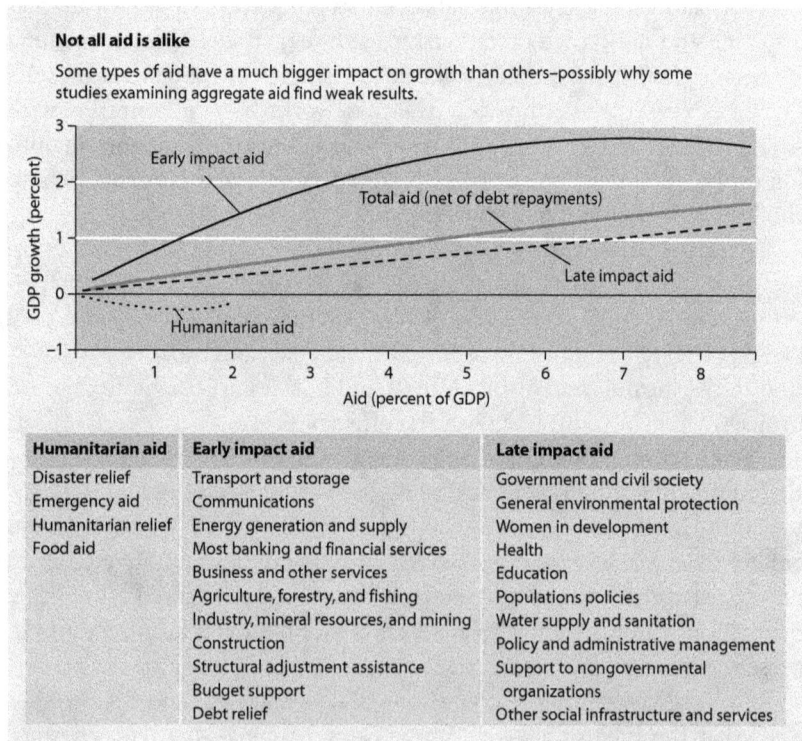

Not all aid is alike

Some types of aid have a much bigger impact on growth than others—possibly why some studies examining aggregate aid find weak results.

Humanitarian aid	Early impact aid	Late impact aid
Disaster relief	Transport and storage	Government and civil society
Emergency aid	Communications	General environmental protection
Humanitarian relief	Energy generation and supply	Women in development
Food aid	Most banking and financial services	Health
	Business and other services	Education
	Agriculture, forestry, and fishing	Populations policies
	Industry, mineral resources, and mining	Water supply and sanitation
	Construction	Policy and administrative management
	Structural adjustment assistance	Support to nongovernmental
	Budget support	organizations
	Debt relief	Other social infrastructure and services

Source: Radelet, Clemens, and Bhavnani (2005), citing Clemens, Radelet, and Bhavnani (2004). Used by permission.
Note: All three curves are estimated using a similar model and include a nonlinear relationship between aid and growth (which is hard to detect visually in the curve for late impact aid). The curve for humanitarian aid is cut off at 2 percent of GDP because there are no data in our sample beyond this point, and to show an upward curve would be misleading. Although only the coefficient on early impact aid is statistically significantly different from zero, the weaker relationships for late impact and humanitarian aid do not necessarily mean these flows have no impact on growth, but rather that a different modeling technique is required to explore these relationships (which we leave for future research).

The findings on the effect of early-impact aid on economic growth include the following:

- The positive effect of early-impact aid on economic growth is not reversed over time.
- Each dollar in early-impact aid yields $1.64 in increased income in the recipient country in net present value terms, or a return of 13 percent per country.
- The relationship between early-impact aid and economic growth is stronger for countries with good policies and institutions.
- Typically, the maximum growth rate occurs when early-impact aid represents 8 to 9 percent of GDP.
- Development assistance is partially fungible—aid flows intended for different purposes have significantly different relationships to economic growth.

Aid has multiple objectives, not often directly related to economic growth. Development aid goals include peacekeeping, fighting terrorism and drug trafficking, disaster relief, and the strategic political and diplomatic support of friendly governments. For example, a large part of development aid received by the Arab Republic of Egypt and Israel is devoted to supporting the Middle East peace process. Aid to conflict-ridden Côte d'Ivoire would be found ineffective if judged only by growth performance. A large fraction of aid to many countries is also designed to support the fight against terrorism. In these situations, there is no immediate effect of aid on growth; instead, it is hoped that aid will promote a more stable economic environment in the long term and thus lead to growth and poverty alleviation. This goes to show that aid effectiveness is to be understood in a larger multidimensional framework. It also leads us to conclude that the seemingly paradoxical effects of aid on growth and poverty reduction are inevitable.

Ensuring That More Aid Means More Growth

There have been increases in official aid in recent years to help developing countries reach, by 2015, the Millennium Development Goals (MDGs) promulgated in the Millennium Declaration of September 2000, which was signed by 189 countries. The MDGs are a set of eight objectives for poverty reduction; improvement in indicators of well-being (health, education, and infant mortality); and the promotion of sustainable development. They represent the international community's commitment to narrowing the gap between rich and poor countries. That commitment has been reaffirmed in successive international meetings, and public aid flows have significantly increased—though still not to the promised levels.[13] It is safe to say, however, that poverty reduction is now firmly back on the global policy agenda, this time with specific targets and deadlines. Rich countries have committed to boosting development aid, canceling debts, and promoting trade access for developing countries.

This section discusses the impact of scaling up aid on government budgets, on national competitiveness, and on the macroeconomic health of recipient countries. The section concludes with an examination of current initiatives to improve aid effectiveness.

Aid and the Government Budget

A scaling up of development aid may facilitate greater expansion of public services, but increased flows also involve the challenges of managing and delivering that extra aid. Aid flows are volatile and may not arrive on schedule, and this can create serious problems for the budgets of individual ministries. When the volume and duration of development aid are not clear, and when questions surround the manner and timing of disbursements, government ministries are hard pressed to produce accurate, sustainable budgets. Celasun and Walliser (2008) found that about 30 percent of development assistance to a sample of 13 countries between 1992 and 2007 did not arrive on time, leading to budgetary shortfalls in countries that had projected these inflows in budget estimates. A 2008 survey by the OECD showed that for the average country, just 45 percent of aid arrives on time. Figure 7.8 shows the wide gaps that exist between the levels of aid scheduled by donors for disbursement and the actual amounts received in five countries.

Complications also arise when the increase in aid is subject to performance criteria or tied to a specific sector or policy. It is difficult to commit to new service delivery under such circumstances, particularly if the government lacks the capacity to substitute domestic funds (either through tax increases or borrowing from domestic banks) in the case of a budgetary shortfall. Donors still practice earmarking, favoring projects and technical cooperation over general budgetary support even at the risk of causing misalignment with recipients' inter- and intrasectoral priorities (figure 7.9).

When development aid is targeted to sectors and projects, the challenge facing the particular sectoral ministry is how to achieve *stability* and

Figure 7.8   Aid Scheduled for Disbursement versus Aid Actually Received in Select Countries

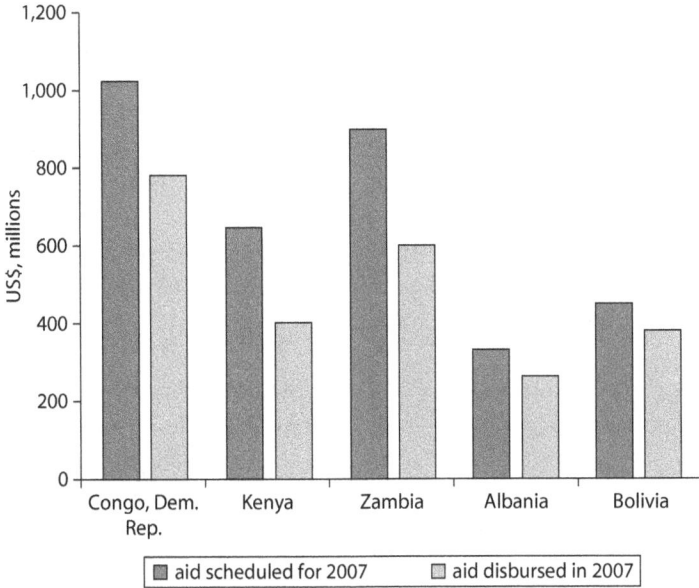

Source: Deutscher and Fyson 2008, citing OECD-DAC 2008a.

Figure 7.9   ODA Commitments by DAC Countries, 2005

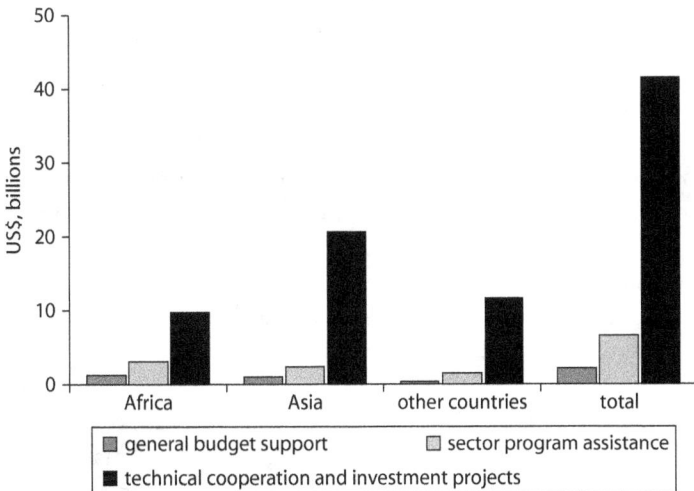

Source: Curto 2007, 20.

sustainability in the sector. Aid spikes may exceed the absorptive capacity of a sector. For example, higher flows to health and education may encounter shortages of staff and personnel. Public financial management systems in many developing countries are ill-equipped to meet the challenges of substantial increases in aid. A 2005 World Bank–IMF study of semiautonomous agencies and extrabudgetary funds found weak budget formulation; weak classification systems; poor commitment controls; and inadequate cash management, budget reporting, auditing, and regulatory capacity (Heller 2005).

A scaling up of aid may also present organizational challenges. As noted by Heller (2005), a department that functions well on one scale may not be able to make the transition to a larger one.

Ensuring That Aid Does Not Compromise Competitiveness

As noted earlier, an increase in development aid flows may generate a Dutch disease effect, whereby the increased inflow of foreign currency boosts demand in both the nontradable and tradable goods sectors, pushing up prices while causing the domestic currency to appreciate and compromising the competitiveness of the recipient country's exports. While increased demand for traded goods can be met by increased imports, this is not the case for nontraded goods, such as housing. We have already noted that excess demand here can lead to production bottlenecks and higher wages, increasing inflation and the real exchange rate. A higher real exchange rate may adversely affect a country's international competitiveness, thus hampering its gains from international trade and its capacity for growth and investment. Heller (2005) identifies three questions a government should ask if an exchange rate is likely to appreciate:

- Does development assistance induce higher productivity in the nontraded goods sector to offset the effect of a currency appreciation?
- Can the effect on exchange rates be moderated by pursuing macroeconomic and microeconomic policies?
- Taking into account adverse effects, will aid's net effect on growth and poverty reduction still be positive?

A nation's central bank may try to keep the pressure off the nominal exchange rate by intervening in the foreign exchange market (buying foreign exchange) and offsetting the monetary impact of increased currency flows by conducting open-market operations. But the capacity of developing countries' central banks to absorb liquidity may be limited by a lack of suitable monetary policy instruments. The result may be an appreciation of the real exchange rate through domestic inflation. Tight fiscal policies—used to keep domestic inflation in check—may also lead to higher interest rates and a crowding out of private investment activities.

In their attempts to ward off a Dutch disease effect, governments may take advantage of resource transfers. Governments may introduce policies that affect the demand for imports. In particular, if resource transfers facilitate the removal of bottlenecks, productivity in the non-traded sector may increase. Furthermore, increasing the supply of nontraded goods in the economy may relieve price pressure and even expand investment and growth in the economy, with the increased supply of nontradables leading to investments in physical infrastructure and human capital.

Heller (2005) argues that it may be sensible for a low-income country to accept some loss in competitiveness by implementing policies that lead to a real transfer of resources from the traded to the nontraded sector. Furthermore, Heller suggests that if increased development assistance is successful in achieving the MDGs, the resulting economic environment will foster productivity and competitiveness. But Heller cautions that uncertainty regarding the continuity of aid may make accepting the loss in competitiveness a risky venture. Thus, governments need to choose their exchange-rate policy in full cognizance of the possibility of future changes, up or down, in the volume of development assistance.

Handling Increases in Aid Successfully at the Macroeconomic Level

Aiyar, Berg, and Hussain (2005) examine the macroeconomic challenges of five African countries—Ethiopia, Ghana, Mozambique, Tanzania, and Uganda—that experienced a large increase in development assistance. All five countries are considered good performers with strong institutions that have benefited from the general rise in aid and from the World Bank's Heavily Indebted Poor Countries (HIPC) initiative, which allowed these countries to greatly reduce their debt burden.

To examine the macroeconomic management of aid inflows, Aiyar, Berg, and Hussain (2005) examine how fiscal and monetary policy interact with ODA. In a typical case, fiscal policy concentrates on directing aid to high-priority projects, while concerns about competitiveness and inflation drive monetary and exchange-rate policies. The trouble is that when undertaken in isolation from each other, fiscal and monetary policies may blunt the positive impact of aid.

The authors concentrate on the classic case, in which aid dollars flow to the government, which immediately sells them to the central bank and then uses local currency to increase spending on domestic goods. Their framework is underpinned by two distinct but related concepts: *absorption* and *spending*.

- *Absorption* is defined as the widening of the current-account deficit (excluding aid) because of the presence of incremental aid. It measures the extent to which aid engenders a real transfer of resources through higher imports or through a reduction in the domestic resources devoted to producing exports. Absorption depends on both exchange-rate policy and on policies that influence the demand for imports. The central bank controls the exchange rate through its sales of foreign exchange, while monetary policy can be used to control aggregate demand—and the demand for imports.
- *Spending* is defined as the widening of the fiscal deficit, excluding incremental aid. The combination of absorption and spending defines the macroeconomic response to a scaling up of aid.

Broadly speaking, there are four possible responses to an aid surge in the short to medium term: (a) absorb and spend; (b) neither absorb nor spend; (c) absorb, but do not spend; and (d) spend, but do not absorb. In their analysis, Aiyar, Berg, and Hussain (2005) look at how the five countries in their sample responded and performed.

Absorb and spend. The government spends the new aid on domestic goods, and the fiscal deficit increases. The central bank then sells foreign exchange to sterilize the local currency spent by the government (that is, to prevent the new spending from causing inflation). In this way, the foreign exchange pays for a widening of the current-account deficit, as the aid is absorbed by the economy. A key point here is that some appreciation of the real exchange rate may be appropriate because, if aid is used to increase net imports, higher aggregate demand or appreciation of the real exchange rate is needed.

In general, absorb-and-spend is the best response to an increase in aid. Absorption ensures a real transfer of resources to the recipient country, while government spending draws resources away from the traded goods sector. Other responses may be justified under particular circumstances for a short time, but in the long run the only sensible alternative to absorbing and spending is to forgo aid altogether.

Aiyar, Berg, and Hussain (2005) found, however, that the absorb-and-spend strategy was surprisingly rare. No country in their sample fully absorbed and spent the incremental aid it received during a surge of assistance. In four of the five countries, less than one-third of the incremental aid was absorbed.

Neither absorb nor spend. In this case, the government does not spend the aid but keeps it in the central bank. Governments may choose this option because they want to build up international reserves from a low level or smooth volatile aid flows. In two of the sample countries—Ethiopia and Ghana—absorption and spending were both very low. Both countries entered the aid-surge period with a low level of reserves—2.2 months of imports in Ethiopia and 1.3 months of imports in Ghana—and used the incremental aid to increase their import coverage. The reserve buildup meant that aid was effectively not available to finance increased domestic spending. But neither was the surge accompanied by a significant widening of the fiscal deficit or an increase in inflation.

Absorb, but do not spend. This response substitutes aid for domestic financing of the government deficit. The government keeps expenditures steady, and the money supply shrinks as the central bank sterilizes liquidity through sale of foreign exchange. Such an approach can help stabilize the economy when domestically financed deficit spending is too high. No country in the sample chose this approach for the entire surge period, but it was used for particular periods—for example, in Ethiopia in 2001, when the strategy helped hold liquidity in check and avoided an inflation surge. This approach can also be used to reduce domestic public debt and "crowd in" the private sector (if there is an increase in private consumption or investment due to the government's action on spending or taxation) if the central bank uses the proceeds from its foreign exchange sales to buy back government debt.

Spend, but do not absorb. This is a suboptimal response that often reflects the inadequate coordination of monetary and fiscal policy. Unfortunately, it is all too common. Under this approach, the government increases expenditures, but keeps aid dollars in the central bank as reserves. This response is similar to fiscal stimulus in the *absence* of aid because the increase in government spending must be financed domestically since there is no real resource transfer (net imports do not increase). This can lead to increases in the money supply and in inflation, unless sterilization is undertaken by sales of government paper (instead of foreign exchange).

Aiyar, Berg, and Hussain (2005) find that Mozambique, Tanzania, and Uganda adopted this suboptimal approach. In all three countries, concerns about the negative impact of a real appreciation of competitiveness dictated the pattern of aid absorption and the monetary response (foreign-exchange sales being held in check to rein in upward pressure on the domestic currency, with sterilization instead being undertaken by sale of government paper).

In these three countries, unlike in Ethiopia and Ghana, the level of import coverage afforded by gross reserves was quite high, with reserves accumulating steadily. A more suitable response to increased aid inflows might have been to combine a widening fiscal deficit with sterilization through sale of foreign exchange. In Tanzania and Uganda, such a strategy would have relaxed the need for open-market operations and the sharp rise in interest rates. In Mozambique, it would have reduced inflation by reining in base money and limiting nominal depreciation.

International Initiatives to Improve the Effectiveness of Aid

In addition to lack of aid predictability and lack of coordination, aid fragmentation further constrains aid effectiveness. Deutscher and Fyson (2008, 16) identify more than "280 bilateral donor agencies, 242 multilateral programs, 24 development banks, and about 40 United Nations agencies working in the development business." Added to that are the increasing number of private foundations, NGOs, and "an estimated 340,000 development projects around the world" (Deutscher and Fyson 2008, 16).

The fragmentation of aid means that (some) countries receive small amounts of aid from a plethora of donors, all requiring adherence to differing procedures and standards. A 2008 OECD survey found that during 2005–06, 38 developing countries received aid from 25 or more DAC and multilateral donors. A 2006 OECD survey found that government authorities in Vietnam in 2005 received 791 visits from donors, while health workers in Tanzania spent a quarter of their working days writing reports for donors (Deutscher and Fyson 2008).

Meanwhile, some countries are ignored altogether.

A series of four high-level meetings since 2002 have produced a promising plan to make aid more effective by 2010 (table 7.5). A major meeting will be held in 2011 to assess whether the targets have been met.

Table 7.5   International Action to Improve Aid Effectiveness

Date	Initiative	Venue	Output
2002	International Conference on Financing for Development	Monterrey	The Monterrey Consensus
2003	High-Level Forum on Harmonization	Rome	The Rome Declaration on Harmonization
2005	2nd High-Level Forum on Aid Effectiveness	Paris	Paris Declaration on Aid Effectiveness
2008	3rd High-Level Forum on Aid Effectiveness	Accra	Accra Agenda for Action
2011	4th High-Level Forum on Aid Effectiveness	TBD	Assessment of whether targets have been met

Source: Authors.
Note: TBD = to be determined.

The International Conference on Financing for Development, organized by the United Nations in Monterrey, Mexico, in March 2002, brought together an unprecedentedly large number of participants involved in development finance—both donors and recipients. The forum yielded recommendations in six areas: mobilizing domestic financial resources for development; mobilizing international resources for development (including FDI and other private flows); international trade as an engine of development; international financial and technical cooperation for development; external debt; and several systemic issues (enhancing the coherence and consistence of the international monetary, financial, and trading systems in support of development). The Monterrey Consensus was adopted by the participants, along with a commitment to a larger volume of more effective aid.

The following year, high-level representatives from the major multilateral and bilateral donor institutions met in Rome with representatives of aid recipients to continue the discussion of how to improve the effectiveness of aid. The resulting Rome Declaration on Harmonization articulated the following goals:

- Ensure that harmonization efforts are adapted to the country context and that donor assistance is aligned with the recipient's priorities.
- Expand country-led efforts to streamline donor procedures and practices.
- Review and identify ways to adapt institutions' and countries' policies, procedures, and practices to facilitate harmonization.

- Implement the good practices, principles, and standards formulated by the development community as the foundation for harmonization.

The same set of participants met again in Paris in early 2005. The Paris Declaration on Aid Effectiveness committed the parties to specific actions that would promote the effective use of aid funds. The Paris Declaration was grounded on 5 mutually reinforcing principles and 12 indicators by which progress was to be assessed. Targets for 11 of those indicators were set in 2010 (see annex). The five principles (and associated indicators) are as follows:

- *Ownership.* Partner countries exercise effective leadership over their development policies and strategies and coordinate development actions (indicator 1).
- *Alignment.* Donors base their overall support on partner countries' national development strategies, institutions, and procedures (indicators 2–8).
- *Harmonization.* Donors' actions are more harmonized, transparent, and collectively effective (indicators 9 and 10).
- *Managing for results.* Managing resources and improving decision making for development results (indicator 11).
- *Mutual accountability.* Donors and partners are accountable for development results (indicator 12).

A first round of monitoring took place in 2006 based on activities undertaken in 2005 in 34 countries where some progress was noted but significant efforts were still needed. A second round of monitoring took place in 56 countries in 2008 prior to the Third High-Level Forum on Aid Effectiveness in Accra.

The Accra Agenda for Action noted that, despite the progress made on reducing poverty, much more needed to be done if the MDGs were to be met. Similarly, much more needed to be done to improve the effectiveness of aid. A 2008 survey conducted by the OECD prior to the Accra meeting examined progress in 33 countries toward the 2010 targets set forth in the Paris Declaration (figure 7.10). Progress was not stellar.

The report identifies three indicators for which targets were on track in 2010. First, good progress has been made in aligning and coordinating technical cooperation (indicator 4). Public financial management systems were also on target (indicator 2): 36 percent of countries within the sample (10 of 28 countries surveyed in 2006 and 2008) had improved their

Figure 7.10 Progress toward the 2010 Paris Declaration Targets

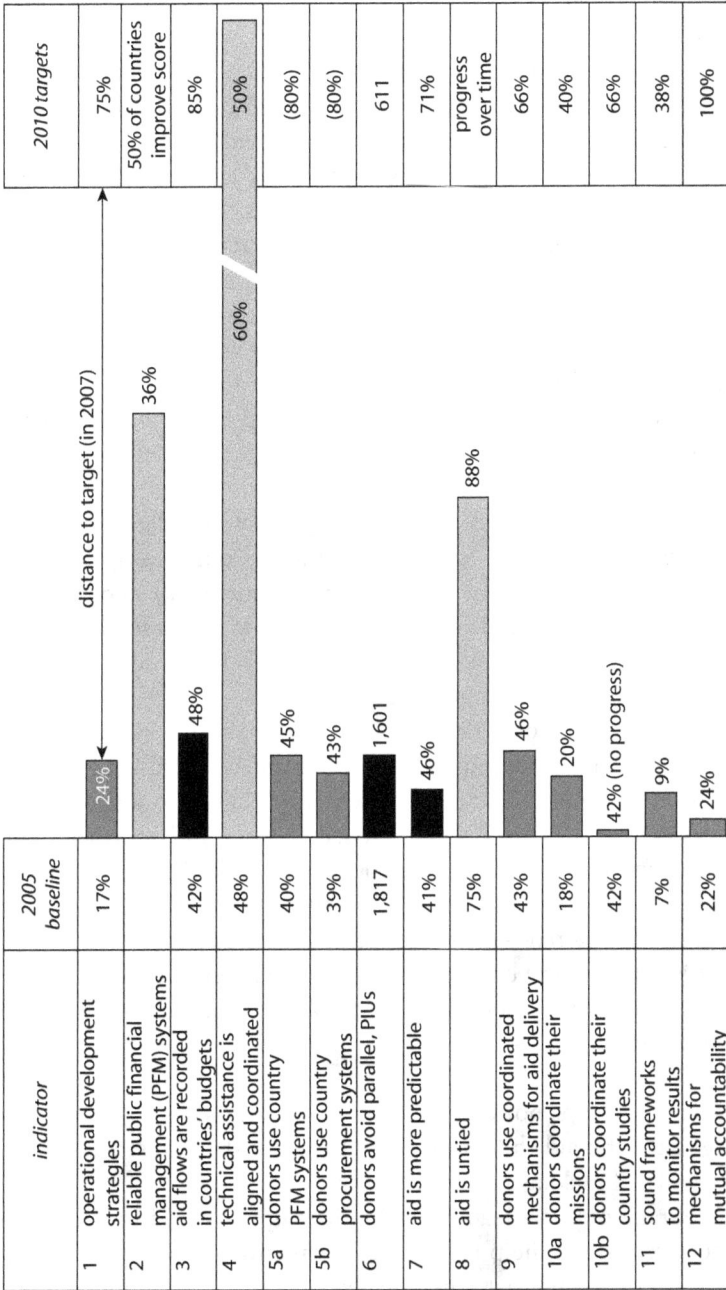

	indicator	2005 baseline	distance to target (in 2007)	2010 targets
1	operational development strategies	17%	24%	75%
2	reliable public financial management (PFM) systems		36%	50% of countries improve score
3	aid flows are recorded in countries' budgets	42%	48%	85%
4	technical assistance is aligned and coordinated	48%	60%	50%
5a	donors use country PFM systems	40%	45%	(80%)
5b	donors use country procurement systems	39%	43%	(80%)
6	donors avoid parallel, PIUs	1,817	1,601	611
7	aid is more predictable	41%	46%	71%
8	aid is untied	75%	88%	progress over time
9	donors use coordinated mechanisms for aid delivery	43%	46%	66%
10a	donors coordinate their missions	18%	20%	40%
10b	donors coordinate their country studies	42%	42% (no progress)	66%
11	sound frameworks to monitor results	7%	9%	38%
12	mechanisms for mutual accountability	22%	24%	100%

Source: OECD-DAC 2008a, 22. Used by permission.

Note: PIU = project implementation unit. For more detail about each indicator, see annex.

systems.[14] Progress has also been made toward untying aid (indicator 8). The share of untied aid increased from 75 percent in 2005 to 88 percent in 2006.

Three further indicators are on track for 2010 if country efforts are significantly scaled up. The incidence of parallel project implementation units (PIUs) has declined, and if no new PIUs emerge, the target should be reached (indicator 6). Improving transparency and accountability in a country's budget by accurately recording aid is the objective of indicator 3. Only marginal progress has been made, but greater coordination at the international level and greater commitment at the country level are needed to ensure that aid flows are accurately recorded in national budgets. Indicator 7 calls for greater predictability in the disbursement of scheduled aid. Despite some improvement, further effort between donors and partner authorities will be needed to reach the target by 2010. The remaining indicators will require significant effort by donors and countries.

The report makes three major policy recommendations aimed at accelerating progress and transforming the aid relationship into a full partnership between donors and recipient countries: (a) step up the use and capability of national institutions as a way of reinforcing country ownership, (b) strengthen accountability for development resources, and (c) make aid management more cost effective.

Deutscher and Fyson (2008) highlight the challenges in meeting these recommendations. Achieving country ownership is difficult in an environment where a country's strategic vision is not linked to a specific fiscal policy or budget process or where capacity is lacking. Even where frameworks for accountability exist, they are often weak. Finally, transparency in how public funds are spent, how contracts are procured, and how results are monitored—all prerequisites for cost-effective aid management—is scarce nearly everywhere in the developing world.

The same authors suggest the following paths for improving aid effectiveness:

- Focus on results, not on getting credit. Donors like to be acknowledged for the aid they provide, but this must not distract from the objective of making aid more effective.
- Encourage political leaders in the developing world to demand aid effectiveness and help reduce the fragmentation of aid, even if this means refusing aid that is not aligned with their development agenda.
- Stem the proliferation of aid agencies—aid effectiveness is compromised by too many donors with too many conflicting systems.

• Increase communication and accountability between donors and the public and between donors and recipient countries.[15]

Conclusion

Development assistance is based on the idea that rich countries can and should help poor countries find the path to sustainable economic growth and poverty reduction—especially those that lack other sources of capital. The chapter began by identifying the sources and composition of net capital flows to developing countries—highlighting the respective roles of private and public flows. We then discussed the arguments and evidence on both sides of the raging debate on whether aid is effective in promoting economic growth. The evidence of a direct effect of aid on growth is not conclusive. Does this mean that aid should be cut back? Not necessarily. The impact of aid should be evaluated not only in relation to its direct effects, but also in terms of its role in improving governance and economic management, and its contribution to social objectives—notably education, health, and infant mortality.

Annex The Five Principles of the Paris Declaration on Aid Effectiveness

Ownership	Target for 2010
1 *Partners have operational development strategies*—Number of countries with national development strategies (including PRSs) that have clear strategic priorities linked to a medium-term expenditure framework and reflected in annual budgets.	**At least 75% of partner countries** have operational development strategies.
Alignment	*Targets for 2010*
2 *Reliable country systems* — Number of partner countries that have procurement and public financial management systems that either (a) adhere to broadly accepted good practices or (b) have a reform programme in place to achieve these.	**(a) Public financial management —** **Half of partner countries** move up at least one measure (i.e., 0.5 points) on the PFM/ CPIA (Country Policy and Institutional Assessment) scale of performance. **(b) Procurement — One-third of partner countries** move up at least one measure (i.e., from D to C, C to B or B to A) on the four-point scale used to assess performance for this indicator.

(continued next page)

(continued)

Alignment	Targets for 2010
3 *Aid flows are aligned on national priorities*—Percent of aid flows to the government sector that is reported on partners' national budgets.	**Halve the gap**—halve the proportion of aid flows to government sector not reported on government's budget(s) (with at least 85% reported on budget).
4 *Strengthen capacity by co-ordinated support*—Percent of donor capacity-development support provided through coordinated programmes consistent with partners' national development strategies.	**50% of technical co-operation flows** are implemented through co-ordinated programmes consistent with national development strategies.

5a *Use of country public financial management systems*—Percent of donors and of aid flows that use public financial management systems in partner countries, which either (a) adhere to broadly accepted good practices or (b) have a reform programme in place to achieve these.

Percent of donors	
Score	Target
5+	**All donors** use partner countries' PFM systems.
3.5 to 4.5	**90% of donors** use partner countries' PFM systems.

Percent of aid flows	
Score	Target
5+	**A two-thirds reduction** in the *% of aid* to the public sector not using partner countries' PFM systems.
3.5 to 4.5	**A one-third reduction** in the *% of aid* to the public sector not using partner countries' PFM systems.

5b *Use of country procurement systems* — Percent of donors and of aid flows that use partner country procurement systems which either (a) adhere to broadly accepted good practices or (b) have a reform programme in place to achieve these.

Percent of donors	
Score	Target
A	**All donors** use partner countries' procurement systems.
B	**90% of donors** use partner countries' procurement systems.

Percent of aid flows	
Score	Target
A	**A two-thirds reduction** in the *% of aid* to the public sector not using partner countries' procurement systems.
B	**A one-third reduction** in the *% of aid* to the public sector not using partner countries' procurement systems.

(continued next page)

(continued)

Alignment	Targets for 2010
6 *Strengthen capacity by avoiding parallel implementation structures* — Number of parallel project implementation units (PIUs) per country.	**Reduce by two-thirds** the stock of parallel project implementation units (PIUs).
7 *Aid is more predictable* — percent of aid disbursements released according to agreed schedules in annual or multi-year frameworks.	**Halve the gap** — halve the proportion of aid not disbursed within the fiscal year for which it was scheduled.
8 *Aid is untied* — Percent of bilateral aid that is untied.	**Continued progress over time.**

Harmonization	Targets for 2010
9 *Use of common arrangements or procedures* — Percent of aid provided as programme-based approaches.	**66% of aid flows** are provided in the context of programme-based approaches.
	(a) 40% of donor missions to the field are joint.
10 *Encourage shared analysis* — Percent of (a) field missions and/or (b) country analytic work, including diagnostic reviews that are joint.	**(b) 66% of country analytic work is joint.**

Managing for results	Target for 2010
11 *Results-oriented frameworks* — Number of countries with transparent and monitorable performance assessment frameworks to assess progress against (a) the national development strategies and (b) sector programmes.	**Reduce the gap by one-third** — Reduce the proportion of countries without transparent and monitorable performance assessment frameworks by one-third.

Mutual accountability	Target for 2010
Mutual accountability — Number of partner countries that undertake mutual assessments of progress in implementing agreed commitments on aid effectiveness including those in this Declaration.	**All partner countries** have mutual assessment reviews in place.

Source: OECD 2009, 161–62.
Note: CPIA = Country Policy and Institutional Assessment; PFM = public financial management; PIU = project implementation units; PRS = Poverty Reduction Strategy.

Notes

1. The objective of the DAC is to improve development assistance through coordination and collaboration with major stakeholders and to collect and synthesize data on aid and foreign assistance before delivering that data to the public.

2. Examples of ODA activities include development projects such as schools, clinics, and water supply systems; emergency aid for natural or man-made disasters; contributions for multilateral development agencies; food aid, both emergency and developmental; aid to refugees and internally displaced persons (IDPs); debt relief under the Paris Club Agreement; and officially financed scholarships for students in developing countries (Smith 2008).

3. The 22 country members are Australia, Austria, Belgium, Canada, Denmark, Finland, France, Germany, Greece, Ireland, Italy, Japan, Luxembourg, the Netherlands, New Zealand, Norway, Portugal, Spain, Sweden, Switzerland, the United Kingdom, and the United States. The 23rd member is the EC. The Republic of Korea joined in January 2010, bringing the number of DAC members to 24. The data discussed in this chapter refer to the 22 members plus the EC.

4. The estimated total from 2004 to 2010 is less than half this—$12 billion (in 2004 prices) (OECD-DAC 2010, 100).

5. Excluding debt relief. Including debt relief the proportions, in real terms, are 24 percent for Sub-Saharan Africa and 22 percent for Africa as a whole (OECD-DAC 2010, 100).

6. Official data are, however, almost certainly understated. Only the officially funded component of aid from NGOs is counted as ODA.

7. AfDB, AfDF, CarDB, Council of Europe, EBRD, EC, GAVI, GEF, Global Fund, IAEA, IBRD, IDA, IDB Sp. Fund, IFAD, IFC, IMF (SAF, ESAF, PRGF), IMF Trust Fund, Montreal Protocol, Nordic Dev Fund, UNAIDS, UNDP, UNECE, UNFPA, UNHCR, UNICEF, UNRWA, UNTA, WFP, and Arab agencies.

8. The Czech Republic, Hungary, Poland, the Slovak Republic, Turkey, the Arab countries, and other countries.

9. The IMFC was established on September 30, 1999, by a resolution of the IMF Board of Governors, to replace the Interim Committee of the Board of Governors on the International Monetary System (usually known simply as the Interim Committee), which had been established in 1974. The IMFC has 24 members appointed by member countries of the IMF.

10. For the poorest recipient countries, ODA has averaged just over 2 percent of GDP since 1996—down from a high of 3.7 percent in 1992 (World Bank 2006a).

11. Global FDI amounts to roughly $1.4 trillion (World Bank 2009, 41).

12. World Bank projections suggest that net private capital flows will be insufficient to meet the external financing needs of 30 of the 40 low-income countries for which data are available. Furthermore, if official capital flows to those countries remain at the 2007–08 levels, they would cover just 2 of the 30 countries in the base-case scenario and not a single country in the low case (World Bank 2009, 84).

13. Deutscher and Fyson (2008) caution that the commitment gap between the spending plans of 23 members of the DAC (the World Bank; the African, Asian, and Inter-American development banks; the main UN organizations; and the global funds for health and the environment) fall short (by $30 billion) of the overall aid targets set by the DAC members individually for 2010.

14. Deutscher and Fyson (2008) disagree, pointing to the Democratic Republic of Congo and the Arab Republic of Egypt, where public financial management systems deteriorated between 2005 and 2007.

15. The process of preparing a Poverty Reduction Strategy Paper—a participatory process involving domestic stakeholders and external development partners, including the World Bank and IMF—facilitates the integration of aid into a country's national plan and offers a good channel for communication. Because the strategy paper is prepared in consultation with donors, the recipient government, and civil society, development assistance should become more focused and targeted.

Bibliography

Accra Agenda for Action. 2008. "Proceedings of the Accra High Level Forum on Aid Effectiveness." Accra, Ghana, September, 2–4. Published on http://www.imf.org.

Aiyar, S., A. Berg, and M. Hussain. 2005. "The Macroeconomic Challenge of More Aid." *Finance and Development* 42 (3): 28–31.

Burnside, A. C., and D. Dollar. 2000. "Aid, Policies and Growth." American Economic Review 90 (4): 847–68.

Bourguignon, François, and Danny Leipziger. 2006. *Aid, Growth and Poverty Reduction: Towards a New Partnership Model.* Washington, DC: World Bank.

Celasun, O., and J. Walliser. 2008. "Managing Aid Surprises." *Finance and Development* 42, No. 3 (September).

Clemens, Michael, Steven Radelet, and Rikhil Bhavnani. 2004. "Counting Chickens When They Hatch: The Short-Term Effect of Aid on Growth." Working Paper 44, Center for Global Development, Washington, DC.

Curto, Stefano. 2007. "Changing Aid Landscape."*Finance and Development* 44 (4): 20–21.

Deutscher, E., and S. Fyson. 2008. "Improving the Effectiveness of Aid." *Finance and Development* 42 (3): 15–19.

Easterly, William. 2001. *The Elusive Quest for Growth—Economists' Adventures and Misadventures in the Tropics.* Cambridge, MA: Massachusetts Institute of Technology Press.

———. 2006. *The White Man's Burden—Why the West's Efforts to Aid the Rest Have Done So Much Ill and So Little Good.* London: Penguin.

Eifert, B., and A. Gelb. 2005. "Coping with Aid Volatility." *Finance and Development* 42 (3): 24–27.

FRIDE (Foundation for International Relations and Foreign Dialogue). 2003. *Towards a New Era in Development Aid.* Madrid: FRIDE.

Gilman, M. G., and J. Wang. 2003. "Official Financing: Recent Developments and Selected Issues." World Economic and Financial Surveys, International Monetary Fund, Washington, DC.

Gupta, S., R. Powell, and Y. Yang. 2005. "The Macroeconomic Challenges of Scaling-Up Aid to Africa." IMF Working Paper WP/05/179, International Monetary Fund, Washington, DC.

Heller, P. S. 2005. "Making Aid Work." *Finance and Development* 42 (3): 8–13.

IMF (International Monetary Fund). 2006. "The Multilateral Debt Relief Initiative (MDRI)." MDRI Factsheet, IMF, Washington, DC.

Isham, Jonathan, Daniel Kaufmann, and Lant Pritchett. 1995. "Governance and Returns on Investment: An Empirical Investigation." Policy Research Working Paper 1550, World Bank, Washington, DC.

Jamison, D. T., and S. Radelet. 2005. "Making Aid Smarter." *Finance and Development* 42 (2): 42–46.

Masud, Nadia, and Boriana Yontcheva. 2005. "Does Foreign Aid Reduce Poverty? Empirical Evidence from Nongovernmental and Bilateral Aid." IMF Working Paper WP/05/100, International Monetary Fund, Washington, DC.

OECD (Organisation for Economic Co-operation and Development). 2009. *Aid Effectiveness: A Progress Report on Implementing the Paris Declaration.* Paris: OECD.

OECD-DAC (Organisation for Economic Co-operation and Development, Development Assistance Committee). 2006. *2006 Survey on Monitoring the Paris Declaration.* Paris: OECD.

———. 2008a. *2008 Survey on Monitoring the Paris Declaration: Making Aid More Effective by 2010. Better Aid,* http://dx.doi.org/10.1787./9789264050839–en, http://www.oecd.org/dac/pdsurvey. Paris: OECD.

———. 2008b. *Scaling Up: Aid Fragmentation, Aid Allocation and Aid Predictability—Report of 2008 Survey of Aid Allocation Policies and Indicative Forward Spending Plans.* Paris: OECD.

———. 2010. *Development Co-operation Report 2010.* http://dx.doi.org/10.1787/dcr-2010-en. Paris: OECD.

Radelet, S., M. Clemens, and R. Bhavnani. 2005. "Aid and Growth." *Finance and Development* 42 (3): 16–20.

Rajan, R., and A. Subramanian. 2005. "Aid and Growth: What Does The Cross Country Evidence Really Show?" IMF Working Paper WP/05/127, International Monetary Fund: Washington DC.

Siddiqi, B. 2005. "Picture This. Aiding Development: Tracking the Flows." *Finance and Development* 42 (3): 14–15.

Smith, K. 2008. *The DAC and ODA (Official Development Assistance) Statistics.* http://www.docstoc.com/docs/1003544/The-DAC-and-ODA-Statistics.

Tressel, Thierry. 2007. "Is There a Foreign Aid Paradox?" *IMF Research Bulletin* 8 (4): 1, 4.

Mishra, P., and D. Newhouse. 2007. "Does Health Aid Matter?" Unpublished paper, International Monetary Fund, Washington, DC.

World Bank. 2005. *Global Development Finance.* Washington, DC: World Bank.

———. 2006a. *Global Development Finance.* Washington, DC: World Bank.

———. 2006b. *Global Monitoring Report.* Washington, DC: World Bank.

———. 2006c. *World Development Indicators.* CD-ROM. Washington, DC: World Bank.

———. 2007. *Global Development Finance.* Washington, DC: World Bank.

———. 2009. *Global Development Finance.* Washington, DC: World Bank.

CHAPTER 8

External Debt

In national finance—as in corporate and personal finance—credit is good, and excessive debt is bad. When a country's debt burden becomes too great, investment evaporates and growth is choked off. Social spending drops and people suffer.

By the late 1980s, many low-income countries had contracted an unsustainable amount of foreign debt; it was widely realized that a wide-ranging program of debt relief would be required if such countries were to avoid becoming hopelessly mired in debt. A round of debt-relief initiatives that began with a summit in Toronto in 1988 culminated in the Multilateral Debt Relief Initiative (MDRI) of June 2005. The MDRI provided for the full cancellation of official debt to qualified low-income countries that agreed to use the savings to reduce poverty, establish sound macroeconomic policies, and improve social outcomes. Between January 2006 and December 2007, 25 heavily indebted developing countries saw $3.3 billion in external debt canceled by private and official creditors, thus freeing up resources to help those countries reach the Millennium Development Goals (MDGs), the major aim of which is to halve poverty by 2015.

But while debt forgiveness brought benefits to many countries, concern persisted that in times of plentiful credit (such as 2002–07), some countries would borrow too much, making themselves vulnerable to sudden increases in interest rates. In 2008, in fact, private investment flows to developing countries shrank by more than 40 percent, as access to international debt markets dried up and inflows of portfolio equity all but ceased (World Bank 2009).

The current crisis has affected the external financing position of all developing countries—but not equally. Those that have high levels of external debt, large current-account deficits, and shallow foreign reserves are more likely to encounter difficulties in obtaining the finance they will need to avoid a severe contraction in growth. Many private firms in the developing world will be hard pressed to service their foreign-currency liabilities with revenues earned in sharply devalued domestic currencies. The World Bank (2009) predicts that the likelihood of balance of payment crises and the restructuring of corporate debt in these countries is very great.

Measures of External Indebtedness

Conventional measures of a country's debt burden are as follows:

- The ratio of external debt to gross domestic product (GDP) or to exports of goods and services, sometimes including workers' remittances and other current-account receipts is used. These measures point to a country's ability to service its debts, particularly in terms of foreign exchange.
- In an elaboration of the simple debt-to-exports ratio, the discounted present value of future debt service is compared with the discounted present value of future export receipts. The calculations of discounted present value include all future debt-service obligations divided by the appropriate discount factors.
- The ratio of scheduled debt service (interest payments and amortization) to government revenues provides an indication of the fiscal impact of external debt and a country's capacity to repay its obligations.

External indebtedness is likely to affect poverty both directly, by shrinking government resources available for poverty-related spending, and indirectly, through its impact on economic growth.

External Indebtedness, Growth, and Poverty

Studies of the link between external debt and growth emphasize the mediating role of investment. According to the "debt overhang" hypothesis, large debts lower growth by hindering investment, as ever-larger shares of a country's resources are transferred abroad to service debts. The debt burden may also raise domestic interest rates, slowing investment. Once the level of debt becomes large enough, investment will remain insufficiently low until the unsustainable portion of the debt is either forgiven or rescheduled. As debt increased in the 1980s, growth slowed in the developing world; it picked up again as debt was reduced in the 1990s (figure 8.1, panels a and b).

As outstanding debt increases beyond a threshold level—to debt over-hang levels—a country's ability or willingness to repay its debts begins to fall, especially as governments begin to default on debt to avoid the damaging effects of very high debt service. As debt rises, the erosion of expected repayments is known as the Laffer debt curve.

International financial markets and aid donors tend to view excessive debt as a sign of economic mismanagement and bad governance, both of which make investment more risky. In this way, high indebtedness can trigger a decline in new flows of external resources, leading, in turn, to a reduction in poverty-related spending.

As debt grows, so does the likelihood that its servicing will be financed through inflationary measures, punitive taxes, arbitrary spending cuts, or other distortionary policies. Expecting such policies, private investors typically choose one of three paths: they invest less, they divert their resources to risky ventures that produce quick financial returns, or they transfer their money into safer investments abroad (capital flight).

Another channel through which debt affects growth is by crowding out social spending. Proponents of debt relief argue that fiscal resources freed up by debt relief can and should be used to support health, education, water, sanitation, and other essential services to the poor, in the belief that increased social spending leads to better social outcomes.[1] In addition, such spending is widely regarded as crucial for low-income countries to achieve the MDGs, which include targets for reducing child and infant mortality, and raising educational enrollment.

Notwithstanding the attractiveness of the debt-overhang hypothesis as an explanation for slow growth in highly indebted countries, empirical evidence of the effects of debt overhang is mixed. For example, Claessens (1990) found that 5 of the 29 middle-income countries in his sample were on the wrong side of the Laffer debt curve, suggesting that partial debt reduction would *decrease* the expected repayment to creditors. For middle-income countries, Warner (1992) concluded that the debt crisis did not depress investment. Several other studies have concluded that it is difficult to disentangle the impact of debt variables on growth.

Figure 8.1   Debt's Inverse Relationship to Growth

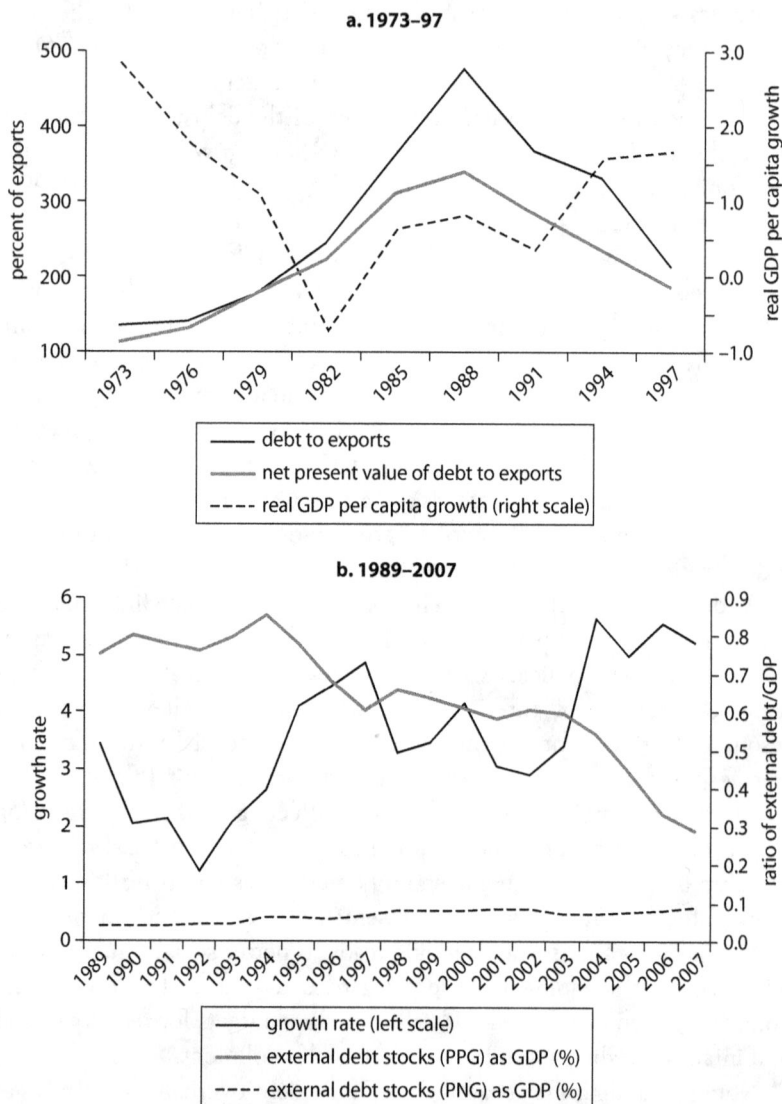

a. 1973–97

b. 1989–2007

Sources: Reprinted from Pattilio, Poirson, and Ricci 2002.
Note: PNG = private nonguaranteed; PPG = public debt and public guaranteed debt. The sample consists of 93 developing countries. The data consist of three-year moving averages over the 1972–88 period.

The second difficulty relates to the "crowding-out" effect. Most studies of the interplay of investment and growth conflate crowding out with the debt-overhang effect. It is important, however, to distinguish between the debt-overhang effect—which can be captured with a variable representing the burden of future debt service, such as the debt stock or the net present value (NPV) of future debt service—and crowding out, the proxy for which is a contemporaneous debt-service ratio in the regression analysis.

Patilio, Poirson, and Ricci (2002) found a nonlinear, Laffer-type relationship between debt and growth in the 93 developing countries that they examined. The average impact of external debt on per capita growth appeared to be negative for debt levels (measured in NPV terms) above 60–70 percent of exports and 35–40 percent of GDP. Furthermore, their results suggest that doubling debt levels slows per capita GDP growth by about 0.5–1.0 percent. The same authors also found that the investment level did not appear to be the main channel through which excessive external indebtedness reduced growth and that the debt-overhang effect was greater than the crowding-out effect.

Debt Relief and Low-Income Countries

External debt emerged as a grave problem for developing countries in the 1980s. Middle-income countries were borrowing from private creditors—chiefly commercial banks—to fund infrastructure projects and cover shortfalls in their balance of payments, while low-income countries without access to private finance borrowed from developed countries—often through export credit agencies or from banks in the form of loans insured by the agencies.[2] Official creditors were willing to take the risks of what was called "national-interest" lending and saw the provision of commercially priced export credit guarantees as a complement to the grants and concessional loans they offered.

Many low-income countries began to have difficulty servicing their debts—paying the interest and principal on the scheduled due dates—in the early and mid-1980s. Their mounting difficulties quickly became a debt crisis. To cope with the crisis, an informal group of official creditors known as the Paris Club[3] agreed to reschedule debt to poor countries (at unchanged interest rates) to preserve growth and economic viability in the affected countries. From 1976 to 1998, the Paris Club rescheduled loans to 81 countries—27 of which came to be identified as heavily indebted poor countries (HIPCs)—delaying payments of about

$23 billion (table 8.1).[4] This approach provided these countries with substantial cash-flow relief for financing reform programs. At the same time, however, their stock of outstanding debt steadily increased. A new approach to the debt problem was initiated in 1988 at the Group of Seven (G-7) summit in Toronto, where, for the first time, it was decided to reschedule the Paris Club commercial loans to low-income countries at below-market interest rates. For the first time, governments were being asked to accept concessional reschedulings on export credit agency debts.[5] A combination of proposals from France, the United Kingdom, and the United States that came to be known as the Toronto terms reduced the NPV of eligible debt by up to one-third.

The Toronto terms were the first of several schemes to provide debt relief to poor countries. Those schemes considerably reduced the external debt of middle-income countries.[6] But many low-income countries— especially in Sub-Saharan Africa—continued to suffer from heavy external debt burdens and high rates of poverty. These countries had difficulty meeting their external debt commitments owing to a confluence of factors, including the accumulation of nonconcessional debt from official export credits, poor debt-management practices, worsening terms of trade, weak macroeconomic policies, poor governance, civil wars, and drought.

During the same period, new initiatives aimed at promoting debt relief for low-income countries were introduced by multilateral institutions. At the G-7 summit in Venice in 1987, the International Monetary Fund (IMF) had unveiled the Enhanced Structural Adjustment Facility (ESAF), designed to provide new concessional IMF lending for low-income countries, financed by grants from wealthier member countries. The ESAF succeeded the Structural Adjustment Facility (SAF) that had been established in 1986. It was itself succeeded by the Poverty Reduction Growth Facility (PRGF) in 1999. Available to low-income member countries facing protracted balance of payment problems, the ESAF provided resources at an annual interest rate of 0.5 percent, repayable over 10 years, including a grace period of 5.5 years. The PRGF offered the same terms.

In September 1996, the World Bank and IMF together launched the HIPC Initiative to reduce the external debt burden of eligible countries "to a sustainable level in a reasonably short period of time" in return for "strong programs of macroeconomic adjustment and structural reforms" (Andrews and others 1999). A country was judged to have reached a sustainable level of external debt if it could meet its current and future

Table 8.1 HIPCs: Paris Club Reschedulings by Type of Terms, 1976–98

Paris club terms	Dates	Number of reschedulings	Number of countries	Amount consolidated (US$, millions)	Stock or flow deals	Stock of debt operations (US$, millions)
Nonconcessional	before Oct. 1988	81	27	22,803	Flow only	—
Toronto terms	Oct. 1988–June 1991	28	20	5,994	Flow only	—
London terms	Dec. 1991–Dec. 1994	26	23	8,857	Flow only	—
Naples terms	since January 1995	34	26	14,664	7 stock deals	2,518
Lyon terms	since December 1996	5	4	2,775	2 stock deals	709

Source: Daseking and Powell 1999, table 1.
Note: Table excludes Nigeria.

external debt-service obligations in full without recourse to debt relief, rescheduling of debt, accumulation of arrears, or curtailment of growth.

At the outset, 41 countries[7] were identified as HIPCs; 32 of these had a gross national product (GNP) per capita of $695 or less in 1993, a debt-to-export ratio of 220 percent or higher, or a debt-to-GNP ratio of 80 percent or higher. The remaining nine countries were those that had received or were eligible for concessional rescheduling from Paris Club creditors. The HIPCs had to be eligible for the ESAF and for loans from the International Development Association (IDA), the World Bank's concessional lending arm. They were required to show a strong record of performance under IMF- and World Bank–sponsored programs (Andrews and others 1999).

After 1999, the Enhanced HIPC Initiative provided deeper, faster, and broader debt relief,[8] and a stronger focus on poverty reduction through the preparation and adoption of a new vehicle—the Poverty Reduction Strategy Paper (PRSP). The PRSP was designed to be a comprehensive, nationally "owned" strategy for reducing poverty through rapid economic growth, macroeconomic stability, and structural reforms. Prepared in consultation with community groups, nongovernmental organizations (NGOs), and donors, the Strategy Paper would identify specific targets tied to the MDGs. At first it was optional for countries to participate in the Enhanced HIPC Initiative, but this was later made a mandatory condition for passing the decision point for obtaining debt relief under the HIPC Initiative.

As of December 2007, debt-reduction packages had been approved for 32 countries (26 of them in Africa), providing $46 billion (in NPV terms, as of the decision point) in debt-service relief over time. Twenty-three[9] had reached the completion point and were receiving irrevocable debt relief. Nine countries[10] had reached the decision point and were receiving interim relief. Social difficulties—internal civil strife, cross-border armed conflict, and governance challenges—prevented the remaining nine countries from obtaining debt relief.

In June 2005, the Group of Eight (G-8) industrial governments proposed canceling the debts of HIPCs under a new measure, the Multilateral Debt Relief Initiative, mentioned at the start of this chapter. The MDRI was designed to provide additional financial support—up to 100 percent debt relief—to countries that had graduated from the Enhanced HIPC Initiative, to better position them to achieve the MDGs. Unlike the HIPC Initiative, the MDRI did not propose any parallel debt relief on the part of official bilateral creditors, private creditors,

Table 8.2   Status of 39 Countries under the Enhanced HIPC Initiative—2010

Post Completion Point Countries (27)		
Afghanistan	Ghana	Niger
Benin	Guyana	Rwanda
Bolivia	Haiti	São Tomé & Príncipe
Burkina Faso	Honduras	Senegal
Burundi	Madagascar	Sierra Leone
Cameroon	Malawi	Tanzania
Central Africa Republic	Mali	Uganda
Congo, Rep.	Mauritania	
Ethiopia	Mozambique	
Gambia, The	Nicaragua	
Interim Countries (Between Decision and Completion Point) (7)		
Chad	Guinea	Togo
Congo, Dem. Rep.	Guinea-Bissau	
Côte d'Ivoire	Liberia	
Pre-Decision Point Countries (5)		
Comoros	Somalia	
Eritrea	Sudan	
Kyrgyz Republic		

Source: Daseking and Powell 2010, 4.

or multilateral organizations except for the IMF, IDA, and the African Development Fund. The bulk of the debt relief was to be provided by the IDA, which began to implement the MDRI in July 2006. The IMF began implementation in January 2006.

All countries that reach the completion point[11] under the Enhanced HIPC Initiative, and those with per capita income below $380 and outstanding debt to the IMF at the end of 2004, are eligible for the MDRI. According to these criteria, 25 countries had qualified as of December 2007. These included 23 HIPCs that had reached completion point and 2 non-HIPCs (Cambodia and Tajikistan) whose per capita income was below $380. The cost of the debt relief under the MDRI was $3.3 billion by the end of December 2007 (Daseking and Powell 2010). Table 8.2 shows the most recent list of countries that are eligible or potentially eligible for HIPC Initiative assistance as of January 30, 2010.

Debt Relief versus Development Assistance

As discussed in chapter 7 of this book, resources for development are directed toward low-income countries through debt relief, development assistance, or both. For example, in Africa in recent years, debt relief has become a more important component of total resource flows, with the bulk of aid increases being channeled to debt relief (figure 8.2). In this context, both donors and policy makers in recipient countries often debate which form of resource flow is more effective in promoting growth and alleviating poverty.

One view is that the relative merits of development assistance versus debt relief depend on the type of country. Debt relief is more effective in countries suffering from a severe debt overhang, where there is an urgent need for resource flows to jump-start the development process. In other countries, development assistance is more efficient than debt relief because it helps develop market institutions and better policies and is more targeted toward projects and sectors that help growth and reduce poverty.

Figure 8.2   Composition of Resource Flows to Africa, 2000–10
US$, billions

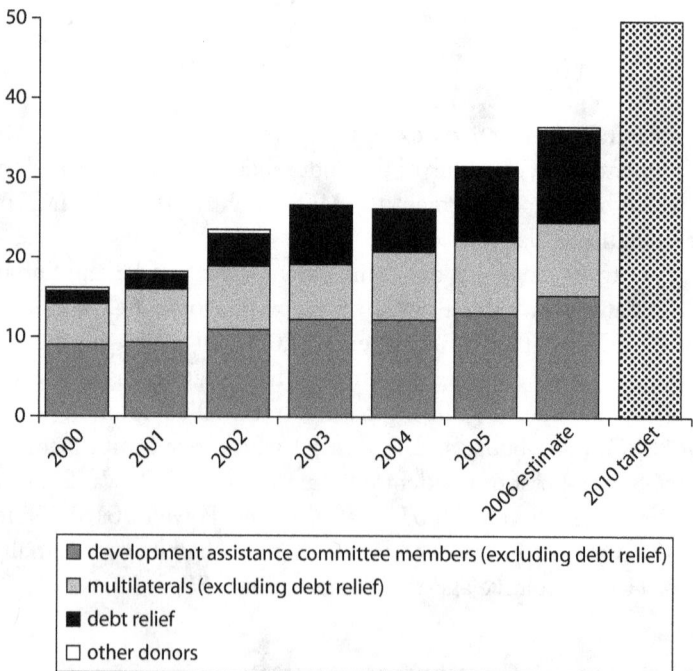

Source: Curto 2007.
Note: Other donors include non-DAC donors reporting to the OECD-DAC.

Another view is that, in general, debt relief is more effective than aid for most developing countries because (a) "tied" aid (for which donors place conditions on recipient countries to purchase goods or services from the donor country) reduces the value of aid by 11 to 30 percent (UN 2005), while debt relief cannot be tied; and (b) debt relief provides flexible budget support and increases government accountability because it makes it possible for governments of recipient countries to set their own priorities instead of focusing on projects proposed by donors.

Debt-relief programs are typically justified on the basis that they free up resources that would otherwise have been used for debt servicing and on the assumption that these freed-up resources will be spent on social programs—such as those focused on education and health—to alleviate poverty and promote growth. There is some evidence that social-service spending has risen in response to past episodes of debt relief. The IMF has estimated that poverty-reducing expenditures in the HIPCs rose from 6.4 percent of GDP in 1999 to 7.9 percent in 2004. But it is far from clear whether the increase was the result of debt relief rather than a boost in development assistance.[12] As seen in the last chapter, donors earmarked much of that boost for sectoral assistance and investment projects, which have a more immediate impact on social sector spending than does debt relief.

It is important to remember that greater health-care spending does not necessarily mean better health, and more money for schools does not necessarily mean more children in school. Other factors such as poor governance and lack of institutional capacity often decide outcomes. IMF chief economist Raghuram Rajan (2005) has argued that if the main obstacle to growth is a bleak investment climate, then reducing the level of debt without providing additional resources or improving policies is unlikely to have any positive effect on growth and poverty reduction.

Individual views on the relative effectiveness of debt relief and development assistance may turn on the perceived value of donor agency involvement. Those who believe that such agencies can increase the positive impact of public expenditure by directing external resources toward the development of better institutions and infrastructure tend to favor development assistance. Those who believe that donor agencies add to bureaucratic and institutional challenges by placing conditions on aid allocation tend to favor debt relief.

We return to this discussion in chapter 15, where we urge that the contribution of both development assistance and debt relief to growth and poverty reduction should be seen in the larger context of the various factors affecting long-term growth in a country, including geography, macroeconomic policies, human capital, infrastructure, institutions, trade, and socioeconomic conditions.

Conclusion

Mounting external debt hobbles economic growth by limiting investment. It also reduces countries' capacity for poverty reduction by curtailing social spending. By the late 1980s, many low-income countries had accumulated such high levels of external debt that their ability to repay that debt—while continuing to grow and fight poverty—was questionable. A host of debt-relief initiatives brought substantial reductions in the official debt of qualified low-income countries. Debt relief effectively provides predictable budgetary benefits and, in this way, has helped countries move toward the MDGs.

Notes

1. In a wide-ranging study of 48 Sub-Saharan African countries for the period 1980–99, Lopes (2002) found that greater social spending did indeed produce better social outcomes (or outputs). The outcomes for education, for example, are gross enrollment rates, pupil-teacher ratios, adult illiteracy rates, and so on; outcomes for health are infant mortality rates, life expectancy at birth, physicians per 1,000 people, number of hospital beds, and so on.

2. The purpose of export credit agencies is to support domestic exports by providing trade loans to developing countries that cannot obtain credit from private lenders, often because of their unstable politics. The provision of export credit guarantees stimulated industrial-country exports and—by extension—domestic employment, while cementing ties with trading partners.

3. The Paris Club is an informal and voluntary gathering of a group of official creditors whose role is to find coordinated and sustainable solutions to the payment difficulties experienced by debtor nations. The first meeting with a debtor country was in 1956, when Argentina agreed to meet its public creditors in Paris. Since then, the Paris Club or ad hoc groups of Paris Club creditors have reached 400 agreements with 83 debtor countries.

4. Subsequent paragraphs discuss the initiatives put in place by the international financial institutions (IFIs) for external debt from 1998 to 2010 and identify the countries that have benefited from these initiatives.

5. Concessional rescheduling on official development assistance was already being provided. "Paris Club practice had always rescheduled aid debts using the concessional interest rate of the original loan contract which implies a reduction in its present value." (Daseking and Powell 1999).

6. The decrease in external debt for middle-income countries has, however, been associated with an increase in domestic debt that has its own inherent risks.

7. The group of 41 countries consisted of Angola, Benin, Bolivia, Burkina Faso, Burundi, Cameroon, the Central African Republic, Chad, the Republic of Congo, Côte d'Ivoire, the Democratic Republic of Congo, Equatorial Guinea, Ethiopia, Ghana, Guinea, Guinea-Bissau, Guyana, Honduras, Kenya, the Lao People's Democratic Republic, Liberia, Madagascar, Mali, Mauritania, Mozambique, Myanmar, Nicaragua, Niger, Nigeria, Rwanda, São Tomé and Príncipe, Senegal, Sierra Leone, Somalia, Sudan, Tanzania, Togo, Uganda, Vietnam, the Republic of Yemen, and Zambia; Malawi was subsequently added to the group (Andrews and others 1999).

8. *Deeper debt relief* involved lowering the debt-to-export ratio from 250 to 150 percent and dropping the requirement for a country-specific vulnerability analysis; lowering the debt-to-fiscal revenue target from 280 to 250 percent; lowering the export-to-GDP ratio from 40 to 30 percent; lowering the revenue-to-GDP ratio from 20 to 15 percent; and changing the basis for debt relief to actual data based on the year prior to the decision point (rather than on projections for the completion point).

   Faster debt relief allowed the IFIs to provide interim relief between the decision and completion points, and the introduction of floating completion points, which allowed assessment of a country's performance to be based on specific outcomes of policy reform and macroeconomic stability, rather than the length of a track record.

   Broader debt relief facilitated a "greater safety margin for the achievement of debt sustainability, providing a clear and permanent exit from unsustainable indebtedness at the completion point." (Andrews and others 1999).

9. Benin, Bolivia, Burkina Faso, Cameroon, Ethiopia, The Gambia, Ghana, Guyana, Honduras, Madagascar, Malawi, Mali, Mauritania, Mozambique, Nicaragua, Niger, Rwanda, São Tomé and Príncipe, Senegal, Sierra Leone, Tanzania, Uganda, and Zambia.

10. Afghanistan, Burundi, the Central African Republic, Chad, the Republic of Congo, the Democratic Republic of Congo, Guinea, Guinea-Bissau, and Haiti.

11. The requirements for an HIPC to reach the completion point include showing satisfactory performance in (a) macroeconomic policies, (b) public expenditure management, and (c) implementation of a poverty-reduction strategy.

12. Development aid inflows averaged nearly 60 percent of total public expenditure in the 14 Sub-Saharan Africa completion-point HIPCs (Moss 2006).

Bibliography

Andrews, D., A. R. Boote, S. S. Rizavi, and S. Singh. 1999. "Debt Relief for Low-Income Countries: The Enhanced HIPC Initiative." Pamphlet Series No. 51, International Monetary Fund, Washington, DC.

Bhattacharya, R., and B. Clements. 2004. "Calculating the Benefits of Debt Relief." *Finance and Development* 41 (4): 48–50.

Claessens, S. 1990. "The Debt Laffer Curve: Some Estimates." *World Development* 18 (12): 1671–77.

Clements, B., R. Bhattacharya, and T. Q. Nguyen. 2005. "Can Debt Relief Boost Growth in Poor Countries?" *Economic Issues* 34, International Monetary Fund, Washington, DC.

Curto, Stefano. 2007. "Changing Aid Landscape." *Finance and Development* 44 (4): 20–21.

Daseking, C., and R. Powell. 1999. "From Toronto Terms to the HIPC Initiative: A Brief History of Debt Relief." Working Paper WP/99/142, International Monetary Fund, Washington, DC.

———. 2007a. "A Factsheet: The Multilateral Debt Relief Initiative (MDRI)." International Monetary Fund, Washington, DC.

———. 2010. "Debt Relief under the Heavily Indebted Poor Countries Initiative (HIPC)." IMF Fact Sheet, February 18, International Monetary Fund, Washington, DC.

Lopes, Paulo Silva. 2002. "A Comparative Analysis of Government Social Spending Indicators and Their Correlation with Social Outcomes in Sub-Saharan Africa." IMF Working Paper 02/176, International Monetary Fund, Washington, DC.

Moss, Todd. 2006. "Briefing: The G8's Multilateral Debt Relief Initiative and Poverty Reduction in Sub-Saharan Africa." *African Affairs*, April 3.

Pattilio, C., H. Poirson, and L. Ricci. 2002. "External Debt and Growth." *Finance and Development* 39 (2): 32–35.

Rajan, Raghuram. 2005. "Debt Relief and Growth." *Finance and Development* 42 (2): 56–57.

UN (United Nations). 2005. *Human Development Report: International Cooperation at a Crossroads: Aid, Trade and Security in an Unequal World.* New York: UN.

Warner, A. M. 1992. "Did the Debt Crisis Cause the Investment Crisis?" *Quarterly Journal of Economics* 107 (November): 1161–86.

WHO (World Health Organization). 2001. *Investing in Health for Economic Development.* Geneva: Commission on Macroeconomics and Health.

World Bank. 2006. "Debt Relief. News and Broadcast." World Bank, http://web.worldbank.org/WBSITE/EXTERNAL/NEWS/0,,contentMDK: 20040942~menuPK:34480~pagePK:34370~theSitePK:4607,00.html.

———. 2009. *Global Development Finance.* Washington, DC: World Bank.

CHAPTER 9

Trade Policy

The share of international trade in developing countries' output grew from 35 percent in 1980 to 57 percent in 2007. Although most economists agree that trade liberalization promotes growth and reduces poverty, concern about its negative effects has not abated among policy makers or the general public. Greater integration of the global economy over the past three decades has opened new markets for producers in the developing world and brought enormous benefits to developing countries, but it has also widened channels through which a slowdown in economic activity in one group of countries can spread to others.

After first presenting the rationale for trade, this chapter reviews the links between openness to trade, growth, and poverty reduction.

The Rationale for Trade

Trade is motivated by the expectation of economic gain. According to the theory of absolute advantage, nations gain by producing goods that require fewer domestic resources and by exchanging their surplus for goods produced abroad with fewer resources. Each country can benefit from specialized production, which encourages trade. The theory of absolute advantage is incomplete, however, because it ignores the gains available through trade even when one party has an absolute advantage in the production of all goods. Those gains are explained by the theory of comparative advantage, which holds that *mutually beneficial trade is always possible between nations whose pretrade relative costs and prices differ*. According to the theory, international trade occurs when two countries begin to explore the benefits of trade. When trading countries concentrate on producing goods and services in which they have a comparative advantage, they benefit, and world output of goods and services is maximized. Differences in endowments of natural resources, human resources, and capital give rise to comparative advantage.

The theory of comparative advantage assumes free trade across countries—that is, free access of each country to the markets of other countries. It also assumes fair trade among countries. Fair trade implies that all countries have perfect market information and perfect access to credit, and that producers have the ability to switch production techniques and outputs in response to market information and demand. The theory recognizes that policies can be "trade creating" or "trade diverting." Outward-oriented policies, which encourage production for export, are trade-creating policies. Trade diversion occurs when policies are oriented inward and do not encourage production for export.

By engaging in trade, most countries expect to increase incomes for their producers and reduce the cost of goods for their citizens. The global value of income and output is maximized if the opportunity costs of producing everything in every country are minimized—that is, if all production inputs have been put to their most efficient use. By encouraging efficient allocations of capital, labor, and land, trade improves the operation of many sectors of the economy, even those that produce goods and services that are not traded internationally.

Additionally, trade is a source of government revenue from license fees and trade taxes. Through exports, it is a source of foreign exchange. Exchanges of goods and services encourage better relationships among countries. Countries that trade with one another are more likely to seek a peaceful solution to conflicts to avoid disrupting trade. Millions of people depend on trade for a livelihood. From production to retail to import and export, trade is a necessary way of life for many people. Efficient trading patterns permit people everywhere to enjoy higher living standards.

A number of factors ensure positive gains from trade at the international level.

Specialization. Specialization gains arise from producing and selling goods for which a country enjoys a comparative advantage and buying other goods from countries that can produce them at a lower cost. Access to export markets widens the scope for specialization gains, while simultaneously giving producers access to intermediate goods at lower costs than would be available solely by means of domestic production.

Uniqueness. In some regions, local sources of certain goods do not exist. Technology gaps, for example, may affect a country's capacity to produce a good or exploit a resource. Gains arise from trading goods that are not locally available.

Scale. Specialization gains may be limited by market size. Moving into the international market permits expanded production. Gains from scale occur when access to export markets stimulates production of larger amounts of goods at lower average costs.

Dynamism. Dynamic gains occur when trade accelerates economic growth and development by spreading technology, accelerating capital formation, or encouraging innovation in the anticipation of succeeding in lucrative export markets.

Political stability. Political gains from trade arise when economic interdependence facilitates international political stability. Mutually beneficial trade is a powerful incentive for countries to avoid conflict by engaging in peaceful negotiations. The interdependence created by trade reduces the likelihood of war.

Trade Barriers

Despite the many gains to be derived from trade, countries erect various barriers to trade. They have a variety of reasons for doing so. States that have limited sources of revenue (because of a narrow tax base, for example, or limited capacity for collecting taxes) use trade barriers as a method of raising revenue. Trade barriers may also be attractive because they protect domestic industries, which may constitute a powerful political constituency, capable of lobbying effectively to protect their interests. Some countries also prefer not to be dependent on other countries, believing that self-sufficiency in as many economic sectors as possible (a largely discredited policy known as *autarky*) will protect their stability and sovereignty.

Barriers to trade come in two basic forms: border barriers (also known as tariff barriers) and behind-the-border barriers (nontariff barriers).

Border Barriers

Border barriers consist of tariffs, quotas, and voluntary export restrictions.

Tariffs. A tariff is an excise tax that applies only to imported goods. Its purpose is either to generate revenue or to protect domestic firms.

Protective tariffs put foreign producers at a competitive disadvantage when selling in domestic markets. By raising the domestic prices of goods, they stimulate domestic production. When a tariff is very high, it becomes a disincentive to trade. A high tariff may divert trade away from the country to other countries where tariffs are lower. Low tariffs encourage trade but generate lower revenue for the state. Unlike nontariff barriers, tariffs are usually transparent; that is, they are of known magnitude.

Quotas. Quotas limit the amount of goods that may be imported or exported, whether absolutely or at a given tariff rate (tariff rate quotas). Quotas raise the price of imported goods. A product may be imported in high quantities despite high tariffs if demand is sufficiently strong, but low absolute import quotas may completely prohibit imports once quotas have been filled. Quotas have particularly pernicious side effects, as profits from import licenses increase the potential for bribery and corruption.

Voluntary export restrictions. These are agreements in which foreign firms "voluntarily" limit the amount of their exports to a particular country. Exporters agree to such restrictions, which have the effect of quotas, in the hope of avoiding more stringent trade barriers.

Behind-the-Border Barriers

Nontariff barriers take many forms, among them licensing requirements, unreasonable standards pertaining to product quality and safety, and cumbersome documentary or administrative requirements designed to discourage imports. Growing concern in some countries about the environment and food safety has led to the adoption of regulatory requirements that in some instances function as nontariff barriers to trade. Poor physical infrastructure (ports, roads) may also have the effect of impeding or limiting trade by raising costs and increasing risks (of spoilage or theft, for example). Creaky financial infrastructure, too, may frustrate trade—for example, if short-term financing for trade transactions is unavailable or onerously expensive.

Trade and Economic Growth

Most economists believe that openness to trade is good for economic growth. Berg and Krueger (2002) cite a number of economists who have found that differences in output per capita across countries are explained by differences in openness to trade. These results hold even when using different measures of openness, adding other variables that might explain differences in income, and controlling for reverse causality (that is, the possibility that growth engenders trade, rather than the other way around).

Openness to trade promotes competition in domestic markets, increases pressure on firms to be competitive and innovative, provides consumers with a wider choice at lower prices, and allows firms to bring in new skills and technologies to fully exploit their comparative advantage. Firms that export are highly productive, and exporting allows them to grow faster. Trade also raises the marginal returns of other reforms, in that better infrastructure, telephones, roads, and ports translate into better performance by the export sector. By contrast, the path of self-reliance, or autarky, followed by many developing countries in the past, causes economic distortions that ultimately hamper growth. Quantitative restrictions, licensing requirements, and prohibitive tariffs keep imports out of the domestic market, leaving the market to inefficient local producers that have little incentive to become more productive.

International trade helped to drive postwar global growth. In the 1950s, global merchandise exports accounted for approximately 8 percent of gross domestic product (GDP), a proportion that had increased to almost 26 percent by 2004 (Krueger 2004). In-depth analyses by Srinivasan and Bhagwati (1999) of country experiences during the 1960s and 1970s show that trade continued to create and sustain higher growth during this period. In the two decades following 1980, international trade continued to drive economic performance, growing twice as fast as worldwide income. Dollar and Kraay (2001b) claim a "statistically significant and economically meaningful effect of trade on growth," finding that when trade as a share of GDP is increased by 20 percentage points, growth increases by between 0.5 and 1 percentage point a year.

The same authors examine the growth experience of countries differentiated by their openness to trade between 1960 and 2000, after controlling for correlation across growth-enhancing variables and addressing difficulties in determining causation. They identify three groups—rich countries, globalizers, and nonglobalizers (figure 9.1). Globalizers are those developing countries that experienced a particularly large proportionate increase in trade as a share of GDP—doubling, on average, from 16 percent of GDP to 33 percent in 20 years. The rich countries showed a 70 percent increase over the same period (from 29 percent to 50 percent). The nonglobalizers, which make up two-thirds of all developing countries, experienced a decline in trade as a share of GDP. The globalizers experienced an increase in their growth rates from 2.9 percent per year in the 1970s to 3.5 percent in the 1980s to 5 percent in the 1990s,

Figure 9.1   Growth in Real Per Capita GDP across Countries

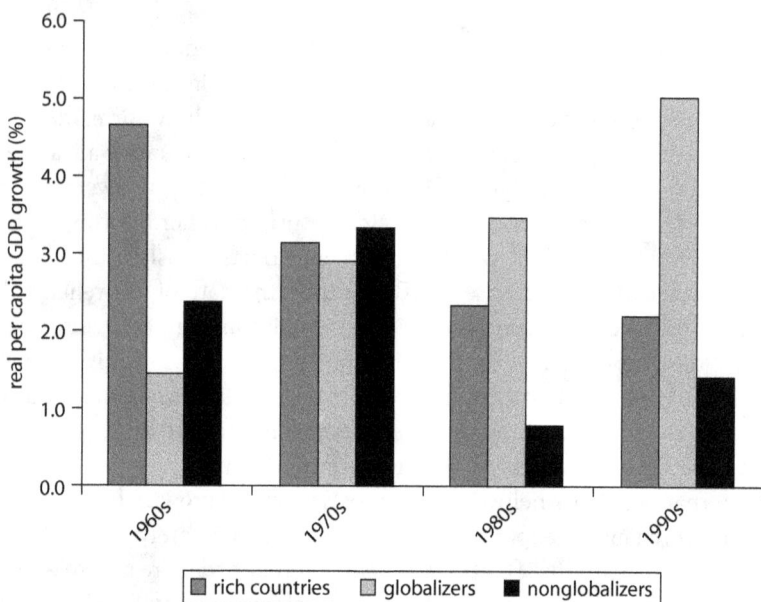

Source: Dollar and Kraay 2001b.

while the nonglobalizers saw annual growth *decline* from 3.3 percent to 0.8 percent over the first two decades, before recovering to 1.4 percent in the 1990s. The results provide robust evidence of the effect of openness on growth.

There are a few dissenters from this positive view of trade and growth, notably Rodriguez and Rodrik (2000), who argue that the high correlation between trade openness and other explanatory variables such as geographic characteristics and domestic policy choices mar the literature's results. Despite these methodological disagreements, it remains generally accepted that trade is good for growth.

Trade certainly is *correlated* with growth. But the direction of causation between trade and growth is unclear. For example, as an economy experiences growth, its opportunities for trading will increase, but the converse is not necessarily true: simply dismantling or reducing tariffs does not guarantee economic growth. The challenge is to provide a framework in which trade can thrive and exert its growth-promoting power. Here, trade liberalization is the key.

Experience with trade liberalization suggests that free trade has to be phased in according to a realistic timetable. The first steps are to eliminate trade bias by adopting a realistic exchange rate and to reduce impediments to exports by eliminating quantitative restrictions on exports and imported inputs. Lowering protection levels and making protection transparent and nondiscriminatory should follow. Zagha, Nankani, and Gill (2006) note that in several South American countries in the 1990s, trade liberalization failed to produce positive economic benefits and poverty reduction because rising exchange rates eroded export competitiveness. In other countries, such as China and India, trade liberalization that was better timed improved economic growth and reduced poverty.

Trade, Inequality, and the Poor

Open trade is good for overall economic growth (and, by extension, poverty reduction), but what effect does it have on inequality? Trade liberalization tends to reduce monopoly rents and the value of personal connections with bureaucrats and politicians, thereby reining in the rich. In developing countries, it may be expected to increase the relative wages of low-skilled workers, who are likely to be scarcer in the world economy than at home. Multilateral liberalization of agricultural trade may increase rural incomes but expose urban dwellers to higher food prices. And, in many countries, trade openness may have adjustment costs with which the poor are ill-equipped to cope. The relationship between trade and inequality is complex.

Trade reform in developing countries took off in the late 1970s. Until then, developing countries had pursued inward-looking policies by promoting import-substituting industrialization strategies. The aim was to encourage domestic production and restrict foreign investment by multinational firms to support the growth of domestic firms. But not only do inward-looking policies create many distortions, as noted above, they also tend to benefit relatively rich and powerful groups at the expense of the poor (Dollar 2004).

Since the late 1970s, developing countries have become more integrated with the world economy through foreign trade, foreign investment, and immigration. Integration has been driven by technological advances in transport and communication and by deliberate policy changes. China's ratio of trade to national income has more than doubled since it opened to the world in the early 1980s, and countries such as Bangladesh, India, Mexico, and Thailand have seen large increases as well.

While the popular press is almost uniform in its view that trade reform is bad for the poor, economists paint a completely different picture. While the relationship between trade and inequality remains unclear, the relationship between trade and growth is strong and positive, as we have seen, meaning that trade is most definitely pro-poor. According to Dollar and Kraay (2001b), increased trade generally accompanies rapid growth, while having no effect on inequality (measured as the income share of the poorest). Thus, increased trade translates into proportionate increases in the income of the poor and goes hand in hand with improvements in the well-being of the poor. This finding is also borne out by Berg and Krueger (2002), who point out that although the vast literature on the effects of trade liberalization on income distribution reveals no systematic relationship between openness and the income of the poorest, the positive effect of openness on overall growth and, in turn, on poverty, is firmly supported.

In support of the pro-poor argument for trade, Dollar (2004) identifies positive trends in growth rates and poverty reduction that followed trade liberalization starting from 1980.

Poor country growth rates have accelerated (developing countries on average grew 3.5 percent per capita in the 1990s and 6.4 percent in the first seven years of the present decade [IMF 2008]) and are higher than rich country growth rates for the first time in modern history. The number of poor people in the world has declined significantly (by 375 million since 1981), and the share of the developing world population living on $1 a day or less has declined by 50 percent since 1981. To what extent can these developments be ascribed to trade? Trends toward faster growth and poverty reduction have been strongest in those developing countries that have embraced trade liberalization.

In contrast to this generally positive picture, there are reasons that trade reform may not benefit the very poorest members of developing countries. The following paragraphs, based on Bannister and Thugge (2001), deal with the possible impacts of trade liberalization on the welfare of the poor.

Trade liberalization normally increases real income by reducing the prices of imports and of substitutes for imported goods. In general, this is seen to have a positive impact on the poor. Imported products such as basic foods, pharmaceuticals, other medical supplies, and used clothing are important for the poor. Moreover, the poor may benefit from the removal of export taxes to the extent that they are net producers of exports, which is often the case in agriculture, for example. An open trade regime improves access to new products and the importation of new technologies and processes that may have positive effects for the poor.

The effect of trade liberalization on wages and employment depends on the level of labor regulation in the country. In a highly regulated labor market, the adjustment to changes in the prices of outputs will translate into changes in real wages. If firms are constrained from reducing their workforces, wages will decline. Where minimum wages prevail and labor mobility is high, the adjustment will take place through changes in employment. Generally, however, the poor work in rural and informal urban sectors that are unregulated and are characterized by flexible labor markets. Here, adjustment to trade shocks will take place through changes in employment rather than in wages. In other words, the poor will suffer higher rates of unemployment. Furthermore, if the impact of trade liberalization is to remove protective barriers from sectors in which the poor predominate, we would expect a lowering of relative wages for the poor. Examples from Latin America (Ravallion and Chen 2004) suggest that trade liberalization has increased wage disparities, benefiting higher income groups more than the poor.

There are concerns that trade reform, by lowering trade taxes, will lead to lower government revenues in the short run. This, in turn, will lead to lower government spending in sectors such as health and education and a decrease in the welfare of the poor. But this concern is unsubstantiated. It is likely, in fact, that reform as actually practiced will raise government revenue by replacing nontariff barriers with tariffs and eliminating tariff exemptions. Moreover, lowering high tariffs may reduce the incentives for smuggling and corruption and therefore increase the amount of goods recorded at customs. Finally, simplifying the tariff regime and thereby promoting transparency may boost fiscal revenue.

In the long run, however, lower tariffs may lead to lower government revenues. In that case, policies to increase revenue—tax reform or spending cuts in other areas—may be needed to minimize the adverse effect of revenue losses on the poor.

Trade liberalization brings about a more efficient allocation of resources that favors economic growth—and, as we have seen, economic growth is one of the best ways to alleviate poverty. Sustaining that growth, however, requires complementary macroeconomic and institutional reforms that are discussed below.

Trade liberalization deepens economic integration. Although integration brings many benefits—such as less dependency on a single export market or product, and less dependency on the domestic market—adverse external shocks can significantly affect economic growth and the welfare of the poor by affecting the sectors in which they are employed.

Thus, it is important that other macroeconomic reforms should be pursued in line with trade reform to maximize and sustain the beneficial effect of trade reform on poverty. For example, if the country's exchange rate is overvalued, policy makers may choose to implement changes to improve competitiveness and avoid impeding the additional growth that would otherwise be possible as a result of trade liberalization.

Most economists agree that the adjustment costs of proposed trade reforms may be high in some countries—and may affect the poor disproportionately. In other words, any reform plan will create some losers among the poor, especially in the short run, as well as many winners. But a transitory loss in income has a deeper impact on the poor than on other citizens and can reduce their chances of escaping poverty. Because the poor are disproportionately vulnerable, trade liberalization policies should include a social safety net.

What poor people lose from trade reform in the short term they may recover later on; in the long run, most researchers agree that changes in investment and technology will lead to higher growth that will benefit the poor. Ravallion and Chen (2004), who found that periods of greater trade liberalization in China did not coincide with periods of poverty reduction, concluded that, over time, trade reform would produce both gainers and losers and that long-run productivity gains would have a positive impact on growth and poverty reduction.

To make trade liberalization more egalitarian, Bannister and Thugge (2001) argue for *broad-based liberalization*, so that the costs of adjustment are spread across a wide range of sectors. It may be necessary to sequence reform at different speeds for different sectors. Furthermore, *exchange-rate flexibility* will facilitate a faster adjustment to trade reform and dissipate reform-related shocks throughout the economy. As already mentioned, trade reform will have a more positive impact if it is accompanied by *other reforms*. The authors identify three areas in particular—infrastructure development, development of markets, and labor mobility and training.

Rich countries can help developing countries achieve and benefit from trade liberalization. The requirements for joining and settling disputes within the World Trade Organization are onerous for poor countries. Meanwhile, the advanced economies maintain extensive and expensive programs of protection for domestic producers, especially in agriculture and labor-intensive products.

In high-income countries, subsidies of various sorts account for nearly one-third of agriculture revenue. The subsidies provided to developed-country farmers amount to some $350 billion per year, almost five times the aid that developed countries send to the developing world. Most agricultural subsidies are provided through mechanisms that artificially boost production and undercut the market for farmers in developing countries. The group known as the West Africa 4 (Benin, Burkina Faso, Chad, and Mali) can produce high-quality cotton at the lowest cost in the world. Despite their productive efficiency, however, the West Africa 4 lag far behind the world's largest producer, the United States, where cotton is heavily subsidized. This leads to paradoxical results. Because of cotton subsidies, which cost the United States up to $4 billion each year, Mali loses $43 million in cotton earnings each year, while receiving $37 million in U.S. aid. As the production of cotton supports 10 million people in West Africa, but just 25,000 farmers in the United States, protectionist policies seriously impair poverty-reduction strategies by depriving farmers in developing countries of their livelihood. Sugar and dairy subsidies provided by the European Union (EU) have the same effect.

In recent years, the apparent unwillingness of the advanced economies to modify protection programs has lowered the incentive for developing countries to pursue multilateral trade liberalization or to undertake unilateral reform. Disputes over this issue led to the collapse of the most recent round of multilateral trade talks in 2003, the Doha Round. The impasse is not likely to be resolved soon. With multilateral progress stalled, the growth of regional trade agreements has proceeded. Such agreements offer many benefits to individual blocs of countries but are not a substitute for further multilateral liberalization.

Conclusion

Trade openness has been an unequivocally positive development for the poor in developing countries. Evidence on the relationship between trade development and inequality, on the other hand, is plentiful but inconclusive. Nevertheless, it is clear that trade is good for growth and that growth is good for the poor, particularly in the long term. To work best, policies that open a country to trade must be sequenced properly and accompanied by complementary reforms, so that the growth benefits of opening to trade can be maximized.

Advanced countries have a role to play in helping developing countries reap the benefits of trade. Trade subsidies provided to agricultural producers in advanced countries are distortionary and hurt poorer countries. Their harmful effects far outweigh the amount of aid typically provided by donor countries. As the same time, it is also fair to say that trade distortions within poorer countries themselves are also highly damaging. Further progress is needed in this area if the full growth potential of international trade is to be realized.

Bibliography

Bannister, Geoffrey J., and Kamau Thugge. 2001. "International Trade and Poverty Alleviation." *Finance and Development* 38 (4): 48–51.

Berg, Andrew, and Anne Krueger. 2002. "Lifting All Boats: Why Openness Helps Curb Poverty." *Finance and Development* 39 (2): 16–19.

———. 2003. "Trade, Growth, and Poverty: A Selected Survey." IMF Working Paper WP/03/30, International Monetary Fund, Washington, DC.

Claessens, S., and R. C. Duncan, eds. 1993. *Managing Commodity Price Risk in Developing Countries*. Baltimore, MD: Johns Hopkins University Press.

Corden, W. M. 1990. "Protection, Liberalization, and Macroeconomic Policy." In *Trade Liberalization in the 1990s*, ed. H. W. Singer, N. Hatti, and R. Tandon. New Delhi: Indus Publishing.

Dollar, D. 2004. "Globalization, Poverty, and Inequality since 1980." Policy Research Working Paper 3333, World Bank, Washington, DC.

Dollar, D., and A. Kraay. 2001a. "Growth Is Good for the Poor." Policy Research Working Paper 2587, World Bank, Washington, DC.

———. 2001b. "Trade, Growth, and Poverty." Policy Research Working Paper 2615. World Bank, Washington, DC.

———. 2006. "Trade, Growth, and Poverty." *Finance and Development* 38 (3): 16–19.

Findlay, Ronald, and Kevin H. O'Rourke. 2003. "Commodity Market Integration, 1500–2000." In *Globalization in Historical Perspective*, ed. M. D. Bordo, A. M. Taylor, and J. G. Williamson. Chicago: University of Chicago Press.

Frankel, Jeffrey A., and David Romer. 1999. "Does Trade Cause Growth?" *American Economic Review* 89 (June): 379–99.

Gourinchas, Pierre-Olivier, and Olivier Jeanne. 2003. "The Elusive Gains from International Financial Integration." NBER Working Paper 9684, National Bureau of Economic Research, Cambridge, MA.

IMF (International Monetary Fund). 2008. *World Economic Outlook. Financial Stress, Downturns and Recoveries*. Washington, DC: IMF.

Krueger, A. 2004. "Expanding Trade and Unleashing Growth: The Prospects for Lasting Poverty Reduction." IMF Seminar on Trade and Regional Integration, Dakar, Senegal, December 6.

Nash, John, and Donald Mitchell. 2005. "How Freer Trade Can Help Feed the Poor." *Finance and Development* 42 (1): 34–37.

O'Rourke, Kevin H., and Jeffrey G. Williamson. 2002. "From Malthus to Olin: Trade, Growth, and Distribution Since 1500." Working Paper 8955, National Bureau of Economic Research, Cambridge, MA.

Ravallion, M., and S. Chen. 2004. "How Have the World's Poor Fared Since the Early 1980s?" Policy Research Working Paper 3341, World Bank, Washington, DC.

Rodriguez, F., and D. Rodrik. 2000. "Trade Policy and Economic Growth: A Skeptic's Guide to the Cross-National Evidence." In *NBER Macro Annual 2000*, ed. Ben Bernanke and Kenneth Rogoff. Cambridge, MA: National Bureau of Economic Research.

Srinivasan, T. N., and J. Bhagwati. 1999. "Outward Orientation and Development: Are Revisionists Right?" Unpublished paper, Economic Growth Center, Yale University, New Haven, CT.

Watkins, K. 2002. "Making Globalization Work for the Poor." *Finance and Development* 39(1): 24–27.

Winters, L. A., N. McCulloch, and A. McKay. 2004. "Trade Liberalization and Poverty: The Empirical Evidence So Far." *Journal of Economic Literature* 42: 73–166.

World Bank. 2002. *Development, Trade, and the WTO: A Handbook*. Washington, DC: World Bank.

———. 2003. *Global Economic Prospects 2004: Realizing the Development Promise of the Doha Agenda*. Washington, DC: World Bank.

———. 2004. *Global Economic Prospects 2005: Trade, Regionalism, and Development*. Washington, DC: World Bank.

Zagha, R., G. Nankani, and I. Gill. 2006. "Rethinking Growth." *Finance and Development* 43 (1): 7–11.

PART III

Factor Accumulation and Structural Policy

CHAPTER 10

Institutions and Growth

At their most fundamental, institutions are the *formal* and *informal* rules and norms that govern economic, social, and political life. Occupying a broad spectrum from the establishment of rules to "actual organizational entities, procedural devices, and regulatory frameworks" (IMF 2003), they provide the predictability needed for societies and markets to function. Institutions can be more or less effective in facilitating exchange, production, and market operations. Studies have shown that institutional quality strongly affects growth—and that institutions are very difficult to change.

Although institutions perform similar functions across societies, the *form* they take in doing so varies considerably. Unfortunately, very little of the empirical work done to date on the importance of institutions examines the link between institutional form and performance. Researchers have instead focused on the link between institutional performance and economic performance.[1] This is important, but it does not tell us how to improve institutional performance and so, in turn, foster economic growth. We do know, however, that adopting in one country the laws and formal regulations of another will not necessarily produce the same institutional performance or, indeed, economic performance. The Washington Consensus that held sway in the 1980s suggested that developing countries would improve their fiscal position by liberalizing their banking systems, reforming and privatizing state enterprises, and reforming tax structures.[2] The success of these policy prescriptions depended, however, on the presence of a complex set of properly functioning institutions. Developing countries that lacked the necessary regulatory and legal frameworks, backed by government policies and commitment—in effect, good governance—ended up in far worse macroeconomic positions after implementing the reforms prescribed by the Washington Consensus.

An important focus of the recent literature on institutional economics is the link between good governance and economic growth and development.[3] This builds on neoclassical economic theory to examine the relationship between buyers and sellers. Every transaction between a buyer and seller carries costs, including uncertainty about the honesty and reliability of one's counterpart and efforts to reduce that uncertainty. "Institutions are formed to reduce uncertainty in human exchange," observes Douglass North (1990). "Together with the technology employed," North continues, institutions "determine the costs of transacting (and producing)."[4] The presence of institutions not only reduces transaction costs but also allows markets for the exchange of goods and services to grow in size and scope.

Unwritten rules—social customs, norms, and religious practices—are informal institutions. Slow to change and enforced by various groups within society, they represent the first level of Williamson's (2000) six-level classification and hierarchy of institutions (figure 10.1). Formal rules, on the other hand, are written into constitutions and laws and enforced by the state. These are political institutions in Williamson's hierarchy. They, too, are slow to change, but not as slow as informal institutions. Legal institutions—many designed to minimize uncertainty—are the fourth level. Examples are institutions that govern market-oriented economic activities, such as stock markets and securities regulators.

In recent years, considerable literature has evolved around the links among economic growth, development, and institutions. Driving this literature has been empirical evidence suggesting that cross-country differences in income are correlated with differences in indicators of institutional quality (figure 10.2).[5] The following section examines measures of institutional quality relating to the perceptions and assessments of public institutions. The chapter concludes with a brief overview of the link between institutions and economic growth.

Figure 10.1   The Williamson Hierarchy of Institutions

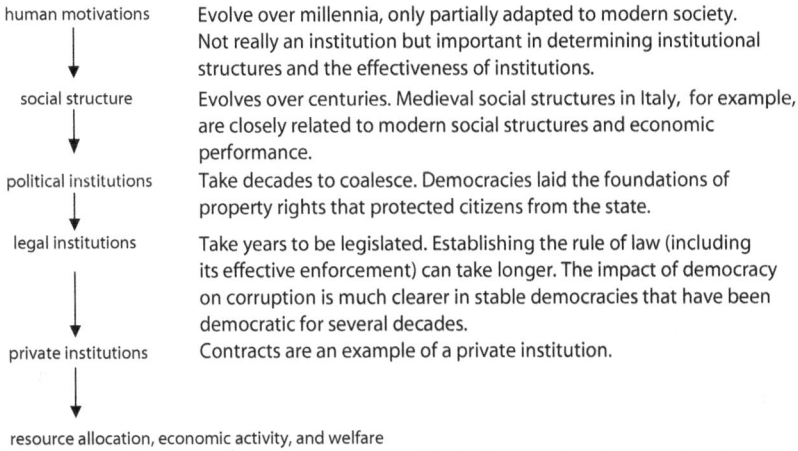

----

human motivations
↓
 Evolve over millennia, only partially adapted to modern society. Not really an institution but important in determining institutional structures and the effectiveness of institutions.

social structure
↓
 Evolves over centuries. Medieval social structures in Italy, for example, are closely related to modern social structures and economic performance.

political institutions
↓
 Take decades to coalesce. Democracies laid the foundations of property rights that protected citizens from the state.

legal institutions
↓
 Take years to be legislated. Establishing the rule of law (including its effective enforcement) can take longer. The impact of democracy on corruption is much clearer in stable democracies that have been democratic for several decades.

private institutions
 Contracts are an example of a private institution.
↓

resource allocation, economic activity, and welfare

Source: Williamson 2000; Azfar 2002.

Figure 10.2   Link between Institutional Quality and Per Capita National Income

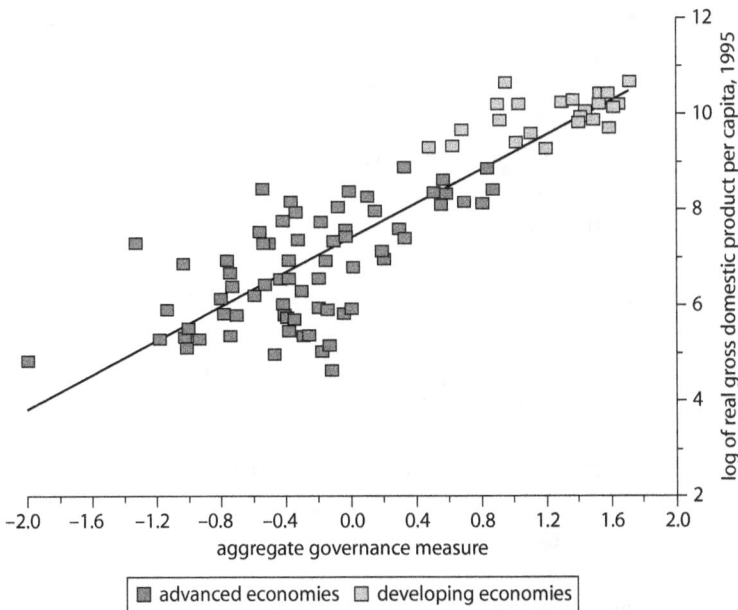

Source: IMF 2003.
Note: Aggregate governance measure represents the overall quality of governance, including the degree of corruption, political rights, public sector efficiency, and regulatory burdens.

Measures of Institutional Quality

In the literature on economics and political science, the concept of institutional quality has been translated into attempts to measure the quality of governance.

Ways of measuring governance have been explored and developed in depth by the World Bank in recent years. The main instrument being used is the country diagnostic study, which tabulates the results of in-depth, country-specific surveys of thousands of public-service users, firms, and public officials to gather specific information about institutional vulnerabilities in a country. The surveys gather information on various dimensions of governance, chiefly corruption in four forms: in the obtaining of services; in public procurement; in the budget process; and in the shaping of the formation of policy, legal, and regulatory frameworks. The latter dimension, also known as "state capture," has occupied a particularly central place in studies of governance in the countries of the former Soviet Union.

Six dimensions of *governance* appear repeatedly in the literature. These are (a) voice and accountability, (b) political stability and absence of violence, (c) government effectiveness, (d) regulatory quality, (e) rule of law, and (f) control of corruption (Kaufmann, Kraay, and Mastruzzi 2007).[6]

Measures of *voice* and *accountability* attempt to gauge the participation of the various strata of a population and how accountable the political regime is to the needs and wishes of its people. Among these measures are various aspects of the political process—notably civil liberties, political rights, and media independence (because independent news sources monitor those in authority and hold them accountable for their actions). Voice and accountability are cornerstones of the emerging literature on social accountability, which seeks to improve the responsiveness of government and other power holders to the needs of the governed—especially those whose voice is weak or obscured. Data on voice and accountability are collected by the World Bank to facilitate cross-country comparisons and changes over time and across countries.

Figure 10.3 examines the percentile ranking of regions for voice and accountability between 1996 and 2008. The Organisation for Economic Co-operation and Development (OECD), the Caribbean, and Eastern Europe and the Baltic states score highest for this indicator of governance, with almost a 30 percentage point difference between the top-scoring OECD and the next highest, the Caribbean. The countries of the former Soviet Union and the Middle East and North Africa score lowest. Eastern Europe and the Baltic states made the most progress

Figure 10.3   Regional Percentile Rank for Voice and Accountability

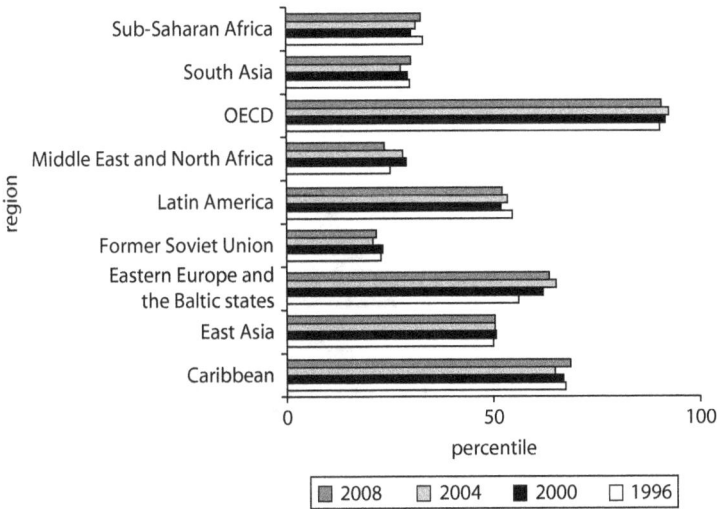

Source: Compiled from Worldwide Governance Indicators (http://info.worldbank.org/governance/wgi/index.asp).

over the 12 years, and East Asia experienced the least amount of change in its percentile rankings.

Political stability, the second of the six common dimensions of governance, captures a population's perception of the stability of its government. The perceived likelihood that the incumbent government could be overthrown by violent or unconstitutional means compromises stability, as does uncertainty about the ability of a country's citizens to peacefully elect and replace those in power. The ability of political and economic institutions to coordinate and to promote stability determines capital accumulation, investment in new technologies, and, thus, economic growth and poverty reduction.

Political stability is weakest in countries wracked by conflict. Once a conflict ends, there is likely to be insecurity both at the household and macroeconomic levels. Conflict usually leaves behind armed civilian populations prone to violence (such as in Somalia and Sudan). At the macro level, whether the conflict has been resolved by military victory (Ethiopia, Uganda) or through a negotiated settlement (Cambodia, Mozambique), there are significant risks that the government may not survive for long.

Figure 10.4 examines the regional percentile rankings for political stability. The top-ranking regions are the same as those for voice and

Figure 10.4   Regional Percentile Rank for Political Stability

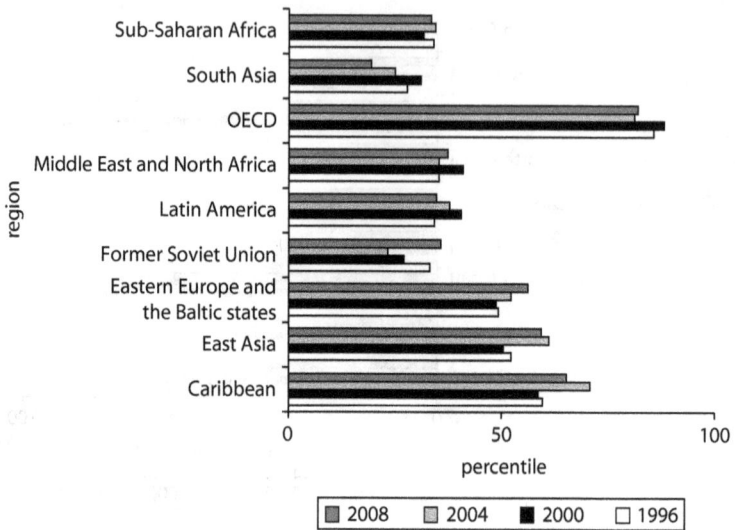

Source: Compiled from Worldwide Governance Indicators.

accountability, with East Asia replacing Eastern Europe and the Baltic states in third place. The percentile ranking for Middle East and North Africa, Sub-Saharan Africa, Latin America, and the countries of the former Soviet Union[7] changed little between 1996 and 2008. The percentile ranking for South Asia has deteriorated over time, while East Asia and the Caribbean have made the most progress toward political stability.

Government effectiveness, as a measure of governance, refers to the inputs that a government needs if it is to produce and implement sound policies and deliver public goods. The competence and independence of the civil service and the government's commitment to the development and implementation of sound policies are keys to effectiveness. An effective government is free of the pitfalls of the predatory state (rent seeking, corruption, theft, conflict, and the risk of expropriation). An effective government is *credible.*

Figure 10.5 examines the percentile rank by region for government effectiveness over the period 1996 to 2008. The OECD ranks highest with relatively little change over the period. The Caribbean, the countries of the former Soviet Union, and Eastern Europe and the Baltic states all improved their percentile rankings, with the countries of the former Soviet Union emerging from a very low base. South Asia and East Asia show a marked deterioration, as did Sub-Saharan Africa to a lesser degree.

Figure 10.5   Regional Percentile Rank for Government Effectiveness

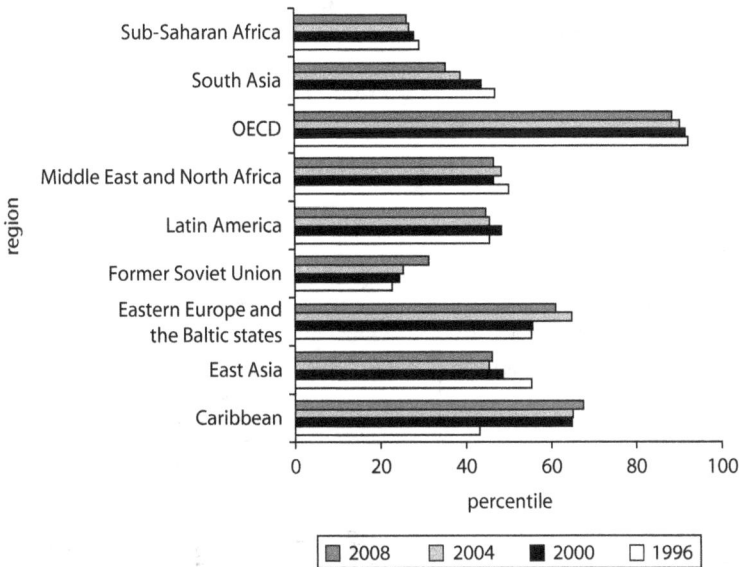

Source: Compiled from Worldwide Governance Indicators.

Regulatory quality refers to the policies developed and implemented by a government. Indexes of regulatory quality reflect how friendly government policies are to growth. Policies that promote red tape, excessive regulation, price controls, and inadequate supervision of the financial sector make for poor governance. They retard growth—if not immediately, then down the road.

Regional regulatory quality is examined in figure 10.6. Eastern Europe and the Baltic states, the Caribbean, and the countries of the former Soviet Union made the most progress in improving their ranking, the last from a low base. Latin America and South Asia declined over time; Middle East and North Africa and East Asia more or less maintained their rankings.

The *rule-of-law* indicator measures the extent to which economic and social interactions are governed by duly constituted, clearly articulated, and reliably enforced laws and regulations. Institutions that protect property rights (both from criminals and from the predatory power of the state) and enforce contracts promote the rule of law and allow economic activity to flourish. Democratic institutions—including an independent, well-trained judiciary and a well-codified legal system—promote freedom, scrutiny, and debate, which in turn reinforce the effectiveness (credibility) of government.

Figure 10.6   Regional Percentile Rank for Regulatory Quality

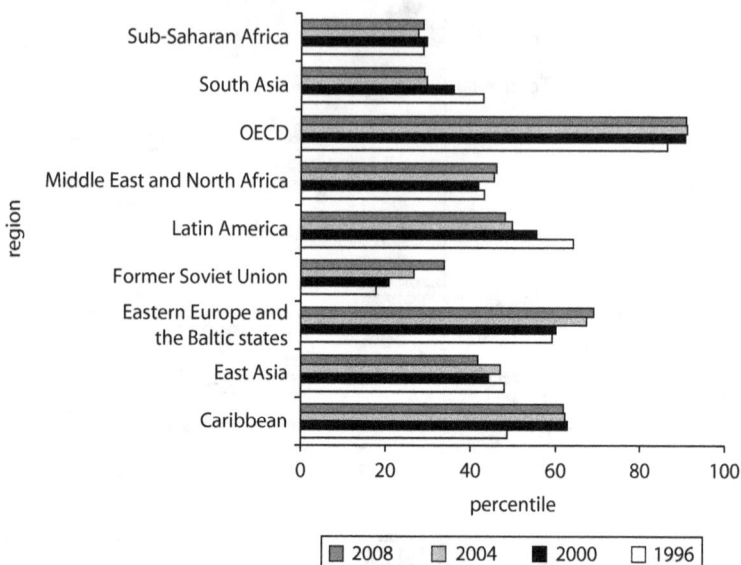

Source: Compiled from Worldwide Governance Indicators.

Figure 10.7   Regional Percentile Rank for Rule of Law

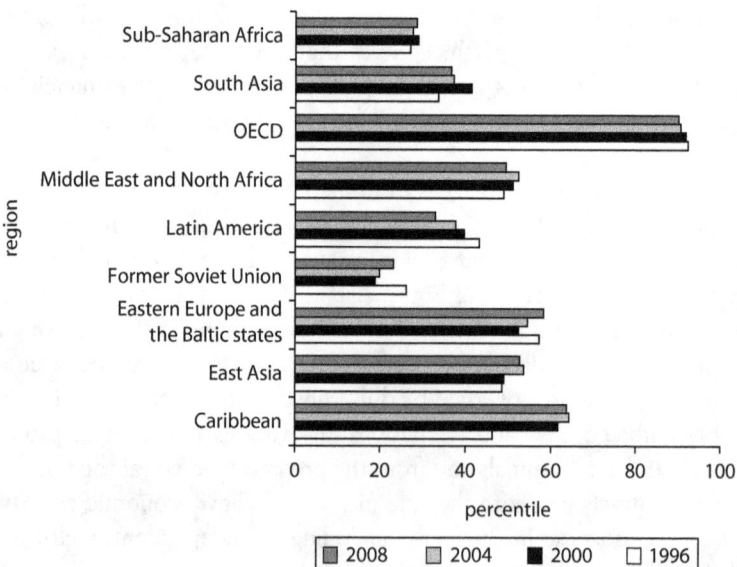

Source: Compiled from Worldwide Governance Indicators.

Percentile rankings for rule of law improved most noticeably for the Caribbean, East Asia, and South Asia when comparing 1996 with 2008. Latin America and the former Soviet countries slipped; Middle East and North Africa, Sub-Saharan Africa, and Eastern Europe and the Baltic states more or less maintained their rankings. These are examined in figure 10.7.

Secure property rights—the protections accorded to private property in a society—are critical to economic development. Without them, investment and trading incentives will be severely curtailed (De Soto 2000), with a deleterious effect on economic activity. Secure property rights have been achieved through a variety of arrangements. China's institutional arrangements differ greatly from those of India, for example. But in both countries, investors and entrepreneurs can be relatively confident of obtaining a return if they do their work well; that security creates a favorable backdrop for market activities and growth. Similarly, financial systems in the United States and the European Union (EU) have different institutional foundations, but both perform at comparable levels of efficiency. In Indonesia under the leadership of Haji Mohammed Suharto, by contrast, the enforcement of property rights depended on closeness to the ruling elite, with adverse consequences for investment and growth.

In many developing countries, the rule of law is spotty, ineffective, or absent. In such countries, private institutions and customs—for corporate governance, long-term relationships, dispute resolution, and information dissemination—have proliferated in place of formal public institutions. Even in countries with strong formal institutions—including legal systems—customary mechanisms may continue to function alongside formal ones. For example, disputes are typically resolved through arbitration and other methods, with the courts left as a last resort.

Measures of *corruption* have generated the most attention in the literature on governance and investment climate. Transparency International, a nongovernmental organization that has fought corruption since its inception in 1993, has become the key source for data and information on the level of corruption in developed and developing countries alike. Transparency International defines corruption as the "misuse of entrusted power for private gain," whether "according to rule" or "against the rule." So-called facilitation payments, whereby a bribe is paid to receive something that the receiver of the bribe is required to do by law, are an example of the former. A bribe paid to obtain services that the bribe receiver is prohibited from providing is an example of the latter.

The incidence of corruption varies widely from country to country and from region to region, according to the measures established by the

Figure 10.8   Regional Percentile Rank for Control of Corruption

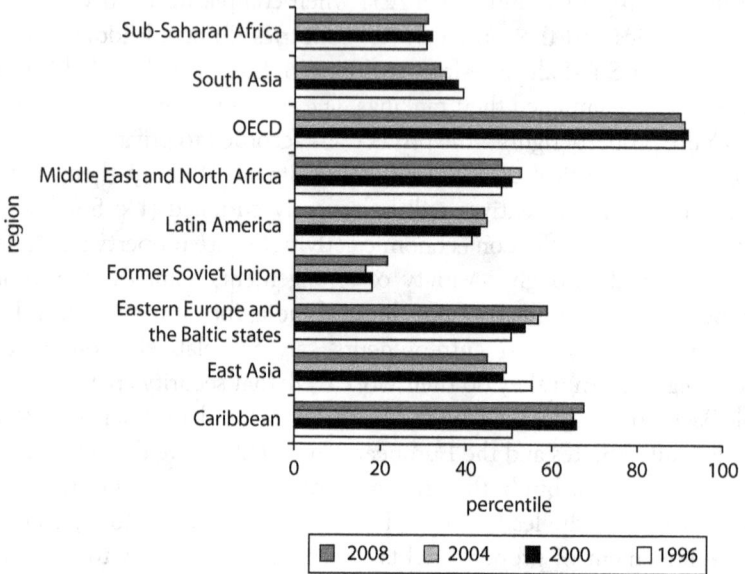

Source: Compiled from Worldwide Governance Indicators.

Governance Group at the World Bank Institute (figure 10.8). The Caribbean and Eastern Europe and the Baltic states have improved their percentile rankings for this indicator while the OECD, Middle East and North Africa, and Sub-Saharan Africa have changed little. Comparing the 1996 percentile score with that of 2008, South Asia and East Asia declined slightly, while Latin America improved.

Institutions and Economic Growth

Differences in the accumulation of economically important inputs such as natural resources, financial capital, and human capital explain some, but not all, of the observed variance in rates of economic growth across countries. Institutions explain much of the rest. A given set of inputs will produce different amounts of growth depending on the institutional filters through which it passes. The right institutions encourage appropriate policies both for the accumulation of inputs themselves (land, capital, and labor) and for developments that improve productivity (new technologies, managerial processes, education)—all of which affect growth.

There is ample evidence that good governance *causes* higher income growth. Edison and others (2002) suggest that improving institutional quality by one standard deviation in their sample would increase average annual growth in income per person by 1.4 percentage points. Rodrik and Subramanian (2003) find that the quality of institutions (measured by a composite that includes protection of property rights and rule of law) is the *only* significant determinant of income levels. If Bolivia and the Republic of Korea had the same institutional quality, they maintain, Bolivia's gross domestic product (GDP) per person would be close to $18,000, more than double its current level of $7,200. Acemoglu (2009) ascribes a key role to institutions (and policies) in determining whether an economy can embark on a growth path. Policies and institutions work together to

- determine society's reward structure, which shapes whether investments in human and physical capital and technological innovation are profitable;
- determine whether the infrastructure and contracting arrangements necessary for modern economic relations are present;
- influence and regulate market structure so that new firms come to the fore and replace less-efficient firms; and
- (sometimes) prevent the adoption of new technologies to protect politically powerful incumbents or stabilize the established political regime (Acemoglu, 2009).

Using an aggregate measure of governance, the International Monetary Fund's (IMF) *World Economic Outlook* (IMF 2003) finds that institutional quality explains almost three-quarters of cross-country variation in income per person. Figure 10.9 shows the benefits to Sub-Saharan Africa in particular of improving institutional quality from −0.49 to the average of developing Asia (−0.19), suggesting an 80 percent increase in its per capita income (from $800 to over $1,400). In fact, differences in GDP per person, the growth rate of GDP, and growth volatility across countries all appear to be closely correlated with indicators of institutional quality (table 10.1).

The level of inequality in a society, as expressed in and transmitted through social institutions, also affects growth, almost always in a negative way (box 10.1).

Improving institutional quality also has positive effects on economic volatility. The higher the quality of institutions, as measured by the

Figure 10.9   Correlation of Economic Performance and Institutional Quality

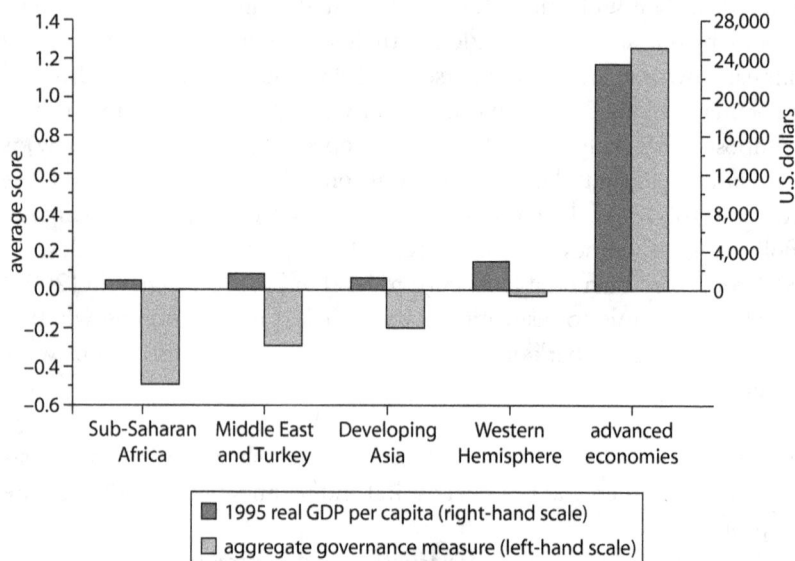

Source: IMF 2003.

Table 10.1   Correlation between Institutions and Economic Performance

Variable	GDP per capita[a]	Growth rate[b]	Growth volatility[c]	Aggregate governance measure[d]	Property rights	Constraint on power of executive
GDP per capita	1.00					
Growth rate	0.65	1.00				
Growth volatility	−0.53	−0.36	1.00			
Aggregate governance measure	0.86	0.59	−0.61	1.00		
Property rights	0.76	0.54	−0.62	0.79	1.00	
Constraint on power of executive	0.72	0.45	−0.64	0.73	0.63	1.00

Sources: Kaufmann, Kraay, and Zoido-Lobatón 1999; Heritage Foundation 2003; Gurr and Marshall 2000; and World Bank 2002.
Note: All correlations are significant at the 5 percent level.
a. Real GDP per capita in U.S. dollars in 1995.
b. Average annual growth rate of real GDP per capita for the period 1960–98.
c. Standard deviation of annual growth rate of real GDP per capita for 1960–98.
d. Aggregate institutional quality measure from Kaufmann, Kraay, and Zoido-Lobatón 1999.

Box 10.1

Inequality, Institutions, and Growth

History shapes the growth of institutions and economies, as well as the role of inequality in this process. In 1800, Argentina's per capita income was equivalent to that of the United States, whereas that of Brazil, Chile, Mexico, and Peru was between 40 and 50 percent of that of the United States. Two centuries later, Argentina's per capita income is one-fifth that of the United States; that of Brazil, Mexico, and Peru are one-fifth or less; and Chile's has remained at about the same relative level.

What accounts for this divergence in economic performance? The answer is that, somehow, the United States was able to create a far greater flow of economic opportunities; that is, access to economic, social, and political opportunities became much greater in the United States than in the other countries. Whereas less than 2 percent of the population of Argentina, Brazil, or Chile voted at the end of the 1800s, more than 10 percent voted in the United States, and the voter participation rate also increased much more rapidly. Three-fourths of the U.S. population owned land, whereas less than one-fifth did in Argentina, and fewer in Brazil. Access to education was similarly better distributed in the United States. Because population densities were much lower in the United States than elsewhere, there were fewer incentives to establish predatory institutions oriented toward extracting rents for the benefit of a small elite.

The conclusion is that, except in the United States and Canada, growth in former European colonies has been influenced by the concentration of economic and political power, which limited access to economic and social opportunities, created less secure property rights, and influenced the course of development for several centuries.

Recent examples of the interplay of institutions, economic growth, and inequality can be found in India. Maharashtra's less fertile western region has sugar cane yields superior to those achieved in the more fertile eastern region because land is more equally distributed there. In the eastern region, the wealthier owners control the sugar cooperatives and set low prices for the other members—thereby reducing incentives for increases in productivity. Another example comes from the Indian state of West Bengal, where tenancy reform in the late 1970s increased the share of output that tenants could retain and strengthened tenancy rights. A sharp increase in yields ensued.

Source: Authors.

aggregate governance measure used in the IMF's (2003) *World Economic Outlook,* the lower the volatility of growth. In the standard growth model used in the *World Economic Outlook,* economic growth measured by the annual average growth rate of GDP per capita is regressed on initial levels of income and schooling to capture the effects of institutions on cross-country growth differentials. Institutional quality is proxied by governance measures and financial development. Improving institutional quality by one standard deviation implies an increase in average annual growth in GDP of 1.4 percentage points and a decrease in volatility of similar magnitude (-1.2 – percentage points). What lies behind the strong correlation of economic growth and institutional quality? One would expect that strong economic performance induces institutional change. Countries with positive growth records are more likely to strengthen their financial and real markets by improving underlying legal and regulatory frameworks. Thus, institutions are endogenous to economic growth. Endogeneity indicates reverse causality—that is, good institutions stimulate growth, and growth encourages the development of good institutions.

Economic policies have important consequences for institutional quality, and vice versa. Openness to trade, stronger competition, and greater transparency are positively associated with institutional quality (Islam and Montenegro 2002; IMF 2003). Consider the positive effect of the EU accession process on institutions in Central and Eastern Europe. Rodrik and Subramanian (2003) find that globalization and international trade also have a positive impact on institutional quality overall.

The success of policies, in turn, depends on the quality of institutions—policies aimed at improving human capital and trade openness are unlikely to be as effective if underlying institutions (political and other) are weak.

Turning to the possible exogenous factors that influence institutional quality, we see that literature has concentrated on "the role played by geographical and historical influences on institutional formation" (IMF 2003).

The effect of these exogenous factors on institutional quality is not conclusive—the success of institutional quality is not a given based on a country's geography or history—although causal links have been found. Geographical factors such as a country's location and its resource endowments are known determinants of economic growth—and institutions are a key intermediary between economic performance and the geographic factors of latitude, distance from main markets, climatic conditions, and resource endowments.

The evolution of institutions and institutional quality has been linked in recent years to historical factors such as settlement and colonization. Acemoglu (2009) suggests that in Australia, Canada, the United States, and other "new worlds" where people settled in large numbers, institutional developments encouraged participative approaches to economic activity that favored innovation, growth, and investment. On the other hand, where settlement was more confined and power rested in the hands of an elite, institutional developments revolved around maintaining that power, which hampered economic growth. Some of the work in this area (see Acemoglu [2009] for references) has considered the legal framework bequeathed by different colonial masters to suggest that common law is more conducive to the development of good institutions than civil law.

Social Capital and Culture

The World Bank defines social capital as a feature of both government and civil society that facilitates collective action for the mutual benefit of a group, whether a household, village, community, province, or country. It includes knowledge, skills, and informal institutions (Dasgupta 2002). Other economists separate the social capital inherent in the government from civic social capital (or culture). The first category includes institutions that support the enforcement of contracts, the rule of law, and the protection of civil liberties.

Government social capital is usually quantified by economic freedom (for example, as measured by the Heritage Foundation index), the political and civil rights index (Gastil 1990), and the Worldwide Governance Indicators generated by Daniel Kaufmann and his team at the World Bank Institute.

Civil social capital, by contrast, encompasses common values, attitudes, and beliefs, including social norms, informal networks, and local associations that affect the ability of individuals to work together to achieve common goals. Savings and credit associations, irrigation management systems, credit cooperatives, and civic associations are also defined as social capital—a productive asset. Other examples may include extended kinship, lobbying organizations, and hierarchical relationships such as those associated with patronage (for example, the Hindu *jajmani* system, the Sicilian Mafia, and even street gangs).

The impact of social capital on welfare may be positive or negative. For example, Olson and Norton (1996) suggest that social capital within one group generally has negative effects on other groups and on a country as a whole. In contrast, Putnam (1993) takes the view that social capital held by one group has positive effects on all groups, because cooperation among members of a group forms habits of serving the greater good that carry over to members' interactions with nonmembers. Most of the evidence supports the hypothesis that social capital, measured at the national level, is associated with improved economic welfare of societies, as measured by growth, investment, and poverty indicators.

Weil (2005) looks at individual aspects of culture, such as openness to new ideas, belief in the value of hard work, saving for the future, and mutual trust. Weil finds that Japan's openness to new ideas and willingness to adopt foreign technology helped the country catch up with Europe and the United States after World War II, whereas India and China were unwilling to adopt new ideas until much later. Weil regrets the absence of data to test this notion.

Asian countries generally have higher savings rates, possibly because Confucianism, Buddhism, and Hinduism all teach moderation in life. But despite high savings, India languished at a low rate of growth for decades (the so-called Hindu rate of growth of less than 2 percent) because of investment policies that were inefficient and unproductive.

Interpersonal trust (as defined by Fukuyama 1995) can affect economic performance by reducing transaction costs, making contracts more effective and secure and improving individuals' access to credit (Greif 1993; Zak and Knack 2001). Trust may also be considered a substitute or complement for the courts and the rule of law. Putnam (1993) demonstrated strong relationships in the regions of Italy between civic community and government performance, and between civic community and citizen satisfaction with government. Helliwell and Putnam (1995) rigorously tested Putnam's (1993) hypothesis on the role of social capital in economic performance by focusing on three alternative indicators of regional social capital—citizen satisfaction, an index of regional government performance, and an index of civic community. They found all three to be positively and significantly related to growth from 1950 to 1990, controlling for initial per capita income. Narayan and Pritchett (1999), by analyzing statistics on household expenditure and social engagements in a sample of some 50 villages in Tanzania, found that households in villages that participated in village-level social organizations on average enjoyed greater income per capita.

Conclusion

This chapter provided a brief overview of how economists think about institutions. In the broadest sense, institutions include the informal rules and norms that govern personal and social behavior, as well as the formal rules and norms that provide the predictability needed for societies to function. Our investigation focused on governance—a multifaceted concept that includes the notions of voice and accountability, political stability, government effectiveness, regulatory quality, rule of law, and control of corruption. We then discussed empirical evidence of how the quality of institutions has a strong impact on economic growth.

Notes

1. In practical terms, a large proportion of the work on institutions and economic growth has focused on measuring how well public institutions function and their impact on private sector behavior.

2. The Washington Consensus is a term coined by the economist John Williamson in 1989 to describe a set of 10 policy prescriptions that he felt should guide the Washington-based international financial institutions as well as the U.S. Treasury when dealing with crisis-wracked countries.

3. The new institutional economics "examines the effects of institutions (rules and rule enforcement) on the behavior of rational individuals in environments with uncertainty and other transactions costs, and examines the consequences of this behavior in terms of individual and collective welfare." (Azfar 2002).

4. North identifies Ronald Coase (1937, 1960) as the scholar who connected institutions, transaction costs, and neoclassical theory.

5. The evidence for this statement is presented later in this chapter.

6. Interactive data-based tools (available at http://www.worldbank.org/wbi/governance/data) allow users to compare countries and world regions on each of these dimensions.

7. Despite a drop in its percentile rank in 2004.

Bibliography

Abed, G., and S. Gupta, eds. 2002. *Governance, Corruption, and Economic Performance.* Washington, DC: International Monetary Fund.

Acemoglu, D. 2009. *Introduction to Modern Economic Growth.* Princeton, NJ: Princeton University Press.

Acemoglu, Daron, Simon Johnson, and James A. Robinson. 2002. "Reversal of Fortune: Geography and Institutions in the Making of the Modern World Income Distribution." *Quarterly Journal of Economics* 117 (November): 1231–94.

Azfar, O. 2002. *The NIE Approach to Economic Development: An Analytic Primer.* Washington, DC: World Bank.

Clark, Gregory. 1987. "Why Isn't the Whole World Developed? Lessons from the Cotton Mills." *Journal of Economic History* 47 (1): 141–73.

Coase, R. H. 1937. "The Nature of the Firm." *Economica* 4 (16): 386–405.

———. 1960. "The Problem of Social Cost." *Journal of Law and Economics* 3 (October): 1–44.

Collier, P., and A. Hoeffler. 2005. "Resource Rents, Governance and Conflict." *Journal of Conflict Resolution* 49 (4): 625–33.

Dasgupta, P. 2002. "Social Capital and Economic Performance: Analytics." University of Cambridge and Beijer International Institute of Ecological Economics, Stockholm, mimeo.

De Soto, Hernando. 2000. *The Mystery of Capital: Why Capitalism Triumphs in the West and Fails Everywhere Else.* New York: Basic Books.

Easterly, William. 1999. "Life during Growth." *Journal of Economic Growth* 4 (3): 239–76.

Edison, Hali, Michael Klein, Luca Ricci, and Torsten Sløk. 2002. "Capital Account Liberalization and Economic Performance: Survey and Synthesis." NBER Working Paper 9100, National Bureau of Economic Research, Cambridge, MA.

Ferguson, Niall. 2003. *Empire: The Rise and Demise of the British World Order and the Lessons for Global Power.* New York: Basic Books.

Fukuyama, Francis. 1995. "The Primacy of Culture." *Journal of Democracy* 6 (1): 7–14.

Gastil, R. D. 1990. "The Comparative Survey of Freedom: Experiences and Suggestions." *Studies in Comparative International Development* 25 (1): 25–50.

Greif, A. 1993. "Contract Enforceability and Economic Institutions in Early Trade: The Maghribi Traders." *American Economic Review* 83 (3): 525–48.

Gurr, Ted R., and Monty G. Marshall. 2000. *Polity IV Dataset.* Center for Systemic Peace, Severn, MD. http://www.cidcm.umd.edu/inscr/polity/.

Helliwell, John F., and Robert D. Putnam. 1995. "Economic Growth and Social Capital." *Eastern Economic Journal* 21 (3): 295–307.

Heritage Foundation. 2003. "Index of Economic Freedom." http://www.heritage.org/.

Hoff, K., and J. Stiglitz. 2001. "Modern Economic Theory and Development." In *Frontiers of Development Economics,* ed. G. Meier and J. Stiglitz. Oxford, U.K.: Oxford University Press.

IMF (International Monetary Fund). 2003. *World Economic Outlook.* Washington, DC: IMF.

Isham, Jonathan, Deepa Narayan, and Lant H. Pritchett. 1995. "Does Participation Improve Performance? Establishing Causality with Subjective Data." *World Bank Economic Review* 9 (May): 175–200.

Islam, Roumeen. 2000. "Institutions to Support Markets." *Finance and Development* 39 (1): 48–51.

Islam, Roumeen, and Claudio E. Montenegro. 2002. "What Determines the Quality of Institutions?" Policy Research Working Paper 2764. World Bank, Washington, DC.

Jorgenson, Dale. 1996. "Technology in Growth Theory." Conference Proceedings: Federal Reserve Bank of Boston (June): 45–89. Boston, MA: Federal Reserve Bank.

Kaufmann, D., A. Kraay, and Massimo Mastruzzi. 2007. "Governance Matters VI: Governance Indicators for 1996–2006." Policy Research Working Paper 4280, World Bank, Washington, DC.

Kaufmann, D., A. Kraay, and P. Zoido-Lobatón. 1999. "Aggregating Governance Indicators." Policy Research Working Paper 2195, World Bank, Washington, DC.

McKinsey Global Institute. 1993. *Manufacturing Productivity*. Washington, DC: McKinsey Global Institute.

Narayan, D., and L. Pritchett. 1999. "Cents and Sociability: Household Income and Social Capital in Rural Tanzania." *Economic Development and Cultural Change* 47 (2): 871–989.

North, Douglass C. 1990. *Institutions, Institutional Change, and Economic Performance*. Cambridge, U.K.: Cambridge University Press.

Olson, David M., and Philip Norton. 1996. "Legislatures in Democratic Transition." In *The New Parliaments of Central and Eastern Europe*, ed. David M. Olson and Philip Norton. London: Frank Cass.

Pinker, S. 1997. *How the Mind Works*. New York: Norton.

Putnam, R. 1993. *Making Democracy Work*. Princeton, NJ: Princeton University Press.

Ridley, M. 1998. *The Origins of Virtue: Human Instincts and the Evolution of Cooperation*. New York: Penguin.

Rodrik, D., and A. Subramanian. 2003. "The Primacy of Institutions." *Finance and Development* 40 (2): 31–34.

Rodrik, D., A. Subramanian, and F. Trebbi. 2002. *Institutions Rule: The Primacy of Institutions over Geography and Integration in Economic Development*. Cambridge, MA: Harvard University Press.

Sachs, Jeffrey D. 2003. "Institutions Don't Rule: Direct Effects of Geography on Per Capita Income." NBER Working Paper 9490, National Bureau of Economic Research, Cambridge, MA.

Weil, D. 2005. *Economic Growth*. New York: Addison-Wesley.

Williamson, O. 2000. "The New Institutional Economics: Taking Stock, Looking Ahead." *Journal of Economic Literature* 38 (3): 595–613.

World Bank. 2002. *World Development Indicators*. Washington, DC: World Bank.

World Economic Forum. 2006. *Information and Communication Technology and Competitiveness*. Davos, Switzerland.

Zak, P., and S. Knack. 2001. "Trust and Growth." *The Economic Journal* 111 (April): 295–321.

CHAPTER 11

Education

Education has a positive effect on economic growth and poverty reduction. Microeconomic literature has established a clear relationship between education (as measured in years of schooling) and income per capita. Education is also positively linked with technological adaptation, innovation, and increased productivity, which help generate economic growth. Yet for many of the world's poor, education remains unattainable.

Achieving universal primary education (UPE) by 2015 is one of the Millennium Development Goals (MDGs) adopted by the international community in 2000. Education for All (EFA), a related international initiative launched in 1990, goes further, committing the nations of the world to provide education for all of their citizens by the year 2015. Because education affects child and reproductive health and enhances human skill and capital, it is critical to the success of the other MDGs.

In this chapter, we examine educational progress in the developing world and the challenges that remain. We examine initiatives for achieving UPE, giving special attention to the financial resources needed to achieve this goal.

Education, Growth, and Poverty Reduction

Education directly benefits its recipients and improves society by increasing productivity, raising rates of innovation and invention, and enabling the adaptation of new technologies. Many developing countries have pursued UPE over the past several decades. Relevant global initiatives include:

- An international commitment, EFA, launched in Jomtien, Thailand, in 1990 to bring the benefits of education to "every citizen in every society." Partners comprised a broad coalition of national governments, civil society groups, and development agencies such as the United Nations Education, Scientific and Cultural Organization (UNESCO) and the World Bank.
- The reaffirmation of this commitment in Dakar, Senegal, in April 2000, and then again in September 2000, when 189 countries and their partners adopted two of the EFA aims within the MDGs, specifying that UPE was to be achieved by all countries by 2015.
- The EFA Fast-Track Initiative (FTI), launched in 2002 by the World Bank in partnership with developing countries and donors to accelerate progress toward UPE by 2015.

Researchers note that while educational attainment may be correlated with economic growth, this does not suggest a causal relationship. Higher overall rates of educational attainment hide disparities connected to family income, gender, and geographic location. Furthermore, rates are often exaggerated because of a high incidence of repeat students. Hence, other considerations such as the enrollment rate versus the completion rate, the quality of education, and the frequency and adequacy of testing and feedback are also important measures of education's effect on economic growth.

Hanushek and Kimko (2000) gathered international test scores in mathematics and science from 1960, formed these into a composite measure of school quality, and related this to differences in cross-country growth rates. They also included income level, years of schooling, and population growth in the model. All of the variables helped explain differences in growth rates—and the quality of schooling proved highly significant. One standard deviation difference in test performance correlated to a 1 percentage point difference in annual growth of gross domestic product (GDP) per capita (Hanushek 2005). Moreover, test scores as a measure of school quality are strongly linked to an individual's earnings and productivity—the higher an individual's test scores, the higher the earning advantage. Although developed countries have supplied most of the data, this relation appears to hold for developing economies as well (Hanushek 2005). The World Bank (2007b) concurs that educational quality, as measured by what people know, positively affects individual earning levels as well as economic growth and the distribution of income. Educational quality is directly related to school attainment.

While school quality and student performance provide a qualitative measure of education, the most common quantitative measure is the net primary enrollment rate (NER). NER is the ratio of the number of children in the official primary school age group enrolled in school to the total number of children in this age group. The NER for developed countries was 96 percent in 2006, a rate matched only by Latin America and the Caribbean among the developing regions (figure 11.1). Among developing regions, Sub-Saharan Africa had the lowest NER—just 71 percent compared to 96 percent for Latin America and the Caribbean. Figure 11.1 shows, however, that between 2000 and 2006, NER increased the most in Sub-Saharan Africa (a 13 percentage point increase) and South Asia (a 10 percentage point increase).

Figure 11.1   Net Primary Enrollment Rates by Region

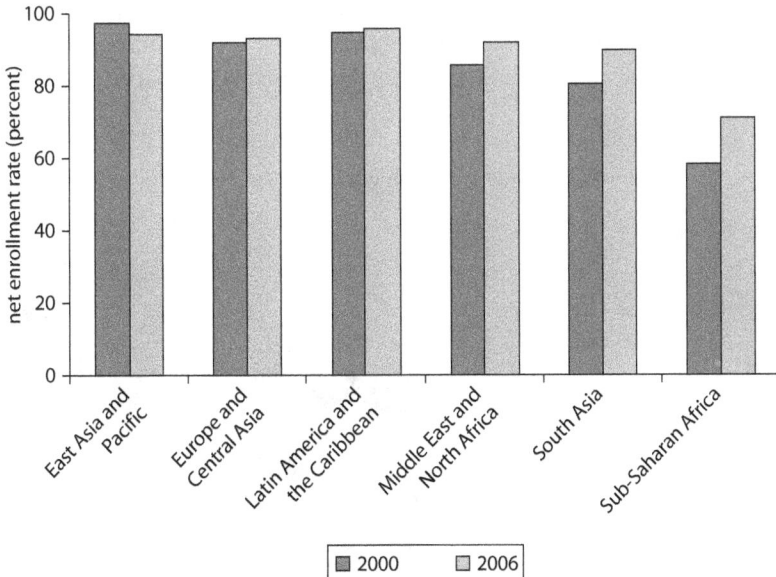

Source: World Bank 2007a.

A less strict standard than the NER is the gross enrollment rate (GER), which captures the ratio of the number of children enrolled in primary education—regardless of age—to the population of the nationally defined primary school age group.

For example, Africa's GER increased remarkably during the 1990s— from 73 percent in 1992 to 83 percent in 2000 and 91 percent in 2002, with partial data for more recent years confirming a continued increase (Fredriksen 2005). Given that 20 percent of students have to repeat grades, however, Africa would need a GER of 120 percent to enroll all children of primary school age (Fredriksen 2005).

Cohen and Bloom (2005) note other advances in school enrollment, including an increase in literacy among developing countries—from 25 to 75 percent in the 20th century—and an increase in average years of schooling, from 2.1 to 4.4 years. Furthermore, the number of students enrolled in secondary school increased from 50 million to 500 million in the past 50 years. Figure 11.2 depicts the average years of schooling completed in various regions.

Although overall enrollment rates have increased in developing countries, they remain subpar. Furthermore, enrollment does not guarantee attendance, and attendance is not necessarily a reliable predictor of education completion (figure 11.3) or high-quality education. Standardized test scores show a huge disparity between children from industrial countries and those from developing countries. The global commitment to achieve UPE as outlined in the MDGs and the even broader education

Figure 11.2   Average Educational Attainment by Region, 2000

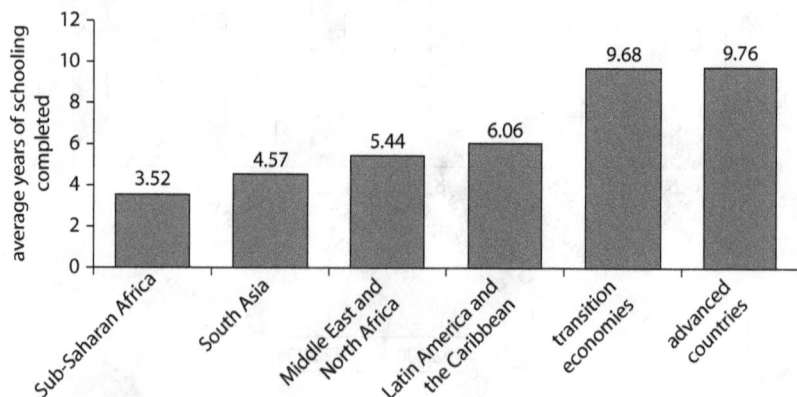

Source: Bruns, Mingat, and Rakotomalala 2003.

Figure 11.3   Primary School Enrollment and Completion Rates for Select Countries

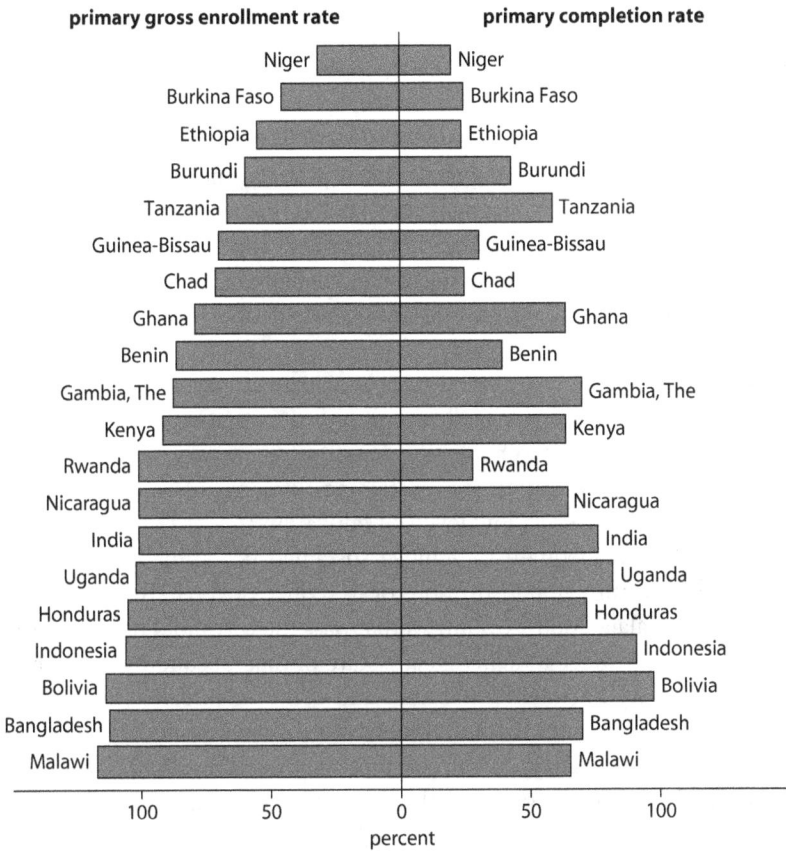

Source: Bruns, Mingat, and Rakotomalala 2003.

goals agreed to at the World Education Forum at Dakar, Senegal, in 2000, are responses to the present, unacceptable situation (Cohen and Bloom 2005; Sperling and Balu 2005). Facts to consider include the following:

- Over 100 million primary school age children are out of school
- Roughly 380 million children are not enrolled in school (28 percent of the primary school age group)
- Of school age children who enter primary school in developing countries, more than one in four drop out before attaining literacy
- Fewer than one-third of children in Africa and South Asia can read and write

- One in five children in primary school in Africa repeat a grade
- Of children enrolled, 150 million are likely to drop out before completing primary school
- More than half of all girls in Africa never enroll in school.

The research on inequality and education is strongly established; illiteracy is one of the strongest predictors of poverty, and unequal access to educational opportunity strongly correlates to income inequality (Bruns, Mingat, and Rakotomalala 2003). O'Connell and Birdsall (2001) and Birdsall and Londoño (1998) suggest that inequality in education has a strong negative effect on growth, independent of education levels and other factors.[1]

Improving school completion rates is of critical importance for developing countries (figure 11.3). Research indicates that completion of five to six years of primary school—the length of a primary school cycle in most countries—is critical to sustaining lifelong literacy and basic numeric skills. Moreover, low levels of education (fewer than six years of schooling) are inadequate to achieve sustained economic development and stable governmental institutions or to reduce poverty (Bruns, Mingat, and Rakotomalala 2003). Countries that pass the threshold of six years of schooling can achieve a higher steady state of macroeconomic growth.

The disparity between enrollment and completion rates (highlighted in figure 11.3) indicates that enrollment rates—whether net or gross—are only weakly correlated with completion rates. Bruns, Mingat, and Rakotomalala (2003) note that the average enrollment ratio masks the fact that many more children begin school than complete it. They cite examples from Brazil and Indonesia in the 1980s. In both countries, close to 100 percent of children were enrolled at grade 1, yet only 60 percent completed five grades in Brazil, compared with 90 percent in Indonesia.

In the decade following 1990, primary school completion in developing countries for boys and girls together increased from 73 percent to 81 percent (table 11.1). In Africa, however, the changes were marginal, with a slight decrease in primary completion for boys offset by a small increase in girls' completion ratios. Completion ratios in Africa are roughly 50 percent and remain far below the developing countries' average.

Explanations for the lack of a strong relationship between enrollment and completion include: (a) family circumstances, (b) geographic location, and (c) gender differences.

Table 11.1   Primary Completion Progress (Population Weighted)
percent

Region	1990			Most recent year [a]		
	Girls	Boys	Both	Girls	Boys	Both
Africa	43	57	50	46	56	51
East Asia and Pacific	92	97	96	98	98	97
Europe and Central Asia	85	95	90	93	95	93
Latin America and the Caribbean	71	64	69	85	81	83
Middle East and North Africa	71	84	78	78	86	83
South Asia	59	77	68	63	84	74
All developing countries	65	79	73	76	85	81

Source: Bruns, Mingat, and Rakotomalala 2003.
a. In most cases, 1999/2000.

Family circumstances. Family illness, a lack of material resources, and family need for communal labor may all play a role in keeping children out of school.

Geographic location. Children from rural areas generally have lower completion rates than children from urban areas. Girls from poor families in rural areas are less likely to complete primary school than boys in similar circumstances, although boys are also at a disadvantage. This could reflect the need for child labor on family farms or cultural factors (rural areas tend to hold more conservative views on the employment of girls) (table 11.2).

Gender differences. The enrollment and completion rates for girls in developing countries are significantly less than those for boys. In the case of India, Filmer (2000) found that the enrollment rate for six-year-old boys in India in 1992 exceeded that of girls by 2.5 percentage points among children of the richest households; the difference for children of the poorest households was 24 percent in favor of boys. Globally, the enrollment rate for girls from rich households exceeded that of girls from poor households by 55.4 percentage points, and the difference for boys was 34 percentage points (Cohen and Bloom 2005). Increasing these rates for

Table 11.2   Proportion of Children Completing Primary School: Averages in Select Countries and Regions
percent

Region or country	Primary gross enrollment rate	Percentage of age group completing primary cycle		
		Total	Rural	Rural girls
Africa	77	45	n.a	n.a
Niger	31	20	12	7
Burkina Faso	45	25	16	10
Guinea	62	34	25	11
Benin	86	39	27	14
Mauritania	88	46	42	38
Mozambique	78	36	21	14
Madagascar	90	26	12	11
Togo	115	68	57	46
South Asia	100	70	n.a	n.a
Latin America and the Caribbean	113	85	n.a	n.a
Middle East and North Africa	95	74	n.a	n.a

Source: Bruns, Mingat, and Rakotomalala 2003.
Note: n.a. = not applicable.

girls is critical given the marked gender differences in schooling that prevail in many developing countries. Studies have shown that the following:

- A year of schooling for the mother reduces child mortality by about 10 percent.
- An additional year of female education reduces the total fertility rate by 0.23 births.
- Educated women are more likely to send their children to school—and keep them there.
- An increase of 1 percentage point in the share of women with secondary education is estimated to raise per capita income by 0.3 percentage points.
- Education increases women's productivity and participation in the workforce.
- Improvements in women's education in 63 countries accounted for 43 percent of the decline in malnutrition from 1970 to 1975 (Smith and Haddad 2000).

The arguments for improving enrollment and completion rates—and achieving UPE—extend beyond economic ones. Education helps in the achievement of all other MDGs, such as poverty reduction, gender equity, child and maternal health, lower rates of HIV/AIDS and other communicable diseases, and environmental stability (Bruns, Mingat, and Rakotomalala 2003). Recent research has found that increases in education for both boys and girls have a strong effect in decreasing the spread of HIV/AIDS (Vandemoortele and Delamonica 2000; Kelly 2000; Gregson, Waddell, and Chandiwana 2001). Researchers also found that better-educated individuals have lower rates of infection, especially among younger people.

Global Education Initiatives

A number of global initiatives currently express the goal of "education for all." How close are we to achieving that goal?[2] The MDG for education, reaffirming the goals established at the Dakar World Education Forum, aims for the following:

- Ensure that, by 2015, children everywhere—boys and girls alike—will be able to complete a full course of primary schooling.
- Eliminate gender disparity in primary and secondary education at all levels of education no later than 2015.

Completing a full course of primary schooling would suggest a UPE rate of 100 percent. Using the progress achieved over the 1990s, Bruns, Mingat, and Rakotomalala (2003) estimate that the global primary completion rate (PCR) in 2015 will not exceed 83 percent. But even this figure masks enormous regional differences (figures 11.4 and 11.5).

By 2000, just over half of all school age children in Africa had completed primary school. In South Asia, the increase between 1990 and 2000 was more dramatic, but the average completion rate leveled off around 70 percent. The Middle East and North Africa experienced a decade of slight decline and stagnation, with the average completion rate settling around 74 percent in 2000. Regional differences also mask country differences—South Africa and The Gambia registered increases in PCRs while Zambia, the Republic of Congo, Cameroon, Kenya, Madagascar, Qatar, the United Arab Emirates, and Bahrain all registered significant declines. Afghanistan dropped from a low 22 percent in 1990 to 8 percent in 1999 (Bruns, Mingat, and Rakotomalala 2003). Emerging Europe and Central Asia were the regions closest to UPE, registering 92 percent in 2000—followed by Latin America and the Caribbean (85 percent) and East Asia and Pacific (84 percent).

Figure 11.4   Primary Completion Progress in Africa, Middle East and North Africa, and South Asia

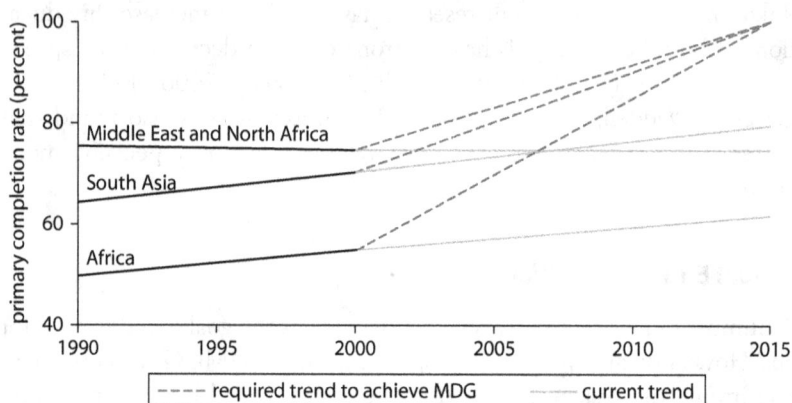

Source: Bruns, Mingat, and Rakotomalala 2003.

Figure 11.5   Primary Completion Progress in Latin America and the Caribbean, East Asia and Pacific, and Europe and Central Asia

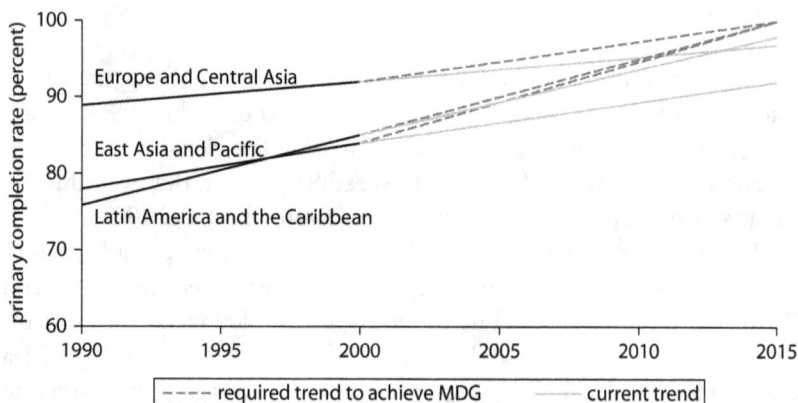

Source: Bruns, Mingat, and Rakotomalala 2003.

How are developing countries progressing toward achieving the target of UPE by 2015? Bruns, Mingat, and Rakotomalala (2003) gauge each country's progress and forecast its potential for achieving this goal (table 11.3 expresses their results). Of the 37 countries that have already achieved—or are close to achieving—UPE, the majority (26) are middle-income countries. Another 32 countries—again primarily

Table 11.3   Prospects for Achieving UPE by 2015

Progress rating	Low-income countries	Middle-income countries	All developing countries
On track	22	47	69
Achieved UPE	11	26	37
On track to achieve UPE by 2015	11	21	32
Off track	51	19	70
Off track to achieve UPE by 2015	28	15	43
Seriously off track	23	4	27
No data available	9	7	16
At risk, subtotal	60	26	86
Total	82	73	155

Source: Bruns, Mingat, and Rakotomalala 2003.

middle income—are on track to achieve it by 2015. The remaining 86 countries—more than 50 percent of the total—are at risk of not achieving UPE. Some of these countries (43) are making good progress, but stagnation in the 1990s makes UPE difficult to reach by 2015. The majority (28) of these are low-income countries. Of greater worry are the 27 countries—23 of which are low income—that are off track. Following current trends, their completion rates will lie at or below 50 percent in 2015. No data were available for 16 countries—including Somalia, Liberia, and Myanmar—but it is highly likely that they are also at risk.

Bruns, Mingat, and Rakotomalala (2003) identified several characteristics of the educational systems in 55 low-income countries that influence enrollment and completion rates:

- Average annual teacher salary
- Pupil-teacher ratio
- Spending other than for teacher salaries
- Average repetition rate
- Government revenues
- Recurrent spending on education
- Recurrent spending on primary education
- Private enrollment.

The 55 low-income countries exhibit enormous variance in these indicators (table 11.4), which translates into huge variance in GERs (ranging between 30 and 120 percent) and PCRs (ranging between

Table 11.4   Benchmarks for Primary Education Efficiency and Quality

| | Sample mean in 1999–2000 | | | |
Variable	Sample range in 1999–2000	Adjusted sample	Highest completion countries	2015 benchmarks
Service delivery				
Average annual teacher salary (as a multiple of per capita GDP)	0.6–9.6	4.0	3.3	3.5
Pupil-teacher ratio	13:1–79:1	44:1	39:1	40:1
Spending on inputs other than teachers (as % of primary education recurrent spending)	0.1–45.0	24.4	26.0	33.0
Average repetition rate (%)	0–36.1	15.8	9.5	10.0 or lower
System financing				
Government revenues (% of GDP)[a]	8.0–55.7	19.7	20.7	14.0/16.0/18.0[b]
Education recurrent spending (as % of government revenues)	3.2–32.6	17.3	18.2	20.0
Primary education recurrent spending (as % of total recurrent spending for education)	26.0–66.3	48.6	47.6	50.0[c]
Private enrollments	0–77.0	9.4	7.3	10.0

Source: Bruns, Mingat, and Rakotomalala 2003.
a. Government current revenues, excluding grants.
b. Staggered targets proportional to per capita GDP.
c. For six-year primary cycle; otherwise, prorated for length of cycle.

20 and 100 percent). Bruns, Mingat, and Rakotomalala (2003) classify the countries into four groups. Members of group 1 were deemed relatively "successful countries," with a GER of 85 percent or above and a PCR of 70 percent or above; group 2 countries were deemed "high inefficiency countries" with a high GER (80 percent or above) but low PCR (60 percent or lower); group 3 countries, or "low coverage countries," had a low GER and PCR (both 60 percent or lower); and group 4 countries fell within the ranges of the other three groups. Figure 11.6 depicts these groups, with the diagonal representing a perfect one-to-one correspondence between GER and PCR.

Figure 11.6   Primary School Completion Rates and Gross Enrollment Ratios in a Sample of Low-Income Countries, 1990–2000

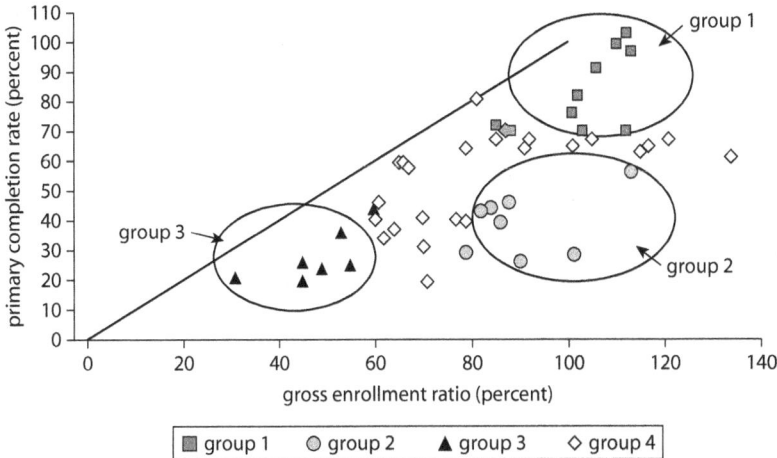

Source: Bruns, Mingat, and Rakotomalala 2003.

Group 1 countries were more likely to

- Devote a higher share of their GDP to public primary education
- Have unit costs that fall in the middle of the range
- Pay teachers an average annual wage of 3.3 times per capita GDP
- Spend slightly more on complementary, non-teacher-salary inputs
- Have an average pupil-teacher ratio of 39:1
- Have average repetition rates below 10 percent.

Group 2 countries had lower average spending and much higher repetition rates (28 percent compared to less than 10 percent for group 1 countries), and group 3 countries had much higher unit costs—about 70 percent higher—than the other groups, primarily due to higher average teacher salaries. These findings provide an outline for educational reform in countries with low PCR and low GER.

Spending on primary education varies widely among the World Bank Regions, ranging from $46 per head in South Asia to $878 per head in Eastern Europe and Central Asia (table 11.5). Public spending on education in low-income countries ranges from less than 2 percent of gross national product in Chad, Guatemala, Guinea, and the Lao People's Democratic Republic to 10 percent in Botswana and Namibia (Mingat

Table 11.5   Current Expenditures on Primary Education

Region	Public spending per student (US$)	Total public spending (US$, million)	Percentage of population covered by public spending data
South Asia	46	6,900	98
Sub-Saharan Africa	68	6,100	98
East Asia and Pacific	103	21,200	96
Latin America and the Caribbean	440	28,200	90
Middle East and North Africa	519	14,200	60
Eastern Europe and Central Asia	878	5,200	22
Developing world	151[a]	81,800	88

Source: Cohen and Bloom 2005.
Note: Public spending figures are more reliable in regions where public spending data are available for a higher fraction of the population.
a. Averages weighted by number of pupils.

and Winter 2005). Usually, greater spending results in higher quality education, although this is not a foregone conclusion[3] (Cohen and Bloom 2005). Mingat and Winter (2005) note that Senegal and Burkina Faso spend almost the same on each primary school student, yet achievement is much higher in Burkina Faso. Moreover, more money for education does not always mean more coverage—public spending on education in El Salvador, Ghana, and Sri Lanka is a relatively small percentage of their respective gross domestic products, yet the coverage is wide.

According to simulations made by Bruns, Mingat, and Rakotomalala (2003), many countries are not in a position to mobilize the resources needed to achieve UPE by 2015. Low-income countries have a small tax base and have difficulty raising revenues because of limited administrative capacity. The cost for 47 countries[4] to reach the education-related MDGs by 2015 would require an increase in domestic funding from approximately $8.5 billion in 2000 to $21 billion in 2015.

Even with maximum effort at the domestic level, the countries surveyed above will not be able to achieve the MDGs in education by 2015 without significant external financing. The 47 countries (plus Afghanistan) require an estimated $2.5 billion a year in external financing. The financing gap ranged from $1 billion in 2000 to $3.6 billion in 2015, which represents 15 percent of total expenditures. Regionally, the estimated annual financing gap ranged from a high of 76 percent in Africa to 1.5 percent in East Asia and Pacific (table 11.6). Africa suffers from the largest financing gap. Thirty-three African countries account for $1.9 billion of the $2.4 billion annual gap internationally (excluding Afghanistan); yet official disbursements have averaged $500 million per year over 1998 to 2000, with new commitments averaging just $600 million per year.

Development Assistance for Education

The Heavily Indebted Poor Countries (HIPC) Initiative (1999), the Poverty Reduction Strategy Paper (PRSP) process (both discussed in chapter 8), and the FTI (2002) should ease developing countries' difficulties in achieving UPE.

The HIPC Initiative directs some of the resources that become available after debt cancellation toward increased social spending. Since countries within the HIPC program are required to prepare PRSPs, these additional resources target education goals within the overall national development priorities set by the PRSPs. Mingat and Winter (2005) note that, in Madagascar, education spending as a proportion of GDP is expected to increase from 2.2 percent to 3.4 percent in 2005, with about one-third of the increase arising from resources freed up under the HIPC Initiative. Fredriksen (2005) notes that countries benefiting from the HIPC program have committed to using an average of 40 percent of their debt payment savings on basic education. A recent review shows that countries are largely meeting this commitment.

Table 11.6   Estimated Annual Financing Gap by Region, 2000
Constant US$, millions

Type of financing	Africa	South Asia	Latin America and the Caribbean	East Asia and Pacific	Middle East and North Africa	Europe and Central Asia	Total	Share of total financing gap (%)
Recurrent	1,127	97	14	30	21	34	1,323	55
Operation	841	97	14	30	21	34	1,037	43
AIDS	286	0	0	0	0	0	286	12
Capital	725	300	34	6	49	0	1,114	45
Total	1,852	397	48	36	70	34	2,437	100
Percentage	76.0	16.3	2.0	1.5	2.9	1.4	100	n.a.

Source: Bruns, Mingat, and Rakotomalala 2003.
Note: n.a. = not applicable

The FTI,[5] agreed upon by developing countries and donors in 2002, aims to achieve UPE for boys and girls by 2015. The FTI functions as a co-coordinating mechanism for disbursing funds once a country has been accepted to the FTI[6] (which requires submitting a country plan for education). The Fast-Track partners (major bilateral donors, regional development banks, the United Nations Children's Fund, and the World Bank) meet regularly to review education plans at the international and country levels. FTI has coordinated with UNESCO to develop uniform benchmarks for an EFA plan, including the allocation of 20 percent of national budgets to education; the elimination of school fees; a targeted 40:1 student-teacher ratio; and repetition rates not above 10 percent.

FTI has been criticized for not doing more to bridge the financing gap. Despite a 2005 increase of $348 million in commitments to the 12 countries included in the initiative, an annual financing gap of $289 million remains. Moreover, the FTI includes only eight countries identified as being off track for reaching UPE by 2015. Sperling and Balu (2005) note that no donor country has made the FTI or even EFA a high priority, although some recent initiatives such as the U.K. Commission on Africa and the UN Millennium Project Task Force on Gender Equality and Education issued reports calling for predictable funding through the FTI.

External financing for education has increased since 2000, when world leaders at Dakar committed to achieving the EFA goals by 2015, although current levels of aid fall far short of the sums required to do so. The International Development Association is the largest source of education assistance to low-income countries. Under the International Development Association, lending for education has grown steadily to reach almost $1.5 billion in 2005. Roughly 86 projects amounting to nearly $4.3 billion in lending were under implementation in 2005. Africa accounted for 40 percent of the total, and Asia accounted for 20 percent. Support for primary education amounted to almost half of total lending over the period 1999 to 2005.

What Do We Know about Educational Policy?

Cross-country data from 1960–90 suggest that (a) richer countries invest a higher proportion of their incomes in education; (b) higher education levels in 1960 (the initial condition) predicted faster subsequent income growth (that is, countries that are better educated are likely to grow faster); and (c) there seems to be little relationship between educational investment (measured by the increase in the number of years an average person spends in school) and income growth.

An individual's level of education, savings rate, and health indicators appear to be strongly correlated. But knowledge of the causal relationships among these variables is limited.

Teacher attendance, quality of education, and test scores in private schools are all higher than those in public schools. In almost all countries, a significant gap between public and private schools is found. Surprisingly, Indian private school teachers have lower salaries than public school teachers, and yet the private teachers perform better as evidenced by student test scores. Clearly, quality of teachers must be an issue.

Community control of public schools and parent-teacher associations can improve public education. Communities and parents are most concerned with the interests of children and know which issues plague local schools; increasingly, they have the authority to monitor, hire, and fire teachers. Unfortunately, parents in rural areas are less educated and may not have the capability to monitor teacher performance. Some evidence suggests that parents in rural areas are not interested in education. Offering cash transfers conditioned on children's school attendance may be one way to lure parents to send their children to school. School choice and vouchers for education are another policy option that could allow parents to decide on public versus private schools and help monitor the quality of education.

Conclusion

Education contributes to economic growth, poverty reduction, and individual economic success. All developing regions, including Africa, have experienced improvements in education, but large educational disparities persist between the developed and the developing worlds, even at the primary level. Research has shown that the development of basic numeric and literary skills requires six years of primary schooling, but even this remains out of reach of most of the poor in the developing countries—particularly in Sub-Saharan Africa. A number of global initiatives have the primary goal of achieving UPE by 2015. The costs of achieving this goal remain high and have implications for domestic and international financial resource mobilization. The chapter ended with a brief discussion on what we know and do not know about inputs, outputs, and outcomes in education.

Notes

1. Including variables such as trade openness and natural-resource endowments.
2. This section is based on research conducted by Bruns, Mingat, and Rakotomalala 2003.
3. Cohen and Bloom (2005) refer to a 2001 Latin America study by Marquis (2001) that showed that although its spending was the lowest in the region (less than $1,000 a student), Cuba was a leader in test scores, literacy, and completion rates.
4. Angola, Armenia, Bangladesh, Benin, Burkina Faso, Burundi, Cambodia, Cameroon, the Central African Republic, Chad, the Democratic Republic of Congo, the Republic of Congo, Côte d'Ivoire, Eritrea, Ethiopia, The Gambia, Georgia, Ghana, Guinea, Guinea-Bissau, Haiti, Honduras, India, Kenya, Lao People's Democratic Republic, Lesotho, Madagascar, Malawi, Mali, Mauritania, Moldova, Mongolia, Mozambique, Nepal, Nicaragua, Niger, Nigeria, Pakistan, Rwanda, Senegal, Sierra Leone, Sudan, Tanzania, Togo, Uganda, the Republic of Yemen, and Zambia.
5. The FTI is a new compact for the education sector that links increased donor support for primary education to recipient countries' policy performance and accountability for results. Initiated by 22 bilateral donors, development banks, and international agencies active in supporting education in low-income countries, the FTI is cochaired on a rotating basis by one Group of Eight and one non–Group of Eight donor, and supported by a steering committee and a secretariat, which is housed in and managed by the World Bank.
6. A first set of 18 low-income countries was invited to join the FTI when it started in 2002: Albania, Bolivia, Burkina Faso, Ethiopia, The Gambia, Ghana, Guinea, Guyana, Honduras, Mauritania, Mozambique, Nicaragua, Niger, Tanzania, Uganda, Vietnam, the Republic of Yemen, and Zambia. Five countries that did not have education plans or national poverty reduction strategies in place were also invited—Bangladesh, the Democratic Republic of Congo, India, Nigeria, and Pakistan (Bruns, Mingat, and Rakotomalala 2003).

Bibliography

Barro, R. J. 2000. "Inequality and Growth in a Panel of Countries." *Journal of Economic Growth* 5 (March): 5–32.

Barro, R. J., and J.-W. Lee. 2000. "International Data on Educational Attainment Updates and Implications." NBER Working Paper 7911, National Bureau of Economic Research, Cambridge, MA.

Birdsall N. and J. J. Londoño. 1998. "No Tradeoff: Efficient Growth Via More Equal Human Capital Accumulation in Latin America." In *Beyond Trade-Offs: Market Reforms and Equitable Growth in Latin America*, ed. Nancy Birdsall,

Carol Graham, and Richard Sabot, 111–206. Washington, DC: Brookings Institution and Inter-American Development Bank.

Bloom, D. E., D. Canning, and D. T. Jamison. 2004. "Health, Wealth and Welfare." *Finance and Development* 41 (1): 10–15.

Bloom, David E., and Joel E. Cohen. 2002. "Education for All: An Unfinished Revolution." *Dædalus* 131 (3): 84–95.

Bruns, B., A. Mingat, and R. Rakotomalala. 2003. *Achieving Universal Primary Education by 2015: A Chance for Every Child*. Washington, DC: World Bank.

Cohen, J. E., and D. E. Bloom. 2005. "Cultivating Minds." *Finance and Development* 42 (2): 9–14.

Deininger, Klaus. 2003. "Does Cost of Schooling Affect Enrollment by the Poor? Universal Primary Education in Uganda." *Economics of Education Review* 22 (3): 291–305.

Filmer, D. 2000. "The Structure of Social Disparities in Education: Gender and Wealth." Prepared as background paper for Engendering Development through Gender Equality in Rights, Resources, and Voice, World Bank, Washington, DC.

Fredriksen, B. 2005. "Keeping the Promise." *Finance and Development* 42 (2): 26–28.

Gregson, S., H. Waddell, and S. Chandiwana. 2001. "School Education and HIV Control in Sub-Saharan Africa: From Discord to Harmony?" *Journal of International Development* 13 (4): 467–85.

Hanushek, E. A. 2005. "Why Quality Matters in Education." *Finance and Development* 42 (2): 15–19.

Hanushek, E. A., and D. D. Kimko. 2000. "Schooling, Labor Force Quality, and the Growth of Nations." *American Economic Review* 90 (5): 1184–208.

Hanushek, E., and L. Woessmann. 2007. *Educational Quality and Economic Growth*. Washington, DC: World Bank.

Kelly, M. J. 2000. The *Encounter Between HIV/AIDS and Education*. UNESCO Sub-Regional Office for Southern Africa: Harare: Zambia.

Marquis, Christopher, "Cuba Leads Latin America in Primary Education, Study Finds." *New York Times*, December 13, 2001.

Mingat, A., and C. Winter. 2005. "Education for All by 2015." *Finance and Development* 42 (2): 32–35.

O'Connell, L., and N. Birdsall. 2001. "Race, Human Capital Inequality, and Income Distribution in South Africa, Brazil and the United States." Discussion Paper 4, Carnegie Endowment for International Peace, Washington DC.

Smith, Lisa C., and Lawrence James Haddad. 2000. "Overcoming Child Malnutrition in Developing Countries: Past Achievements and Future Choices."

2020 Vision Discussion Papers 30. Washington, DC: International Food Policy Research Institute.

Sperling, G., and R. Balu. 2005. "Designing a Global Compact on Education." *Finance and Development* 42 (2): 38–41.

Vandemoortele, J., and E. Delamonica. 2000. "Education, 'Vaccine' Against HIV/AIDS." *Current Issues in Comparative Education* 3 (1): 6–13.

Viaene, J. M., and I. Zilcha. 2003. "Human Capital Formation, Income Inequality and Growth." In *Growth and Inequality: Issues and Policy Implications*, ed. T. Eicher and S. Turnovsky, 89–118. Cambridge, MA: MIT Press.

World Bank. 2002. "Fast Track Initiative Indicative Framework." World Bank. http://www1.worldbank.org/education/efafti/harmonization.asp.

———. 2006a. "IDA Support for Education Fact Sheet." World Bank. http://web.worldbank.org/WBSITE/EXTERNAL/EXTABOUTUS/IDA/.

———. 2006b. *World Development Report: Equity and Development.* Washington, DC: World Bank.

———. 2007a. *World Development Indicators.* Washington, DC: World Bank.

———. 2007b. *Education Quality and Economic Growth.* Washington, DC: World Bank.

CHAPTER 12

Health

International law guarantees the basic human right to receive health care, which is a critical component of economic progress (Sen 1999). Yet for millions of the world's poor, basic health care remains out of reach. Developing countries account for 90 percent of the world's disease burden (Gottret and Schieber 2006). HIV/AIDS, malaria, tuberculosis (TB), maternal and prenatal conditions, childhood infections, tobacco-related illnesses, and nutritional deficiencies caused roughly 16 million deaths in 1998 (WHO 2006). Almost 11 million children under age five, mostly in developing countries, died from diseases in 2000; of these, 8 million were infants—half of whom were just one month old or less. Many of these diseases are, however, treatable. The international community's commitment to the Millennium Development Goals (MDGs)—three of which are directly related to health[1]—attest to its recognition that investment in health is vital to human development, economic growth, stability, and reduced poverty.

This chapter examines health within a macroeconomic context, addressing indicators, the disparity between low-income countries and the rest of the world, economic growth, and policy solutions for low-income countries. The chapter finishes with an examination of some current global health initiatives and the status of development assistance for health (DAH).

Macroeconomics and Health

The examination of health in the macroeconomic framework of developing countries is a recent phenomenon. Critics of the old Structural Adjustment Facility (SAF)[2] noted its lack of emphasis on health in programs that targeted macroeconomic adjustment and structural reforms. The international financial community has increased its focus on poverty reduction in recent years, and recognized the role of health in economic growth and development. Initiatives such as the Poverty Reduction Strategy Paper (PRSP) in 1999 and the Heavily Indebted Poor Countries (HIPC) Initiative reflect this development. The World Health Organization (WHO) established the Commission on Macroeconomics and Health (CMH) to examine how investment in health could tackle mass premature death and thereby improve economic development. Other global initiatives on health—such as the Global Alliance for Vaccines and Immunizations (GAVI) and the Global Fund for AIDS, TB, and Malaria (GFATM)—reflect the critical connections among health, poverty reduction, and economic growth.

The disparity in health indicators among the various country development categories is stark (table 12.1). The combined population of the least-developed and lower-middle-income countries in which many of the world's poor live (such as India and China) was approximately

Table 12.1 Life Expectancy and Mortality Rates by Country Development Category

Development category	Population (millions)		Life expectancy at birth (years)		Infant mortality (deaths before age 5 per 1,000 live births)		Under-five mortality (deaths before age 5 per 1,000 live births)	
	CMH	2003	CMH	2003	CMH	2003	CMH	2003
Least-developed	643	675	51	51	100	94	159	150
Lower-middle-income	2,094	2,655	70	69	35	31	39	39
Upper-middle-income	573	333	71	74	26	18	35	22
High-income	891	972	78	78	6	5[a]	6	7[a]
Sub-Saharan Africa	642	705	51	46	92	101	151	171

Source: CMH 2001; updated for 2003 (2002a) using World Development Indicators (WDI), World Bank 2005.
Note: CMH data refer to a year between 1995 and 2000.
a. Data are for 2002.

3.3 billion in 2003. An individual born in a least-developed country can expect to live to the age of 51, compared with 78 in a high-income country. The health indicators for Sub-Saharan Africa have dramatically worsened over the study period (1995–2000 and 2003). Life expectancy at birth has fallen from 51 to 46 years of age, and infant mortality deaths (before the age of 1) have increased from 92 per 1,000 live births to 101. Mortality rates of children under 5 have likewise worsened in Sub-Saharan Africa—from 151 per 1,000 live births to 171. By contrast, life expectancy and mortality rates have improved or remained constant for the remaining country groupings.

Based on current projections, low-income countries are unlikely to meet the MDGs. Hsiao and Heller (2007) note that to meet the MDG of reducing under-five mortality,[3] mortality rates would have to fall on average by 4.3 percent per year; the current annual rate is 2.3 percent. For a reduction of maternal mortality by three-quarters between 2000 and 2015, maternal mortality rates would have to fall 5.4 percent per year compared to the present rate of 2.4 percent.

Common factors that prevent developing countries from making health progress are HIV/AIDS, low levels of tax resources available for discretionary spending, and limited resources for health (Hsiao and Heller 2007, 31). HIV/AIDS has had enormous negative macroeconomic effects on labor supply, human capital, foreign investments, and economic growth. Table 12.2, taken from Hsiao and Heller (2007), documents a number of studies that highlight the macroeconomic impact of HIV/AIDS.

Furthermore, basic health-care services in low-income countries have suffered as resources are diverted toward treating and preventing HIV/AIDS, especially in Africa, where the pandemic is especially prevalent. While various global initiatives have increased funding for health care (see below), their targeted nature has taken away from spending on other preventive and curative services.

Widespread disease stunts farming, migration, and trade. Bad health saps job productivity and retards intellectual, physical, and emotional development. In other words, ill-health pushes the poor deeper into poverty. A diminished threat of disease would ease the pressure to have many children, and families could invest more in the health of each child. These improvements in health would, in turn, translate into higher incomes, higher economic growth, and reduced (and more sustainable) population growth.

Table 12.2 Summary of Studies of the Macroeconomic Impact of HIV/AIDS in Africa

Growth	Country and period of economic data	Period of most recently used HIV/AIDS data	Results (comparison with non-HIV/AIDS scenario)	
			Growth of GDP	Growth of GDP per capita
Dixon, McDonald, and Roberts (2001)	41 countries (1960–98)	late 1990s	GDP growth rates reduced by 2%–4% a year; large variation across countries, in line with prevalence of HIV	—
World Bank (2001b)	Swaziland	early 1990s	Average annual growth rate of GDP during 1991–2015 will be 1.3% lower	Average annual growth rate of GDP per capita during 1991–2015 will be 0.2% higher
World Bank (2001a)	Namibia	early 1990s	Average annual growth rate of GDP during 1991–2015 will be 0.8% lower	Average annual growth rate of GDP per capita during 1991–2015 will be 0.1% higher
World Bank (2000)	Lesotho	early 1990s	Average annual growth rate of GDP during 1991–2015 will be 1.4% lower	Average annual growth rate of GDP per capita during 1991–2015 will be 0.3% higher
Bonnel (2000)	About 50 countries (1990–97)	mid-1990s	—	Rate of growth of GDP per capita in Africa reduced by 0.7% per year in the 1990s (1.2% for a country with HIV prevalence of 20%)
Quattek and Fourie (2000)	South Africa	mid-1990s	Average rate of GDP growth over next 15 years will be 0.3%–0.4% lower per year	—
Arndt and Lewis (2000)	South Africa	—	Annual growth rate of GDP is lowered by about 0.5% in the late 1990s, rising to 2.5%–2.6% during 2008–10	GDP per capita will be 8% lower in 2010 than in the absence of AIDS; implies that AIDS lowers average annual growth rate of GDP per capita by 0.7% during 1997–2010

Study	Country		Effect on GDP growth	Effect on per capita GDP growth
Greener, Jefferis, and Siphambe (2001)	Botswana	late 1990s	During 1996–2001, annual growth rate of GDP reduced by 1.1%–2.1%, 1.5% in the scenario considered most likely	Little effect; annual per capita GDP growth rate between 0.6% lower and 0.4% higher due to AIDS; 0.1% lower in the scenario considered most likely.
BIDPA (2000)	Botswana	late 1990s	Average rate of growth of GDP in 2000–10 reduced by 1.5% per year	—
Bloom and Mahal (1995)	51 countries (1980–92)	early 1990s	Statistically insignificant effect on income growth	—
Cuddington and Hancock (1994)	Malawi	early 1990s	Average rate of growth of GDP in 1985–2010 reduced by up to 1.5% per year	Average growth of per capita GDP reduced by up to 0.3% per year [a]
Cuddington (1993a, 1993b)	Tanzania	early 1990s	Average annual rate of growth of GDP in 1985–2010 reduced by up to 1.1%.	Average annual growth reduced by up to 0.5%
Kambou, Devarajan, and Over (1992)	Cameroon	—	GDP growth rate over 1986–91 reduced by 1.9% per year	—
Over (1992)	30 Sub-Saharan countries	early 1990s	Average annual growth rate of GDP during 1990–2025 reduced by 0.9% on average (up to 1.5% in 10 worst affected countries)	Average annual growth rate of GDP per capita reduced by 0.15% per year (up to 0.6% in 10 worst affected countries)

Source: Hsiao and Heller 2007, 33.

Note: References to effect on GDP growth or per capita GDP growth rates refer to average annual growth rates for the period mentioned, expressed as percentage-point differences from a "no AIDS" scenario. — = not available.

a. For "extreme" assumption about future AIDS prevalence.

Health and Economic Growth

Health and economic growth have a reciprocal relationship. On the one hand, individuals with higher incomes can afford better nutrition, sanitation, and health care.[4] On the other hand, a healthier individual is less likely to miss work for health reasons and is likely to be more productive. Healthier children have higher rates of school attendance and higher cognitive abilities.[5]

Individuals are also less likely to save for retirement when mortality rates are high. Falling mortality rates in many developing countries have opened up new incentives to save. Consequently, national saving rates have risen, which has boosted investment rates and per capita income.

Bloom and Canning (2009) identify four difficulties faced by studies examining the relationship between health and economic growth:

- The use of morbidity (chiefly used in microeconomic studies) versus mortality (chiefly used in macroeconomic studies).
- The issue of causality.
- The issue of timing based on growing evidence that indicates early childhood health affects productivity as an adult; therefore, health effects in the macroeconomy may have long lags.
- Partial versus general equilibrium—some studies focus on the former while others focus on the latter, again making comparisons difficult.

Income and Health

In examining the cross-country relationship between average income and increases in life expectancy, Preston (1975) finds that increases in average income among poor countries are strongly associated with increases in life expectancy. Figure 12.1 shows the relationship between income and life expectancy for 2005. As income per capita rises, this relationship flattens: for rich countries, the relationship is weak or absent. Deaton (2001) finds income has a much stronger effect on reducing the probability of death at the lowest-income distribution bracket than at the highest. Thus, a redistribution of income in poorer countries—even without an increase in average income—should improve average health and reduce infant and child mortality. As Deaton (2001) notes, however, *average* income matters more for population health than *income inequality* in poor countries.

A number of authors[6] quoted in Bloom and Canning (2009, 55) find that "the major forces behind health improvements have been improvements in health technologies and public health measures that prevent the spread of infectious disease, and not higher income." They further find

Figure 12.1   Income and Life Expectancy

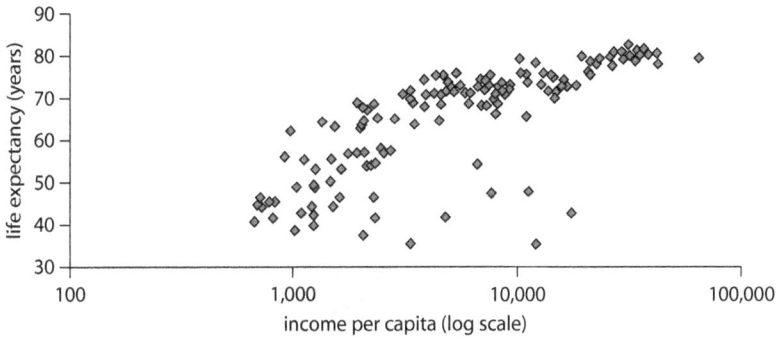

Source: World Bank 2007.
Note: Data are for 155 countries in 2005. Income is in current international dollars, measured at purchasing power parity.

that by plotting the relationship between population health and national income at different points in time, upward movements of the curve account for 75 percent of health gains, while movements along the curve explain less than 25 percent of gains, suggesting that health interventions can improve population health without requiring higher incomes.

Health and Income

Poor health reduces gross domestic product (GDP) per capita by reducing or restricting labor productivity, investment in physical capital, access to natural resources and the global economy, and schooling and cognitive capacity. Figure 12.2 illustrates this relationship. Adult illness, malnutrition, and early retirement also reduce the labor force. The lower ratio of workers to dependents that results from a reduced labor force translates directly into lower GDP per capita. The HIV/AIDS epidemic in Sub-Saharan Africa has already increased adult mortality and could eventually follow the pattern illustrated in figure 12.2, with consequent adverse effects for investment, education, and retirement savings.

Bloom, Canning, and Sevilla (2004) identify the initial health of a population as one of the most robust factors contributing to future economic growth[7]: one extra year of life expectancy raised steady-state GDP per capita by about 4 percent; and a 10 percent improvement in life expectancy at birth is associated with a rise in economic growth of between 0.3 and 0.4 percentage points per year, all other growth factors being constant. Therefore, the difference in annual growth between a high-income country (where life expectancy at birth is around 77 years on average), and a typical poor country (where it is 49 years on average) is

Figure 12.2   Health and Gross Domestic Product

Health's links to GDP
Poor health reduces GDP per capita by reducing both labor
productivity and the relative size of the labor force.

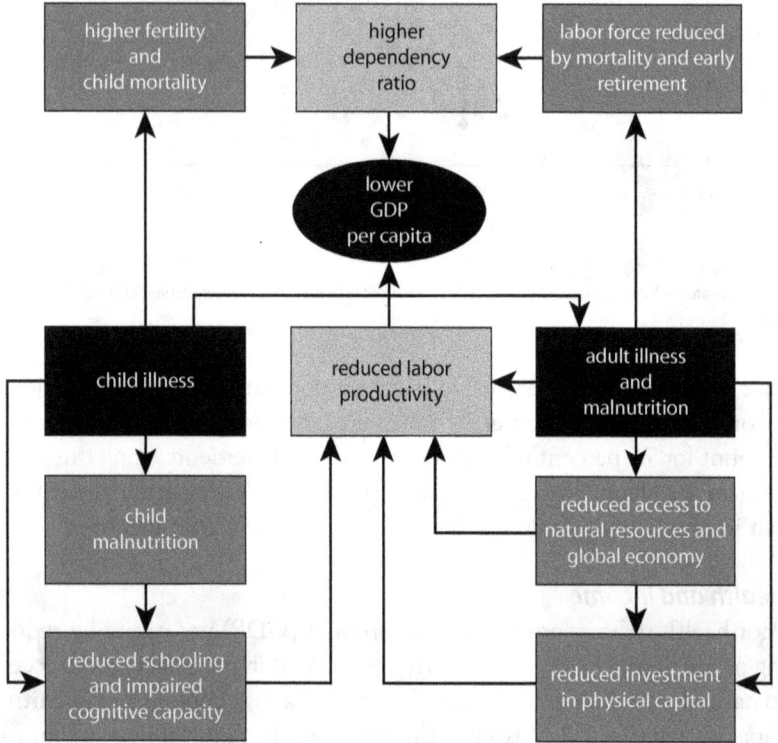

Source: Reprinted with permission from Bloom, Canning, and Jamison 2004.

about 1.6 percent a year. The effects compound over time. Thus, even after
controlling for other macroeconomic variables, health status can explain
part of the difference in growth rates between rich and poor countries.

Table 12.3, taken from Bloom and Canning (2009), provides further
evidence that health is a predictor of economic growth. Countries with
higher initial levels of life expectancy experience more rapid economic
growth at each level of income.

Various studies disagree on how to interpret the link between measures of population health and future economic growth.[8] Health does not
have a direct effect on growth but acts as a proxy for European settlement
that was more successful in countries with a low burden of infectious

Table 12.3. Annual Growth Rate of Per Capita Income
% growth (number of countries)

Initial income, 1960 (constant 2000 US$, PPP)	Initial infant mortality rate			
	50 and under	51–100	101–150	151+
1,000 and under	—	3.9 (1)	2.0 (11)	0.8 (9)
$1,001–$2,000	—	4.8 (3)	1.5 (7)	0.5 (7)
$2,001–$3,500	—	1.6 (6)	1.7 (6)	1.0 (4)
$3,501–$7,000	3.5 (6)	2.1 (9)	0.7 (2)	1.0 (1)
Greater than $7,001	2.5 (17)	0.9 (1)	—	—

Source: Bloom and Canning 2009.
Note: The number reported is the average growth rate of countries in that income and infant mortality rate interval. The numbers in parentheses represent the number of countries in the interval that are used in constructing the average. PPP = purchasing power parity, — = not available.

diseases (Bloom and Canning 2009). Acemoglu and Johnson (2007, 2009), using the initial disease burden and worldwide technological progress in disease-specific interventions as a measure of health, find no predictive impact on the level of income. Bloom and Canning (2009) attribute this to the fact that health improvements have delayed effects. Acemoglu and Johnson (2009) concur but note that improved population health leads to greater longevity and population growth that places a strain on other factors and causes income per capita to decline.

In their review of the empirical macroeconomic literature, Jack and Lewis (2009) note that national public health investments, such as vaccinations, improve a country's overall health and can therefore have a small effect on improved investment opportunities that are linked to economic growth. But they caution that the lack of a solid macroeconomic link between health and growth is insufficient reason to withdraw money from the health sector. As noted earlier, improved health may have a delayed effect on economic growth. On the other hand, they find much more robust evidence at the microeconomic level that points to a strong causal relationship between health, earning potential, and income. At the margin, investments in nutrition, early childhood education, education in general, and mother's education improve productivity.

Macroeconomic Policy and Health

Increased health spending does not always correlate with improved health outcomes. Hsiao and Heller (2007, 83) note that this is especially true in a low-income setting where the "systematic lack of information on many issues relating to the health sector" prevents macroeconomists and country policy makers from formulating sound health policy. They suggest the following steps for low-income countries:

- Ensure the availability and collection of crucial health information—National Health Accounts should be collected annually and a report issued on the health and education outcomes of the poor. Data can be collected with Rapid Field Assessment instruments.[9]
- Warn policy makers of market anomalies in the health sector. Health care consists of more than a dozen markets, most of which are susceptible to serious market failures.[10]
- Promote rational health policies. Sound health policy requires a well-designed combination of regulation and competition, public and private financing, and institutional capacity building.

On a broader level, Hsiao and Heller (2007) make the point that huge gaps in knowledge[11] prevent macroeconomists from prescribing anything other than "blunt policy instruments"[12] to close budgetary financing gaps. They argue that all countries face similar problems when financing or investing in health care based on limited evidence. In their eyes, "evidence-based health care" as a global public good may be underfunded, and they suggest creating a commonly financed agency to disseminate knowledge of health-care policy.

Beyond GDP

Health indicators can vary widely for the same income level. Therefore, GDP is a limited measure of a country's economic performance. A more accurate measure is full income, which captures changes in life expectancy by including them in a measure of economic welfare.[13] A proxy for full income is the value of a statistical life (VSL), or the willingness to pay to avoid risks, defined as the observed amount required for accepting a risk divided by the level of the risk. Bloom, Canning, and Jamison (2004) give the example of a worker who demands $500 more a year to accept a more risky but similar job for which the increase in the mortality rate is 1 in 10,000. Thus, the VSL is [$500/(1/10,000)] = $5,000,000. Based on research by Viscusi and Aldy (2003), a country's VSL values range between 100 to 200 times its GDP per capita. The willingness to pay to avoid risks increases with income, and richer countries therefore tend to have higher VSLs. Since lower mortality rates translate into higher VSLs, the benefits of health investment can be described in terms of a monetary gain.

Bloom, Canning, and Jamison (2004) estimate full income for Africa in an attempt to measure the impact of AIDS. Even though life expectancy in Sub-Saharan Africa has declined to 46 years, and almost 21 percent of deaths were directly attributable to AIDS (2001 figures), little impact was found on GDP per capita.[14] Using the change in GDP per capita and the value of changes in mortality rates (calculating the impact of AIDS on mortality rates) as a measure of full income, the authors suggest that income declined by 1.7 percent a year from 1990 to 2000—much higher than existing estimates of this effect. Furthermore, prior to 1990, improvements in adult health suggested larger economic benefits relative to changes in GDP per capita. When one compares full income with GDP per capita, Kenya's economic performance before 1990 was significantly underestimated and has been overestimated since (figure 12.3).

Although AIDS has undone earlier health progress in some regions (table 12.4), the challenges to further improving health indicators are not insurmountable. The CMH (2001, 4) noted that the "epidemiological evidence conveys a crucial message: the vast majority of the excess disease burden is the result of a relatively small number of identifiable conditions, each with a set of existing health interventions that can dramatically improve health and reduce the deaths associated with these conditions."[15]

Figure 12.3   Comparison of Full Income and GDP per Capita, Kenya

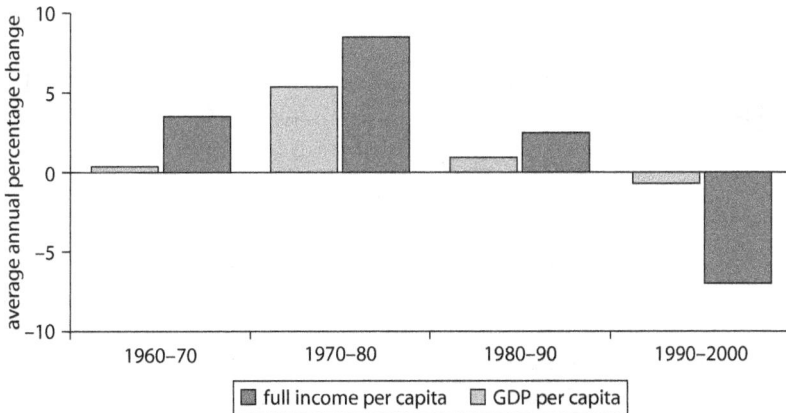

Source: Bloom, Canning, and Jamison 2004.

Table 12.4   Life Expectancy

Region	Life expectancy (years)				
	1960	1990	2001	2002	2003
East Asia and Pacific	39	67	69	69	70
Europe and Central Asia	—	69	69	69	68
Latin America and the Caribbean	56	68	71	71	71
Middle East and North Africa	47	64	68	69	69
South Asia	44	58	63	63	63
Sub-Saharan Africa	40	50	46	46	46
Low- and middle-income	44	63	64	65	65
High-income	69	76	78	78	78
World	50	65	67	67	67

Source: World Bank 2005.
Note: — = not available.

While corruption, mismanagement, and a weak public sector hinder improvements in health, the poor often lack the financial resources necessary to utilize existing interventions. The CMH (2001) estimated that the cost of these health interventions, including those for AIDS, would amount to $30–$40 per person annually. Yet average health spending in least-developed countries is only $13 per person annually—of which budgetary outlays account for $7. For comparison, average health spending in high-income countries is at least $2,000 per person annually. More efficient and greater resource mobilization among poor countries will not bridge the gap in financing; donor finance is needed. The CMH (2001) suggested that a scaling up of health investments would require $27 billion per year in donor grants by 2007, compared to $6 billion in 2001.

As noted in previous chapters, rapidly scaling up aid flows may generate inflation and macroeconomic instability, increase the debt burden (when the aid comes in the form of loans rather than grants), and create short-term volatility in exchange and interest rates. In particular, where aid is used to purchase local goods and services, costs may rise faster than supply. This would especially affect the health sector in which "local costs are typically 70 to 75 percent of total spending and where the number of skilled staff cannot be increased quickly" (WHO 2005, 64). Therefore, aid flows are most effective when they are predictable and persistent, when disbursement timing matches national budget cycles, and in countries that have already initiated improvements in health and macroeconomic stability. In addition, increased aid inflows may target other sectors, such as road construction and sanitation, that indirectly affect health and have less potential for inflationary and macroeconomic instability.

Investing in Health

The relationship between health investment and economic growth is cyclical: improvements in health directly affect productivity, which increases the economic growth that in turn facilitates further health improvements. This pattern of cumulative causation increases for a time before diminishing returns to health set in as the population ages. Bloom and Canning (2009) review the literature on health and welfare, focusing on four components of productivity—human capital, education and cognitive ability, savings, and demographics.

Studies that view health as a part of human capital find that early childhood health significantly influences adult health and earnings.[16] Schultz (2002) measures health by comparing adult height with childhood height and considering nutrition an input. He finds that each centimeter gain in height due to improved inputs as a child in Ghana and Brazil leads to a wage increase of between 8 and 10 percent (Bloom and Canning 2009, 57). Other referenced studies,[17] using different methods of analysis, reach similar conclusions on the importance of early childhood investment in health for later adult productivity. But it is unclear which types of early interventions are most important or what the likely rate of return on health investment in human capital would be in all cases (Bloom and Canning 2009).[18] Jack and Lewis (2009, 31) also suggest that at the macroeconomic level, health and income are "at least as likely to be jointly determined by such intangible features as institutional quality, corruption, and public sector accountability."

Health affects education and cognitive ability through two channels. First, improved health directly affects school attendance, cognitive ability, and learning. Poor childhood health and poor nutrition directly affect children's ability to attend school and prevent the development of cognitive abilities necessary for success at school.[19] Poor maternal nutrition and health can also have adverse consequences for the health of offspring.[20] Bloom and Canning (2009) identify helminthic infections, micronutrient deficiencies, and chronic protein malnutrition as the most important causes of morbidity among children.

Second, impaired health directly affects savings. Medical expenses arising from health problems can consume a large part of disposable income, which limits saving. This is especially worrisome in developing economies with underdeveloped or absent private and public health insurance markets. In "India[,] 83 percent of health spending comes from the private sector and 94 percent of private sector spending comes from out-of-pocket expenses" (Bloom and Canning 2009, 59). Moreover, because poor health is associated with shorter life spans, households may choose not to save.[21] Bloom and Canning also consider household investment behavior and note that investment is critical for accumulating wealth. Household savings in poor economies may be invested in assets that directly affect productivity.

At the national level, foreign investors are more likely to shun environments in which the labor force suffers from a high disease burden. Infrastructure projects and entire industries—such as agriculture, mining, manufacturing, and tourism—suffer from a lack of investment when disease is prevalent. Endemic diseases (such as river blindness) can prevent individuals from exploiting land and other natural resources.

The association between health and demography has implications for economic growth. Conclusions from Bloom and Canning (2009), who note that the 20th century global population explosion initially stemmed from a fall in infant mortality, suggest the following:

- Improvements in health and decreases in infant mortality rates can catalyze a transition from high to low rates of fertility.[22]
- Subsequent health improvements tend to primarily affect the elderly, reducing old age mortality and lengthening life spans.
- High birth and low death rates generate population growth but have different effects on economic growth given their differing effects on the age structure; for example, as long as the baby boomers are of working age and productively employed, economic growth increases.
- Healthy aging leads to a later onset of physical dependency among the elderly.
- Consequences for economic growth depend on the policy environment.

Many of the benefits of health investment remain beyond the reach of developing economies. Through global initiatives and DAH, the global economy is addressing the poor's right to basic health care.

Global Health Initiatives

The CMH (2001) concluded that health spending in low-income countries was insufficient to address their health challenges and that a scaling up of financing was needed *in tandem* with government-wide reform programs. Reforms should establish better planning and coordination within and between ministries of health and ministries of finance and planning. Stronger collaboration among development partners in the international community can in turn support a concerted effort at the national level.

The following subsections examine the contributions of multilateral and bilateral donors toward raising the profile of health in the national development objectives of low-income countries.

Development Assistance for Health

Bilateral and multilateral agencies provide approximately 90 percent of total DAH (Michaud 2003). Total DAH from sources such as the European Community, the GFATM, and the Bill and Melinda Gates Foundation (BMGF) increased from $6.4 billion on average during 1997–99 to $8.1 billion in 2002—an increase of almost a quarter (table 12.5). The majority of funds from both public and private sources were allocated for HIV/AIDS and TB.

Table 12.5   Trends in Development Assistance for Health
Selected major sources of funds (US$, thousands)

	1997–99	*2002*	*2003*
Bilateral agencies	2,559.8	2,875.2	—
U.S. Agency for International Development	920.8	1,134.9	1,474.0
Multilateral agencies	3,401.5	4,649.2	—
United Nations	1,575.5	2,036.3	—
World Health Organization	864.2	1,140.5	—
Regular budget	406.1	461.1	—
Extrabudgetary contributions	458.1	776.5	—
Pan American Health Organization	84.3	93.4	—
United Nations Program on HIV and AIDS	58.2	91.9	—
United Nations Children's Fund	275.8	391.0	—
United Nations Fund for Population Activities	293.0	319.5	—
Development Banks	1,522.0	1,405.5	—
World Bank	1,124.9	983.0	1,171.8
International Development Association	713.5	536.4	586.2
International Bank for Reconstruction and Development	411.4	446.6	585.5
Inter-American Development Bank	245.7	205.0	0.0
Asian Development Bank[a]	287.7	—	—
African Development Bank	151.4	217.5	—
Other multilateral	304.1	1,207.4	—
European Commission	304.1	244.5	—
Global Fund to Fight AIDS, Tuberculosis and Malaria	0.0	962.8	979.2
Private nonprofit			
Bill and Melinda Gates Foundation	458.0	595.9	—
Total	6,419.3	8,120.3	—

Source: Michaud 2003.
Note: — = not available.
a. Not included in totals (pending update) to increase comparability of total DAH.

Bilateral aid for health initiatives has fared better than aid as a whole.[23] Bilateral commitments to official development assistance (ODA) for health increased from an average of $2.6 billion in 1997–99 to $2.9 billion in 2002. The largest increase in commitments came from the United States, which pledged $1.5 billion in 2003—up from $920 million three years previous (1997–99). In 2003, the United States committed a further $300 million to other multilateral agencies and the GFATM.

The United Nations (UN) agencies increased funding from $1.6 billion to $2 billion over the study period—thanks largely to the extrabudgetary contributions of the WHO. Contributions from the World Bank, after increasing over the 1990s, now stand at $1 billion. The BMGF is the major nonprofit donor agency focusing on global health. The BMGF has focused its funding in two main areas: (a) improving the poor's access to existing vaccines, drugs, and other tools to fight diseases common in developing countries; and (b) funding research projects to develop health solutions that are effective, affordable, and practical. Commitments from the BMGF amounted to $0.6 billion in 2002.

Of the $6.5 billion provided by the above donors, the largest share went to support country and regional activities ($5.2 billion), with the remainder going to interregional and global activities (Michaud 2003). More than one-third of the funds went to Africa, and $1.25 billion was allocated to HIV/AIDS, malaria, and TB. The United States was the largest donor for HIV/AIDS, committing $790 million—more than double that of the next-largest donor in 2002. The GFATM allocated over half (56 percent) of total commitments to HIV/AIDS, with 27 percent going to malaria and 15 percent to TB (Michaud 2003). The largest increase in DAH was allocated toward fighting AIDS in Sub-Saharan Africa (table 12.6).

Michaud (2003) reaches the following conclusions in his study on DAH:

- DAH maintained a steady level during the 1990s even when total ODA was falling.
- DAH allocation has responded to geographical needs, at least for HIV/AIDS, malaria, and TB.
- The establishment of the GFATM (as suggested initially by the CMH) has generated increased commitment from the developed world to fight major health problems in developing countries.
- Funds increased by $1.7 billion from 1997 to 2002 but continue to fall short of needs.

Table 12.6   Development Assistance for Health in Select Countries, 2002

Country	Population (thousands)	Per capita ($)	DAH total ($ thousands)	HIV/AIDS ($ thousands)	Malaria ($ thousands)	Tuberculosis ($ thousands)
			Development Assistance for Health			
El Salvador	6,154	28.0	172,187	500	0	250
Zambia	8,976	16.7	150,222	25,933	5,978	27
Namibia	1,695	12.7	21,445	4,287	41	15
Gambia, The	1,268	12.2	15,488	47	57	6
Jamaica	2,560	11.9	30,368	12,728	0	4,009
Senegal	9,240	11.7	107,986	6,001	2,726	1,000
Honduras	6,316	9.6	60,820	3,888	220	650
Benin	5,937	7.3	43,250	2,861	1,564	3
Burundi	6,565	7.0	45,902	189	437	2,019
Lesotho	2,108	6.6	13,926	1,239	0	0

Source: Michaud 2003.
Note: Countries with populations of less than 1 million were not included.

- Political commitment is at an unprecedented high—for example, in the early 2000s, the United States committed $15 billion to fight AIDS in 14 countries over a five-year period.

Poverty Reduction Strategies and Funding for Health

Since the late 1990s, multilateral organizations—working through the Enhanced HIPC Initiative and the PRSP—have recognized the importance of social spending on health in the macroeconomic framework. According to Gupta and others (2001), countries can use the savings freed up by debt relief toward social spending, which could substantially increase public spending on health from its present level of 2.1 percent of GDP in the HIPCs (figure 12.4). Many countries include measures to increase access to health care in their PRSPs. By contrast, total public spending and total revenues (including grants) were almost 24 percent and 21 percent, respectively (figure 12.4). However, the increased focus on poverty-reduction programs in the PRSP will likely change the composition of total public spending and increase the budget allocation for health.

Twenty-three countries reached their decision point in 2001,[24] and their PRSPs contain measures for increased spending on primary and preventive health care.[25] These countries have significantly increased their public health-care spending in per capita terms compared to non-HIPCs (figure 12.5). But health-care spending as a proportion of GDP in the HIPCs still lagged behind that of other non-HIPC countries eligible for debt relief under the IMF's Poverty Reduction Growth Facility (PRGF). For example,

Figure 12.4   Spending on Health in the HIPCs That Have Reached the Decision Point[a], 1999

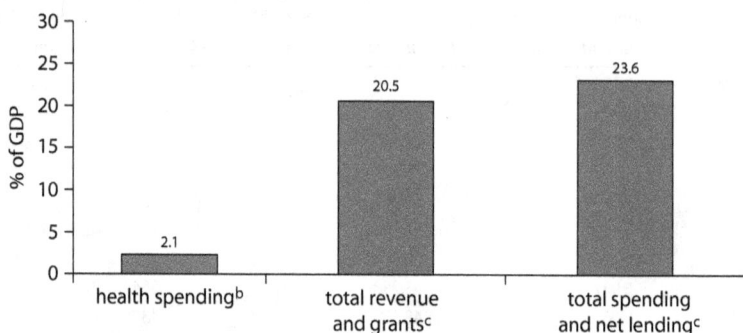

Source: Gupta and others 2001.
a. 1999 or the most recent data available.
b. Refers to 19 of the 23 decision-point HIPCs.
c. Refers to all decision-point HIPCs, except São Tomé and Príncipe.

Figure 12.5   Annual Percentage Change in Health Spending and Social Indicators, 1985–99[a]

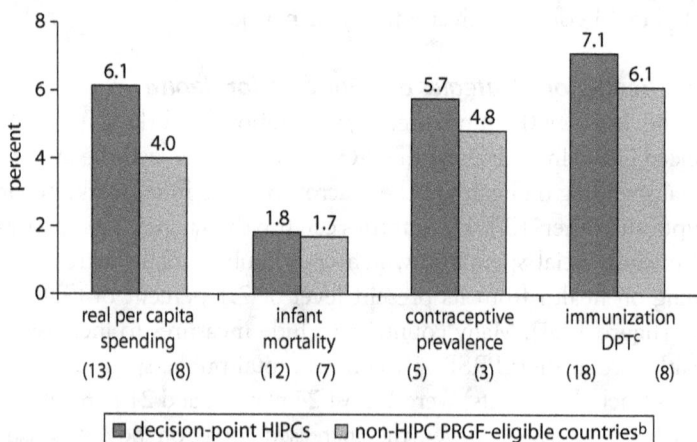

Source: Gupta and others 2001.
Note: a. Average improvement between the first year since 1985 in which the country embarked on an IMF-supported program and the most recent year for which data are available. Number of countries are in parentheses.
b. Excludes transition economies.
c. Diphtheria, pertussis, tetanus.

in 1999, non-HIPCs spent about 1 percent more of GDP on health care than the HIPCs. In per capita terms, the HIPCs' spending on health ranged from $3 a person in Madagascar to $35 a person in Bolivia and Guyana.

Targeting public health care alone may not be the most judicious use of funds made available under debt relief; improvements in other high-priority areas such as water, sanitation, and nutrition can also improve the health of the poor. In fact, available evidence suggests that increased outlays on health care do not always translate into better health-care indicators, although indicators as a measure of government policy alone can be misleading. Limited data and changes in the methodologies used can affect these indicators, as well as factors other than government expenditures, such as household income, general economic conditions, improvements in health technology, and the activities of nongovernmental organizations and other private sector providers (Gupta, Clements, and Tiongson 1998). A more comprehensive strategy for improving health-care spending would focus on removing inefficiencies and reallocating funds to programs more beneficial to the poor, such as prenatal care and vaccinations against preventable diseases (Gupta and others 2001).

President's Emergency Plan for AIDS Relief

In January 2003, U.S. President George W. Bush announced the President's Emergency Plan for AIDS Relief (PEPFAR/Emergency Plan), the largest commitment ever by any nation for an international health initiative dedicated to a single disease. It is a five-year, $15 billion, multifaceted approach to combating the disease around the world. The cumulative disbursements in fiscal years 2004–06 were $8.3 billion (table 12.7). The PEPFAR/Emergency Plan now leads the world in its level of support for the fight against HIV/AIDS, along with other international agencies such as the GFATM, BMGF, the World Bank, and UN agencies, led by the Joint United Nations Programme on HIV/AIDS (UNAIDS).

The most recent available information from PEPFAR's website (www.pepfar.gov) suggests:

- Through its partnerships with more than 30 countries, as of September 30, 2009, the PEPFAR directly supported life-saving antiretroviral treatment for over 2.4 million men, women, and children. They represent more than half the estimated 4 million individuals in low- and middle-income countries on treatment.
- In addition, through September 30, 2009, the PEPFAR partnerships have directly supported care for nearly 11 million people affected by HIV/AIDS, including 3.6 million orphans and vulnerable children.
- In fiscal year (FY) 2009, the PEPFAR directly supported prevention of mother-to-child transmission programs that allowed nearly 100,000 babies of HIV-positive mothers to be born HIV-free, adding to the nearly 240,000 babies born without HIV because of the PEPFAR support during FY2004–08.

Table 12.7   U.S. President's Emergency Plan for AIDS Relief (PEPFAR)
US$, millions

Programs	FY2004 enacted	FY2005 enacted	FY2006 enacted	FY2004–06 cumulative total
Focus countries	845	1,370	1,756	3,971
Global Fund	547	347	545	1,439
Other bilateral programs	444	455	428	1,327
Other activities (including National Institutes of Health research and TB programs)	475	547	561	1,583
Total emergency plan (without malaria)	2,311	2,719	3,290	8,320

Source: PEPFAR 2007.
Note: FY = fiscal year.

- In FY 2009, the PEPFAR also directly supported HIV counseling and testing for nearly 29 million people, providing a critical entry point to prevention, treatment, and care.
- From FY 2010 onward, the PEPFAR will report on partner countries' national achievements in service delivery and health systems strengthening, as well as the PEPFAR's direct contributions to those achievements. The new national health systems indicators are being developed in collaboration with partner countries and multilateral organizations.

Conclusion

The provision of basic health care is critical for economic progress, yet it remains out of reach for many of the world's poor. Health indicators vary widely across countries, and many early deaths in developing countries are preventable. Corruption, mismanagement, weak public sectors, and a lack of financial resources inhibit prevention and proper care. The international community increasingly recognizes the costs of substandard health care in both human suffering and forgone economic growth. Even as some forms of development assistance are being scaled back, donors have increased their provision of health assistance in line with new health reforms included in country-owned PRSPs.

Notes

1. MDG 4 targets the child mortality rate; MDG 5 targets the maternal mortality rate; MDG 6 targets the number of people living with HIV/AIDS.

2. The International Monetary Fund (IMF) began providing financial assistance on concessional terms to low-income member countries in the mid-1970s, first through the Trust Fund, and then, beginning in 1986, through the SAF. Starting in December 1987, the IMF provided concessional financial assistance through the Enhanced Structural Adjustment Facility (ESAF). The ESAF was replaced by the Poverty Reduction and Growth Facility (PRGF) in November 1999.

3. The MDG calls for reducing under-five mortality by two-thirds between 1990 and 2015.

4. Bloom and Canning (2009) reference Fogel (2004) on the role of access to food, Deaton (2006) and Cutler and Miller (2005) on public health measures such as clean water and sanitation, and Cutler and McClellan (2001) on the increasing contribution of medical care to health outcomes.

5. A number of studies have shown the positive effects of health and nutrition on school attendance and cognitive ability (Pollitt 1997, 2001; Bhargava and Yu 1997; Kremer and Miguel 1999).

6. Easterly (1999); Cutler, Deaton, and Lleras-Muney (2006).

7. Among the other factors identified by Bloom, Canning, and Jamison (2004) are the initial level of income per capita, geographic location, institutional environment, economic policy, initial level of education, and investments in education.

8. See Jack and Lewis (2009) for a review of the literature on interpreting the correlations between health and income that highlights the methodological challenges in measurement and estimation.

9. "Despite intense efforts made by WHO and [the World Bank], most low and middle-income countries are not compiling [National Health Accounts] on a regular basis." (Hsiao and Heller 2007, 84).

10. See Evans (1984), Massaro, Nemac, and Kalman (1994), and Hsiao (1995) for a review. Hsiao and Heller (2007, 84) state that "health policy cannot automatically follow the free market strategy often used in economic development for economic goods."

11. Knowledge relating to what policy makers are doing in other countries, what problems they face, and how they may have resolved these problems. Similarly, public and private health insurance organizations have an interest in knowing about the cost effectiveness of new drugs and technologies.

12. For example, rationing, limits on wage rates, controlling prices, and global budget constraints.

13. Alleyne (2009, 50) notes, citing Nordhaus (2003), "in the first half of the past century, more than half of the growth in the United States, if measured in terms of full income, was due to health inputs and that, in the second half, almost as much growth in full income was due to health improvements."

14. This does not preclude GDP per capita from decreasing in the long run, as education and savings rates may fall because of high mortality rates. Two studies undertaken for the WHO and IMF concluded "that the AIDS epidemic in the 1990s had far more adverse economic consequences than its effects on per capita GDP would suggest" (Bloom, Canning, and Jamison 2004).

15. The CMH identifies HIV/AIDS, malaria, TB, childhood infectious diseases, maternal and prenatal conditions, tobacco-related illnesses, and micronutrient deficiencies.

16. Case, Fertig, and Paxon (2005), quoted in Bloom and Canning (2009, 57).

17. Basta, Soekirman, and Scrimshaw (1979) find sizable effects on worker productivity in Indonesia when iron supplementation was used to reduce iron deficiency. Bleakley (2003) found that children in the American South not exposed to hookworm and malaria after eradication of these diseases had higher incomes as adults compared with those born before eradication.

18. Alleyne (2009) laments the lack of a "vulgar metric" for health and worries that too little attention is being paid to developing a useful metric such as years of schooling for education. Hsiao and Heller (2007, 83) note that "most non-[Organisation for Economic Co-operation and Development] countries have not gathered the basic data on inputs and outputs of their health system, for example, total health spending; the poor's access to health care; the efficacy of resources used; operations in the private market; the proportion of households that may be driven into poverty by the need to incur large medical outlays; and consumer satisfaction."

19. Behrman (2009), referencing Walker and others (2007), identifies the following risk factors for children under five born into poverty: stunting, inadequate cognitive stimulation, iodine deficiencies, and iron deficiency anemia.

20. The United Nations (UN) estimates that, every year, roughly 30 million children born in developing countries have impaired physical development as a result of poor nutrition in utero (Bloom and Canning 2009).

21. A longer life span suggests greater savings for retirement.

22. Lee (2003) refers to this as the demographic transition.

23. The share of total bilateral aid allocated to the health sector increased from 3.8 percent in 1990 to 6.8 percent in 2002 (Michaud 2003).

24. Benin, Bolivia, Burkina Faso, Cameroon, Chad, The Gambia, Guinea, Guinea-Bissau, Guyana, Honduras, Madagascar, Malawi, Mali, Mauritania, Mozambique, Nicaragua, Niger, Rwanda, São Tomé and Príncipe, Senegal, Tanzania, Uganda, and Zambia reached the decision point in 2001, and they became eligible for interim debt relief.

25. "Some PRSPs also call for increased spending on water and sanitation (9 countries), roads and road maintenance (7 countries), and rural development

(8 countries), and some include programs that provide housing for the poor and measures to strengthen social safety nets" (Gupta and others 2001).

Bibliography

Acemoglu, D., and S. Johnson. 2007. "Disease and Development: The Effect of Life Expectancy on Economic Growth." *Journal of Political Economy* 115 (6): 925–85.

———. 2009. "Disease and Development: The Effect of Life Expectancy on Economic Growth." In *Health and Growth*, ed. M. Spence and M. Lewis, 77–130. Commission on Growth and Development. Washington, DC: World Bank.

Alleyne, G. 2009. "Health and Economic Growth: Policy Reports and the Making of Policy." In *Health and Growth*, ed. M. Spence and M. Lewis, 41–52. Commission on Growth and Development. Washington, DC: World Bank.

Arndt, C., and J. D. Lewis. 2000. "The Macro Implications of HIV/AIDS in South Africa: A Preliminary Assessment." *South African Journal of Economics* 68 (5).

Basta, S. S., K. Soekirman, and N. S. Scrimshaw. 1979. "Iron Deficiency Anemia and Productivity of Adult Males in Indonesia." *American Journal of Clinical Nutrition* 32 (4): 916–25.

Behrman, J. R. 2009. "Early Life Nutrition and Subsequent Education, Health, Wage, and Intergenerational Effects." In *Health and Growth*, ed. M. Spence and M. Lewis, 167–84. Commission on Growth and Development. Washington, DC: World Bank.

Bhargava, A., and J. Yu. 1997. "A Longitudinal Analysis of Infant and Child Mortality Rates in Developing Countries." *Indian Economic Review* 32 (2): 141–51.

BIDPA (Botswana Institute for Development Policy Analysis). 2000. "The Macroeconomic Impact of the HIV/AIDS Epidemic in Botswana." Gaborone.

Bleakley, H. 2003. "Disease and Development: Evidence from the American South." *Journal of the European Economic Association* 1 (2–3): 376–86.

Bloom, D. E., and D. Canning. 2009. "Population Health and Economic Growth." In *Health and Growth*, ed. M. Spence and M. Lewis, 53–76. Commission on Growth and Development. Washington, DC: World Bank.

Bloom, D. E., D. Canning, and D. Jamison. 2004. "Health, Wealth and Welfare." *Finance and Development* 31 (March): 10–15.

Bloom, D. E., D. Canning, and J. Sevilla. 2004. "The Effect of Health on Economic Growth: A Production Function Approach." *World Development* 52 (January): 1–13.

Bloom, D. E., and Ajay S. Mahal. 1995. "Does the AIDS Epidemic Threaten Economic Growth?" *Journal of Econometrics* 77.

Bloom, D. E., and J. D. Sachs. 1998. "Geography, Demography, and Economic Growth in Africa." *Brookings Papers on Economic Activity* 2: 207–95. http://www.cid.harvard.edu/.

Bonnel, Rene. 2000. "HIV/AIDS and Economic Growth: A Global Perspective." *South African Journal of Economics* 68.

Case, A., A. R. Fertig, and C. Paxson. 2005. "The Lasting Impact of Childhood Health and Circumstance." *Journal of Health Economics* 24 (March): 365–89.

CMH (Commission on Macroeconomics and Health). 2001. *Macroeconomics and Health: Investing in Health for Economic Development.* Washington, DC: World Health Organization (WHO).

Cuddington, J. T. 1993a. "Modelling the Macroeconomic Effects of AIDS, with an Application to Tanzania." *World Bank Economic Review* 7 (2).

_____. 1993b. "Further Results on the Macroeconomic Effects of AIDS: The Dualistic, Labour-Surplus Economy." *World Bank Economic Review* 7 (3).

Cuddington, J. T., and J. D. Hancock. 1994. "Assessing the Impact of AIDS on the Growth Path of the Malawian Economy." *Journal of Development Economics* 43: 363–68.

Cutler, D. M., and M. McClellan. 2001. "Productivity Change in Health Care." *American Economic Review* 91 (2): 281–86.

Cutler, D. M., and G. Miller. 2005. "The Role of Public Health Improvements in Health Advances. The Twentieth Century US." *Demography* 42 (1): 1–22.

Cutler, D. M., A. S. Deaton, and A. Lleras-Muney. 2006. "The Determinants of Mortality." *Journal of Economic Perspectives* 20 (3): 71–96.

Deaton, A. 2001. "Health, Inequality and Economic Development." Working Paper Series WGI:3, CMH and WHO, Geneva, Switzerland.

_____. 2006. "The Great Escape: A Review Essay on Fogel's 'The Escape from Hunger and Premature Death, 1700–2100.'" *Journal of Economic Literature* 44 (1): 106–44.

Dixon, Simon, Scott McDonald, and Jennifer Roberts. 2001. "AIDS and Economic Growth in Africa: A Panel Data Analysis." *Journal of International Development* 13.

Easterly, W. 1999. "Life during Growth." *Journal of Economic Growth* 4 (3): 239–76.

Evans, R. 1984. *Strained Mercy—the Economics of Canadian Health Care.* Toronto: Butterworths.

Fogel, R. W. 2004. *The Escape from Hunger and Premature Death, 1700–2100: Europe, America and the Third World.* Cambridge, U.K.: Cambridge University Press.

Gottret, P., and G. Schieber. 2006. *Health Financing Revisited: A Practitioner's Guide*. Washington, DC: World Bank.

Greener, Robert, Keith Jefferis, and Happy Siphambe. 2001. "The Macroeconomic Impact of HIV/AIDS in Botswana." *AIDS Analysis Africa* 11 (4).

Gupta, S., B. Clements, and E. Tiongson. 1998. "Public Spending on Human Development." *Finance and Development* 35 (3): 10–13.

Gupta, S., B. Clements, M. T. Guin-Siu, and L. Leruth. 2001. "Debt Relief and Public Health Spending in Heavily Indebted Poor Countries." *Finance and Development* 38 (3): 10–13.

Hsiao, W. 1995. "Abnormal Economics in the Health Sector." *Health Policy* 32 (1–3): 125–39.

Hsiao, W., and P. S. Heller. 2007. "What Should Macroeconomists Know about Health Care Policy?" IMF Working Paper WP/07/13, International Monetary Fund, Washington, DC.

Jack, W., and M. Lewis. 2009. "Health Investments and Economic Growth: Macroeconomic Evidence and Microeconomic Foundations." In *Health and Growth*, ed. M. Spence and M. Lewis, 1–40. Commission on Growth and Development. Washington, DC: World Bank.

Jamison, Dean. 2004. "External Finance of Immunization Programs: Time for a Change in Paradigm?" In *Vaccines: Preventing Disease and Protecting Health*, ed. C. de Quadros, 325–32. Washington, DC: Pan American Health Organization.

Kambou, Gerard, Shantayanan Devarajan, and Mead Over. 1992. "The Economic Impact of AIDS in an African Country: Simulations with a General Equilibrium Model of Cameroon." *Journal of African Economies* 1 (1).

Kremer, M., and T. Miguel. 1999. "The Educational Impact of De-Worming in Kenya." Paper presented at the Northeast Universities Development Conference, Harvard University, October 8–9.

Lee, R. 2003. "The Demographic Transition: Three Centuries of Fundamental Change." *Journal of Economic Perspectives* 17 (4): 167–90.

Massaro, T. A., J. Nemac, and I. Kalman 1994. "Health System Reform in the Czech Republic—Policy Lessons from the Initial Experience of the General Health Insurance." *Journal of the American Medical Association* 271 (23): 1870–74.

Michaud, C. 2003. "Development Assistance for Health (DAH): Recent Trends and Resource Allocation." Paper prepared for the Second Consultation of the CMH, Geneva, Switzerland, October 29–30.

Nordhaus, W. 2003. "The Health of Nations: The Contribution of Improved Health to Living Standards." In *Measuring the Gains from Medical Research: An Economic Approach*, ed. K. M. Murphy and R. H. Topel, 9–40. Chicago: University of Chicago Press.

Ntozi, J. P. M., and F. E. Ahimbisibwe. 1999. "Some Factors in the Decline of AIDS in Uganda." In *The Continuing African HIV/AIDS Epidemic*, ed. J. C. Caldwell, I. O. Orubuloye, and J. P. M. Ntozi, 93–107. Canberra: Australian National University, National Centre for Epidemiology and Population Health, Health Transition Centre.

Over, M. 1992. "The Macroeconomic Impact of AIDS in Sub-Saharan Africa." Technical working paper No. 3, World Bank, Washington, DC.

PEPFAR (President's Emergency Plan for AIDS Relief). 2007. "The Power of Partnerships." Third Annual Report to Congress on PEPFAR, Washington, DC.

Pollitt, Ernesto. 1997. "Iron Deficiency and Educational Deficiency." *Nutrition Reviews* 55 (4): 133–41.

———. 2001. "Nutrition in Early Life and the Fulfillment of Intellectual Potential." *Journal of Nutrition* 125 (4 Supplement): 1111S–1118S.

Preston, S. 1975. "The Changing Relation Between Mortality and Level of Economic Development." *Journal of Population Studies* 29 (2): 231–48.

Quattek, K., and T. Fourie. 2000. *Economic Impact of AIDS in South Africa: A Dark Cloud on the Horizon.* Johannesburg, South Africa: ING Barings, South African Research.

Sala-i-Martin, X., G. Doppelhofer, and R. I. Miller. 2004. "Determinants of Long-Term Growth: A Bayesian Averaging of Classical Estimates (BACE) Approach." *American Economic Review* 94 (4): 813–35.

Schultz, T. P. 2002. "Wage Gains Associated with Height as a Form of Human Capital." *American Economic Review, Papers and Proceedings* 92 (2): 349–53.

Sen, A. K. 1999. *Development as Freedom.* New York: Knopf.

Viscusi, W. K., and J. E. Aldy. 2003. "The Value of a Statistical Life. A Critical Review of Market Estimates from Around the World." *Journal of Risk and Uncertainty* 27 (August): 5–76.

Walker, S. P., T. Wachs, J. M. Gardner, B. Lozoff, G. Wasserman, E. Pollitt, and J. Carter. 2007. "Child Development: Risk Factors for Adverse Outcomes in Developing Countries." *Lancet* 369 (9556): 145–57.

World Bank. 2000. "Lesotho: The Development Impact of HIV/AIDS: Selected Issues and Options." Macroeconomic Technical Group, Africa Region, Report No. 21103-LSO, Washington, DC.

———. 2001a. "Namibia: Selected Development Impact of HIV/AIDS." Macroeconomic Technical Group, Africa Region, Report No. 22046-NAM, Washington, DC.

———. 2001b. "Swaziland: Selected Development Impact of HIV/AIDS." Macroeconomic Technical Group, Africa Region, Report No. 22044-SW, Washington, DC.

World Bank. 2005. *World Development Indicators*. Washington, DC: World Bank.

———. 2007. *World Development Indicators*. Washington, DC: World Bank.

World Health Organization. 2001. "Key Facts and Findings on the Linkages of Health and Development." World Health Organization. http://www.who.int/macrohealth/background/findings/en/print.html.

———. 2003. "Increasing Investments in Health Outcomes for the Poor." Second Consultation on Macroeconomics and Health, Geneva.

———. 2005. "Health and the Millennium Development Goals." World Health Organization, Geneva.

———. 2006. "Working Together for Health." World Health Report 2006, World Health Organization, Geneva.

CHAPTER 13

Labor Markets

The labor market is one of the main conduits through which economic growth can help reduce poverty. Economic growth arises from increased employment and productivity. On the flip side, an economy's failure to translate economic growth into employment opportunities can retard efforts to reduce poverty. Labor is the main asset of the poor, and jobs are the highway out of poverty.[1]

The functioning of countries' labor markets is affected by a wide array of factors, among them labor market conditions (affected by labor and tax regulations, among other things), natural resources, cultural factors, and long-run economic performance. In addition, external factors such as globalization and technology play an increasing part in determining labor market outcomes within countries.

Improving labor market conditions to tangibly reduce poverty requires both immediate and long-term actions. In the short run, the labor market must be made more flexible; in the long run, closing the gap between labor supply and demand requires improvements in human capital and training.

This chapter first analyzes the "labor friendliness" of economic growth—a recurring theme in the literature on developing economies. We will see that such employment-intensive economic growth, while sometimes effective, is a double-edged sword—as it may also impede improvements in labor productivity. After analyzing the link between investment climate and labor market performance, we conclude by examining labor supply trends of particular interest to developing countries, including trends in labor force growth rates, unemployment, wages, skills, and gender issues.

Labor-Friendly Economic Growth

If economic growth is to reduce poverty, it must be labor friendly. What does this mean? If growth in output is not translated into growth in employment, unemployment may actually increase or more people may be driven into marginal jobs in the informal sector. In recent years, strong economic growth in the economies of the former Soviet Union has been accompanied by large and increasing rates of unemployment. The unemployment rate in Montenegro, Poland, Serbia, and the Slovak Republic has been close to 20 percent, with declining labor force participation rates. A similar tale can be told in Latin America, where the unemployment rate doubled to more than 10 percent in Argentina, Brazil, and Chile during the 1990s—accompanied by an expansion of the informal sector, an increase in the ranks of the working poor, and rising wage and income inequality. Although many countries in East and South Asia managed to successfully combine strong economic growth with increasing employment, for many other developing regions (especially Sub-Saharan Africa), increases in the working-age population outstripped the growth of job opportunities in the formal sector, resulting in an increase of informal sector jobs.

In developing countries, where social protection for unemployment is inadequate or absent, unemployment is not really an option for most people living in poverty. For the *working poor*, insufficient compensation means living below an accepted poverty line. Meanwhile, *vulnerable employment* is characterized by inadequate earnings, low productivity, and difficult work conditions that undermine workers' fundamental rights (ILO 2010, 18).

Vulnerable employment shares are indicative of informal economy employment in developing regions (ILO 2010, 18). Vulnerable employment shares in the world and by region are examined in table 13.1. As would be expected, the share of vulnerable employment in the developed economies and the European Union (EU) pales in comparison to that in the developing world. South Asia and Sub-Saharan Africa suffer most, with over three-quarters of employment deemed vulnerable.

Table 13.1   Vulnerable Employment Shares, World and Regions
percent

	1998	1999	2000	2005	2006	2007	2008*	2009* S1	2009* S2	2009* S3
World	53.4	53.3	52.8	51.3	50.8	50.6	49.5	49.4	50.6	52.8
Developed economies and EU	11.1	10.9	10.7	10.1	9.9	9.8	9.7	9.9	10.3	10.7
Central and Southeastern Europe (non-EU) and CIS	22.2	25.0	24.6	22.0	21.5	20.5	19.5	18.0	21.5	26.2
East Asia	61.5	60.2	59.0	56.4	55.9	55.9	53.2	52.0	53.3	56.4
Southeast Asia and Pacific	63.4	65.8	64.9	62.5	62.2	61.8	60.7	59.7	61.5	64.1
South Asia	80.2	79.8	80.3	78.8	78.6	78.0	76.9	76.9	77.4	78.6
Latin America and the Caribbean	34.7	35.0	34.4	32.4	32.4	31.1	31.0	31.8	31.9	33.6
Middle East	51.1	46.6	43.7	39.9	39.9	39.1	38.1	38.3	39.0	45.5
North Africa	43.8	42.1	40.7	40.7	40.7	39.0	37.9	37.3	40.4	43.1
Sub-Saharan Africa	81.9	81.4	81.1	77.2	77.2	76.7	75.5	75.7	76.9	79.6

Source: ILO 2010, 53.
Note: * = preliminary estimate; CIS = Commonwealth of Independent States; EU = European Union; S = scenario.

Against the background of favorable growth rates in the developing world (see table 13.2) and prior to the ongoing global financial crisis, vulnerable employment shares were declining across all regions. Vulnerable employment decreased globally by 3.9 percentage points between 1998 and 2008. Between 2007 and 2008, vulnerable employment fell by 10.5 million people (ILO 2010, 18). This trend is unlikely to continue in the wake of the financial crisis; the International Labour Organization (ILO) suggested two possible outcomes for 2009[2]—either a reversal of the gains since 2007 (table 13.1, S2) and a worldwide vulnerable employment share of 50.6 percent, or a reversal of the gains since 2000 (table 13.1, S3) and a vulnerable employment share of 52.6 percent. These shares are equivalent to 1.48 and 19.59 billion vulnerable workers, respectively, worldwide (ILO 2010, 18). Moreover, the ILO expected that the crisis would further increase the share of vulnerable workers, particularly males, in the three Asian regions and Sub-Saharan Africa, given the lack of job security in these regions. It expected that Central and Southeastern Europe (non-EU), the Commonwealth of Independent States (CIS) members, and the Middle East and North Africa would be worst hit, with vulnerable employment increasing by more than 5 percentage points in the worst-case scenario (table 13.1, S3).

The number of working poor was also on a downward trend prior to the global financial crisis, suggesting a 16.3 percentage point decline between 1998 and 2008 for those falling below the $1.25 a day line and a 17 percentage point decline for those falling below the $2 a day poverty line (tables 13.2 and 13.3, respectively). Worldwide, the share of working poor was 21.2 percent, or 633 million people living on less than $1.25 a day (table 13.2); meanwhile, 39.7 percent of workers, or 1.2 billion people, were classified as working poor (living on $2 a day) (table 13.3).

It is likely that the global financial crisis has also had an impact on the numbers of working poor. Refuting the small decreases that might have occurred in 2009 had the working poor maintained their historical downward trend,[3] the ILO suggests that at the $1.25 a day poverty line, an increase of 7 percentage points in the working poor was possible. This would translate into an additional 215 million workers (table 13.2). At the $2 a day poverty line, the ILO estimates an additional 5.9 percent of workers joining the working poor, or 185 million (table 13.3). Again, the regions likely to suffer most are South Asia, Southeast Asia, and Sub-Saharan Africa, reflecting the fact that many workers are just above the poverty line there (ILO 2010, 22).

Employment and Productivity during Economic Growth

An examination of the concept of employment elasticity sheds some light on the employment intensity of growing output. Employment elasticity measures (in percentage points) the change in the number of employed persons in a country or region associated with an increase in economic output, measured by gross domestic product (GDP). Essentially a ratio of the growth in employment (numerator) to the growth in output (denominator), employment elasticity varies across countries and across time. Research at the ILO shows that labor supply growth, the size of a country's service sector, instability, uncertainty, and taxes on labor earnings are relevant in explaining the intensity of a country's growth in employment (Kapsos 2005).

Examining changes in output, along with changes in employment elasticity, helps explain whether growth is bringing gains in employment and labor productivity, or whether it is balanced between the two. Globally, employment elasticities ranged between 0.3 and 0.38 percentage points from 1991 to 2003 (Kapsos 2005). Thus, for every percentage point increase in GDP, employment growth grew by one-third and productivity

Table 13.2 Working Poor Indicators, World and Regions ($1.25 a Day)

| | Numbers of people (millions) | | | | | | Share in total employment (%) | | | | | | |
| | | | | 2009* | | | | | | | 2009* | | |
	1998	2003	2008*	S1	S2	S3	1998	2003	2008	S1	S2	S3
World	945	778	633	632	744	849	37.5	28.5	21.2	21.1	24.8	28.3
Central and Southeastern Europe (non-EU) and CIS	11	9	7	7	8	10	7.3	6.1	4.0	4.1	5.3	6.3
East Asia	372	201	87	78	100	124	52.0	26.5	11.0	9.7	12.6	15.6
Southeast Asia and Pacific	101	81	64	64	78	92	44.9	32.5	23.3	23.0	27.8	32.7
South Asia	276	285	274	275	328	374	56.7	53.0	45.5	44.9	53.5	61.0
Latin America and the Caribbean	26	28	17	18	21	25	13.4	12.8	6.6	7.0	8.5	9.9
Middle East	4	5	5	5	7	8	9.5	9.5	8.1	8.1	10.4	12.7
North Africa	10	10	9	9	10	12	19.9	19.9	13.7	13.6	15.6	17.7
Sub-Saharan Africa	146	160	172	177	191	204	66.5	63.0	58.6	58.7	63.5	67.7

Source: ILO 2010, 54.

Note: * = preliminary estimate; CIS = Commonwealth of Independent States; S = scenario.

273

Table 13.3 Working Poor Indicators, World and Regions ($2 a Day)

	Numbers of people (millions)			2009*			Share in total employment (%)			2009*		
	1998	2003	2008*	S1	S2	S3	1998	2003	2008	S1	S2	S3
World	1,429	1,328	1,185	1,187	1,283	1,368	56.7	48.6	39.7	39.5	42.8	45.6
Central and Southeastern Europe (non-EU) and CIS	31	24	21	22	25	29	21.2	15.6	12.8	13.6	15.5	18.0
East Asia	549	390	231	214	244	272	76.7	51.4	29.3	26.8	30.6	34.1
Southeast Asia and Pacific	158	156	142	144	161	175	70.0	62.6	51.5	51.4	57.4	62.5
South Asia	419	454	479	485	510	529	86.2	84.4	79.5	79.1	83.2	86.2
Latin America and the Caribbean	54	57	38	41	47	53	27.7	26.0	15.3	16.2	18.7	21.3
Middle East	11	13	14	15	17	20	24.3	24.5	22.9	22.8	26.6	30.7
North Africa	20	20	20	20	24	29	40.6	36.9	30.7	30.4	36.9	43.5
Sub-Saharan Africa	188	214	239	246	255	262	85.8	84.4	81.6	81.6	84.7	86.9

Source: ILO 2010, 54.

Note: * = preliminary estimate; CIS = Commonwealth of Independent States; S = scenario.

growth by two-thirds. Positive economic growth accompanied by an employment elasticity of greater than one indicates declining labor productivity and an increase in lower-productivity jobs. Opinion varies on whether employment-led or productivity-led growth is more advantageous from a development perspective.

The employment elasticity in individual sectors—where value added in an economic sector such as agriculture, manufacturing, or services replaces GDP in the denominator—links employment growth to changes in the sectoral composition of employment. Low employment elasticity and positive sectoral growth for a given sector suggest productivity growth. If this scenario continues and is accompanied by reduced employment in the given sector—and if overall economic growth is positive—then it is probable that structural change is occurring. At the early stages of development, structural change is indicative of a movement away from agriculture to manufacturing, and, at later stages of development, low-employment elasticities and positive sectoral growth suggest a movement out of manufacturing into services. Based on data from 139 countries, table 13.4 shows employment elasticities by sector and value-added growth rates in each sector during the period 1991–2003 (Kapsos 2005).

The services sector was the fastest growing (3 percent) in the 139 countries; it also provided the most job-intensive growth: for every percentage point of growth in the services sector, employment increased by 0.57 percentage points, as shown in table 13.4.

On the other hand, productivity growth contributed more to growth in the agricultural and industrial sectors over the period. Structural change—that is, a movement from agriculture and industry to service sectors—played an important role in these divergent results; nevertheless, new jobs were created in both agriculture and industry, and agriculture remains the world's largest employment sector (1.2 billion workers in 2003), reflecting its importance in developing economies.

Gutierrez and others (2007) find that what matters for poverty reduction is the sectoral pattern of employment and productivity growth. In the

Table 13.4   Employment Elasticities by Sector for 139 Countries, 1991–2003

	Agriculture	Industry	Services
Sector value-added elasticity	0.41	0.28	0.57
Average annual value-added growth rate (%)	2.0	2.1	3.0

Source: Kapsos 2005.

short run, the overall employment intensity of growth is largely irrelevant for poverty reduction. Employment-intensive growth in the manufacturing sector was associated with decreases in poverty, whereas productivity growth in agriculture promoted poverty reduction. Thus, focusing solely on employment intensity of overall growth misses the details. Examining manufacturing employment and agricultural productivity has lessons for poverty reduction.

Turning to a regional analysis, East Asia witnessed the most growth over the period 1991–2003, with average annual GDP growth of almost 10 percent, while Latin America experienced a declining growth rate, reflecting, in part, deep financial crises across several countries during the study period (table 13.5). In terms of the employment intensity of growth, economic growth in Latin America was much more employment intensive than growth in East Asia. Employment elasticities ranged from 0.45 to 0.70 in Latin America compared with 0.14 to 0.16 in East Asia, suggesting that growth in East Asia was driven by increased labor productivity. The high employment elasticities shown for the Middle East (in excess of 1) suggest that labor productivity actually declined over the majority of the study period. Similarly, the high employment elasticities for North Africa and Sub-Saharan Africa suggest a high employment intensity of economic growth, reflecting the region's very high population growth rate.

Trends in employment elasticities can also indicate structural shifts in an economy (table 13.6). For example, a 1 percentage point increase in GDP in South Asia between 1991 and 2003 was associated with

Table 13.5   Employment Elasticities and Average Annual GDP Growth by Developing Region

	Total employment elasticity			Average annual GDP growth		
	1991–95	1995–99	1999–2003	1991–95	1995–99	1999–2003
East Asia	0.14	0.14	0.16	11.6	7.4	7.7
Southeast Asia and Pacific	0.39	0.20	0.38	7.4	1.6	4.8
South Asia	0.40	0.49	0.49	6.0	5.8	5.1
Latin America	0.65	0.70	0.45	3.5	2.7	1.4
Caribbean	0.43	0.37	−0.42	1.9	5.2	2.5
Middle East	1.10	1.29	0.91	3.9	3.0	4.1
North Africa	0.30	0.74	0.51	2.2	4.8	4.1
Sub-Saharan Africa	0.73	0.82	0.53	1.1	3.2	3.2

Source: Kapsos 2005.

Table 13.6   Employment Elasticities and Growth by Sector and Region, 1991–2003

	Employment elasticity			Average annual value-added growth rate (%)		
	Agriculture	Industry	Services	Agriculture	Industry	Services
East Asia	0.23	0.06	0.50	3.7	12.5	8.8
Southeast Asia and Pacific	0.20	0.68	0.99	2.1	5.4	4.6
South Asia	0.71	0.37	0.36	2.9	5.9	6.9
Latin America	−0.33	0.54	1.04	2.5	2.2	2.6
Caribbean	−0.11	0.05	0.99	2.5	3.7	3.8
Middle East	1.94	0.26	0.70	3.9	1.3	4.6
North Africa	0.55	0.43	0.76	2.4	3.2	4.0
Sub-Saharan Africa	0.82	0.90	0.79	2.3	2.0	2.8

Source: Kapsos 2005.

an increase in agricultural employment of 0.71 percent, an increase in industrial employment of 0.37 percent, and an increase in service sector employment of 0.36 percent. This trend suggests that South Asia is not exhibiting a significant degree of structural economic change away from agriculture and into industry and services. On the other hand, in Latin America and the Caribbean, a 1 percentage point increase in GDP was associated with a decrease in agricultural employment of –0.33 percent and –0.11 percent, along with an increase in service sector employment of 1.04 and 0.99 percent. This evidence indicates ongoing structural changes in the region—in particular a movement away from jobs in agriculture toward those in the service sector.

There was unprecedented growth over the 2003 to 2007 period (see table 13.7); all regions, except the developed economies and EU, recorded growth rates in excess of 5 percent in 2007. But given the vagaries of the regional labor markets,[4] translating this growth into employment is not always easy. We return to this point below.

Following the onset of the financial crisis in 2007, growth rates were down in all regions in 2008, with the largest decline in East Asia—almost a 4 percentage point decrease. Preliminary estimates for 2009 showed that the developed economies and the EU, Central and Southeastern Europe (non-EU), and the former CIS were particularly hard hit. Estimates for all other regions, except East and South Asia, were below 5 percent in 2009. Projections for 2010 suggest a recovery in late 2009 that will see growth rates increase for all regions, albeit at significantly lower rates than those prevailing in the mid-2000s.

Table 13.7   Annual Real GDP Growth Rates, World and Regions
percent

	2004	2005	2006	2007	2008	2009*	2010p
World	4.9	4.5	5.1	5.2	3.0	−1.1	3.1
Developed economies and European Union	3.1	2.6	2.9	2.6	0.6	−3.5	1.1
Central and Southeastern Europe (non-EU) and CIS	8.3	7.0	7.9	7.6	4.5	−6.5	2.4
East Asia	8.9	8.9	10.0	11.2	7.3	6.1	7.9
Southeast Asia and Pacific	6.5	5.9	6.2	6.5	4.4	0.5	4.0
South Asia	7.6	8.8	9.1	8.7	6.6	5.0	6.0
Latin America and the Caribbean	6.0	4.7	5.7	5.7	4.2	−2.5	2.9
Middle East	6.4	5.8	5.5	6.1	4.9	1.4	4.1
North Africa	4.7	5.0	6.1	5.8	5.5	3.7	4.3
Sub-Saharan Africa	7.2	6.1	6.3	6.8	5.4	1.2	4.1

Source: ILO 2010, 45.
Note: * = preliminary estimate; p = projection.

Examining output per worker sheds some light on how employment responded to the impressive growth rates experienced over the period. Table 13.8 shows output per worker for the world and regions. Labor productivity in 2006 and 2007 was greater than that in the previous five years (2000–05) for all regions, except the developed economies and EU. Following the crisis, labor productivity declined in all regions and while most (except Southeast Asia and Pacific and the developed economies and EU) maintained a productivity level greater than that in 2000–05, the percentage point difference between 2007 and 2008 ranged from a fall of 0.3 percentage points in Central and Southeastern Europe (non-EU) and CIS to a fall of 3 percentage points in East Asia. The Middle East and North Africa actually increased their labor productivity in 2008 over 2007. Preliminary estimates for 2009 show negative growth, suggesting that the declines in GDP were greater than the declines in employment in all regions except East Asia, South Asia, and North Africa. Declines in output per worker put downward pressure on working conditions, with implications for wages and earnings, especially in regions with low labor productivity.

So far, we have emphasized the distinction between labor productivity and employment intensity in contributing to overall growth and sectoral value-added growth. In fact, *both* goals should be pursued in tandem

Table 13.8   Output per Worker, Level, and Growth Rate

	Annual growth (%)				2009*		
	2000–05	2006	2007	2008	CI lower bound	Preliminary estimate	CI upper bound
World	1.9	2.9	3.0	1.8	−2.9	−2.5	−2.2
Developed Economies and European Union	1.4	1.3	1.0	0.2	−1.4	−1.3	−1.2
Central and Southeastern Europe (non-EU) and CIS	4.9	6.3	5.3	5.0	−4.9	−4.7	−4.3
East Asia	7.3	9.4	10.6	7.6	3.6	4.0	4.3
Southeast Asia and Pacific	3.3	4.0	3.8	2.1	−2.1	−1.8	−1.6
South Asia	4.4	6.3	6.1	4.4	2.2	2.6	2.9
Latin America and the Caribbean	0.2	2.1	3.3	1.9	−3.9	−3.5	−3.2
Middle East	1.7	2.2	2.9	3.7	−3.1	−2.5	−1.9
North Africa	1.0	1.8	2.9	3.2	−0.2	0.6	1.3
Sub-Saharan Africa	1.8	3.1	3.4	2.0	−2.1	−1.7	−1.4

Source: ILO 2010, 49.
Notes: * = preliminary estimate; CI = confidence interval. Calculations are based on constant 2005 purchasing power parity–adjusted international dollars.

to further economic development. To do this, one needs information on other labor market indicators—job quality, demographics (labor supply), labor demand, and so on—to be able to fully examine the link between labor market improvements and economic development. Economic growth reduces poverty when there is a strong link between labor market improvements and economic development.

Job Quality, the Informal Labor Market, and the Investment Climate

Employment intensity and labor productivity offer no information on the quality of jobs created. Yet the type of jobs created is important in a developing economy, where so much of the labor market is in the informal sector. The mismatch between job gains and losses in this context often swells the informal sector. Minimal unemployment benefits mean that dismissed workers cannot afford to be unemployed and are left with no choice but to seek work in the informal sector.

Macro and structural reforms in the labor market should strive for greater equity and efficiency to increase workers' economic opportunities and broaden access to the labor market. As noted in the World Bank's

World Development Report for 2006, the "playing field may be uneven if protection for formal-sector workers, while bringing valued benefits to some, slows processes of restructuring and job creation for other workers" (World Bank 2006)—and if it maintains a large informal sector dominated by undesirable jobs.

Besley and Burgess (2002) analyze the link between labor regulations (including the bargaining power of labor and modes of settlement of labor disputes) and the output of registered manufacturing firms in several Indian states over a long period. Their evidence shows that regulating in a pro-worker direction was associated with lower levels of investment, employment, productivity, and output. Regulation that is too favorable to labor can also affect the investment climate.

It is widely accepted that investment-climate reforms—including changes in trade barriers, products, and labor markets—are essential to set countries on a path to growth that is sustainable in the long term. Where the investment climate is good and the labor market functions well, one finds greater employment opportunities, lower levels of informal work, better working conditions, and the potential for rising wages. But in the short run, efforts to improve the investment climate can be costly to workers. As the investment climate improves, for example, domestic firms may experience a reduction in trade barriers, reduced state support, and increased competition from foreign-owned firms, which may lead them to cut jobs, at least in the short run.

Labor Markets in Developing Countries

Eighty percent of the world's labor force works in developing countries, where labor markets are very different from those in developed countries. In many developing countries, more than half the population of working age labors in the informal economy, where working conditions can be poor (World Bank 2005). Behrman (1999) notes additional differences. In the developing world, agriculture and other rural labor activities are much more important than they are in the industrial world. Nonwage labor (such as that of unpaid family workers) plays a much more important role in the economy, particularly in agriculture. Labor forces grow more rapidly, and labor force participation rates among those ages 15–64 are higher (particularly for low-income countries, in part because of lower school enrollment rates). Human capital investment is lower, with larger gender gaps, and nonlabor production inputs per worker are much smaller. In the developing world, social protection such as unemployment insurance either does not exist or has very limited coverage. Few households have the resources to weather a period of unemployment. Therefore, many who lose their jobs must look for work in the informal sector and have no option but to choose undesirable jobs (Bourguignon 2005).

The ILO (2010), in a synopsis of regional developing labor markets, noted the following:

- The limited increase in the unemployment rate in Sub-Saharan Africa (to 8.2 percent in 2009 from 8.0 percent in 2008, see below) is not indicative of the true state of the labor market—the share of vulnerable and working poor should also be consulted. Furthermore, discouraged workers are an important phenomenon in Sub-Saharan Africa.

- The labor market in North Africa continues to face a large number of challenges, namely, a rapidly growing labor force (2.6 percent annually over the past 10 years); high unemployment rates, especially among youth; low labor force participation rates among women; slow increases in productivity, with repercussions for wages and earnings; and large shares of the vulnerable and working poor.

- Youth unemployment and large shares of vulnerable and working poor also characterize the labor market in the Middle East. Furthermore, there are large gaps between the sexes in labor force participation rates, with female participation rates just over one-third of male rates. The 2009 estimate of 25.4 percent of women is the lowest among all regions.

- Favorable economic conditions in Latin America and the Caribbean— rapid economic growth, rising exports, high commodity prices, and abundant financing—yielded positive spin-offs for the labor market over the past decade as seen in reduced rates of vulnerable employment and reduced unemployment rates. This has been curtailed in the wake of the global financial crisis with negative effects for the working poor, vulnerable employment, and unemployment.

- East Asia boasts the highest employment-to-population ratio among all the regions—almost 70 percent of the working-age population is employed. The figure has been declining, however, as young people spend longer in school and older workers retire and exit the labor market. The share of workers in salaried employment has grown significantly in East Asia in recent years, reaching 45 percent in 2008. Significant gains have been made among the working poor in the past decade, with an estimated 29 percent living with their families on less than $2 a day and 11 percent living with their families on less than $1.25 a day in 2008—versus 75 percent and 50 percent, respectively, a decade earlier. The negative impacts of the ongoing crisis are expected to be offset by declining commodity prices, and economic growth is expected to rebound sharply with unemployment expected to decline slightly to 4.3 percent (see below).

- Southeast Asia and Pacific are heavily dependent on foreign trade and investment flows, and thus have been hit hard by the ongoing crisis. Unemployment has increased, especially among men. Youth unemployment is a big concern in this region and there is a large gender gap in labor force participation. Labor force participation among the youth has declined, which may suggest more youth staying on in education or becoming discouraged. Vulnerable employment and the working poor remain big issues in this region.

- South Asia suffered least from the recent crisis, due principally to the fact that its two largest countries—India and Pakistan—are less reliant on exports than many of the other countries in the Asian regions. The region's workforce has a large proportion of working poor and many in vulnerable employment. Progress has been made in extending social protection in the region but much remains to be done.

Labor Supply and Unemployment

Labor supply depends on population—its age composition, gender composition, skill level, global distribution, and migration patterns. Table 13.9 examines labor supply trends by region for 1990 and 2006 and forecasts for 2016. Developing economies account for 64 percent of the global working-age population (World Bank 2008); these economies' labor forces are expected to expand very rapidly. Across the regions, the labor force in Sub-Saharan Africa, South Asia, and the Middle East and North Africa increased by at least 2 percent per year. Population growth is the principal factor driving labor force growth, and while the rate of population increase has slowed in most developing countries, the working-age population continues to grow, at least for the time being. (Changes in population growth affect the labor force only after a lag of some years.)

We know little about rates of unemployment and underemployment in the developing world, compared with the wealth of data collected by

Table 13.9   Labor Supply Trends by World, Region, and Income

	Working-age (15–64 years) population (millions)	Average annual labor force growth (%)	Average annual population growth (%)		Share of women in labor force (%)	
	2006	1990–2006	1990–2006	2006–16p	1990	2006
East Asia and Pacific	1,317.8	1.4	1.1	0.8	44.1	43.5
Eastern Europe and Central Asia	317.3	–0.1	0.1	0.0	45.7	44.7
Latin America and the Caribbean	356.5	2.6	1.5	1.1	33.9	40.8
Middle East and North Africa	195.7	3.4	2.0	1.7	22.9	28.0
South Asia	928.1	2.0	1.8	1.4	29.7	29.3
Sub-Saharan Africa	419.0	2.7	2.6	2.3	43.0	42.2
High-income economies	691.6	0.9	0.7	0.4	41.4	43.4
World	4,223.6	1.6	1.4	1.1	39.7	39.9

Source: World Bank 2008.
Note: p = projection.

labor economists in the industrial economies. The data that do exist are often unreliable and not susceptible to cross-country comparison. They are notoriously incomplete in Africa and South Asia, where large rural and informal sectors exist. In Latin America, the term unemployment often refers to urban unemployment only.

Unemployment increased in all the developing countries during the 1990s (Betcherman 2002). The scenario during 2000 to 2007 was much different, reflecting the favorable growth rates experienced by the regions, as outlined in table 13.7. The unemployment rates in 2007 represented a marked decrease from those in 1999 (table 13.10) across all regions except South Asia and to a lesser extent Southeast Asia and Pacific.

Following the onset of the global financial crisis, in 2008, a number of the developing regions had the same unemployment rate as in 2007 or only a marginally lower rate (the Middle East, South Asia, Southeast Asia and Pacific, North Africa, and Sub-Saharan Africa). The preliminary estimates for 2009 indicated an increase in unemployment in all regions; some regions—Sub-Saharan Africa, the Middle East, Latin America and the Caribbean—were expected to return to 1999 rates (table 13.10). Those regions reliant on international trade were hard hit, and the progress made over 2000–07 was reversed in many regions, with adverse implications for the working poor and those in vulnerable employment.

Meanwhile, the issue of youth unemployment continues to be a major worry for many regions. Table 13.11 examines the share of youth

Table 13.10 Unemployment Rates by World, Region, and Economy

percent

For men and women	1999	2000	2004	2005	2006	2007	2008	2009* CI lower bound	2009* Preliminary estimate	2009* CI upper bound
World	6.4	6.2	6.4	6.3	6.0	5.7	5.8	6.3	6.6	6.9
Developed economies and European Union	7.0	6.7	7.2	6.9	6.3	5.7	6.0	8.3	8.4	8.5
Central and Southeastern Europe (non-EU) and CIS	12.4	10.6	9.7	9.4	9.0	8.3	8.3	10.0	10.3	10.6
East Asia	4.7	4.5	4.2	4.2	4.0	3.8	4.3	4.1	4.4	4.8
Southeast Asia and Pacific	5.1	5.0	6.4	6.5	6.1	5.4	5.3	5.4	5.6	5.9
South Asia	4.3	4.5	5.2	5.3	5.1	5.0	4.8	4.8	5.1	5.5
Latin America and the Caribbean	8.5	8.4	8.4	8.0	7.4	7.0	7.0	7.9	8.2	8.5
Middle East	9.3	9.5	9.3	10.0	9.5	9.3	9.2	8.8	9.4	10.0
North Africa	13.1	14.0	12.3	11.5	10.4	10.1	10.0	9.8	10.5	11.1
Sub-Saharan Africa	8.2	8.3	8.2	8.2	8.2	8.0	8.0	7.9	8.2	8.5

Source: ILO 2010, 46.

Notes: * = preliminary estimate; CI = confidence interval.

Table 13.11 Unemployment Rates for Youth by World, Region, and Economy

percent

	1999	2000	2004	2005	2006	2007	2008	2009*		
								CI lower bound	Preliminary estimate	CI upper bound
World	12.6	12.5	13.0	13.0	12.4	11.8	12.1	12.7	13.4	14.0
Developed economies and European Union	13.9	13.2	14.4	14.1	13.0	12.2	13.1	17.5	17.7	17.8
Central and Southeastern Europe (non-EU) and CIS	22.7	19.9	19.6	19.1	18.5	17.5	17.1	20.9	21.5	22.0
East Asia	9.2	8.9	8.5	8.4	8.2	7.8	8.7	8.3	9.0	9.7
Southeast Asia and Pacific	13.1	13.2	17.0	17.9	17.2	14.9	14.4	14.6	15.3	16.0
South Asia	9.8	10.2	10.3	10.4	10.0	9.9	9.9	10.0	10.7	11.5
Latin America and the Caribbean	15.6	15.5	16.5	16.1	15.1	14.1	14.3	16.1	16.6	17.5
Middle East	20.5	21.1	20.8	22.6	21.6	21.4	21.7	20.9	22.3	23.8
North Africa	27.3	29.9	27.2	26.8	24.2	23.6	23.5	23.2	24.7	26.1
Sub-Saharan Africa	12.6	12.6	12.6	12.4	12.4	12.3	12.3	12.0	12.6	13.0

Source: ILO 2010, 47.

Notes: * = preliminary estimate; CI = confidence interval.

unemployment in recent years and its estimated response to the onset of the global financial crisis.

Similar to the total unemployment rate (table 13.10), the largest increases in youth unemployment between 2008 and 2009 (estimated) occurred in the developed economies and the EU (an increase of 4.6 percentage points between 2008 and 2009), in Central and Southeastern Europe (non-EU) and CIS (a 4.4 percentage point increase), and in Latin America and the Caribbean (a 2.3 percentage point increase). Youth unemployment is a major concern in the Middle East and North Africa, with one in five of the regions' youth classified as unemployed.

Wages

Conclusions on wages and worker compensation in developing countries are also difficult to make owing to poor and incomplete data. Often the only data collected are for manufacturing. In countries with large rural and informal sectors, such data fail to give an accurate picture of worker compensation. It is difficult to compare trends over time and across countries because of data inconsistencies and differences in productivity, the bargaining power of workers, and social security (Betcherman 2002). Nevertheless, the ILO and the World Bank do the best they can to collect data on workers' compensation, as measured by payroll costs, not just wages.

Keeping these caveats in mind, let us consider some of the disparities that appear across countries. For example, an average worker in manufacturing in Kenya earned less than $100 a year in the early 1990s, whereas an average worker in Brazil earned more than $14,000 a year. In terms of earnings growth, East Asian countries experienced increases in real wages of between 25 and 31 percent in the early 1990s, while real wages declined in South Asia and Sub-Saharan Africa, with mixed trends in the Latin American region.[5]

Within regions, the best measure of wage inequality is income inequality (because, in most countries, wages are the primary source of income). Data on various inequality measures, and in particular the Gini coefficient—as quoted in Betcherman (2002)—show that inequality varies dramatically across countries, with developing countries exhibiting much higher and increasing levels than developed countries.

The United Nations Development Programme (UNDP 2009) tabulates the Gini coefficient for 148 countries for the period 1992–2007 (figure 13.1). We selected a number of countries to show the range of values. Denmark had the lowest Gini coefficient of 24.7 and Namibia had the highest, 74.3. The greatest proportion of the 148 countries had

Figure 13.1   Income Inequality (Gini Coefficient) in Select Countries, 1992–2007

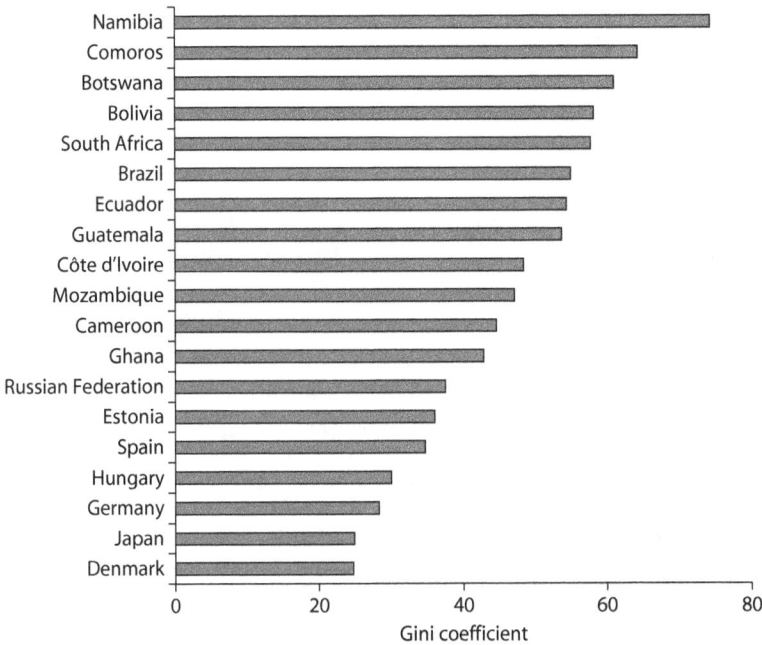

Source: UNDP 2009.

values between 30 and 39. Many countries in Africa scored in the 40s and 50s, as did some Latin American economies.

Skills

The link between education (and other forms of human capital invest-ment) and sustainable long-run economic growth is strong, as we saw in chapter 11 of this book. Pierre and Scarpetta (2004b) note that "a simple decomposition of the sources of economic growth over the past decades suggests that the combined effect of greater utilization of labor and enhancement in human capital have generally made a significant contri-bution to improvements in output per capita." No wonder, since a skilled workforce attracts new firms while enabling existing firms to become more efficient and productive. Surveys[6] conducted regularly by the World Bank reveal that many firms in developing countries rate inadequate worker skill and education as a major obstacle to their operations.

Although educational attainment has improved in all developing regions—particularly in East Asia and Pacific and the Middle East and

North Africa—it remains low in many developing countries. In Sub-Saharan Africa and South Asia, more than 40 percent of those aged 25 and over in 2000 had not completed any formal education. And while there have been significant improvements in the proportion of adults who have completed secondary and higher education in all regions, their share in the working-age population remains very low in many countries (figure 13.2).

The link between education and growth can break down under extreme circumstances, in developing and developed countries alike. Many African countries have seen poor growth performance even with rapid increases in education. For investments in education to reap positive returns, the investment climate must be favorable, the *quality* of education must be high, firms must have incentives to hire more skilled workers, and graduates must have opportunities to use their newly acquired skills in productive settings, rather than in bloated bureaucracies and overstaffed state enterprises (World Bank 2005).

The World Bank (2007) notes the following:

• Educational quality—measured by what people know—has powerful effects on individual earnings, on the distribution of income, and on economic growth.

Figure 13.2   Educational Attainment by Region

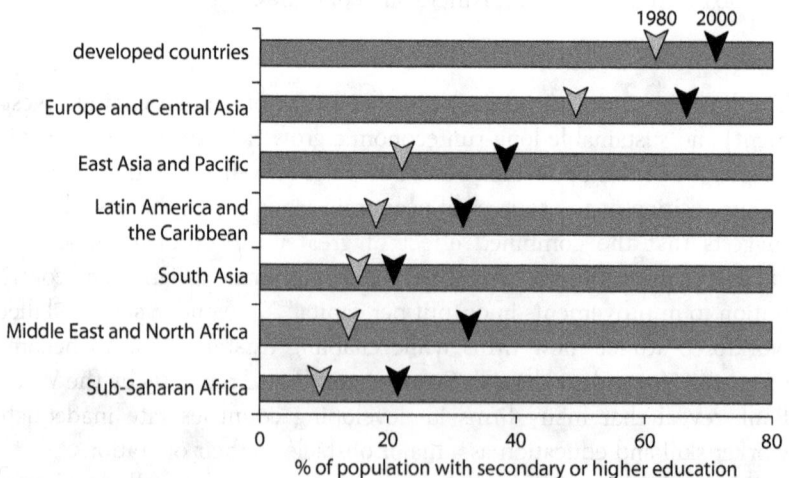

Source: World Bank 2005.
Note: Population is persons age 25 and over with secondary or higher education attainment as a share of total population age 25 and over.

- The educational quality in developing countries is much worse than the educational quantity (school enrollment and attainment)—a picture already quite bleak.
- Just providing more resources to schools is unlikely to be successful—improving the quality of education will take major changes in institutions (World Bank 2007, 2).

Investments in education also yield higher returns when combined with or preceded by investments in health and nutrition. Behrman (1999) shows that initial 1965 investments in health and nutrition—represented by life expectancies at birth relative to those predicted by per capita income in a cross-section for that year—had more predictive power for economic growth over the coming quarter-century than did initial investments in schooling. It is reasonable to expect that with better health and nutrition, the expected returns on schooling would be far greater. The links between skill and health generate a cycle in which good education and health enable growth, which in turn promotes further investment in them (World Bank 2005).

Women and Children in the Labor Force

Between 1999 and 2008, the proportion of women in the labor force increased in all regions except East Asia and Southeast Asia and Pacific (see table 13.12). Globally, the proportion of women in the labor force decreased by 0.1 percentage points during the same period. There is a great deal of variation across the regions. The relatively low share in the Middle East and North Africa—24.9 percent and 27.5 percent, respectively, in 2008—compared with the other regions has been linked to the nonenforcement of legislation protecting women's employment rights and family laws that translate into women being less employable than men. On the other hand, women are more likely than men to be employed in the informal sector, with the result that their overall weight in the labor force is greater than official statistics would suggest.

Child labor is primarily a rural and agricultural phenomenon, with children working either on family land or as hired farm laborers, and is found disproportionately in poor countries (figure 13.3). Girls work in the household or are hired out as domestic help. While they are working, children are not in school, which limits their own potential and that of their social group. Even where free schooling is available, parents may prefer that their children help out on the farm or in the household. If fees must be paid for education, many parents worry that their

Table 13.12   Labor Force Participation Rates of Females by World, Region, and Economy
percent

	1999	2000	2001	2002	2003	2004	2005	2006	2007	2008	2009*
World	51.8	51.6	51.6	51.5	51.4	51.4	51.5	51.6	51.6	51.7	51.6
Developed economies and European Union	51.8	51.9	51.9	51.9	52.0	52.0	52.4	52.7	52.8	53.2	52.9
Central and Southeastern Europe (non-EU) and CIS	49.8	49.4	49.7	50.1	49.9	49.7	49.9	50.2	50.5	50.7	50.6
East Asia	69.9	69.6	69.2	68.8	68.3	67.9	67.5	67.1	66.8	66.6	66.5
Southeast Asia and Pacific	58.0	57.5	57.7	57.4	57.3	57.1	57.2	57.0	57.2	57.4	57.4
South Asia	34.3	34.1	34.0	33.9	33.9	33.8	34.2	34.6	34.8	35.1	34.9
Latin America and the Caribbean	46.6	46.8	47.0	47.9	48.3	49.3	50.0	50.8	51.0	51.6	51.7
Middle East	22.6	22.8	23.1	23.4	23.7	24.1	24.4	24.6	24.8	24.9	25.4
North Africa	26.6	26.6	26.2	26.3	26.7	26.9	26.9	27.1	27.3	27.5	27.4
Sub-Saharan Africa	60.4	60.8	61.1	61.3	61.5	61.6	61.8	61.8	61.9	62.1	62.6

Source: ILO 2010, 50.
Note: * = preliminary estimate.

Figure 13.3   Child Labor Participation and GDP per Capita

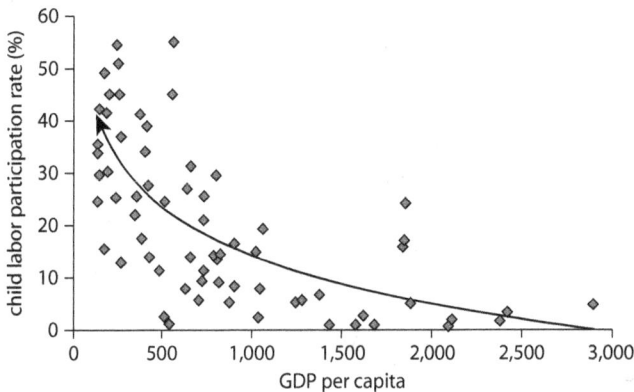

Source: World Bank 2006.

investments will not be repaid, particularly if employment prospects are bleak. Mothers are more likely than fathers to make sacrifices and invest in children. Therefore, transfer programs that help women (such as Mexico's Progresa program) are also likely to benefit children. Bans on child labor, trade sanctions, and boycotts have proven to be ineffective, even where they are enforced, as children wind up working in illegal or unregulated activities.

Conclusion

The labor market represents one of the main conduits through which economic growth can help reduce poverty in developing countries. While labor-friendly economic growth can be useful—especially where demand for jobs is high and rising—an accompanying cost may be slow growth in labor productivity. The labor force is growing rapidly in many developing countries, accompanied in many cases by an ongoing shift from agricultural employment. This would appear to call either for some form of labor-intensive growth or for a marked increase in growth itself, if an increase in unemployment or a shift to the informal sector is to be avoided. Other notable developing-country concerns highlighted in this chapter are wage inequalities across countries and marked differences in labor market access for men and women.

Notes

1. Narayan and others (2002), quoted in Pierre and Scarpetta (2004a), "found that for more than 70 percent of the poor, finding a job—whether salaried or self-employed—is the main way out of poverty. And in most developing and emerging economies about 90 percent of jobs are created by private firms."

2. The ILO dismisses the first scenario—which includes revisions to GDP growth—as unlikely. The ILO suggests that "vulnerable employment is a long-term trend indicator that tends to lag changes in GDP growth. Accordingly, the lower bound of the range (which is based on the historical relationship between vulnerable employment and GDP growth in each country) should be viewed as the long-term path that the world was on prior to the onset of the crisis, rather than a likely estimate for 2009" (ILO 2010, 18). Nevertheless, the share of vulnerable employment is shown in the S1 column.

3. Tables 13.2 and 13.3, S1.

4. For example, the large proportions of vulnerable and working poor.

5. The data refer to the periods before the financial crises in Asia and Latin America.

6. The World Bank maintains an index of the ease of doing business in 183 economies and select cities at the subnational and regional level and publishes these reports. See http://www.doingbusiness.org for further details.

Bibliography

Behrman, J. R. 1999. "Labor Markets in Developing Countries." In *Handbook of Labor Economics*, ed. O. Ashenfelter and D. Card, 2859–939. Amsterdam: Elsevier Science Publishers.

Besley, T., and R. Burgess. 2002. "Can Labor Regulation Hinder Economic Performance? Evidence from India." Unpublished paper, London School of Economics.

Betcherman, G. 2002. "An Overview of Labor Markets World-Wide: Key Trends and Major Policy Issues." Discussion Paper 0205, Social Protection Unit, World Bank, Washington, DC.

Bourguignon, F. 2005. "Development Strategies for More and Better Jobs." Presentation at the Carnegie Endowment for International Peace conference "Help Wanted: More and Better Jobs in a Globalized Economy," Washington, DC, April 14.

Gutierrez, C., C. Orecchia, P. Pierell, and P. Serneels. 2007. "Does Employment Generation Really Matter for Poverty Reduction?" Poverty Reduction Group, World Bank, Washington, DC.

ILO (International Labour Office. 2010. *Global Employment Trends*. Geneva: ILO.

Kapsos, S. 2005. "The Employment Intensity of Growth: Trends and Macroeconomic Determinants." Employment Strategy Paper 12, International Labour Office, Geneva.

Narayan, D., and P. Petesh. 2002. *Voices of the Poor—From Many Lands*. Washington, DC: World Bank.

Pierre, G., and S. Scarpetta. 2004a. "Employment Regulations Through the Eyes of Employers: Do They Matter and How Do Firms Respond to Them?" Background note for *World Development Report 2005: A Better Investment Climate for Everyone*, World Bank, Washington, DC.

———. 2004b. "How Labor Market Policies Can Combine Workers' Protection with Job Creation: A Partial Review of Some Key Issues and Policy Options." Background paper for *World Development Report 2005: A Better Investment Climate for Everyone*. World Bank, Washington, DC.

Ravallion, M., and G. Datt. 1999. "When Is Growth Pro-Poor?" Policy Research Working Paper 2263, World Bank, Washington, DC.

UNDP (United Nations Development Programme). 2009. *Human Development Report*. New York: United Nations.

World Bank. 2004. "Unlocking the Employment Potential in the Middle East and North Africa: Toward a New Social Contract." Middle East and North Africa Development Report, World Bank, Washington, DC.

———. 2005. *World Development Report: A Better Investment Climate for Everyone*. Washington, DC: World Bank.

———. 2006. *World Development Report: Equity and Development*. Washington, DC: World Bank.

———. 2007. *Education Quality and Economic Growth*. Washington, DC: World Bank.

———. 2008. *World Development Indicators*. Washington, DC: World Bank.

CHAPTER 14

Land and Agriculture

Land is of critical importance to the poor, particularly in rural areas. Owners of land have an incentive to make it productive, raising household incomes and contributing to national growth. Land can be exchanged in the market, as well as through nonmarket channels such as inheritance. It can also be used as collateral to raise funds for further investment. In short, land widens the economic choices open to those who possess it.

But inequality in access to and ownership of land is a serious problem in most developing countries. When inequality becomes a serious brake on growth, the state may step in to achieve socially desirable land allocation and utilization, in particular where unequal land distribution has kept large sections of the population in poverty.

We begin this chapter by looking at why land inequality is so prevalent in the developing world, then go on to explore the impact of inequality on economic growth and poverty, particularly among the rural poor. Land inequality has been shown to affect three key aspects of economic development: education, institutions, and financial development. We examine the relevant literature on these subjects. The final section examines the role that government can play in bringing about a more equal distribution of land. The chapter concludes with an examination of the pros and cons of land titling, a modern property rights tool.

Land Distribution in Poor Countries

The history of land ownership in many developing countries has the notable fault of excluding much of the population, especially the rural poor, from secure tenure. Formal tenure covers only 2 to 10 percent of the land in Africa, for example. Property rights are often imposed by outside forces or local elites, whose objective is to seek surpluses from local populations or force them into wage labor without promoting opportunities for land ownership. The result is an unequal distribution of land and a large landless population. Of the periurban population, more than 50 percent in Africa and more than 40 percent in Asia live under informal tenure, with highly insecure land rights (World Bank 2003a).

Paralleling the exclusion of the poor from land access and ownership is the absence of institutional systems for titling land. Overlapping institutions have evolved over long periods and often provide little clarity on how land rights are defined, how ownership and possession are determined, and how conflicts are resolved. Some forms of land distribution that add ambiguity to an already murky picture of access and ownership are land owned by communities (for example, communal land among indigenous people), land handed down from generation to generation through customary practices (for example, primogeniture, where the eldest son inherits the father's land), and land taken over by the state (for example, "crown land").

In many countries, the state continues to own a large portion of valuable land despite evidence that such ownership is conducive to mismanagement, underutilization of resources, and corruption. Because discretionary bureaucratic interventions and controls remain a major source of corruption and a barrier to the start-up of small enterprises in many developing countries, campaigns to achieve broad, egalitarian ownership can significantly improve governance by strengthening the voice of the poor, allowing them greater participation in the political process, and improving public services, especially at the local level. Land is the primary physical asset of poor households. In Uganda, for example, it constitutes between 50 and 60 percent of their total assets. Securing title to that land is critical for improving welfare and stimulating investment and the accumulation of wealth for current and future generations. As noted by the World Bank (2003a), a secure title to land enables households to survive and generate a marketable surplus, defines their social and economic status and often their collective identity, increases their incentive to use land in a sustainable manner, and enables them to self-insure and maintain access to financial markets.

The scope for economic growth is limited where land tenure is not secure or property rights poorly defined. For example, in many African countries, the vast majority of land (more than 90 percent on average) remains under customary tenure, which often lacks legal recognition. To avoid leaving the occupants of this land effectively outside the rule of law, many African countries have recently given legal recognition to land tenure arrangements that have been in operation for generations as well as to the institutions administering it. But lack of institutional capacity to administer and implement these laws remains a major challenge (World Bank 2003a).

Informality is also widespread in urban areas. This is of particular concern because, in many countries, growing populations and expanding nonagricultural demand lead to an appreciation of land values and increase the potential for land-related conflict. Defending one's land becomes a costly endeavor that diverts efforts from more productive pursuits, such as investment.

Where land titles are secure, by contrast, economic opportunities and social advantages multiply (figure 14.1). In other words, economic growth follows secure land titles. First, greater security against eviction is likely to increase land-related investment. Second, greater ability to transfer land will increase the payoff from land-connected investments because it allows investors to benefit even if they are unable to use the land themselves. Third, greater security of tenure can improve access to credit, thereby increasing investment in situations in which limited credit supply may have constrained it.

Land ownership is particularly important for women's welfare, though women's ownership rates are disproportionately low. In addition to ensuring a more equitable society, more attention to women's land rights would have far-reaching economic consequences in areas where women are the main cultivators, male emigration rates are high, control of productive activities is differentiated by gender, or high adult mortality rates and unclear inheritance regulations undermine widows' livelihoods. Several studies have shown that productivity increases when women both own and control land. Udry (1996) showed that the transfer of plots from men to women in Burkina Faso increased output by 6 percent. But Adesina and Djato (1997) found no significant difference between the efficiency of women and men on plots in Côte d'Ivoire.

Figure 14.1   Initial Land Distribution and Growth by Economy, 1960–2000

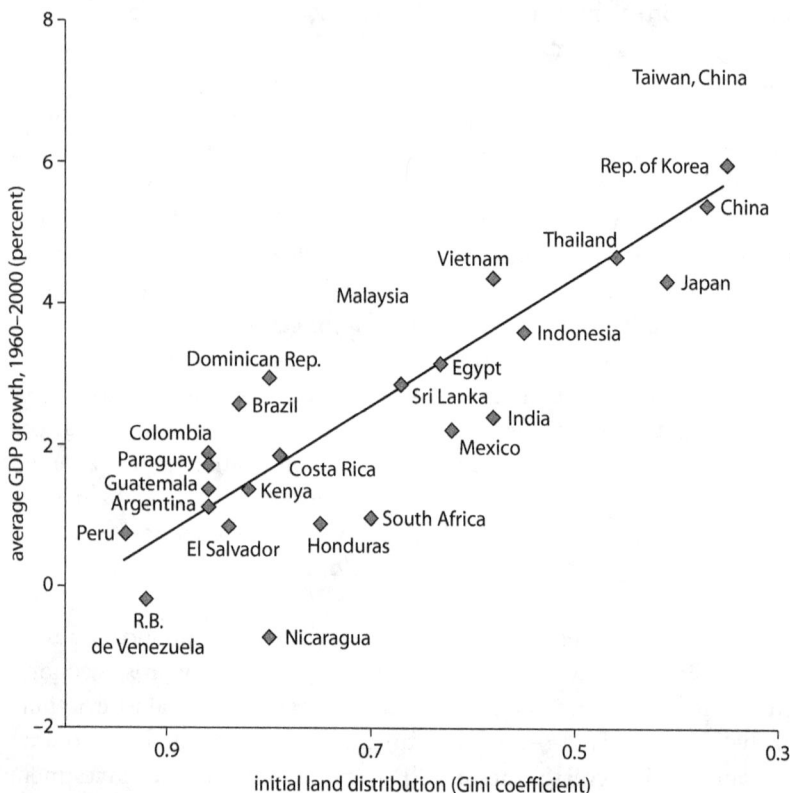

Source: Deininger 2003, 18.
Note: The Gini coefficient measures the degree of concentration (inequality) of a variable in a distribution of its elements. It compares the Lorenz curve of a ranked empirical distribution with the line of perfect equality. This line assumes that each element has the same contribution to the total summation of the values of a variable. The Gini coefficient ranges between 0, where there is no concentration (perfect equality) and 1, where there is total concentration (perfect inequality).

Women's land rights in many developing economies are acquired through husbands or male relatives. Widows often have only indirect access to land, and even this access is insecure. In India, for example, laws and prevailing practices are often heavily biased against women (Saxena 1999). A woman's right to own land still needs to be legally recognized and enforced in many developing countries. Reforming inheritance laws is one way of achieving this goal. Embedding gender equality in the constitution (to supersede contrary legislation) is another. Developing countries in Asia, Latin America, and Africa have embraced some of these options, but much more needs to be done.

Land-policy initiatives targeted at women also play a positive role in enhancing nutrition and accumulating human capital. A study by Quisumbing and Otsuka (2001) shows that the introduction of export crops in Ghana increased the demand for female workers and resulted in improved spending on female education and health.[1]

Land Inequality and Rural Poverty

On average, rural poverty accounts for nearly 63 percent of poverty worldwide (see box 14.1). The rural poor account for 90 percent of those in poverty in China and Bangladesh and between 65 and 90 percent in Sub-Saharan Africa. In Latin America, by contrast, poverty is concentrated in urban areas (Khan 2000). Among the rural poor, those who are landless suffer more than landholders. Because the rural poor depend mainly on income from agriculture, forestry, fishing, and, in some cases, small-scale industries, agricultural growth has almost always contributed to a reduction in poverty, even when land holdings are small and technology is sparse (Khan 2000; Gaiha 1993; and Datt and Ravallion 1998). In spite of this, government policy has often disfavored the agricultural sector and rural infrastructure, both social and physical.

Box 14.1

How Rural Poverty Is Created

- Political instability and civil strife
- Systemic discrimination on the basis of gender, race, ethnicity, religion, or caste
- Ill-defined or unfair enforcement of rights to agricultural land and other natural resources
- High concentration of land ownership and asymmetrical tenancy arrangements
- Corrupt politicians and rent-seeking public bureaucracies
- Economic policies that discriminate against or exclude the rural poor from the development process and accentuate the effects of other poverty-creating processes
- Large and rapidly growing families with high dependency ratios
- Market imperfections caused by distortionary public policies and the high concentration of land and other assets
- External shocks stemming from natural causes (for example, climatic changes) and fluctuations in the international economy

Source: Khan (2000), drawing on Jazairy, Alamgir, and Panuccio (1992) and Gaiha (1993).

Land differentiates the rural poor. *Cultivators* have access to land as small-scale landowners and tenants, whereas *noncultivators* are landless, unskilled workers (Khan 2000). Cultivators account for the majority of the rural poor and are directly involved in agricultural production. In most cases, they are unable to sustain themselves on their own holdings and therefore offer their labor to larger-scale landholders. Noncultivators are generally the poorest of the rural poor, and their numbers have been increasing in developing countries because of a natural increase in population and "depeasantization"[2]—public policies aimed at moving small-scale landholders out of agricultural production. Noncultivators are particularly vulnerable to changes in the demand for labor, wage rates, and food prices. Furthermore, they are typically isolated from public infrastructure services and public safety nets, such as food rations. As noted in the previous section, rural women suffer more than rural men because of their lower social status and because of institutional discrimination, such as in inheritance laws.

Khan (2000) offers some policy prescriptions to deal with the problem of rural poverty. These include

- land reform through titling, redistribution, and fair and enforceable tenancy contracts;
- improvements in health, education, and infrastructure (including irrigation, transport, and communications) and the involvement of local government and civil society in devising and implementing these improvements;
- rural credit programs that target the needs of the rural poor, perhaps through the extension of community-based credit programs;
- a flexible public works program to smooth out household consumption and decrease the poverty of the landless; and
- public safety nets, such as food-supplement programs, that could be provided through schools, health-care clinics, and community centers in times of need.

Land Inequality and Economic Development

Land inequality has been linked to low levels of economic development, with adverse consequences for the poor. The facets of the economy that appear to suffer most from the unequal distribution of land are education, institutions, and finance. According to theories that attempt to explain the relative success of developing countries in raising incomes over time, no part of the economy develops optimally in the face of land inequality. These theories have been bolstered by empirical cross-country studies (using a Gini coefficient to measure the distribution of land within groups of landowners across countries) that found a negative relationship between land inequality and institutional development, education, and financial development (Deininger and Squire 1998).

The theory linking land inequality and economic development is quite clear in differentiating between those who own land (and the inequality in land distribution within this group of landowners) and those who are landless. But, until recently, empirical work failed to make this distinction. Erickson and Vollrath (2004) derived a measure of land inequality that encompassed both agricultural landowners and landless individuals.[3] They found a significant negative relationship between education and land inequality—but only for landless individuals. They found no significant relationship between land inequality and financial institutions for either landholders or landless persons.

So the jury is still out. The following sections examine the literature behind the hypothetical relationships between land inequality, on the one hand, and institutional development, education, and financial development on the other.

Institutions and Land Inequality

Engerman and Sokoloff (1997, 2000) first highlighted the negative relationship between institutions and land inequality. Examining the economic development of Latin America following colonization, they found that land inequality dated from the existence of vast plantations worked by slave labor—a system that perpetuated inequality in access to resources. Unequal resource allocation led to the development of institutions designed specifically to protect the interests of the elite, hampering economic growth and development.

The hypothesis that land inequality favored such allocation practices and promoted the development of bad institutions was taken up by Easterly (2002), who suggested that this relationship held across time and regions. Easterly and Levine (2003) also found that natural resource endowments affected growth through institutions. For example, environments where crops were most effectively produced, such as on large plantations, quickly developed political and legal institutions that protected a landholder minority from a peasant majority—some even included slavery. Even when agriculture receded from the economic spotlight, enduring institutions continued to thwart competition and, hence, economic development. In colonies with inhospitable climates, the colonial powers established extractive institutions so that a few colonialists could exploit available natural resources. Where the climate was more hospitable, colonial powers established settler institutions. According to this view, the institutional structures created by colonialists in response to particular environments endured even after the end of colonialism. Thus, the impact of the environment on economic development is felt through the shaping of institutions.

Education and Land Inequality

Empirical work on the relationship between land inequality and education has focused on land inequality and the public provision of education. Mariscal and Sokoloff (2000)—in extending the work of Engerman and Sokoloff (1997, 2000)—found a negative relationship between the public provision of education and land inequality. Their hypothesis was that, assuming education to have a smaller complementarity with agriculture than with manufacturing, landowners were reluctant to fund education because they believed the costs to outweigh the benefits, particularly in an agricultural setting. Galor, Moav, and Vollrath (2003)—examining the incentives of landowners to provide education—argue that the provision of education decreases as land distribution becomes more unequal. Deininger and Squire (1998) found a negative relationship between levels of education attained and land inequality. But their study was not able to distinguish whether this was due to poor public provision of educational resources or limited demand for education based on available assets—or a combination of both factors.

Erickson and Vollrath (2004) tested the hypothesis that the public provision of education—as measured by spending as a proportion of gross domestic product (GDP)—is limited by land inequality. Between 1965 and 1979, they found that greater land inequality across the agricultural population was associated with lower spending on education for landless populations.

Financial Development as a Constraint to Land Equality

The effects of inequality in physical assets such as land can be transmitted through financial markets. For example, access to credit is conditional on ownership of assets, and—in the context of a developing economy—land is the most common asset. The distribution of assets, as well as average income, will determine how many people are able to undertake investment in, for example, physical and human capital. In societies where the distribution of land is unequal, fewer people will be able to take up investment opportunities, thus leading to lower stocks of human and physical capital and lower levels of economic growth in the long run.

The literature on land inequality and the financial sector is extensive. A broad consensus suggests that land inequality (a) hampers financial development, (b) results from and persists because of poor financial development, and (c) implies fewer potential users of financial sector products, such as credit, deposits, insurance, and so on.

The literature also finds that, where rural elites prevail, the government may be the main provider of credit, thus retarding the development of the private financial sector.

The absence of a properly functioning financial sector with markets for risk and credit contributes to unequal land allocation. Individuals have no choice but to retain their holdings in the face of external price shocks. As noted by Erickson and Vollrath (2004), farm workers may have no incentive to change the status quo of land concentration, given that production risks are borne by the landowner. In a society where land is concentrated among a landholding minority, there are few incentives to provide financial services because demand is so low.

The Role of Government in Land Markets

The rights to own and exchange land are established and protected by governments. Governments may also have a role in equalizing land allocation and use if inequalities have led to widespread poverty or stifled economic growth. The World Bank (2003a) suggests that property rights in land should have the following characteristics:

- The *time frame* for securing land rights should be long enough to ensure an adequate return on investment. The potential for investment in urban areas is greater than in rural areas, so the time frame should reflect this. Although property rights given for an indefinite period are the best option, long-term rights that can be renewed automatically are the next-best alternative.

- Property rights should be defined in a way that makes them easy to *observe, enforce,* and *exchange.* This requires the existence of recognized institutions that are accessible by the general populace and that render decisions backed by the power of the state. The need for universal legitimacy is particularly evident in Africa, where rights to 90 percent of the land are determined outside the legal system. Informal institutions of land administration cannot offer universally recognized mechanisms for enforcing property rights. On the other hand, formal institutions make little difference to the lives of ordinary people if their scope is limited.

- If the government is engaged in *land allocation reforms*, it must decide whether it is more appropriate to confer property rights on individuals or on groups. Group rights are more appropriate in situations characterized by economies of scale in resource management and high-risk markets. While a group system of property rights may be advantageous in the early stages of development, the likelihood of technical progress and demographic changes suggests that one should expect property rights to become individualized over time. This is not an automatic evolution, however, but one that will be shaped by political and economic factors.

The governments of many developing countries have already started implementing a first generation of reforms encompassing significant steps toward greater economic liberalization—including the establishment and protection of property rights. But there is a further role for government in the implementation of second-generation reforms that address through registration and titling the persistent insecurity of land rights. Formalizing land ownership can deliver large productivity gains. It is especially beneficial where indigenous tenure systems are weak, the potential return on investment on land is high, and collateralized lending is in place. Second-generation reforms have been progressing over the past decade in Latin America, for example, where unequal distribution of land is historically common. Both the World Bank and the Inter-American Development Bank have funded projects in land titling and registration.

While land titling and registration have been largely positive in Latin America, it is not clear whether similar reforms are successful in every region. In particular, the effectiveness of titling and land registration has been questioned for Sub-Saharan Africa (Atwood 1990; Migot-Adholla and others 1991). Jacoby and Minten (2005, 1) write that "Sub-Saharan Africa lacks the infrastructure, factor market development, and other prerequisites for land tenure reform to promote agricultural intensification and productivity growth."

Incidences of land titling in Africa are relatively rare. This is unsurprising given that most land in the region is unsecured. Some tenure reform has taken place in Kenya, but the resulting literature suggests little economic impact (Carter, Weibe, and Blarel 1997; Place and Migot-Adholla 1998). Based on their study of investment, productivity, and value between titled and untitled plots worked by the same household, Jacoby and Minten (2005) conclude that a formal land-titling system should not be extended to rural Madagascar. They find that the presence of a title has no significant effect on land-specific investment, with weak effects on land productivity and values.

Indeed, as noted by Jacoby and Minten (2005), proceeding with land titling and registration in an unsecured, indigenous tenure system may not reduce insecurity to any appreciable extent and might even increase it. In most cases of unsecured land, an informal system evolves over time to govern community land use and transfer. Imposing a formal structure on arrangements that have worked for years may do no more than create opportunities for rent seeking. These concerns are captured by Atwood (1990) and quoted in Jacoby and Minten (2005, 2) as follows:

> Members of a local community may face far fewer risks of loss of land under the existing informal system than an outsider would face. In addition, while land registration might reduce the risks faced by an outsider, it may increase the risks and insecurity faced by local people as family members or peripheral land claimants jockey to see in whose name a parcel will be registered . . . For many local people, therefore, registration can create rather than reduce uncertainty and conflict over land rights.

To strengthen development and reduce poverty, land policies must take history and traditional customs into consideration. Without exceeding institutional capacity, they should aim to provide secure tenure to land to improve the welfare of the poor. Government land policy also has a key role in promoting and contributing to socially desirable land allocation and utilization. For example, in the countries of the former Soviet Union, farm restructuring was a necessary step in decollectivization and land reform. In some East and West African countries with a highly unequal distribution of land ownership, where land issues are often key elements of social strife, a clear and equitable postconflict land policy is needed. Land policy also has a central role to play in devising appropriate incentives for sustainable land use, which is required to avoid the irreversible degradation of nonrenewable natural resources.

The Role of Agriculture in Reducing Rural Poverty[4]

Agricultural development is vital for achieving the first Millennium Development Goal (MDG): to halve by 2015 the share of people suffering from extreme poverty and hunger. As noted, three out of every four poor people in developing countries live in rural areas, and most of them depend directly or indirectly on agriculture for their livelihoods.

Two world regions offer great promise but present acute challenges. For much of Sub-Saharan Africa, agriculture is a strong option for spurring growth, overcoming poverty, and enhancing food security. Improvements in agricultural productivity are vital for stimulating growth in other parts of the economy. But accelerating growth will require a sharp increase in the productivity of smallholder farming, combined with more effective support to the millions coping as subsistence farmers, many in remote areas.

In Asia, the challenge of overcoming widespread poverty hinges on confronting widening rural-urban income disparities. Asia's fast-growing economies remain home to more than 600 million rural people who live in extreme poverty. Despite massive rural-urban migration, rural poverty will remain dominant for several decades to come. It is therefore essential to generate many more rural jobs by diversifying into labor-intensive, high-value agriculture linked to a dynamic rural, nonfarm sector.

With land and water becoming scarcer in all regions of the world, the future of agriculture is tied to better stewardship of natural resources. With the right incentives and investments, agriculture's environmental footprint can be lightened, and environmental services harnessed to protect watersheds and biodiversity. Today, rapidly expanding domestic and global markets; institutional innovations in markets, finance, and collective action; and revolutions in biotechnology and information technology all offer exciting opportunities for agriculture to promote development. But seizing these opportunities will require the political will to move forward with reforms that change how agriculture is managed.

Assessing Agriculture's Contribution to Growth

How much can agriculture be expected to contribute to economic growth? To answer that question, we group the countries of the developing world into three categories: agriculture-based countries (including India and many of the world's poorest countries), transforming countries (including China and Indonesia), and urban countries (such as Brazil). Key characteristics of each of the three groups of countries are presented in table 14.1.

Table 14.1   Characteristics of the Three Economies

	Agriculture-based countries	Transforming countries	Urban countries
Rural population (millions), 2005	417	2,220	255
Share of rural population (%), 2005	68	63	26
GDP per capita (2000 US$), 2005	379	1,068	3,489
Share of agriculture in GDP (%), 2005	29	13	6
Annual agricultural GDP growth, 1993–2005 (%)	4.0	2.9	2.2
Annual nonagricultural GDP growth, 1993–2005 (%)	3.5	7.0	2.7
Number of rural poor (millions), 2002	170	583	32
Rural poverty rate, 2002 (%)	51	28	13

Source: Compiled from table 1.1. in World Bank 2007, 31.
Note: Poverty line is $1.08 a day, in 1993 purchasing power parity dollars.

Agriculture's average contribution to GDP growth differs markedly by category (figure 14.2). The sector accounts for 32 percent of growth on average in agriculture-based countries, 7 percent in transforming countries, and 5 percent in urban countries.

Toward Effective Agricultural Development Policies
Given agriculture's leading role in the growth of the poorest countries, the size of the rural population in the agriculture-based and transforming countries, and high rates of rural poverty in both groups of countries, policy makers need to implement effective policies of agricultural development. Several areas where good policies are needed are described below.

Increase access to assets. Among household assets, land, water, and human capital are the major determinants of the rural poor's ability to participate in agricultural markets, secure livelihoods in subsistence farming, compete as entrepreneurs in the rural nonfarm economy, and find employment in skilled occupations. Enhancing assets requires significant public investments in irrigation, health, education, and institutional development, such as enhancing the security of property rights and the quality of land administration. Increasing assets may also require affirmative action to equalize chances for disadvantaged or excluded groups, such as women and ethnic minorities.

Improve land markets. Land rental markets in many areas are hobbled by insecure property rights, poor contract enforcement, and legal restrictions

Figure 14.2   Agriculture's Contribution to Growth

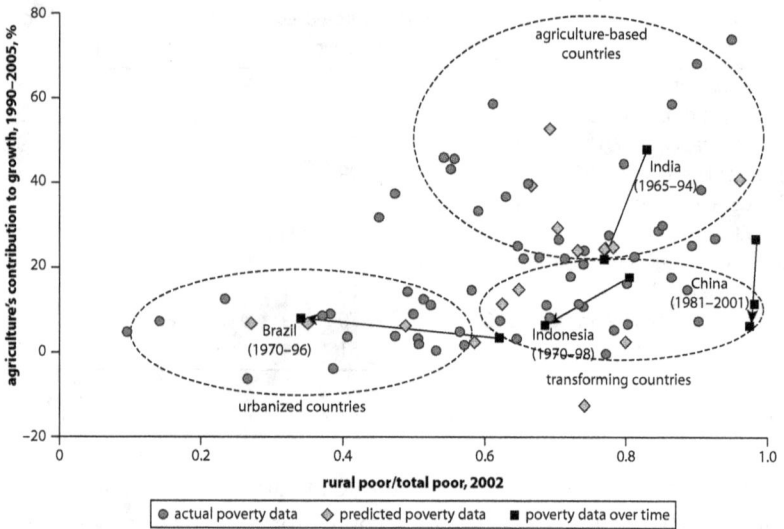

Note: Arrows show paths for Brazil, China, India, and Indonesia.

that discourage those who work the land from raising productivity, diversifying their incomes, or abandoning agriculture for another pursuit. Safety nets and access to credit are widely needed to minimize distressed land sales because of shocks. Land reform is needed to promote smallholder entry into the market, reduce inequalities in land distribution, increase efficiency, and recognize women's rights. Targeted subsidies to facilitate market-based land reform are already used in Brazil and South Africa.

Expand irrigation, and make it more efficient. Irrigated land is more than twice as productive as rainfed land, on average, yet in Sub-Saharan Africa only 4 percent of cultivated land is under irrigation, compared with 39 percent in South Asia and 29 percent in East Asia. Among the essential steps are revamping existing irrigation schemes, expanding small-scale schemes, and improving measures to harvest and store water.

Encourage technical education. Education levels in rural areas tend to be dismally low worldwide, yet rural people need education to pursue opportunities, obtain skilled jobs, start businesses in the rural nonfarm economy, and migrate successfully. Demand for education, including vocational training that can provide technical and business skills, can be enhanced through cash transfers conditioned on school attendance (as in Bangladesh, Brazil, and Mexico).

Protect the health of rural dwellers. Illness and death from HIV/AIDS and malaria have greatly reduced agricultural productivity and devastated livelihoods in many countries. In Zambia, for example, 19 percent of people age 15–24 in 1990 were dead by 2000. Irrigation may have contributed to the spread of malaria. Avian influenza caused by the proximity of humans and animals poses a growing threat to human health.

Raising Productivity among Smallholders

Harnessing agriculture to promote economic growth and move the large numbers of smallholder farmers and those coping as subsistence farmers in remote areas out of poverty is a key development challenge. A broad array of policy instruments can be used to raise productivity among commercial smallholders and subsistence farmers. Those policies include

- improving price incentives for poor farmers by liberalizing agricultural trade;
- improving product markets, including those for food staples, bulk exports, and high-value items for domestic consumption;
- widening access to financial services and reducing exposure to uninsured risks;
- enhancing the performance of producer organizations; and
- promoting innovation through science and technology.

We will expand briefly on these points below.

Improving price incentives for poor farmers by liberalizing agricultural trade. International trade in agriculture is heavily distorted by the subsidies that most developed-country governments provide to their domestic producers. Those subsidies cost the average family in the European Union, Japan, and the United States more than $1,000 each year, while depressing global prices for the products that poor farmers produce in the developing world. Further distortions are caused by the taxation and tariff policies of governments in much of the developing world. The challenge of unwinding those distortions for the greater good of the world's producers and consumers proved to be so politically sensitive that, in September 2003, it scuttled the Doha Round of international trade talks, launched in 2001. An effort to revive the talks was unsuccessful.

Considered as a purely technical matter, the World Bank (2003b) believes that rich and poor countries alike stand to benefit greatly from full multilateral liberalization of agricultural trade. The Bank estimated that a "pro-poor tariff reduction program," combined with an end to agricultural subsidies as presently practiced, had the potential to produce gains for developing countries of nearly $350 billion in additional income by 2015 (the target date of the MDGs). Those gains would mean that by 2015, 140 million fewer people would be living in poverty (that is, living on less than $2 a day). The same program would also have produced gains for rich countries on the order of $170 billion. Although the prospect for implementation of such a multilateral program are presently almost nil, *developing countries have many opportunities to benefit from unilateral liberalization.*

Improving product markets, including those for food staples, bulk exports, and high-value items for domestic consumption. Amid structural changes in agricultural markets and the entry of powerful new actors, a key issue for development is enhancing the participation of smallholders.

Reducing transaction costs and risks in food staples markets can offer the promise of quick improvements to promote faster growth and benefit the poor (comparatively faster than infrastructure investments, for example). Innovations include commodity exchanges, market information systems based on rural radio and short messaging systems, and market-based risk management tools. Insurance through exchange-traded futures contracts can sometimes manage price risks.

The long downward trend in world market prices of exports such as coffee and cotton threatens the livelihoods of millions of producers. Reduced taxation, greater liberalization of export markets, more efficient production and supply-chain processes, and better quality have improved incomes in many settings, including Zambia.

High-value markets for domestic consumption are the fastest-growing agricultural markets in most developing countries, expanding up to 6 to 7 percent a year, led by livestock products and horticulture.[5]

Widening access to financial services and reducing exposure to uninsured risks. Recently, the range of financial products[6] available to the rural poor has broadened to include savings, money transfers, insurance services, and leasing options. Information technologies are reducing transaction costs and making loans less costly in rural areas.

Exposure to uninsured risks—the results of natural disasters, health shocks, demographic changes, price volatility, and policy changes—has high costs for rural households, sapping efficiency and welfare. Farmers tend to forgo actions that might offer higher incomes if they have no way of guarding against the associated risk. Index-based insurance for drought risk (in India and elsewhere) could reduce risks and unlock agricultural finance. Children suffer long-term consequences when they are taken out of school in response to shocks or are malnourished. But despite multiple initiatives, progress has been slow in reducing uninsured risks in small-holder agriculture, largely because state-managed schemes have been ineffective.

Enhancing the performance of producer organizations. For smallholders, producer organizations are essential to achieve competitiveness, market-ing, input provision and credit, greater civil society participation, and governance.[7] But they must overcome legal restraints, low managerial capacity, elite capture, exclusion of the poor, and nonrecognition by the state.

Promoting innovation through science and technology. Developing countries invest far too little in agricultural research and development.[8] The agro-ecological features of Sub-Saharan Africa limit the degree to which the region can benefit from international technology transfers, while the small size of many African countries prevents them from cap-turing economies of scale in agricultural research and development. These factors have resulted in a widening cereal yield gap with the rest of the world. In addition, many public research organizations face leadership, management, and financial constraints that require urgent attention if Africa's producers are to take advantage of openings in higher-value mar-kets. Less-favored regions require better technologies for soil, water, and livestock management and more sustainable and resilient agricultural systems, including crop varieties more tolerant of pests, diseases, and drought. The potential benefits of technologies such as genetically modi-fied organisms will be missed unless the international development community sharply increases its support to interested countries.

Making Agriculture More Sustainable

The environmental agenda is inseparable from the broader agenda of agri-cultural development for the simple reason that agriculture cannot con-tinue to prosper without better stewardship of the natural resource base on which it depends. Agriculture poses a multiplicity of environmental problems linked to agricultural intensification (reduced biodiversity, mis-managed irrigation water, agrochemical pollution, and health costs and deaths from pesticide poisoning) and livestock breeding (pollution and contamination from animal waste and the spread of animal diseases such as avian influenza). Less-favored areas suffer from deforestation, soil erosion, desertification, and degradation of pastures and watersheds.[9]

More sustainable production systems and enhanced environmental services in agricultural areas will depend in large part on whether we can learn to handle water more wisely. Necessary steps include reducing water pollution and arresting the unsustainable mining of groundwater while meeting the demands of all users. We can start by discouraging wasteful water usage, devolving water management to local user groups, investing in better technologies, and regulating water usage (and agricultural production in general).

Better water measurement (remote sensing) and quality of irrigation services reforms could gain support for otherwise unpopular reforms. Payments by beneficiaries for environmental services can help overcome market failures in managing environmental externalities such as watershed and forest protection to create environmental services (clean drinking water, table water flows to irrigation systems, carbon sequestration, and protection of biodiversity).[10]

Conclusion

Access to and ownership of land shapes the capacity of the poor to escape from poverty. In most of the developing world, however, both access and ownership are very unequally distributed, with negative consequences for economic growth and poverty reduction. Certain groups, notably the rural poor and women, suffer disproportionately from land-related inequality. Governmental efforts to reduce inequality in access to land have focused on improving land titling and registration. Such efforts—while generally positive in the long run—have carried negative implications in some cases, as poor people have lost access to land without gaining ownership.

Agriculture remains a potent weapon in the fight against poverty. Countries with a predominant agricultural base and close to two-thirds of their population living in rural areas experience a high incidence of poverty. Growing and developing the agricultural sector in a sustainable manner represents the only viable way out of poverty. Policy makers have a critical role to play in making agriculture work for the rural poor. Unleashing the full development effect of agriculture calls for a number of policies in different areas of the economy. Among the initiatives discussed were achieving higher productivity, improving access to education and resources, and better stewardship of natural resources. Moreover, the gains from a pro-poor tariff reduction program, combined with a multilateral liberalization of agricultural trade, would decrease the numbers of people living in poverty.

Notes

1. Other studies—in West Africa and Kenya—show that the introduction of export crops actually decreased the demand for female laborers, with men taking over the land previously farmed by women—thus weakening women's rights to land (Kevane and Gray [1999] for West Africa; Dolan [2001] for Kenya). In Ghana, the demand for women's labor increased in the face of export crops, leading to an improvement in women's rights to land. Husbands had to make a gift of the plots to their wives in return for labor on the cocoa plots (Quisumbing and Otsuka 2001).

2. Khan (2000, 27) states that small-scale landowners and tenants are under pressure to get out of the agriculture sector altogether because of the underlying "market forces and policies affecting landholdings, rents, prices, credit, inputs, and public investment in the social and physical infrastructure."

3. Erickson and Vollrath (2004) argue that given the significant role that agriculture plays in the lives of the poor—agricultural production continues to account for a substantial fraction of total production in most developing countries, particularly the poorest—it is critical to examine the role of agricultural inequality and how, or whether, it relates to institutional development.

4. This section draws on *World Development Report 2008* (World Bank 2007). The focus of the report was on agriculture for development. We summarize here the overview to this report highlighting the contribution that agriculture can make to development.

5. Fresh and processed fruits and vegetables, fish and fish products, meat, nuts, spices, and floriculture now account for 43 percent of agricultural and food exports from developing countries, worth about $138 billion in 2004.

6. Credit reporting bureaus covering microfinance institutions and the lower tier of commercial banks also help smallholders capitalize on the reputations they establish as microfinance borrowers to access more commercial loans. Many of these innovations are still at the pilot stage, requiring evaluation and scaling up to make a real difference for smallholder competitiveness.

7. Between 1982 and 2002, the percentage of villages with producer organizations rose from 8 percent to 65 percent in Senegal and from 21 percent to 91 percent in Burkina Faso. The Indian Dairy Cooperatives Network has

12.3 million individual members (many of them landless and women) and produces 22 percent of India's milk supply.

8. Investment in agricultural research and development tripled in China and India over the past 20 years, but increased by barely a fifth in Sub-Saharan Africa (declining in about half of the countries there).

9. In the East African highlands, soil erosion can result in productivity losses as high as 2 to 3 percent a year, in addition to creating off-site effects such as the siltation of reservoirs.

10. In Nicaragua, payments induced a reduction in the area of degraded pasture and annual crops by more than 50 percent in favor of silvopastoralism, half of it by poor farmers. Environmental certification of products also allows consumers to pay for sustainable environmental management, as practiced under fair trade or shade-grown coffee.

Bibliography

Adesina, A. A., and K. K. Djato. 1997. "Relative Efficiency of Women as Farm Managers: Profit Function Analysis in Côte d'Ivoire." *Agricultural Economics* 16 (1): 47–53.

Agarwal, B. 1994. *A Field of One's Own: Gender and Land Rights in South Asia.* South Asian Studies. Cambridge, U.K.: Cambridge University Press.

Arnold, J. E. M. 2001. "Devolution of Control of Common Pool Resources to Local Communities: Experiences in Forestry." In *Access to Land, Rural Poverty, and Public Action*, ed. A. de Janvry, G. Gordillo, J. P. Plateau, and E. Sadoulet, 163–95. Oxford, U.K.: Oxford University Press.

Atwood, D. A. 1990. "Land Registration in Africa: The Impact on Agricultural Production." *World Development* 18 (5): 659–71.

Bardhan, P. 1995. "Research on Poverty and Development Twenty Years after Redistribution with Growth." In *Annual World Bank Conference on Development Economics*, ed. M. Bruno and B. Pleskovic, 59–72. Washington, DC: World Bank.

Bruce, J., S. Migot-Adholla, and J. Atherton. 1997. "The Findings and Their Policy Implications: Institutional Adaptation or Replacement." In *Searching for Land Tenure Security in Africa*, ed. J. Bruce and S. Migot-Adholla, 114–21. Dubuque, IA: Kendall/Hunt.

Buckley, S. 1996. "No Somali Government? No Problem." 1996. *Washington Post*, March 3.

Carter, M., K. Weibe, and B. Blarel. 1997. "Tenure Security for Whom? Differential Effects of Land Policy in Kenya." In *Searching for Land Tenure Security in Africa*, ed. J. Bruce and S. Migot-Adholla, 215–22. Dubuque, IA: Kendall/Hunt.

Coleman, J. 1988. "Social Capital in the Creation of Human Capital." *American Journal of Sociology* 94 (Supplement): S95–S120.

———. 1990. *Foundations of Social Theory*. Cambridge, MA: Harvard University Press.

Datt, G., and M. Ravallion. 1998. "Farm Productivity and Rural Poverty in India." *Journal of Development Studies* 34 (4): 62–85.

Deere, C. D., and M. Leon. 2001. *Empowering Women: Land and Property Rights in Latin America*. Pitt Latin America Series. Pittsburgh, PA: University of Pittsburgh Press.

Deininger, K. 2003. "Land Policies for Growth and Poverty Reduction." World Bank Policy Research Report, World Bank, Washington, DC.

Deininger, Klaus, and Lyn Squire. 1996. "A New Data Set Measuring Income Inequality." *World Bank Economic Review* 10: 565–92.

———. 1998. "New Ways of Looking at Old Issues: Inequality and Growth." *Journal of Development Economics* 57 (2): 259–87.

De Janvry, A., G. Gordillo, J. P. Plateau, and E. Sadoulet, eds. 2001. *Access to Land, Rural Poverty, and Public Action*. Oxford, U.K.: Oxford University Press.

Dolan, C. S. 2001. "The 'Good Wife': Struggles Over Resources in the Kenyan Horticultural Sector." *Journal of Development Studies* 37 (3): 39–70.

Easterly, W. 2002. "The Middle Class Consensus and Economic Development." *Journal of Economic Growth* 6 (4): 317–35.

Easterly, W., and R. Levine. 2003. "Tropics, Germs, and Crops: How Endowments Influence Economic Development." Working Paper W9106, National Bureau of Economic Research, Cambridge, MA.

Engerman, S. L., and K. L. Sokoloff. 1997. "Factor Endowments, Institutions, and Differential Paths of Growth Among New World Economies: A View from Economic Historians of the United States." In *How Latin America Fell Behind*, ed. S. Harber, 260–96. Palo Alto, CA: Stanford University Press.

———. 2000. "Institutions, Factor Endowments and Paths of Development in the New World." *Journal of Economic Perspectives* 14 (3): 217–32.

Erickson, L., and D. Vollrath. 2004. "Dimensions of Land Inequality and Economic Development." Working Paper 04/158, International Monetary Fund, Washington, DC.

———. 2005. "How Are Land Inequality and Development Related?" *IMF Survey* 34 (1): 12–13.

Gaiha, R. 1993. "Design of Poverty Alleviation in Rural Areas." United Nations Food and Agricultural Organization, Rome.

Galor, O., O. Moav, and D. Vollrath. 2003. "Land Inequality and the Origin of Divergence and Overtaking in the Growth Process: Theory and Evidence." Brown Economics Working Paper, Brown University, Providence, RI.

Grootaert, Christiaan. 1998. "Social Capital: The Missing Link?" Social Capital Initiative Working Paper 3, Social Development Family, Environmentally and Socially, Sustainable Development Network, World Bank, Washington, DC.

Jacoby, H., and B. Minten. 2005. "Is Land Titling in Sub-Saharan Africa Cost-Effective?" World Bank, Washington, DC. http://siteresources.worldbank.org/DEC/Resources/LandTitles_Mad.pdf.

Jazairy, I., M. Alamgir, and T. Panuccio. 1992. *The State of World Rural Poverty: An Inquiry into its Causes and Consequences.* New York: New York University Press.

Kevane, M., and L. C. Gray. 1999. "A Woman's Field is Made at Night: Gendered Land Rights and Norms in Burkina Faso." *Feminist Economics* 5 (3): 1–26.

Khan, H. M. 2000. "Rural Poverty in Developing Countries." *Finance and Development* 37 (4): 26–29.

Lipton, M. 1998. *Successes in Anti-Poverty.* Geneva: International Labour Office.

Mariscal, E., and K. L. Sokoloff. 2000. *Schooling, Suffrage and the Persistence of Inequality in the Americas, 1800–1945.* Palo Alto, CA: Hoover Institution Press.

Migot-Adholla, S. 1993. *Indigenous Land Rights Systems in Sub-Saharan Africa: A Constraint on Productivity?* Oxford, U.K.: Oxford University Press.

Migot-Adholla, Shem E., Peter Hazell, Benoit Blarel, and Frank Place. 1991. "Indigenous Land Rights Systems in Sub-Saharan Africa: A Constraint on Productivity?" *World Bank Economic Review* 5 (1): 155–75.

North, D. 1990. *Institutions, Institutional Change, and Economic Performance.* Cambridge, U.K.: Cambridge University Press.

Olson, Mancur. 1982. *The Rise and Decline of Nations: Economic Growth, Stagflation, and Social Rigidities.* New Haven: Yale University Press.

Pathan, R., N. Arul, and M. Poffenberger. 1993. "Forest Protection Committees in Gujarat—Joint Management Initiatives." Reference Paper 8, prepared for Sustainable Forest Management Conference, sponsored by the Ford Foundation, Delhi.

Place, F., and S. Migot-Adholla. 1998. "The Economic Effects of Land Registration on Smallholder Farms in Kenya: Evidence from Nyeri and Kakamega Districts." *Land Economics* 74 (3): 360–73.

Putnam, R. 1993. "The Prosperous Community—Social Capital and Public Life." *American Prospect* 13 (Spring): 35–42.

Putnam, R., R. Leonardi, and R. Nanetti. 1993. *Making Democracy Work: Civic Traditions in Modern Italy.* Princeton, NJ: Princeton University Press.

Quisumbing, A. R., and K. Otsuka. 2001. "Land, Trees, and Women: Evolution of Land Tenure Institutions in Western Ghana and Sumatra." Research Report 121, International Food Policy Research Institute, Washington, DC.

Ravallion, Martin, Shaohua Chen, and Prem Sangraula. 2007. "New Evidence on the Urbanization of Global Poverty." Policy Research Paper 4199, World Bank, Washington, D.C.

Saxena, N. C. 1999. "Rehabilitation of Degraded Lands in India through Watershed Development." Government of India, Planning Commission, New Delhi, India.

Stiglitz, J. 1996. "Some Lessons from the East Asian Miracle." *World Bank Research Observer* 11 (2): 151–77.

Udry, C. 1996. "Gender, Agricultural Production, and the Theory of the Household." *Journal of Political Economy* 104 (5): 1010–46.

World Bank. 1997. "Expanding the Measure of Wealth: Indicators of Environmentally Sustainable Development." Environmentally Sustainable Development Studies and Monographs Series 17, World Bank, Washington, DC.

———. 2003a. *World Development Report 2003—Sustainable Development in a Dynamic World: Transforming Institutions, Growth, and Quality of Life.* Washington, DC: World Bank.

———. 2003b. *Global Economic Prospects 2004: Realizing the Development Promise of the Doha Agenda.* Washington, DC: World Bank.

———. 2006. *World Development Indicators.* Washington, DC: World Bank.

———. 2007. *World Development Report 2008: Agriculture for Development.* Washington, DC: World Bank.

CHAPTER 15

Technology, Entrepreneurship, and Productivity

More than six decades of empirical evidence from developing countries suggests that total factor productivity (TFP, defined as the efficiency with which physical and human capital, land, and natural resources are used to produce outputs) influences growth more than the accumulation of physical and human capital. But economists do not know which factors (such as national policies and institutions) drive the accumulation of new technology, nor do they agree on a definition of technology (box 15.1).

This chapter explores whether the adoption of new technology prompts growth in income, employment, and productivity or if such adoption—especially if it takes place too rapidly—leads to job insecurity and job losses as old skills become obsolete. Some evidence suggests that the factors most important for growth differ depending on the income level of the country: physical capital is most important in low-income countries (at the early stages of development), human capital in middle-income countries, and new ideas and technology in advanced countries.

Total Factor Productivity

Cross-country differences in TFP lead to different rates of gross domestic product (GDP) growth. Unfortunately, measuring TFP is difficult because

Box 15.1

What Is Technology?

Technology is usually thought of as a process of invention, innovation, development, and diffusion/adoption (also called knowledge). Organizational structures, management skills, and culture (including social organizations) are considered part of technology. Technological inventions and innovations are extremely unpredictable (for example, which research is relevant and for what purpose is usually not known except in hindsight); therefore, the time path of technological change is uncertain. Also, the various components of technology interact with the growth process in different ways. While most growth has historically been attributed to exogenous technological changes, some recent research, particularly by Dale Jorgenson (2001), who treats technology as knowledge, indicates that improved measures of physical and human capital can reduce the importance of innovation and knowledge-based spillovers in explaining growth. In contrast, some economists believe that the knowledge that leads to technological advances differs from physical and human capital, as investors cannot fully internalize the benefits of accumulating knowledge (that is, spillovers from private investment in knowledge). The rate of accumulation of knowledge is an important factor in the growth process even with modest spillover effects.

Source: Authors.

(a) small differences in assumptions can lead to big differences in TFP growth estimates; (b) data on the depreciation rate, flows of new investment, and initial stocks of human and physical capital, among other things, are limited and subject to measurement errors; and (c) increasing returns to scale, imperfect competition in labor and product markets, and gains from sectoral reallocation of inputs can skew results. Further, there are econometric problems, as the residuals of TFP in a simple regression are correlated with the growth of inputs. In other words, the ordinary least squares method of regression is invalid and an instrumental variables approach must be used to obtain meaningful estimates.

For example, Ethiopia, Kenya, Mozambique, Senegal, and Tanzania, as a group, have exhibited relatively fast growth during the past 15 years (table 15.1). But because of slower TFP growth, these fast-growing African countries trail other developing countries in real GDP growth. The aggregate TFP growth of these five economies averaged 0.41 per year

Table 15.1   Indexes of Average Gross and Net TFP–Adjusted Prices in Selected African Countries Relative to China, 2000–04

	Gross TFP	Net TFP
Ethiopia	0.50	0.25
Kenya	0.70	0.35
Mozambique	0.30	0.25
Senegal	0.80	0.65
Tanzania	0.65	0.40

Source: Eifert, Gelb, and Ramachandran 2005, 26.

during the 1990s. More detailed firm-level TFP estimates by Eifert, Gelb, and Ramachandran (2005) show that the gross TFP growth of several fast-growing African countries from 2000 to 2004 was 40 to 80 percent lower than that of China and that net TFP (gross TFP growth adjusted for indirect costs of infrastructure, transport, and other costs external to the firms) was 20 to 40 percent lower.

As shown in table 15.1, Senegal has the highest TFP growth among the few countries for which data are available. Eifert, Gelb, and Ramachandran (2005) argue that the relatively low economic performance of African countries is due largely to inadequate private sector activities. In their view, collusion between African private business elites and political elites, who depend on rent-seeking activities aided and abetted by a deep-seated and widely accepted bureaucracy, keep the economies of these countries at a lower equilibrium level than otherwise.[1]

Spending on Research and Development

The production function of each country differs depending on its diffusion of technology, infrastructure stock and human capital, and natural resources endowment. Theoretically, a country can experience growth for a long period without technological progress by accumulating physical and human capital. But productivity growth of this sort cannot continue indefinitely. The large sums spent on research and development (R&D)—which may be distorted by tax credits that encourage firms to classify current expenditure as investment—and variations in incentives for innovators lead to varying levels of innovation endogenous to firms and the economy.

Broadly defining technology as the difference in productivity across countries explains most of the disparities in per capita income across countries (De Long 1996), whereas defining technology as most modern machinery and manufacturing processes does not. For example, Clark (1987) shows that during the early twentieth century, textile mills in different countries used the same machinery but experienced large differences in output per hour. Similarly, with comparable technology, Japan is 47 percent more productive than the United States in steel production but 67 percent less productive in food processing (McKinsey Global Institute 1993). Recent growth theories emphasize the importance of endogenous technological change to explain growth patterns. Increasing R&D expenditures while effectively using human capital and the existing knowledge stock leads to innovation and inventions, which firms use to permanently increase the growth rate of output.

Data available on 20 Organisation of Economic Co-operation and Development (OECD) and non-OECD countries indicate that innovation has a positive effect on the per capita output of both developed and developing countries. Not only are the OECD countries with large markets able to increase their innovation by investing in R&D, but the remaining OECD countries seem to promote their innovation by using the know-how of other OECD countries. In particular, a 1 percent increase in innovation raises per capita income by around 0.05 percent in both OECD and non-OECD countries, while a 1 percent increase in the R&D stock increases innovation by about 0.2 percent only in the OECD countries with large markets (which includes the Group of Eight). This finding implies that innovation, such as capital stock, leads to only short-term increases in the growth rate of output and cannot explain perpetual economic growth. As neither patent nor R&D data are complete measures of innovation, these figures should be interpreted cautiously.

In both advanced and emerging economies, government is a large source of financing for research. The social rate of return to innovation is substantial in leading industries, indicating that governments should provide modest incentives for R&D only for these industries and not for traditional or declining industries or sectors. Also, links between public R&D spending and private industries should be encouraged, except in the case of strategic technology (for example, nuclear technology).

Questions still remain that require further research. How strong is the causal link between research activity and innovation? Would growth lead to more R&D and therefore technological change, or do more R&D and technological change lead to growth? Is innovation more dependent on technological opportunities and luck than on incentives and spending on R&D?

Technology Diffusion and Adoption

Technology has driven economic and social progress since the industrial revolution. Measuring technology as TFP explains most of the differences in both the level and rate of income growth across countries (see, for example, Hall and Jones 1999). Defining technology as scientific innovation and invention, however, delegates it almost exclusively to richer countries, albeit ones in which many developing-country nationals do much of the research (for example, a large proportion of engineers in Silicon Valley and researchers at the National Aeronautics and Space Administration, or NASA, are foreign born). Firms throughout the rest of the world then adopt and adapt the preexisting technologies. Openness to trade, foreign direct investment (FDI), and domestic investments in human capital are critical to rapid diffusion. Technology is therefore both a determinant and an outcome of rising incomes.

Older technologies such as fixed-line telephones, electric power, transportation, and health-care services remain in high demand in low- and middle-income developing countries. Because of the large initial investments, high maintenance costs, and need for highly skilled engineers, the government usually provides these services. In contrast, newer technologies such as the Internet, cell phones, and computers are cheaper to adopt and easier to maintain and use. Still, technology adoption remains very uneven in most developing countries, creating rural-urban gaps such as that in India.

Why does rapid diffusion of ideas fail to eliminate cross-country technological differences as predicted by economic theory? For one, the technologies of the world frontier may not serve the needs of specific countries. The OECD countries conduct more than 90 percent of the world's R&D. Accordingly, new technologies tend to be less appropriate for the conditions, skills, and capital intensity of developing countries. A notable exception is the case of pharmaceuticals (for example, HIV drugs), which could be used both in the OECD and developing countries. Similarly, the technologies developed for the capital-intensive production processes in the OECD countries may be of little use in labor-abundant, less-developed countries.

One theory suggests that the entry of new and more productive plants and the exit of less productive plants—the process that Joseph Schumpeter (1934) dubbed "creative destruction"—can explain productivity differences across firms. But available evidence indicates that entry and exit account for only about 25 percent of average TFP growth, with the remaining 75 percent attributable to existing plants, where firms regularly invest in technology and productivity.

A review of empirical evidence on technological adoption by Chandra (2006) concludes that (a) latecomers can leapfrog over several stages of development—India and Ireland appear to be riding on a wave of outsourcing of international business operations, while Taiwan, China, increased its per capita income tenfold within four decades largely due to the rapid expansion of electronic exports—and (b) technological learning, involving technological mastery first and deepening later, was key to the latecomers' success. The channels of technology transfer included the following:

- Intrafirm transfers through FDI (from parent to subsidiaries—for example, wine in Chile; floriculture in Kenya; electronics in Malaysia and Taiwan, China; and Nile perch fisheries in Uganda)
- Licensing, contracting, and subcontracting because buyers must develop their own marketing capabilities (this, however, appears to be a more limited channel)
- Technology embodied in capital goods imports
- Formal R&D
- Harnessing of the diasporas to disseminate technological knowledge to local firms (for example, software from India and electronics from Taiwan, China).

Information and Communication Technology

Information and communication technology (ICT) is now the main technological driver for productivity growth in a number of developing countries. According to a study by the Centre for Economic Policy Research, countries with mobile phone penetration of 10 percent of the population have a 0.59 percent higher GDP per capita growth rate. Furthermore, strong empirical evidence suggests that investment in ICT and higher education—partly by allowing for the better use of ICT—strongly improves competitiveness (figure 15.1).

Are Entrepreneurship and Growth Linked?

North (1990, 83) explicitly links economic growth and the entrepreneur: "The agent of change is the individual entrepreneur responding to the incentives embodied in the institutional framework." Schumpeter (1934) defines the entrepreneur as the bearer of the mechanism for change and economic development and entrepreneurship as the undertaking of new

Figure 15.1   Global Competitiveness Index

Impact of Investment in ICT

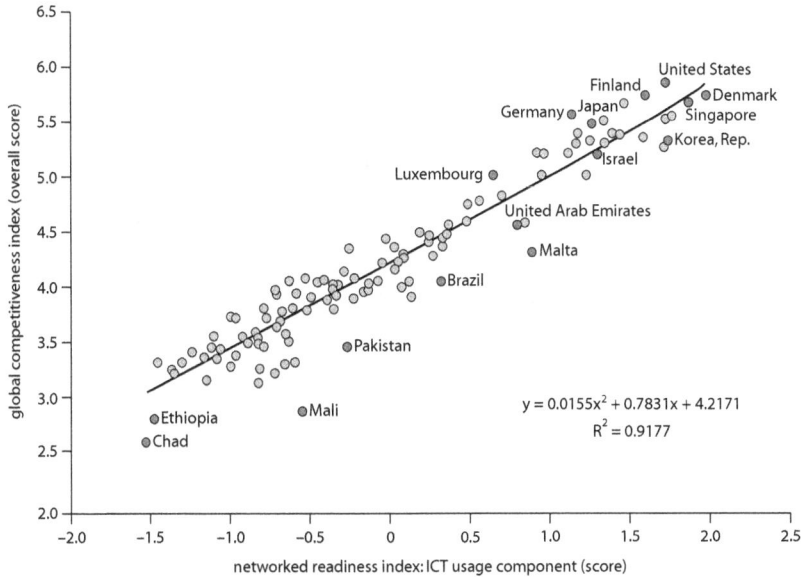

Source: Ndulu and others 2007, 172.

ideas and new combinations (that is, innovations). He describes five man-ifestations of entrepreneurship (Schumpeter 1934, 66): a new good, a new method of production, a new market, a new source of supply of intermediate goods, and a new organization. Kirzner (1973, 17) argues that "entrepreneurship is inherent in the competitive market process" and that the entrepreneur's activities are essentially competitive: "The 'pure' entrepreneur observes the opportunity to sell something at a higher price than that at which he can buy it."

Vosloo (1994, 147) offers another view, describing the entrepreneur "as a person who has the ability to explore the environment, identify opportunities for improvement, mobilize resources and implement action to maximize those opportunities." Several studies (Acs 1996; Baldwin and Johnson 1999; Audretsch and Thurik 2001) support the view that smaller firms (employing fewer than 500 persons) have contributed more toward innovative products[2] than larger firms.

Yu (1997) argues that Schumpeter's entrepreneur, the creative destroyer, prevents the economy from reaching a stationary equilibrium, while Kirzner's entrepreneur brings the economy into equilibrium by spotting and profiting from disequilibria. Landström (1999) illustrates their differences on a production possibility curve (figure 15.2).

Figure 15.2   Changes in the Production-Possibility Frontier

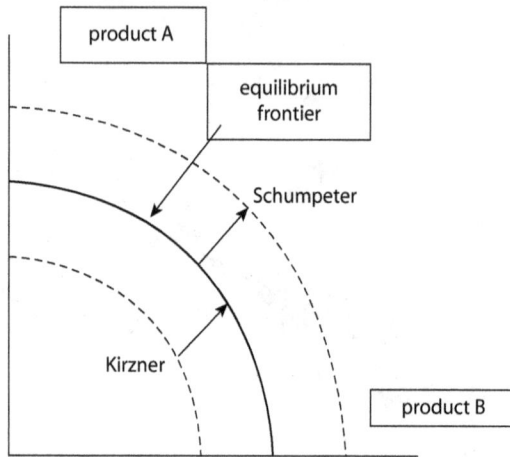

Source: Landström 1999, 49.

By introducing new ideas, processes, and products and services, Schumpeterian entrepreneurs renew the economic activities of firms, industries, and—on a larger scale—regions. Aggregated and evaluated in terms of their economic impact at a territorial level, these entrepreneurial initiatives could spur economic growth. Furthermore, the larger the share of innovative entrepreneurs in the workforce, the faster the pace of economic growth.

Karlsson, Friis, and Paulsson (2004) observe a structural shift in the OECD countries from "managed economies," dependent on large companies, to "entrepreneurial economies," populated by smaller companies relying on knowledge, initiative, and flexibility. This transition appears to have taken place between the mid-1970s and the early 1990s.

The researchers use Chandler's (1990, 3) characterization of the economy as the "three-pronged investment in production, distribution and management that brought the modern industrial enterprise into being."[3] Competitive advantage remains in economies of scale or scope, which allow the product to reach a large market. Therefore, large firms drive the economy, while the entrepreneurial economy depends on knowledge and flexibility as the key factors of production.

Successful entrepreneurship, combined with dynamic corporations, contributes to a nation's economic development, though in different ways depending on the national income level as measured by GDP per capita. At low levels of national income, self-employment provides job opportunities and scope for the creation of markets. As per capita income increases, the emergence of new technologies and economies of scale allows larger and more established firms to satisfy both the demand of growing markets and their role in the overall economy.

Entrepreneurship results in new businesses; creates new jobs, products, and services; and may increase productivity through technological change. Therefore, higher entrepreneurship can be associated with higher economic growth. Acs (2006) describes two types of entrepreneurship: "necessity entrepreneurship," which emerges when other options are lacking, and "opportunity entrepreneurship," in which a new enterprise exploits an existing or latent opportunity. Using data from 11 countries, Acs claims that necessity entrepreneurship has no effect on economic development, while opportunity entrepreneurship has a significant positive effect.

The Global Entrepreneurship Monitor (GEM) model research program, initiated in 1999 with data on 10 countries, expanded in 2005 to cover 39 developed and developing countries. In a "harmonized assessment" (that is, one applying uniform definitions), the GEM surveys a large sample of entrepreneurs (1,000 to 27,000 individuals) from each participating country. To counter enthusiasm bias and ensure accuracy, the GEM uses a ratio of "opportunity-necessity" as a composite indicator of entrepreneurial activity and economic development.[4] The GEM shows that some developing countries have higher levels of both opportunity and necessity entrepreneurship than high-income countries.

Economists attribute the "patterns of structural change" (Syrquin 1988) to three stages in development. The first stage is agriculture. The second stage is marked by a shift toward small-scale manufacturing with increasing specialization, followed by a move toward services. The decline in entrepreneurial activity results in decreasing employment rates, including self-employment (Kuznets 1966); marginal managers can earn more money being employed by someone else.

In the third stage, entrepreneurial activity in developed, industrial countries moves toward larger organizations. Interestingly, a series of studies found that in the mid-1970s, this trend began to reverse itself (Blau 1987). More studies have confirmed that, in developed countries, firm-size distribution shifted away from larger corporations toward entrepreneurial activity. Acs (2006) lists three explanations. First, in the past 30 years, all industrial economies have experienced a decline in manufacturing and a relative increase in the service sector. But while service firms are generally smaller than manufacturing firms (leading to an overall decrease in firm size across the economy), their growth provides more entrepreneurship opportunities, as in the case of the European Union and the United States. Second, technological changes, especially in communications, have been favorably biased toward industries in which entrepreneurial activity is important and associated with increased returns (Jorgensen 2001). Third, in contrast to Lucas's (1978) finding that higher development leads to larger firm size, recent research (Aquilina, Klump, and Pietrobelli 2006) suggests that the high value of the elasticity of factor substitution leads to capital concentration (more capital per capita), easier entrepreneurship, and smaller firms.

Therefore, economies in the early or middle stage of development are likely to have relatively little entrepreneurial activity, since workers are moving from self-employment to wage employment, whereas developed economies are likely to experience entrepreneurial activity as people shift from wage work to entrepreneurship. As figure 15.3 indicates, this framework implies a U-shaped relationship between entrepreneurial activity and economic development in the global economy. Colombia, Indonesia, and Jamaica have high levels of entrepreneurial activity and low per capita income, while Ireland, Slovenia, and Sweden have precisely the opposite situation: high per capita income and relatively low entrepreneurial activity. Countries in the midst of the transformation from a middle-income level to a higher-income level have rising entrepreneurial activity and compose the middle. High-income countries such as Belgium, Finland, France, Germany, and Italy have relatively low levels of entrepreneurial activity, while Japan and the United States are outliers.

Figure 15.3 illustrates the association between entrepreneurship and the level of economic development: (a) early-stage entrepreneurial activity is generally higher in those countries with lower levels of GDP; (b) early-stage entrepreneurial activity is relatively low in high-income countries, especially for the core countries of the European Union and Japan; and (c) countries with the highest levels of GDP show increasing early-stage entrepreneurial activity, suggesting a new increase in opportunity-related entrepreneurship. But this cross-sectional approach does not imply any specific causal relationships between entrepreneurial activity and economic development.

Entrepreneurial Activity and Growth

Traditional analyses of economic development tend to focus on large corporations and neglect the innovations and competition that small

Figure 15.3   Early-Stage Entrepreneurial Activity Rates and GDP per Capita

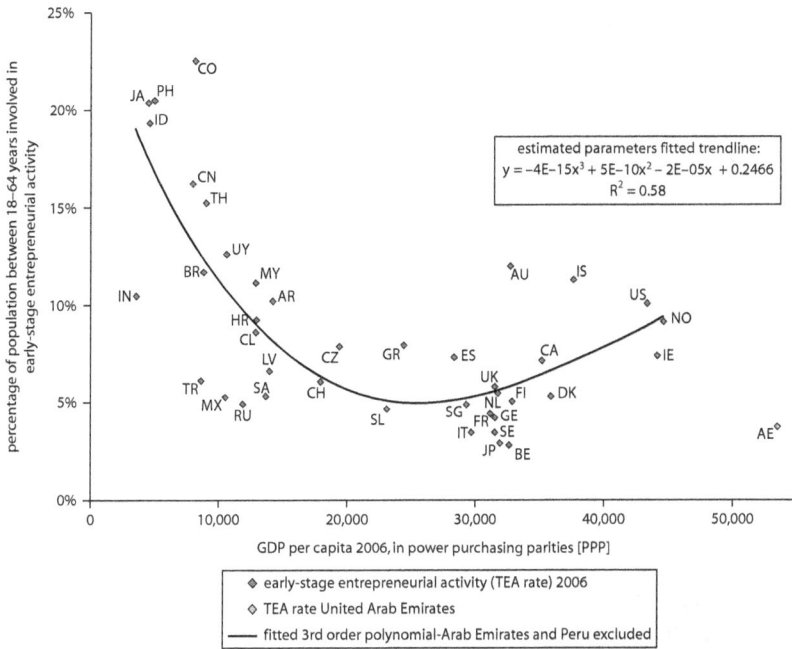

estimated parameters fitted trendline:
$y = -4E-15x^3 + 5E-10x^2 - 2E-05x + 0.2466$
$R^2 = 0.58$

percentage of population between 18–64 years involved in early-stage entrepreneurial activity

GDP per capita 2006, in power purchasing parities [PPP]

◆ early-stage entrepreneurial activity (TEA rate) 2006
◇ TEA rate United Arab Emirates
—— fitted 3rd order polynomial-Arab Emirates and Peru excluded

Source: Reprinted with permission from GEM 2006, 11; GDP levels were taken from IMF 2006.
Note: Permission to reproduce this figure from the *Global Entrepreneurship Monitor 2006 Summary Results* has been kindly granted by the copyright holders. The GEM is an international consortium and this report was produced from data collected in, and received from, 42 countries in 2006. The report was made possible by contributing authors, national teams, researchers, funding bodies, and others.
    AR = Argentina; AU = Australia; BE = Belgium; BR = Brazil; CA = Canada; CL = Chile; CH = China; CO = Colombia; CN = Croatia; CZ = Czech Republic; DK = Denmark; FI = Finland; FR = France; GE = Germany; GR = Greece; HR = Hungary; IS = Iceland; IN = India; ID = Indonesia; IE = Ireland; IT = Italy; JA = Jamaica; JP = Japan; LV = Latvia; MY = Malaysia; MX = Mexico; NL = Netherlands; NO = Norway; PH = Philippines; RU = Russian Federation; SG = Singapore; SL = Slovenia; SA = South Africa; ES = Spain; SE = Sweden; TH = Thailand; TR = Turkey; AE = United Arab Emirates; UK = United Kingdom; US = United States; UY = Uruguay. Peru not shown in this graph.

firms contribute to the economy. Country-specific business conditions influence large corporations' ability to affect national economic growth. These corporations influence economic growth primarily through the construction of new plants and the creation of jobs. When an old plant is replaced, the use of new technologies results in increased productivity and contributes to the country's growth. In general, "national framework conditions" apply to ongoing business operations, while start-ups encounter "entrepreneurial framework conditions" (figure 15.4). These conditions together affect the entrepreneurial process and can lead to

Figure 15.4   Global Entrepreneurship Monitor Model

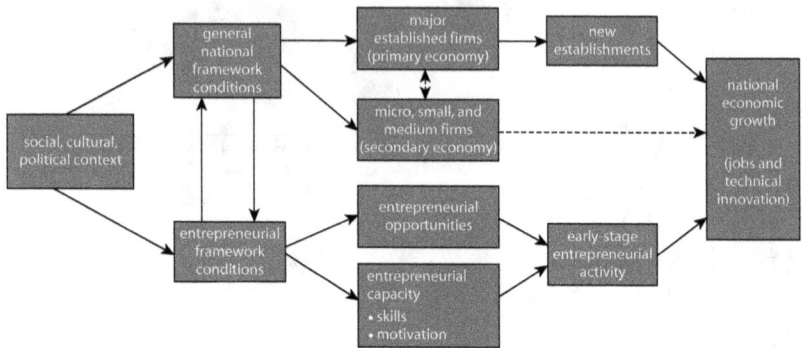

Source: Reprinted with permission from GEM 2007, 8.
Note: Permission to reproduce this figure from the *Global Entrepreneurship Monitor 2007 Global Report*, which appears here, has been kindly granted by the copyright holders. The GEM is an international consortium and this report was produced from data collected in, and received from, 42 countries in 2007. The report was made possible by contributing authors, national teams, researchers, funding bodies, and others.

innovation, competition, and development in the marketplace and contribute to economic growth.

Figure 15.4 suggests a complicated relationship among entrepreneurship, corporations, and economic development. Note also the importance of GDP per capita. At low levels of national income, self-employment provides market opportunities. Increasing GDP per capita will result in new technologies, while economies of scale allow large and established firms to satisfy the increasing demand of growing markets. At the same time, the number of business start-ups decreases as more people find stable employment.

Policy Implications

Karlsson, Friis, and Paulsson (2004) suggest organizing the "institutional rules of the game" to provide and support incentives for innovation and facilitate the entry and growth of new and small firms (Davis and Henrekson 1999; Fölster 2002; and Henrekson 2002). They recommend several means of support: (a) encourage immigration of individuals with key knowledge; (b) provide education and training to nationals in foreign countries where critical new technology and knowledge is being used; and (c) provide loan guarantees for rapid adoption of critical foreign technology (Baumol 1993) to encourage changes in entrepreneurial behavior according to the "rules of the game." Karlsson, Friis, and Paulsson (2004) also suggest the following policy measures:

- The wage formation and labor markets, in general, should be deregulated. This would support the growth of firms by making it easier to hire (and fire) staff.
- The tax system should not discourage small and new firms. Furthermore, low income taxes promote the accumulation of wealth necessary for the birth of new firms.
- Entry of firms should be free across the entire economy—that is, regulated public sector monopolies should be abolished.

As income increases, more individuals have the resources to go into business for themselves (provided that the business environment encourages the exploitation of opportunities). In high-income economies, through lower costs and accelerated technology development, entrepreneurial firms will enjoy a newfound competitive advantage. Therefore, entrepreneurs in countries with different levels of GDP per capita face different challenges and, as a result, policies and conditions favorable to entrepreneurship in one country (or region) may not be effective or favorable in another.

Before focusing on the entrepreneurial sector, less-developed countries should develop policies that reduce the number of self-employed workers and strengthen existing small and medium-size firms. For example, improved working conditions, the rule of law, labor market flexibility, infrastructure, financial market efficiency, and management skills attract FDI and thus promote employment, technology transfer, exports, and tax revenues. Similarly, a strong commitment to education is important. Those with less education in developing countries tend toward necessity entrepreneurship.

To encourage opportunity entrepreneurship, developing economies must improve technology transfer; increase the availability of early-stage funding; and support entrepreneurial activity in the state, corporate, and educational sectors (especially at the university level). The higher education systems need to play an important role in R&D and technology commercialization.

Conclusion

Total factor productivity is the main driver of growth. But we know little about innovation and its contribution to productivity and growth.

Most developing countries adopt new technologies generated by advanced economies. Several policies may encourage technological innovation and adoption, but there is little empirical evidence of a strong causal link between a particular policy and technological success. Entrepreneurship appears to be a key driver of technological innovation and commercialization. Small firms, not large companies, are still at the center of technological innovation and adoption.

Notes

1. Eifert, Gelb, and Ramachandran (2005, 31) use the findings of the Afrobarometer surveys to validate this assertion. A majority of the respondents in several countries prefer government-led growth and job creation and a large bureaucracy even when the government cannot pay decent wages. Further, only 35 percent of respondents support the privatization of public enterprises, and only 32 percent support civil-service reform.

2. *Innovative products* are defined here as electronic computing equipment, process control instruments, electronic components, engineering and scientific instruments, and plastic products.

3. See Acs 1996, 1999; Acs and Audretsch 2001; Audretsch and Elston 2002; Carree, Thurik, van Stel, and Wennekers 1998; Carree, Klomp, and Thurik 1999; Carree, van Stel, Thurik, and Wennekers 2002; Thurik 1996; Thurik, Verheul, and Uhlaner 2003.

4. Stating that the program's inability to effectively compare entrepreneurial activity in developed and developing countries is a "major shortcoming," the GEM cites the example of low-income countries such as Ecuador, Peru, and Uganda (which have very high levels of self-employment and therefore high levels of entrepreneurial activity) versus high-income countries such as Germany, Japan, and Sweden (which have much lower levels of entrepreneurial activity). As a solution, the "opportunity-necessity ratio" is used as a composite indicator of entrepreneurial activity and economic development.

Bibliography

Acs, Zoltan. 1996. "Small Firms and Economic Growth." In *Small Business in the Modern Economy*, ed. Z. J. Acs, B. Carlsson, and R. Thurik, 1–62. Oxford, U.K.: Blackwell Publishers.

———. 1999. "The New American Evolution." In *Are Small Firms Important? Their Role and Impact*, ed. Z. J. Acs, 1–20. Dordrecht, The Netherlands: Kluwer Academic Publishers.

———. 2006. "How Is Entrepreneurship Good for Economic Growth?" *Innovations: Technology, Governance, Globalization* 1 (1): 97–107.

Acs, Zoltan, and D. B. Audretsch. 2001. *The Emergence of the Entrepreneurial Society*. Stockholm: Swedish Foundation for Small Business Research.

Aquilina, M., R. Klump, and C. Pietrobelli. 2006. "Factor Substitution, Average Firm Size and Economic Growth." *Small Business Economics* 26 (3): 203–14.

Audretsch, D. B., and J. A. Elston. 2002. "Does Firm Size Matter? Evidence on the Impact of Liquidity Constraints on Firm Investment Behavior in Germany." *International Journal of Industrial Organization* 20 (1): 1–17.

Audretsch, D. B., and A. R. Thurik. 2001. "What is New About the New Economy?: Sources of Growth in the Managed and Entrepreneurial Economies." *Industrial and Corporate Change* 10: 267–315.

Baldwin, J. R., and J. Johnson. 1999. "Entry, Innovation and Firm Growth." In *Are Small Firms Important? Their Role and Impact*, ed. Z. J. Acs. Dordrecht, 51–78. The Netherlands: Kluwer Academic Publishers.

Baumol, W. J. 1993. *Entrepreneurship, Management, and the Structure of Payoffs*. Cambridge, MA: Massachusetts Institute of Technology Press.

Blau, D. 1987. "A Time-Series Analysis of Self-Employment in the U.S." *Journal of Political Economy* 95 (3): 45–67.

Carree, M. A., L. Klomp, and R. Thurik. 1999. "Productivity Convergence in OECD Manufacturing Industries." Tinbergen Institute Discussion Papers 99-065/3, Tinbergen Institute, The Netherlands.

Carree, M. A., R. Thurik, A. van Stel, and S. Wennekers. 1998. "Business Ownership and Economic Growth: An Empirical Investigation." Paper 9809/e, Neuhuys— Research Institute for Small and Medium-Sized Business, The Netherlands.

Carree, M.A., A. van Stel, R. Thurik, and S. Wennekers. 2002. "Economic Development and Business Ownership: An Analysis Using Data of 23 OECD Countries in the Period 1976–1996." *Small Business Economics* 19 (3): 271–90.

Chandler, A. 1990. *Scale and Scope: The Dynamics of Industrial Capitalism*. Cambridge, MA: Harvard University Press.

Chandra, V. 2006. *Technology, Adaptation and Exports, How Some Developing Countries Got It Right*. Washington, DC: World Bank.

Clark, G. 1987. "Why Isn't the Whole World Developed? Lessons from the Cotton Mills." *Journal of Economic History* 47 (1): 141–73.

Davis, S., and M. Henrekson. 1999. "Explaining National Differences in the Size and Industry Distribution of Employment." *Small Business Economics* 12 (1): 59–83.

De Long, J. B. 1996. "A Positive Program for Better Economic Growth." J. Bradford De Long's Working Papers 106, Economics Department, University of California at Berkeley, Berkeley, California.

Eifert, Benn, Alan Gelb, and Vijaya Ramachandran. 2005. "Business Environment and Comparative Advantage in Africa: Evidence from the Investment Climate Data." Center for Global Development (CGD). Working Paper 56, CGD: Washington, DC.

Fölster, S. 2002. "Do Lower Taxes Stimulate Self-Employment?" *Small Business Economics* 19 (2): 135–45.

GEM (Global Entrepreneurship Monitor). 2006. *Results 2006*. Babson Park, MA: Babson College; London: London Business School.

———. 2007. *Results 2007*. Babson Park, MA: Babson College; London: London Business School.

Hall, R. E., and C. I. Jones. 1999. "Why Do Some Countries Produce So Much More Output Per Worker than Others?" *Quarterly Journal of Economics* 114 (1): 83–116.

Henrekson, M. 2002. "Entrepreneurship—A Weak Link in the Mature Welfare State." SSE/EFI Working Paper 518, Stockholm School of Economics, Stockholm.

Holcombe, Randall G. 1998. "Entrepreneurship and Economic Growth." *Quarterly Journal of Austrian Economics* 1 (2): 45–62.

Hülsmann, Jörg Guido. 1997. "Knowledge, Judgment, and the Use of Property." *Review of Austrian Economics* 10 (1): 1–22.

———. 1999. "Entrepreneurship and Economic Growth: Comment on Holcombe." *Journal of Austrian Economics* 2 (2): 63–65.

IMF (International Monetary Fund). October 2006. *World Economic Outlook Database*. IMF, Washington, DC.

Jorgenson, D. W. 2001. "Information Technology and the U.S. Economy." *American Economic Review* 91 (1): 1–32.

Karlsson, Charlie, Christian Friis, and Thomas Paulsson. 2004. "Relating Entrepreneurship to Economic Growth." Electronic Working Paper Series, Royal Institute of Technology, Centre of Excellence for Science and Innovation Studies, Stockholm.

Kirzner, I. M. 1973. *Competition & Entrepreneurship*. Chicago: University of Chicago Press.

———. 1994. "The Entrepreneur in Economic Theory." In *The Dynamics of Entrepreneurship*, ed. E. Dahmén, L. Hannah, and I. M. Kirzner, 45–59: Lund University Press.

Kuznets, S. 1966. *Modern Economic Growth*. New Haven, CT: Yale University Press.

Landström, H. 1999. "Entreprenörskapets rötter." Studentlitteratur, Lund University, Sweden.

Lucas, Robert E., Jr. 1978. "On the Size Distribution of Business Firms." *Bell Journal of Economics* 9 (2): 508–23.

McKinsey Global Institute. 1993. *Manufacturing Productivity*. Washington, DC: McKinsey Global Institute.

Ndulu, B. J., Lopamudra Chakraborti, Lebohang Lijane, Vijaya Ramachandran, and Jerome Wolgan. 2007. *Challenges of African Growth: Opportunities, Constraints, and Strategic Directions*. Washington, DC: World Bank.

North, D. C. 1990. *Institutions, Institutional Change and Economic Performance*. Cambridge, MA: Harvard University Press.

North, D. C., and R. P. Thomas. 1973. *The Rise of the Western World: A New Economic History*. Cambridge, MA: Harvard University Press.

Runge, I. 2000. *Capital and Uncertainty*. Cheltenham, U.K.: Edward Elgar.

Schumpeter, J. A. 1934. *The Theory of Economic Development*. Cambridge, MA: Harvard University Press.

Syrquin, M. 1988. "Patterns of Structural Change." In *Handbook of Development Economics*, ed. H. Chenery and T. N. Srinivasan, 203–73. Amsterdam/New York: North-Holland.

Thurik, A. R. 1996. "Determinants of Small Firm Debt Ratios: An Analysis of Retail Panel Data." In *Small Firms and Economic Growth*, ed. Z. J. Acs, vol 1. Cheltenham, U.K.: Edward Elgar.

Thurik, A. R., I. Verheul, and L. Uhlaner. 2003. "Business Accomplishments, Gender and Entrepreneurial Self-Image." Scales Research Reports N200312, EIM Business and Policy Research, Zoetermeer, The Netherlands.

von Mises, Ludwig von. 1985. *Theory and History*. 3rd ed. Auburn, AL: Ludwig von Mises Institute.

Vosloo, W. B., ed. 1994. *Entrepreneurship and Economic Growth*. Pretoria, South Africa: HSRC Publishers.

WEF (World Economic Forum). 2006. *The Global Competitiveness Report*. Davos, Switzerland: WEF.

Yu, T. F. L. 1997. *Entrepreneurship and Economic Development in Hong Kong*. London: Routledge.

CHAPTER 16

Urbanization and Growth[1]

A number of countries on high and sustained growth paths share common strategic factors. These factors include the maturation and deepening of market institutions, effective macroeconomic policy management, high levels of savings and investment, openness to trade and financial flows (and adoption of technology), and the presence of fast-growing urban areas.[2] This chapter will analyze the urbanization process, discuss its contribution to growth and poverty alleviation, and outline emerging issues in the urbanization of developing countries.

Trends in Urbanization

The year 2008 was a landmark in history: for the first time, more than 50 percent of the world's population was living in urban areas (figure 16.1). Cities cover just 2 percent of the world's land area, but they consume more than 75 percent of the world's resources and generate more than 70 percent of the world's greenhouse gases. Urbanization signals modernization and industrialization and is viewed as a natural part of an economy's transition from low-productivity agriculture to higher-productivity industry and services. Historically, no country has industrialized without urbanizing. At the same time, many critics view urbanization as the result

Figure 16.1   Urban and Rural Populations of the World

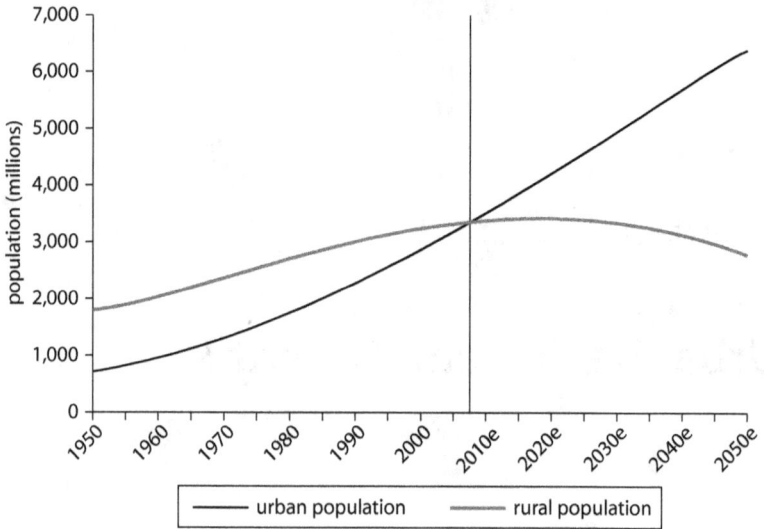

Source: United Nations 2007b.
Note: e = estimated.

of a bias toward cities in government policies and investment, a bias that presses people to migrate from rural areas to cities in search of jobs. Rapid urbanization places stress on cities' basic infrastructure—water, sanitation, electricity, and roads—and, when unplanned, can lead to sprawling slums and rising levels of inflation, poverty, crime, and environmental damage. Given the current and projected global trends in urbanization, it is important to understand and resolve these opposing viewpoints and develop effective programs and policies for sustainable economic development in the years ahead.

Rapid urbanization first started in today's more developed regions. In 1920, just under 30 percent of Europe, North America, and Oceania's population lived in urban areas, compared to more than half in 1950. By 2007, over 70 percent of the population of Australia and New Zealand and over 80 percent of the population of North America lived in urban areas. Among the less-developed regions, Latin America and the Caribbean had a similarly high level of urbanization—78 percent in 2007—even higher than that of Europe. Africa and Asia, in contrast, remained mostly rural, with 38 percent and 41 percent, respectively, of their populations living in urban areas (table 16.1). Over the coming decades, urbanization is expected to increase in all the major areas of the developing world,

Table 16.1   Rate of Regional Urbanization

Major areas	Percentage urban						Rate of urbanization (percentage)			
	1950	1975	2007	2025	2050	1950–75	1975–2007	2007–25	2025–50
Africa	14.5	25.7	38.7	47.2	61.8	2.28	1.28	1.10	1.08
Asia	16.8	24.0	40.8	51.1	66.2	1.42	1.66	1.24	1.04
Europe	51.2	65.7	72.2	76.2	83.8	1.00	0.29	0.30	0.38
Latin America and the Caribbean	41.4	61.1	78.3	83.5	88.7	1.56	0.78	0.36	0.24
Northern America	63.9	73.8	81.3	85.7	90.2	0.58	0.30	0.29	0.20
Oceania	62.0	71.5	70.5	71.9	76.4	0.57	-0.05	0.11	0.24

Source: United Nations 2007b.

with Africa and Asia urbanizing more rapidly than the rest. Nevertheless, by midcentury, Africa and Asia are expected to have the lowest levels of urbanization in the world.

Despite its low level of urbanization, Asia was home to about half of the world's urban population in 2007; Europe had the second-highest share, at 16 percent (figure 16.2). It is estimated that over the next four decades, Africa's urban population will triple and Asia's will more than double. By midcentury, most of the world's urban population will be concentrated in Asia (54 percent) and Africa (19 percent).

Urbanization and Growth

The world's urban population is expected to nearly double by 2050, increasing from 3.3 billion in 2007 to 6.4 billion in 2050—the same size as the world's total population in 2004. Urban areas of the less-developed regions, whose population is projected to increase from 2.4 billion in 2007 to 5.3 billion in 2050, will absorb most of the world's population

Figure 16.2   Distribution of the World's Urban Population

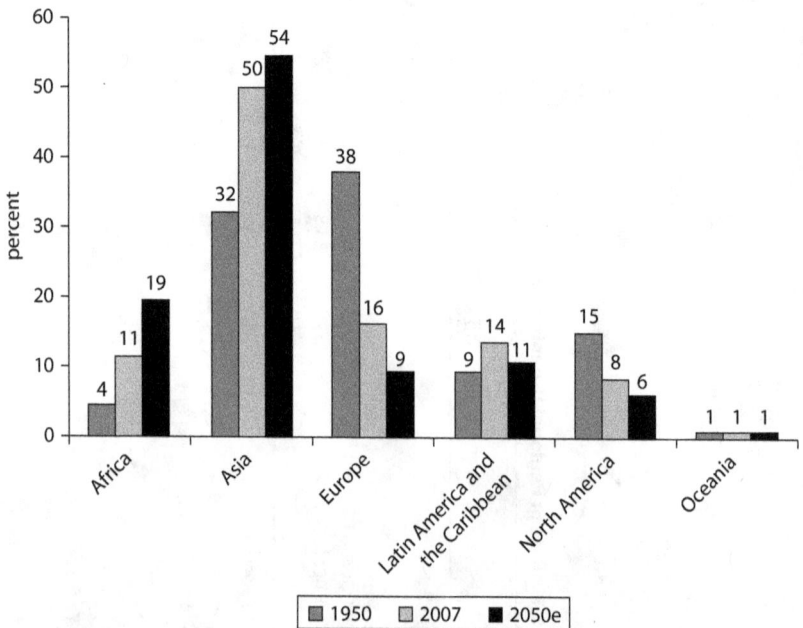

Source: United Nations 2007b.
Note: e = estimated.

growth. The urban population of the more-developed regions is projected to increase modestly, from 0.9 billion in 2007 to 1.1 billion in 2050.

The urban growth rate of less-developed regions reached a high in 1995–2000 of 3 percent per year, compared to 0.5 percent in the more developed regions. The urban growth rate in less-developed regions is expected to be particularly rapid, averaging 2.4 percent per year during the period 2000–30.

Productivity gains can explain some of the economic growth associated with urbanization. According to Quigley (2008), these gains arise from specialization; lower transaction costs and complementarities in production; education, knowledge, and mimicking; and greater proximity to large numbers of economic actors. Productivity gains translate to higher per capita incomes. Bloom and Khanna (2007) find a positive cross-country association between income and urbanization, as shown in figure 16.3, which plots country-level data on the real gross domestic

Figure 16.3   Urbanization and Economic Growth

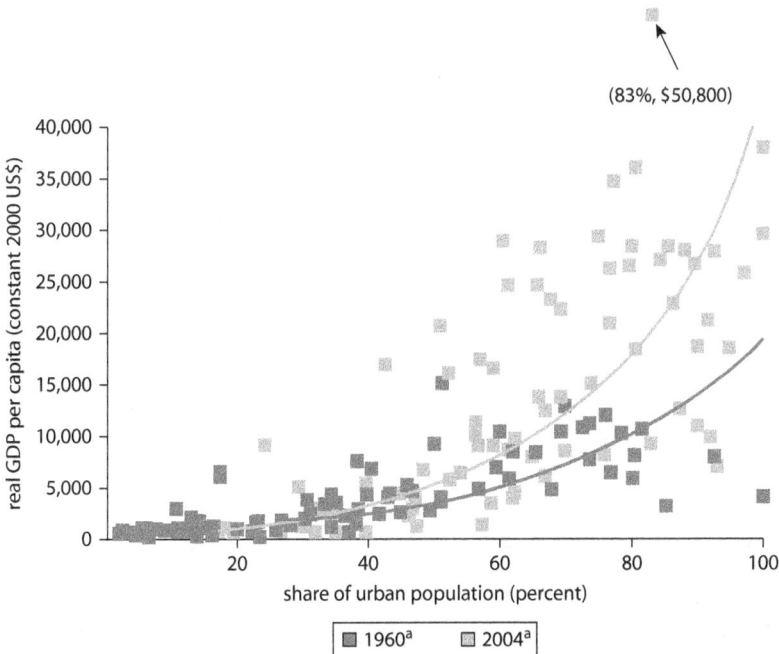

(83%, $50,800)

Source: Bloom and Khanna 2007, 11.
a. Sample size N = 97 in 1960 and N = 79 in 2004.

product (GDP) per capita and the share of the population living in urban areas during 1960 and 2004. The curves are initially very flat, implying that the links between urbanization and income are relatively weak at low levels of development. In a study on urbanization in the East Asia region (Iimi 2005), the elasticity of economic growth to urbanization rate was estimated at 2.71—in other words, a 1 percent increase in the urbanization rate raises the GDP per capita by 2.71 percent. This figure supports the view that urbanization is an engine for growth.

But this may not be true for all countries. While rapid economic growth has accompanied urbanization in Asia over the past 45 years, in Africa, where urbanization has been nearly identical, economic growth has been sluggish. This does not rule out a link between urbanization and economic growth (incomes in Africa might have grown even more slowly without urbanization, for example), but it does suggest that factors other than urbanization are more important determinants of income growth.

Urbanization and Poverty

An estimated one-third of urban residents are poor, representing one-quarter of the world's total poor (Baker 2008). Many of these people live in small cities and towns, where poverty is more prevalent than it is in big cities. With continued urbanization, however, the number of urban poor is predicted to rise, and poverty will become an increasingly urban phenomenon.

The incidence of urban poverty (the share of the poor as a proportion of the urban population) is highest for South Asia (35 percent) and Sub-Saharan Africa (40 percent), as shown in table 16.2. Latin America and the Caribbean and Europe and Central Asia have the greatest proportion of urban poor relative to total poor because of high urbanization rates in these regions. The urban poor account for 66 percent and 50 percent of the total poor in these two regions, respectively. Overall, the Middle East and North Africa has the lowest incidence and share of urban poverty. The incidence of urban poverty is notably lower in East Asia and Pacific, Europe and Central Asia, and the Middle East and North Africa compared to the other regions, reflecting better initial conditions.

Key Issues in Urbanization

Rapid urbanization has raised some key issues that have to be addressed if urban growth is to be sustainable. These include limited access to

Table 16.2   Urban Poverty Estimates, 2002

	Number of urban poor (millions) $1/day	Number of urban poor (millions) $2/day	Headcount index (%) $1/day	Headcount index (%) $2/day	Urban share of the poor $1.08/day	Urban share of the poor $2.15/day	Urban share of the population
East Asia and Pacific	16	126	2.2	17.7	6.7	15.1	38.8
China	4	53	0.8	10.7	2.2	9.5	37.7
Europe and Central Asia	2	32	0.8	10.7	33.4	49.9	63.5
Latin America and the Caribbean	38	111	9.5	27.5	59.0	65.6	76.2
Middle East and North Africa	1	20	0.7	12.4	19.9	29.3	55.8
South Asia	135	297	34.6	76.2	24.9	25.2	27.8
India	116	236	39.3	80.1	26.0	26.0	28.1
Sub-Saharan Africa	99	168	40.4	68.5	30.2	31.1	35.2
Total	291	754	13.2	34.0	24.6	26.4	42.3

Source: Baker 2008, 3 (citing Ravallion, Chen, and Sangraula 2007).
Note: Table uses $1.08/day and $2.15/day poverty lines in 1993 purchasing power parity values. The headcount index represents the urban poor as a proportion of the total poor.

income and employment in urban cities; urban slums; megacities and urban agglomeration; and urban land management and housing. The following subsections discuss these issues in detail.

Income and Employment

Cities draw rural migrants seeking more economic opportunities. Duranton (2008) points out that labor mobility generates new ideas and opportunities and is crucial to growth. Labor mobility responds to wage differentials across different locations. A study by Prud'homme (1996) indicates that the GDP per capita in most cities in Asian developing countries is higher than the average national income. As seen in table 16.3, the per capita income in Shanghai was 3.66 times the national average, and in Seoul it was 1.13 times the national average.

But not everyone who lives in an urban area gets a job in the formal sector. In fact, evidence shows that the bulk of urban jobs are in the informal sector, which accounts for 30 to 70 percent of the GDP in developing countries. While the informal sector provides employment for many who cannot enter the formal labor market and supplies goods and services typically not offered by the formal sector, it is also characterized by relatively poor working conditions, lack of social insurance, operations outside the legal system, and vulnerability to economic fluctuations, which particularly affect the poor, who have relatively little savings. The majority of the urban poor work in the informal sector.

Unemployment and underemployment are typically higher for the urban poor than for urban residents who are not poor. For example, a World Bank (2007) study found that the unemployment rate for the

Table 16.3   GDP of Urban Areas Compared with National GDP

City	(A) National GDP per capita ($)	(B) City GDP per capita ($)	(B/A)	City GDP ($ billion)
Tokyo	25,430	35,600	1.40	890.1
Osaka	25,430	32,300	1.27	339.1
Seoul	5,400	6,080	1.13	66.9
Bangkok	1,420	4,900	3.45	34.8
Shanghai	370	1,350	3.66	18.0
Manila	730	1,400	1.92	12.5
Jakarta	570	1,230	2.15	11.3
Calcutta	350	875	2.50	9.4

Source: Prud'homme 1996, 101–03.

poorest male workers in Dhaka, Bangladesh, is about 10 percent—double the rate for the wealthiest (5 percent). About 25 percent of poor women in Dhaka are unemployed, compared to 12 percent of the nonpoor.

Youth unemployment is a major problem in many cities and is increasingly linked to social unrest. An International Labour Organization (ILO 2004) study indicated that average youth unemployment rates in 2003 were highest in the Middle East and North Africa region (25.6 percent) and Sub-Saharan Africa (21 percent) and lowest in East Asia (7 percent). The United Nations Population Fund (UNFPA) predicts that by 2030, 60 percent of those living in urban areas will be under the age of 18. The proportion of young people is particularly high in slum areas, where employment opportunities are limited. This combination of youth and poverty can lead to high crime rates. Some demographers have forecast that the increasing concentration of populations in big cities will lead to major conflicts affecting both urban areas and entire countries.

Child labor also goes hand in hand with urban poverty in many countries, particularly in Sub-Saharan Africa. The latest International Labour Organization estimates for several African countries indicate that more than 26 percent of children ages 5–14 were economically active in 2004. While child labor typically had been a rural phenomenon, with children working overwhelmingly with their families, it now also exists in cities, with children working in the service sector, construction, and manufacturing. Girls are typically the most vulnerable, as they are often sent to work in the informal economy and as domestic workers. High levels of child labor translate into very low levels of school enrollment, which affects the children's opportunities later in life.

Urban Slums

Because quality urban housing is costly, increasing numbers of urban poor live in slums where water and sanitation facilities are inadequate and living conditions are crowded and often unhealthy. The United Nations (UN) (UN-Habitat 2006, *vi*) estimates that the number of people living in slums exceeded 1 billion in 2007 and could reach 1.39 billion in 2020, although there are large variations among regions. In Asia and the Pacific, two out of five urban dwellers live in slums; in Africa, the figure is three out of five.

In Sub-Saharan Africa, about 72 percent of city dwellers live in slums. Asia has by far the highest number of city dwellers living in slums, and the problem is worst in South Asia, where half of the urban population is

Figure 16.4   Share of Slum Population in Urban Areas in Select Asian and Pacific Countries

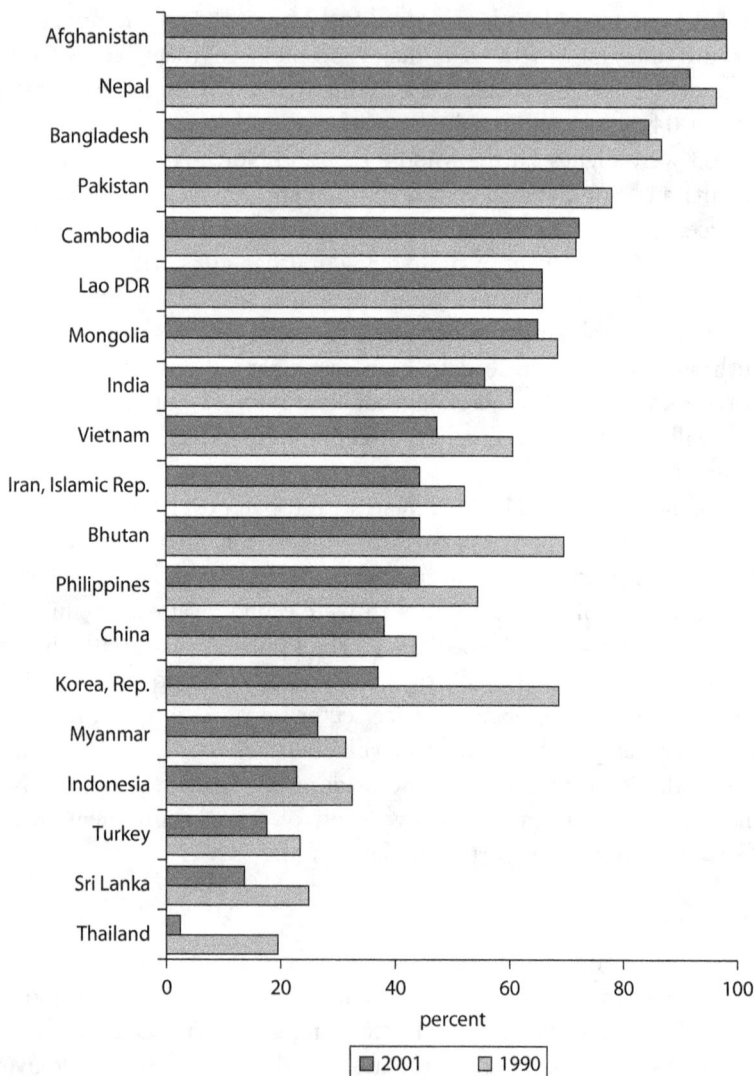

Source: United Nations 2007a.

composed of slum dwellers. Figure 16.4 illustrates the share of slum population in some Asian and Pacific countries. In 2001, as much as 99 percent of Afghanistan's urban population lived in slums, while 92 per-cent and 85 percent of urban populations lived in slums in Nepal and

Bangladesh, respectively, two countries that have had some success in containing the problem since 1990.

Understanding slums has become a priority for policy makers. The Millennium Development Goals (MDGs)—in particular, goal 7, target 11—call for the improvement of the lives of at least 100 million slum dwellers through a rapid, sustained decline in slum-growth rates.[3] Few countries are on track for reaching these goals, however. According to Baker (2008), the countries that are farthest behind are mainly in Sub-Saharan Africa (table 16.4), where slums grew at an annual rate of 4.53 percent over the period 1990–2001, mainly because of local governments' inability to accommodate a rapid increase in migration to cities. The largest and most overwhelming slum in Africa is Kibera in Nairobi, where between half a million and a million people reside. The UN-HABITAT statistics are both illustrative and alarming: in Zambia, 74 percent of urban dwellers live in slums; in Nigeria, 80 percent; in Sudan, 85.7 percent; in Tanzania, 92.1 percent; in Madagascar, 92.9 percent; and in Ethiopia, an astounding 99.4 percent.

The burgeoning slums are partly attributable to the lack of an appropriate urban-planning strategy. Most governments have moved away from the ill-advised policy of eliminating city slums through demolition and now attempt to upgrade or relocate them. Very few governments, however, are actively planning at the appropriate scale to prevent future slums. One exception is Malawi, which has set aside decent land in cities such as Lilongwe for low-income housing projects. With urbanization set to rapidly increase in the near future, it is imperative that other governments plan for the influx of new urban residents with policies that promote growth and ensure a higher quality of life for the urban poor.

Table 16.4   Regional Characteristics of Slums, 2001

Region	Estimate of slum dwellers (millions)	Slum dwellers as proportion of urban population (%)	Slum annual growth rate (1990–2001)
Sub-Saharan Africa	166.2	71.9	4.53
Middle East and North Africa	21.3	28.2	−0.15
Latin America and the Caribbean	127.5	31.9	1.28
South Asia	253.1	59.0	2.20
Southeast Asia	56.8	28.0	1.34
East Asia	193.8	36.4	2.28
Europe and Central Asia	45.2	6.0	0.72
World	912.9	31.2	2.22

Source: Baker 2008, 7 (citing UN-HABITAT 2006).

Megacities and Urban Agglomeration

Dramatic decreases in the costs of information and communication technology and transport should have reduced spatial disparities in economic activities and moved us toward a "global village." Yet in both industrial and developing countries, economic activities are concentrated in a few centers, and regional disparities persist. For example, only about 15 percent of the world's population live in temperate zones, but they produce 50 percent of the world's GDP. In the United States, counties occupying only 2 percent of the land area account for more than half of GDP. Similarly, in a few countries, poverty is concentrated in a few pockets. It was Krugman (1991) who deduced that agglomeration economies accrue at the plant level; hence, firms are located in a single area near consumer demand in large urban areas, minimizing transport costs. In other words, the location of economic activity matters, and a tiny (initial) difference may soon lead to the concentration of economic activity around a center and ultimately to the formation of an industry cluster in the same space. Agglomeration economies accrue at the level of the plant, industry, city, or region.

Successful cities are centers of entrepreneurship and innovation that attract talented and skilled workers and foster productivity and growth. But as cities grow bigger and develop into megacities—those with more than 10 million people—they can also develop megaproblems. Most megacities are in Asia (figure 16.5). The concentration of population, which partly accounts for a metropolitan area's dynamism, also causes congestion, environmental degradation, housing shortages, and the formation of ghettos. The governance of a sprawling metropolitan area can be complex and difficult.

The Commission on Growth and Development (2008, 58) has noted that "cities thrive because of . . . *agglomeration economies*. When activities are clustered closely together, they can reap economies of scale and scope." There is substantial evidence that urban agglomeration improves productivity and promotes economic growth. Au and Henderson (2006) used aggregate data on 285 Chinese cities to estimate the effects of urban agglomeration on productivity. As expected, the authors found that the aggregate productivity relationship exhibits an inverted U shape in metropolitan size and scale. The estimated urban agglomeration benefits are quite high, and it appears that a large fraction of cities in China are undersized due to migration controls imposed at the national level. Lall, Koo, and Chakravorty (2003) also provide strong evidence, using plant-level data from India, that urbanization helps reduce costs per unit of output.

Figure 16.5   Global Distribution of Megacities

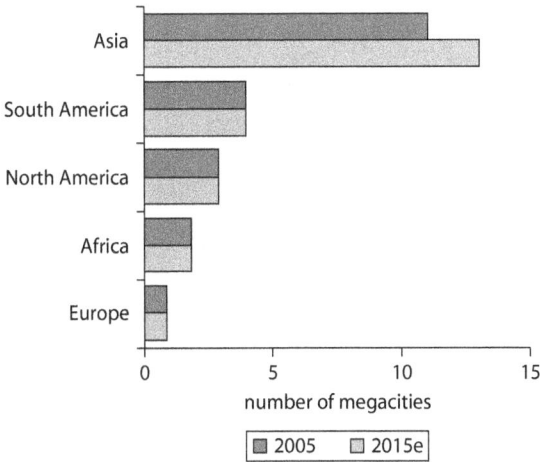

Source: United Nations 2007b.
Note: e = estimated.

This finding is consistent across all industries and size classes of Indian plants and is perhaps applicable to other developing economies as well.

The increasing population in urban areas, however, can lead to decreasing returns over the long term. Quigley (2008) suggests that while larger cities facilitate greater complementarities and specialization, land and transport costs and unpriced externalities such as greater congestion, pollution, and the risks of epidemics limit cities' size and efficiency. In addition, urban agglomeration requires huge concomitant increases in urban infrastructure, especially in Asia. Deutsche Bank Research (2008) estimates that by 2030, Asia's energy networks and power stations will require an investment of nearly $4.5 trillion (figure 16.6). This represents nearly half of the global investment required in this sector.

Duranton (2008) asks whether cities actually favor economic efficiency. He concludes that while megacities provide large efficiency benefits and do not appear to systematically hurt particular groups, they can nonetheless be a drag on growth. In his recommendations to the Commission on Growth and Development, Duranton suggests shifting the focus of public policy from *within-city* efficiency to *between-city* efficiency by favoring the mobility of resources across cities and regions rather than their concentration in only one city. This would enable a more efficient and equitable distribution of scarce public funds over a longer time horizon.

Figure 16.6   Investment Needs for the Energy and Water Sectors, 2005–30
US$ trillions

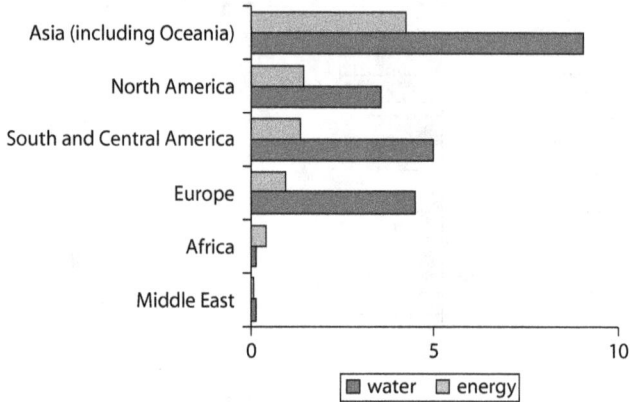

Source: Deutsche Bank Research 2008.

Urban Land Management and Housing

It is not easy to control migration into a city. Therefore, cities become overcrowded and marked by intense competition for space, mobility, and resources. In the past 30 years, the urban population in East Asia and Pacific has increased by 560 million people (or 260 percent), and in the next 30 years it is expected to increase by about 1.45 billion people (or 250 percent). This unprecedented urbanization process has been fueled by rapid economic growth and even more rapid industrialization.

Well-functioning cities, however, require efficient and equitable land markets. Most cities in developing countries suffer from land market distortions caused by poor land development and management policies. These include a lack of planning, slow provision of infrastructure and services, substandard land information systems, cumbersome and slow land transaction procedures, and underregulation of private land development, which leads to unplanned or ribbon/corridor development of land in the urban periphery. In addition, the natural population growth in urban areas and the influx of new migrants have made urban land scarcer.

Together, a scarcity of urban land and distortions in the land markets give rise to land speculation, which often forces the poor out of the formal land markets and into informal markets such as slums, squatter settlements, and illegal subdivisions on the periphery of cities. This leads to longer commutes, higher commuting costs, and very poor living conditions (because of a lack of adequate infrastructure and services) that cause poor health, thereby entrenching the cycle of poverty. The Commission on Growth and Development (2008) has noted that urban land management is crucial to creating sustainable cities, preventing spiraling prices, and reducing poverty.

Rapid urbanization severely strains urban housing, particularly in countries with a large informal sector. Unauthorized housing violates regulations concerning land ownership, land use and zoning, and building construction. Arnott (2008), while studying the housing patterns in developing countries, notes that in 1990,[4] about two-thirds of housing units in low-income countries were unauthorized, while practically none were in high-income countries (table 16.5). The large proportion of unauthorized housing affects the government's housing policy. If the government were to simply regularize unauthorized housing, developers would have little incentive to conform to regulations in the first place. Thus, the government must strike a balance between discouraging unauthorized housing and ensuring that such housing is safe once built.

Conclusion

Urbanization is rapidly increasing. Between 2005 and 2030, the world's urban population is expected to grow at an average annual rate of 1.78 percent—almost twice the growth rate of the world's total population. The proportion of people living in rural areas will shrink significantly after 2015. While increasing urbanization has led to greater per capita income and productivity, it has also led to a growing informal sector, greater urban poverty, more slums, scarcity of housing, spiraling urban real-estate prices, and inadequate infrastructure facilities. Given this phenomenon of economic concentration in one area and spatial disparities elsewhere, should rural labor move for jobs or should jobs move to rural

Table 16.5   Housing Rates by Type and Country Income Group, 1990
percent

	Country type			
Housing type	Low-income	Lower-middle income	Upper-middle income	High-income
Owner occupancy	33	59	57	59
Unauthorized housing	64	27	9	0
Squatter housing	17	16	4	0

Source: Arnott 2008.

areas? Finance and labor do not automatically move toward poorer areas. Evidence from across the world suggests that policy makers should strive to remove impediments to capital and labor flows and reinforce agglomeration economies. This can be done by encouraging labor movement, abolishing national minimum wages, cutting unemployment benefits and social benefits, and abolishing rent control to increase the supply of housing. Similarly, governments can affect firms' decisions on where to locate their productive activities by improving the business climate, increasing access to finance (including microfinance and availability of credit to small enterprises), and developing infrastructure services. Strengthening provincial and local governments' ability to provide essential services is particularly key to reducing economic concentration and spatial disparities.

Addressing these development issues in cities is essential to meeting the MDGs. Urban planning is no longer a luxury; it is a necessity. The Commission on Growth and Development (2008, 60) summarizes the urbanization process as follows:

> [I]f history is any guide, large-scale migration to the cities is part and parcel of the transformation economies must go through if they are to grow quickly . . . Ultimately a successful city will need urban planning, building codes, and robust property rights. It will need drainage, sewerage, rapid transit, and a sophisticated financial system capable of mobilizing the funds for these. But accumulating this infrastructure, expertise, and sophistication takes time. Governments should avail themselves of whatever shortcuts they can find, including the experience and expertise of other cities that have gone through this turmoil before them.

Notes

1. This chapter was written by Raj Nallari and Indira Iyer.
2. The Commission on Growth and Development identified 13 economies with successful growth experiences, defined here as achieving at least a 7 percent rate of growth over 25 years or more. These economies are Botswana; Brazil; China; Hong Kong SAR, China; Indonesia; Japan; the Republic of Korea; Malaysia; Malta; Oman; Singapore; Taiwan, China; and Thailand.
3. This target actually represents a relatively small proportion of existing slum dwellers, approximately 10 percent.
4. Data for other years are yet to be compiled. Data for 1990 are from Angel (2000).

Bibliography

Ahmad, E. 2007. "Big or Too Big?" *Finance and Development* 44 (3): 20–23.

Angel, S. 2000. *Housing Policy Matters: A Global Analysis.* Oxford, U.K.: Oxford University Press.

Arnott, Richard. 2008. "Housing Policy in Developing Countries: The Importance of the Informal Economy." Working Paper 13, Commission on Growth and Development, World Bank, Washington, DC.

Au, Chun-Chung, and J. V. Henderson. 2006. "Are Chinese Cities Too Small?" *Review of Economic Studies* 73 (3): 549–76.

Baker, J. L. 2008. "Urban Poverty, A Global View." Urban Papers UP-5, World Bank, Washington, DC.

Bloom, D., and T. Khanna. 2007. "The Urban Revolution." *Finance and Development* 44 (3): 8–14.

Commission on Growth and Development. 2008. *The Growth Report: Strategies for Sustained Growth and Inclusive Development.* Washington, DC: World Bank.

Deutsche Bank Research. 2008. "Megacities: Boundless Growth?" March 12, Germany.

Duranton, Gilles. 2008. "Cities: Engines of Growth and Prosperity for Developing Countries?" Working Paper 12. Commission on Growth and Development, World Bank, Washington, DC.

Iimi, Atsushi. 2005. "Urbanization and the Development of Infrastructure in the East Asian Region." *JBICI Review* 10 (March): 88–109.

ILO (International Labour Office). 2004. "Global Employment Trends." Geneva, Switzerland (ILO).

Krugman, Paul. 1991. "Increasing Returns and Economic Geography." *Journal of Political Economy* 99 (3): 483–99.

Lall, Somik V., Jun Koo, and Sanjoy Chakravorty. 2003. "Diversity Matters: The Economic Geography of Industry Location in India." Policy Research Working Paper 3072, World Bank, Washington, DC.

Prud'homme, R. 1996. "Management of Megacities: Institutional Dimensions." In *Megacity Management in the Asian and Pacific Region: Policy Issues and Innovative Approaches, Vol. 1,* ed. J. Stubbs and G. Clarke, 99–132. *Proceedings of the Asian Development Bank and the World Bank Regional Seminar on Megacities Management in Asia and the Pacific,* Asian Development Bank, Manila, October 24–30, 1995.

Quigley, John. 2008. "Urbanization, Agglomeration and Economic Development." Working Paper 19, Commission on Growth and Development, World Bank, Washington, DC.

Ravallion, Martin. 2007. "Urban Poverty." *Finance and Development* 44 (3): 15–17.

Ravallion, Martin, Shaohua Chen, and Prem Sangraula. 2007. "New Evidence on the Urbanization of Global Poverty." Policy Research Working Paper 4199, World Bank, Washington, DC.

United Nations. 2007a. *Statistical Yearbook for Asia and the Pacific 2007*. New York: Economic and Social Commission for Asia and the Pacific, UN.

———. 2007b. *World Urbanization Prospects: The 2007 Revision*. New York: Department of Economic and Social Affairs/Population Division 5, UN.

UN-HABITAT. 2006. "State of the World's Cities 2006/7." *The Millennium Development Goals and Urban Sustainability*. London: Earthscan.

World Bank. 2003. "Urban Poverty in East Asia: A Review of Indonesia, the Philippines, and Vietnam." Urban Development Working Paper 11, World Bank, Washington, DC.

———. 2007. *Dhaka, Improving the Living Conditions for the Urban Poor.* World Bank Report 35824-BD, World Bank, Washington, DC.

CHAPTER 17

Corruption and Poverty

The literature on corruption is large and growing. This chapter provides some empirical evidence on the impact of corruption on growth and poverty reduction. Corruption—which includes bribery, rent seeking, extortion, and embezzlement—is perceived as a major problem in many countries. It is commonly defined as the misuse of public office for private gain. This does not mean that corruption is nonexistent in the private sector; in fact, it is quite common in (private) financial firms. But corruption is more severe in the public sector. One of the first known articles on corruption and its punishment is in Kautilya's *Arthasastra*, which dates back to 14 BC.[1] In that work, corruption is intertwined with a country's social norms, formal and informal rules, culture, and legal environment. Corruption connotes illegal or immoral behavior and is treated as "socially and culturally deviant." If it is not controlled, high-level corruption can lead to political instability and reduce citizens' trust and faith in institutions.

Detection and Measurement of Corruption

Indirect measures must be used to quantify corruption because the measured corruption index is subject to the victimization bias—that is, only aggrieved parties speak out, while the vast majority who benefit from corruption do not. Firms may bribe officials to avoid legal problems, avoid paying taxes, or hide their noncompliance with regulations. Obviously, such transactions are not reported or recorded.

Attempts at measuring corruption include the corruption perception index (CPI) of Transparency International (TI), the "control of corruption" indicators of the World Bank Institute (WBI), the Business Environment and Enterprise Performance Survey (BEEPS, a World Bank survey of 26 countries on the extent of bribe payments in 1999), and the bureaucratic efficiency index. Some estimates of the worldwide scope of corrupt practices (Kaufmann, Kraay, and Mastruzzi 2006) are reported below.

Worldwide Bribery: Around $1 Trillion

Kaufmann (2005, 81) estimates worldwide corruption to be around $1 trillion, with a confidence interval ranging from $600 million to $1.5 billion. He bases his estimate on data from surveys in which firms and households report "average annual bribery payments as a share of sales (for enterprises), or incomes (households)." Working under the assumption that the overall population exhibits patterns similar to those of the sampled population, Kaufmann (2005) extrapolated the results to include countries not covered in the surveys.

Kaufmann (2005) included two enterprise surveys for his estimate: the World Bank Enterprise Survey (World Bank 2000), which was carried out in 2000 in 81 countries and elicited 10,033 responses from firms, and the Global Competitiveness Survey (2004), which was carried out in 104 countries and elicited 8,729 responses. He also used the results from household surveys carried out by the World Bank in the context of 16 governance and corruption diagnostic surveys. The main objective of the exercise was to arrive at a preliminary range of estimates rather than a precise estimate.

Unofficial Economy: Between $3.4 Trillion and $5.1 Trillion Worldwide

Estimates on the size of the "unofficial economy" rely on studies by Schneider and Enste (2002) and Friedman and others (2000). For money laundering, Kaufmann (2005) used an International Monetary Fund (IMF) study (Camdessus 1998), as well as a paper by John Walker (1999); for other bribery estimates, he used the results of an online survey and a report on a recent survey of corruption in the Russian Federation. Kaufmann computed the unofficial economy as the sum of the products of individual countries' unofficial economy figures in 1997 and the associated gross domestic product (GDP) in 2002. The higher estimate was drawn from Schneider and Enste (2002), who provided estimates of the large shadow economy in 76 developing and developed economies. For 21 Organisation for Economic Co-operation and Development economies, they estimated the size of the underground economy as having grown from $2 trillion (12.7 percent of GDP) in 1989 to $3.4 trillion (16.7 percent of GDP) in 2001. Kaufmann notes that unofficial economy transactions are not necessarily corrupt and, conversely, that bribes and corrupt transactions do not necessarily take place in the unofficial economy.

Worldwide Money Laundering: $600 Billion to $2.8 Trillion

A 1998 IMF study estimated that the world's money-laundering economy could be as large as 2 to 5 percent of the world's GDP, or $600 billion to $1.5 trillion (Vogl 1998). In an unrelated study, John Walker (1999) estimated a worldwide money-laundering economy of $2.8 trillion.

Other Bribery Estimates: $1 Trillion and Up

An estimate of bribes and inappropriate fees paid worldwide in procurement processes was made using data from an online governance survey carried out in 2003 by the WBI. The estimate was computed as the sum of the products of regional procurement figures (using 1998 worldwide procurement figures of $5.5 trillion) and the associated bribe share in procurement. The resulting estimate was about $1 trillion. It should be noted that this estimate focuses on one area of bribery and that margins of error and sample biases may be particularly large because the figures were derived from voluntary surveys on the Web.

Analytical Framework for the Study of Corruption

The principal-agent relationship is the main framework under which Kaufmann (2005) studies corruption. Under this framework, the principal (employer, owner, government, or banker) must induce the agent (employee, contractor, tax inspector, or borrower) to act in the principal's best interest. Difficulties arise when missing or incomplete information, unforeseen contingencies, or informational asymmetry prevent the principal from writing a complete contract or establishing incentives that induce the agent to act optimally on the principal's behalf. The agent has an opportunity to raise money for himself in relationships involving a government tax inspector and a taxpayer, a regulator (of, say, pollution) and a firm, a police officer and a potential criminal, a government provider of services and a consumer, and so on. Corruption occurs when a third party, such as a polluting firm, offers money to the inspector (agent) that is not passed on to the principal (regulator or government).

Some economists use the principal-agent-client relationship, the principal-supervisor-agent relationship or the provider-consumer relationship to reflect the three-tier connection. Several scenarios of principal-agent corruption are prevalent in the real world. First, the supervisor's role may be limited to information gathering (say, the estimating of individual incomes or pollution levels among firms). As such, his power comes from an ability to distort such information (for example, in enforcement cases involving taxes, regulations, or policing).

Second, the principal (government) sets broad objectives (say, tax revenue targets) for the supervisor but delegates to the supervisor the authority to put in place any incentive mechanism for the agent. This is a common situation in large bureaucracies involving policy design and provision of social services.

Third, the principal (government) may transfer all the power to the supervisor (for example, monopoly power to issue permits or licenses or set import-export quotas). The supervisor and his inspectors can vary the price of permits sold to businesses, especially when the government does not or cannot monitor the number of permits sold and the price of each permit.

Fourth, in several such cases, the supervisor, who has information-gathering responsibility (for instance, estimation of income tax), and the agent (inspector), who uses the information to collect taxes, can collude. The principal (government) must use incentives to prevent such collusion or must hire additional monitoring staff. Collusion possibilities expand bureaucracy further and limit the principal's ability to implement policy and incentive mechanisms.

Fifth, in the real world, the supervisor can collude with the agent to produce a report favorable to the agent—or use the threat of an unfavorable report to demand a bribe from the agent (for example, extortion of a lower-level staff member by a higher-level official).

Several forms of corruption and many complex economic scenarios cannot be understood within this framework. For example, with political corruption—in which the citizens are the principals and the elected politicians the agents—the incentive system is different. The citizens' control is limited to their ability to reelect or vote out the corrupt

politician. The citizens here are multiple principals, and the assets captured by a powerful few add to the complexity of the problem, which
cannot be analyzed using the principal-agent theory.

Causes of Corruption

Corruption is likely when one or more of the following conditions are in
place: (a) the motivation to earn more income is extremely strong, compounded by poverty and low, declining civil service salaries; (b) public
officials with broad discretion in economic matters exhibit rent-seeking
behavior; (c) accountability is weak; (d) political competition and civil
liberties are restricted; and (e) laws and penalties are poorly developed
and enforced.

Low wages are often cited as a major inducement for corrupt behavior among government employees. When low-paid employees meet
wealthier private sector clients, they look for ways to close the gap in
living standards and climb the social ladder; hence, they turn to corruption. Higher wages for government employees effectively work as a fine
for bribe taking and act as "efficiency wages" that could deter corrupt
behavior. In countries where corruption is harder to eliminate, however,
higher public sector wages, more bureaucracy, and widespread corruption may coexist.

The causes of corruption can be quite complex, including rational but
inconsistent human behavior (as proclaimed by behavioral economists).
For example, officials may resort to bribery to avoid noncompliance with
pollution regulations or taxes. Honest firms threatened with extortion by
inspectors may be similarly tempted to avoid taxes. Finally, several layers
of government corruption—including, for example, collusion between
supervisors and inspectors—combined with an inept judiciary can leave
the average citizen little choice but to pay bribes.

What wage and commission rates are optimal to prevent bribery and
ensure better monitoring and more truthful reporting (say, of pollution
levels or tax evasion)? What happens when corruption's rewards exceed
the penalty for taking bribes or the compensation for truthful reporting?
The best way to contain corruption is to impose a large penalty for
bribery. Providing a commission or incentive for truthful reporting can
also induce corruption; for example, a corrupt inspector could extort a
firm by overreporting its pollution level. Van Rijckeghem and Weder
(2001) find that an increase in civil service salaries relative to those paid
in the manufacturing sector also has a favorable impact on the corruption

index. Civil service wages are highly correlated with the measures of rule of law and quality of bureaucracy as well. (Other studies did not find strong support for this negative relationship between relative wages and corruption, however.)

Would paying higher wages to employees in a bloated bureaucracy be fiscally sustainable in developing countries, or would doing so entail comprehensive civil service reforms that pare down the number of employees while modernizing the financial management and human resource systems? A related issue is whether government officials responsible for the fiscal management of a country should be paid bonuses, particularly when public sector wage levels are relatively low. Chand and Moene (1997) find that such bonus payments help promote less-corrupt outcomes, but corruption at higher levels of government needs to be contained as well, and that means reforming the state.

There is some evidence that countries dependent upon the extraction of natural resources have high economic rents, which are a breeding ground for corruption. The same is true for countries with high per capita aid flows. While one study has found that high educational spending does not coincide with high corruption, other studies indicate that the social sectors and infrastructure sector are more prone to corruption than the agriculture, industry, and services sectors because they are largely financed by aid and involve brick-and-mortar activities (Mauro 1995, 1998, 2002; Kenny 2009).

Corruption varies across countries as well as within countries. In a study examining the pattern of corruption across public agencies of eight countries using microdata, Recanatini, Prati, and Tabellini (2005) found that the internal design of the organization is perceived by agency insiders and by customers to be systematically corrupt. However, corruption is lower when internal decisions on budget, procurement, and personnel are regularly audited, when these same decisions are made in an open and transparent manner, and when personnel decisions are based on merit and clearly stated professional criteria.

Opportunities for corruption can depend on a country's organizational structure. While a centralized state may reward the bribe-paying rich in a country, decentralization may not necessarily reduce corruption because the capture of the state by local elites is an obvious possibility. In a randomized experiment in India, however, Duflo and Hanna (2005) find little state capture by powerful elites in villages. They also find that the inclusion of minorities in decision making increases the likelihood that some resources will be redistributed to disadvantaged groups.

Economic and Political Competition

Increased competitiveness within an economy generally means lower profit margins and lower corruption (especially in pollution or other areas of market failure). But this does not preclude corruption in other sectors. For example, high-cost, low-profit firms forced to pay bribes may exit the market, thereby reducing competition and increasing the profit margins for the remaining firms. Inspectors may also be willing to accept smaller bribes from low-profit firms.

Ades and Di Tella (1997) find evidence of a negative relationship between the competitiveness of firms and the CPI. When firms enjoy higher rents, bureaucrats will have greater incentive to engage in corruption. But despite deregulation and price liberalization under the adjustment programs of the 1980s and 1990s, most countries have experienced an increase in corruption. It is therefore possible for greater competition to coexist with higher corruption. The degree of political competition also matters. For example, proportional representative elections with lower weight for individual accountability of candidates are associated with higher corruption.

Charap and Harm (1999) contend that corruption is endogenous to political structures and helps maintain equilibrium among different population groups. Elimination of corruption in such instances could then destabilize existing political systems and lead to anarchy, rather than enhancing economic efficiency. Under these conditions, a comprehensive reform of the civil service could be implemented only if a ruler gains stability from benevolence, rather than patronage. If the survival of the regime is threatened, this reform program is likely to be rejected.

Costs and Benefits of Corruption

The argument that corruption is ultimately beneficial because it cuts down red tape and bureaucratic inefficiency has no empirical basis. Corruption tempts even honest officials to slow down the processing of requests in an effort to avoid responsibility and put off decisions that they might regret in the future. If corruption were beneficial to society, such corrupt practices would be legal.

How does one explain the high level of corruption in a large number of countries despite repressive laws to control it? Everyone now accepts that some level of corruption is inevitable in every combination of market and government. Politicians and bureaucrats have a vested interest in increasing and overextending their reach into the marketplace. Therefore, a minimalist state helps curb corruption and corrupt practices.

There appears, however, to be a link between government corruption and market failures. Governments intervene with the best of intentions in the case of market failures and use subsidies and transfers to divert resources from gainers to losers or vulnerable groups. This flow of money creates corruption opportunities that undermine the very purpose of government intervention. Government intervention requires bureaucrats (agents) to collect information, make decisions, and implement policies and programs. Hiring officials to control corruption diverts talented individuals away from productive activity. Corruption in the form of rents for bureaucrats clearly induces a misallocation of resources and rapidly expands the size of the bureaucracy. Because it is difficult to eliminate completely, however, we must reconcile ourselves to a "second-best" world in which some bureaucrats will always be taking bribes.

Transaction costs related to corruption are also higher than those for legal contracts. Also, corruption does not allow for legal recourse; therefore, partners are locked in long after the exchange of goods and services has been completed.

Impact of Corruption on Economic Performance

Bribery is widespread in many countries, to varying extents. Bribery raises transaction costs and uncertainty in an economy, leads to inefficient economic outcomes, impedes long-term foreign and domestic investment, misallocates talent to rent-seeking activities, diverts assets from important projects such as agricultural and rural development to "roads to nowhere" and large defense projects, pushes firms underground, lowers revenue collection, and acts as a regressive tax against smaller firms, with the cumulative effect of sending the economy into a vicious downward spiral.

The World Economic Forum's (WEF) Global Competitiveness Survey for 1997 indicates that enterprises reporting a greater incidence of bribery also tend to spend a greater share of their management time with bureaucrats and public officials negotiating licenses, permits, signatures, and taxes.

In a seminal paper, Murphy, Shleifer, and Vishny (1993) postulate that corruption reduces the returns of productive activities. This is especially true when corruption and rent seeking yield higher returns than productive activities, thereby draining human resources away from the productive sector. Mo (2001) estimates that this tendency accounts for about 14.8 percent of the negative effect of corruption on growth. Mauro

(1995) also shows the negative impact of corruption on investment and thereby on growth. Pak (2001) estimates that a 1 percent increase in corruption could reduce the growth rate (through the investment channel) by about 0.72 percent, which translates to about 21.4 percent of the effect of corruption on growth.

In a recent IMF book titled *Governance, Corruption, and Economic Performance*, edited by Abed and Gupta (2002), cross-country analysis shows that high-corruption countries have lower tax revenues, lower per capita income, a higher incidence of poverty, and worse social indicators than low-corruption countries. The book further illustrates that corruption and rent-seeking behavior affect both the expenditure and revenue sides of the budget. By using cross-sectional data, Mauro (2002) shows that corruption is negatively associated with government expenditure on education. An increase in corruption by one unit (on a scale of 0 to 10) lowers the ratio of public spending on education by 0.2 percent of GDP. Corruption, therefore, could lead to a suboptimal composition of government expenditure. The reason for this is that education programs are less prone to rent seeking.

Gupta, Davoodi, and Tiongson (2002) show that a high level of corruption has adverse consequences for a country's child and infant mortality rates, the percentage of low-birthweight babies in total births, and primary school dropout rates. For example, an increase in corruption by one unit (on a scale of 0 to 10) raises the child mortality rate on average by 1.1 to 2.7 deaths per 1,000 live births. These results are consistent with predictions stemming from theoretical models and service-delivery surveys. An important implication of the results is that improvements in health and education outcomes do not necessarily require higher public spending, but rather better control over existing resources that are being diverted through corrupt channels.

Tanzi and Davoodi (2002) provide further evidence on how corruption leads to allocations in favor of less-productive investment projects and against nonwage operations and maintenance expenditures, such as books and medicines, thereby reducing the quality and productivity of existing infrastructure.

Corruption affects other types of public spending as well. Gupta, de Mello, and Sharan (2002) show that corruption is associated with higher military spending as a share of both GDP and total government spending, as well as with arms procurement in relation to the GDP and total government spending. Military spending is a monopoly of the state, and contracts are often drawn up in secret, with authorities exercising considerable discretionary power over how money is spent. The results from the study suggest governance indicators should account for defense spending.

A considerable and growing amount of public spending takes place at subnational levels in a number of countries. De Mello and Barenstein (2002) find that decentralization of control over expenditure to subnational governments can enhance governance. The higher the share of total government expenditures that is spent on a subnational level, the stronger the positive association between decentralization and governance. The relationship between decentralization and poor governance also depends on how subnational expenditures are financed—in general, the higher the share of nontax revenues in total revenues as well as grants and transfers from higher levels of government in total expenditure, the stronger the association between decentralization and corruption.

Poor governance also affects a country's income distribution and poverty. Dabla-Norris and Wade (2002) present a model to explain why relatively wealthy people choose to engage in rent-seeking activities such as employment in the government bureaucracy, army, or police rather than in productive and entrepreneurial activities. Given imperfect capital markets and lump-sum entry fees associated with rent seeking, those who are relatively wealthy to begin with tend to engage in rent seeking to protect their wealth from expropriation. Deregulation, liberalization, privatization, strengthening of the budgetary process, and institution building have helped to improve economic governance and reduce the opportunities for rent-seeking behavior.

Corruption impedes growth by limiting the development of small and medium-size enterprises: rather than building their businesses, entrepreneurs have to devote their valuable time to bribing officials. Of course, causation is an issue in all such countries. Are poor countries with weak implementation capacity in all facets of economic management likely to have high levels of corruption, or are corrupt countries likely to have low per capita income and a high incidence of poverty? Do stagnating countries breed corruption, or does corruption cause countries to stagnate?

A high degree of income inequality, as in Latin American countries, gives poor people a strong incentive to engage in illegal or corrupt activities. This situation threatens the institution of private property as well as law and order and could have a negative effect on growth. Mo (2001) estimates that the uncertainty induced by such threats accounts for more than 53 percent of the total effect of corruption on growth. Using a sample of worldwide governance indicators, such as corruption, voice and accountability, and rule of law, covering 175 countries for the period 2000–01, Kaufmann, Kraay, and Mastruzzi (2006) show (a) a strong positive causal effect running from better governance to higher per capita income, thereby confirming the importance of good governance for economic growth, and (b) a weak—even negative—causal effect running in the opposite direction from per capita income to good governance, indicating that the absence of higher income leads to further improvement in governance. Economic growth is possible without improved governance.

The above discussion depicts the complexity of dealing with corrupt behavior. While some studies show that providing higher wages to government employees (along with giving incentives and imposing penalties) can reduce bribery, other studies indicate the need for bolder policy changes to reduce opportunities for corruption (box 17.1). These include enhancing transparency in public transactions and increasing the accountability of public officials, with the media and civil society playing a "watchdog" role. The following are some of the major economic policy changes that will unambiguously reduce opportunities for corruption:

- lowering tariffs and other barriers to international trade;
- unifying market-determined exchange rates and interest rates;
- eliminating enterprise subsidies;
- minimizing regulations, licensing requirements, and other barriers to entry for new firms and investors;
- demonopolizing and privatizing government assets; and
- transparently enforcing prudent banking regulations and auditing and accounting standards.

Corruption cannot be substantially reduced without modifying the way governments are organized and operate. Such modifications require a multipronged strategy, including a reduction in excessive and complex regulations; reform of the civil service; improved budgeting, financial management, and tax administration; and stronger legal and judicial systems. Such reforms should involve changing government structures and procedures, placing greater emphasis on competition and incentives within the public sector, and strengthening internal and external checks and balances. As a complement to these broader reforms, the transparent implementation of enforcement measures, such as prosecuting some prominent corrupt figures, can also have an impact.

Other studies point to the role of timely audits and monitoring. For example, a randomized field experiment examined several approaches to

Box 17.1

How to Reduce Corruption

Transparency improves governance and reduces corruption and is required for better development and faster economic growth. A basic checklist of concrete reforms to promote transparency might include the following items:

- Public disclosure of assets and incomes of candidates running for public office, public officials, politicians, legislators, judges, and their dependents
- Public disclosure of political campaign contributions by individuals and firms and of campaign expenditures
- Public disclosure of all parliamentary votes, draft legislation, and parliamentary debates
- Effective implementation of conflict of interest laws separating business, politics, legislation, and public service, and the adoption of a law governing lobbying
- Public blacklisting of firms in public procurement (as done by the World Bank) that have been shown to bribe and a requirement to "publish what you pay" for multinationals working in extractive industries
- Effective implementation of the freedom of information laws, with easy access for all to government information
- Freedom of the media (including the Internet)
- Public disclosure of central and local budgets, adoption of the IMF's reports on the standards and codes framework of fiscal transparency, detailed government reporting of payments from multinationals in extractive industries, and open meetings involving the country's citizens
- Disclosure of the actual ownership structure and financial status of domestic banks
- Transparent (Web-based) competitive procurement
- Periodic implementation and publicizing of country governance, anticorruption, and public-expenditure tracking surveys, such as those supported by the World Bank
- Transparency programs at the city level, including budget disclosure and open meetings

Source: Kaufmann 2005, 92.

reducing corruption in more than 600 village road projects in Indonesia by having engineers independently estimate the prices and quantities of all inputs used in each road and then comparing these estimates to villages' official expenditure reports (Olken 2005). Announcing the certainty of a government audit (top-down monitoring) reduced theft by 8 percent of expenditures, and increasing grassroots participation in the monitoring process reduced theft of villagers' wages (but this was almost entirely offset by corresponding increases in theft of materials, which are public goods).

The scorecard method advanced by an Indian nongovernmental organization from Bangalore, whereby users rated local service-providing agencies, has already resulted in the firing of officials, improved service delivery, and a decreased incidence of bribery (Van der Meer-Kooistra and Vosselman 2004). This approach has been found to be effective in a number of other states and cities in India and in several developing countries. At least in some cases, the free press disseminated information about corruption and triggered some changes.

Persistence of Corruption

Is corruption the norm in certain countries, or is it a deviation from the norm? The very definition of corruption as a misuse of public duties for private gain implies a deviation. It also raises questions of ethics, cultural values, and social behavior. Norms are persistent social traditions or behaviors. Does corruption persist because of imperfect information, underlying beliefs, the ease of collusion at all levels, or because it is self-replicating? Does the introduction of a few corrupt individuals into an otherwise honest society lead to pervasive corruption over time? Mishra (2006) suggests that self-replicating behavior may be the problem, as youth look up to corrupt but successful people, wanting to assume their role.

Economists view this as a multiple equilibria problem—different societies at similar levels of economic and political development (per capita income, political structure, judicial efficiency) may exhibit varying degrees of corruption, tax evasion, and other noncompliant behavior. This multiplicity of equilibria may arise because of complementarities, but why do some societies get trapped in such a bad equilibrium? The answers are complex. If people in a country expect corruption, then the expected cost of being corrupt and getting caught will be low, which then will lead to more corruption. While incentives and rewards can get one out of a bad equilibrium and move from high to low corruption, they do not solve other problems, such as agency costs and expensive information gathering, which also lead to multiple equilibria.

We may have a low-corruption equilibrium if few firms choose to pollute or if the inspector spends substantial time and effort gathering information on when and how firms pollute. On the other hand, we may have a high-corruption equilibrium if the inspector is uninformed about firms (and wants to be uninformed) and a high proportion of firms take a chance and pollute.

Evolutionary social dynamics can also explain a multiplicity of equilibria. An individual chooses to be corrupt because everyone else is corrupt and this is an accepted social norm. How does an honest leader, say, bring about a new social norm of low corruption?

Recanatini, Prati, and Tabellini (2005) find that both corruption and the design of an organization can be influenced by the individuals at the very top of the agency. In fact, the procedure for appointing the head of the agency is one of the major determinants of both corruption and the design of the agency's internal organization. Agencies whose head is popularly elected are systematically more corrupt and have worse internal organization than agencies whose head is appointed by a political body. Finally, the data show that corruption is influenced by demand-side factors. Agencies that provide services to firms are more prone to corruption than those that provide services to households, particularly if alternative providers are not readily available in the marketplace or elsewhere.

Conclusion

Despite all the checks and balances, the imposition of penalties, the enforcement of civil service rules, and other major reforms, both private sector representatives (givers) and public employees (receivers) find ingenious and unique ways of colluding for profit—and avoiding charges. A high level of corruption is only one indicator of misgovernance. Therefore, any study of corruption may have to cover other institutional and governance issues such as rule of law, crime and violence, voice and accountability, transparency, and so on. Rapid technological changes, the changing role of media in society, and the use of the Internet for information dissemination have brought about greater transparency. But given that the rich and powerful own the media, and that the media are likely targets of corruption, how can one ensure truthful reporting and transparency? There is much more to know about corruption in the private sector and its motives.

Note

1. "Just as it is impossible not to taste honey or poison that one may find at the tip of one's tongue, so it is impossible for one dealing with government funds not to taste, at least a little bit, of the king's wealth" (Shamasastry 1961).

Bibliography

Abed, George, and Sanjeev Gupta, eds. 2002. *Governance, Corruption, and Economic Performance*. Washington, DC: International Monetary Fund.

Ades, Alberto, and Rafael Di Tella. 1997. "National Champions and Corruption: Some Unpleasant Interventionist Arithmetic." *Economic Journal* 107 (443): 1023–42.

Camdessus, M. 1998. "Good Governance Has Become Essential in Promoting Growth and Stability." *International Monetary Fund Survey* 27 (February 9): 36–38.

Chand, Sheetal K., and Karl O. Moene. 1997. "Controlling Fiscal Corruption." IMF Working Paper WP/97/100, International Monetary Fund, Washington, DC.

Charap, J., and C. Harm. 1999. "Institutionalized Corruption and the Kleptocratic State." IMF Working Paper 91, International Monetary Fund, Washington, DC.

Dabla-Norris, Era, and Paul Wade. 2002. "Production, Rent Seeking, and Wealth Distribution." In *Governance, Corruption, and Economic Performance*, ed. G. Abed and S. Gupta, 439–57. Washington, DC: International Monetary Fund.

de Mello, Luiz, and Matias Barenstein. 2002. "Fiscal Decentralization and Governance: A Cross-Country Analysis." In *Governance, Corruption, and Economic Performance*, ed. G. Abed and S. Gupta, 333–67. Washington, DC: International Monetary Fund.

Duflo, E., and Rema Hanna. 2005. "Monitoring Works: Getting Teachers to Come to School." NBER Working Paper Series 11880, National Bureau of Economic Research, Cambridge, MA.

Friedman, E., S. Johnson, D. Kaufmann, and P. Zoido-Lobatón. 2000. "Dodging the Grabbing Hand: The Determinants of Unofficial Activity in 69 Countries." *Journal of Public Economics* 76 (3): 459–93.

Global Competitiveness Survey. 1997. *Global Competitiveness Report*. Geneva: World Economic Forum.

———. 2004. *Global Competitiveness Report*. Geneva: World Economic Forum.

———. 2007. *Global Competitiveness Report*. Geneva: World Economic Forum.

Gupta, Sanjeev, Hamid R. Davoodi, and Erwin R. Tiongson. 2002. "Corruption and the Provision of Health Care and Education Services." In *Governance, Corruption, and Economic Performance*, ed. G. Abed and S. Gupta, 111–40. Washington, DC: International Monetary Fund.

Gupta, Sanjeev, Luiz de Mello, and Raju Sharan. 2002. "Corruption and Military Spending." In *Governance, Corruption, and Economic Performance*, ed. G. Abed and S. Gupta, 300–32. Washington, DC: International Monetary Fund.

Katz, Lawrence F., and Kevin M. Murphy. 1992. "Changes in Relative Wages, 1963–1987: Supply and Demand Factors." *Quarterly Journal of Economics* 107 (1): 35–78.

Kaufmann, Daniel. 2003. "Rethinking Governance: Empirical Lessons Challenge Orthodoxy." *Global Competitiveness Report 2002–2003*, Geneva: World Economic Forum.

———. 2005. "Myths and Realities of Governance and Corruption." *Global Competitiveness Report 2005–06*, chapter 2.1. Geneva: World Economic Forum.

Kaufmann, Daniel, Art Kraay, and M. Mastruzzi. 2005. "Governance Matters IV: Governance Indicators for 1996–2004." Policy Research Working Paper 3630, World Bank, Washington, DC.

———. 2006. "Measuring Governance Using Cross-Country Perceptions Data." In *International Handbook on the Economics of Corruption*, ed. S. Rose-Ackerman, 52–104. Cheltenham, U.K.; Northampton, MA: Edward Elgar.

Kenny, C. 2009. "Measuring Corruption in Infrastructure: Evidence from Transition and Developing Countries." *Journal of Development Studies* 45 (3): 314–32.

Mauro, Paulo. 1995. "Corruption and Growth." *Quarterly Journal of Economics* 110 (3): 681–712.

———. 1998. "Corruption and the Composition of Government Expenditure." *Journal of Public Economics* 69 (August): 263–79.

———. 2002. "The Persistence of Corruption and Slow Economic Growth." IMF Working Papers 02/213, International Monetary Fund, Washington, DC.

Mishra, A. 2006. "Corruption, Hierarchies and Bureaucratic Structures." In *International Handbook on the Economics of Corruption*, ed. Susan Rose-Ackerman, 189–215. Cheltenham, UK; Northampton, MA: Edward Elgar.

Mo, P. H. 2001. "Corruption and Economic Growth." *Journal of Comparative Economics* 29 (1): 66–79.

Murphy, K. M., A. Shleifer, and R. W. Vishny. 1993. "Why Is Rent-Seeking So Costly to Growth?" *American Economic Review* 83 (2): 409–14.

Olken, B. A. 2005. "Monitoring Corruption: Evidence from a Field Experiment in Indonesia." NBER Working Paper Series 11753, National Bureau of Economic Research, Cambridge, MA.

Pak, Hung Mo. 2001. "Corruption and Economic Growth." *Journal of Comparative Economics* 29 (1): 66–79.

Recanatini, F., A. Prati, and G. Tabellini. 2005. "Why are Some Public Agencies Less Corrupt than Others? Lessons for Institutional Reform from Survey Data." Paper presented at Sixth Jacques Polak Annual Research Conference, International Monetary Fund, Washington, DC, November 3–4.

Schneider, F., and D. Enste. 2002. *Hiding in the Shadows: The Growth of the Underground Economy*. Washington, DC: International Monetary Fund.

Shamasastry, R., trans. 1961. *Kautilya's Arthasastra*. Mysore, India: Mysore's Printing and Publishing House.

Tanzi, Vito, and Hamid R. Davoodi. 2002. "Corruption, Growth, and Public Finances." In *Governance, Corruption, and Economic Performance*, ed. G. Abed and S. Gupta, 197–224. Washington, DC: International Monetary Fund.

Van der Meer-Kooistra, J., and E. G. J. Vosselman. 2004. "The Balanced Scorecard: Adoption and Application." In *Advances in Management Accounting*, vol. 12 ed. Marc J. Epstein, John Y. Lee, 287–310. Amsterdam; Boston: Elsevier.

Van Rijckeghem, Caroline, and Beatrice Weder. 2001. "Bureaucratic Corruption and the Rate of Temptation: Do Low Wages in Civil Service Cause Corruption?" *Journal of Development Economics* 65 (2): 307–31.

Vogl, F. 1998. "The Supply Side of Global Bribery." *Finance and Development* 35 (2): 30–33.

Walker, J. 1999. "Measuring the Extent of International Crime and Money Laundering." Paper prepared for Kriminal Expo Conference, Budapest, June 9.

WEF (World Economic Forum). *Global Competitiveness Survey for 1997*. Davos, Switzerland: WEF.

World Bank. 2000. *World Bank Enterprise Survey*. Washington, DC: World Bank.

CHAPTER 18

Regulation and Economic Growth

Since the 1980s, developing countries have regulated and deregulated infrastructure, production, labor, security, finance, and banking sectors in an effort to liberalize their public services. Effective regulation encourages competition while mitigating the adverse impact of market failures; yet the regulations of most developing countries in fact limit productivity, growth, and service delivery—and cost three times more than those of advanced economies.

At the same time, property rights protection in developing countries is half that of advanced economies. Costly labor-market regulations protect jobs rather than people. For example, minimum wage requirements limit the creation of new low-skill jobs, especially in the services sector. Similarly, land and property regulations hamper private investment, industrial expansion, and growth. In several developing countries, 60–70 percent of people do not have legal title to their land, which limits the use of land as collateral for access to financing. While product safety standards protect consumers (for example, by ensuring that appliances are not fire hazards), product-market regulations limit firms' productivity (for example, Germany restricts the hours during which retail stores can be open).

Regulations should encourage competition and break up monopolies where possible; be simple and transparent yet dynamic and responsive to specific industries and changing markets over time; and be evenly enforced across sectors and industries. They should protect people and not jobs; be customized to national needs (and not simply mimic those in advanced economies); and be explicit, particularly in the regulation of prices and natural monopolies (for example, utilities).

Product-Market Regulation

Schiantarelli (2005) provides a critical overview of recent empirical research on how regulations affect the product market. He suggests that regulations affect allocative efficiency—that is, the allocation of resources among sectors producing different goods and among firms with different productivity within each sector, the productivity of existing firms, and the pace of productivity growth—by altering the incentives to innovate and determining the speed with which new products and processes replace old ones. As regulations reduce the gap between prices and marginal costs and allocate capital and labor to produce those goods most demanded by consumers, markets become more competitive. This competitive climate pressures less-efficient firms to exit, and market share shifts from lower- to higher-productivity firms, leading to a more efficient allocation of the factors of production.

Product-market reforms[1] have both short- and long-term effects. For instance, an increase in the degree of substitutability between goods leads to lower markups and allows firms to exit the market with no long-term effects on the economy. It also increases employment and higher real wages. Product-market reforms that decrease entry costs thus have positive long-term effects: as new firms enter the market, markups fall and employment and real wages rise.

Labor Regulation

Boeri, Helppie, and Macis (2008) claim that labor regulations are detrimental to economic efficiency and therefore impede growth and prosperity. Others claim that they correct market imperfections and allow for redistribution without hampering efficiency (Freeman 2005).

Considerable changes in income distribution have accompanied recent globalization. But contrary to what most trade models predict, the distributional changes have not favored the less-skilled workers abundant in developing countries (Goldberg and Pavcnik 2007). With the rise of globalization, labor-market protection—especially of the most vulnerable segments of the population—has become increasingly important.

Economic theory cannot always predict the effects of labor-market regulation in developing countries. Standard competitive models of the labor market predict that minimum wages reduce employment. On the other hand, in models that include some form of modern monopsony or other market imperfection that results in job matches yielding economic rents (for example, Mortensen and Pissarides 1994), minimum wages redistribute the rent without necessarily affecting employment levels or overall economic efficiency. In some circumstances, minimum wages might even increase employment. Because of the ambiguities of theoretical predictions, any assessment of the effects of labor-market regulations ultimately relies on empirical studies.

Labor-market regulations can affect firms' choices of inputs, investments, technology, and output and can influence the allocation of resources across firms and sectors. Because of job reallocation's critical role in economic development (see Caballero and Hammour 2000; Krizan, Haltiwanger, and Foster 2002; Bartelsman, Haltiwanger, and Scarpetta 2004), understanding whether labor market institutions help or hinder reallocation is an important task. Strict labor regulations are associated with larger unofficial economies, which in turn may suggest worse working conditions and poorer job quality. It is important to assess whether stricter regulations actually cause such conditions.

Minimum Wages

To improve the earnings of disadvantaged workers, governments typically set minimum wage limits and mandate that employers provide nonwage benefits to their workers, such as health care, paid vacations, and maternity leave. Minimum wage regulations are most likely to affect females, teenagers, minorities, and other low-wage earners.

As indicated in figure 18.1, if wage and employment are determined in a competitive labor market, a legal minimum wage set above the market-clearing wage level will result in an employment reduction, the magnitude of which depends on the actual wage increase and on the elasticity of labor demand. If this is the case, the cost of higher wages for employed workers is unemployment for other workers. The net effect on total welfare is then ambiguous, depending on the magnitude of the employment effect and the alternatives available to those who remain without a job.

Figure 18.1   Effect of (Higher) Minimum Wage on Employment

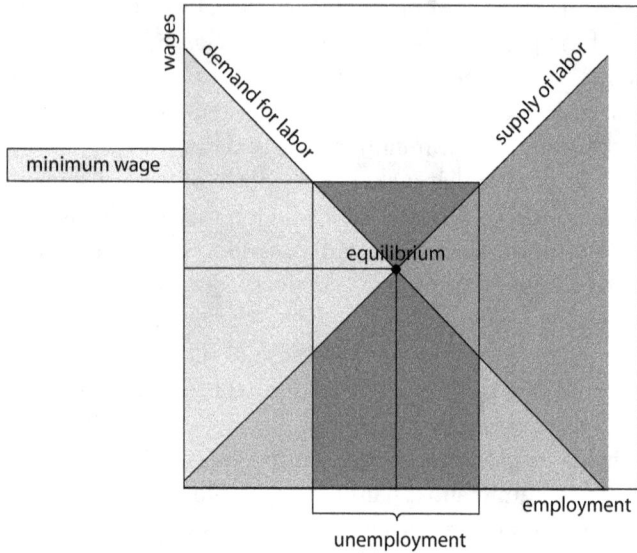

Source: Authors.

The predicted effects depend on a series of institutional variables, including the degree of compliance, enforcement, penalties for noncompliance, and the existence (and size) of uncovered sectors (more relevant in developing countries). Because of some market frictions, a mandated minimum wage can result in a redistribution of the surplus from employers to workers without reducing employment. If enforcement is ineffective or if the penalties for paying wages below the minimum are only modest, there is little reason to expect compliance—and so the effects of minimum wages will be negligible. Moreover, minimum wage limits and other labor-market regulations do not apply or are not enforced in the informal sector.

Competitive models predict that a binding minimum wage prices out workers whose marginal product falls below the wage floor into the sector where the minimum wage is not applicable. Boeri, Helppie, and Macis (2008) find that the minimum wage reduces the employment rates of young and unskilled labor and raises those of older and skilled workers. In Mexico, the minimum wage adversely affected employment for females of all ages and had positive employment effects for males ages 55–64 years (Feliciano 1998). In Indonesia, the minimum wage negatively affected the employment of blue-collar workers and positively affected that of white-collar workers.

Efficiency-wage-type models suggest how minimum wages could reduce poverty. In very low-income countries where workers' malnutrition is often an issue, higher wages could increase productivity through improved nutrition. Empirical evidence on the effects of the minimum wage on poverty and welfare is scant and displays mixed results. But two studies—cross-sectional data from several countries in Latin America (Morley 1995) and longitudinal data from Latin America, Asia, and Africa (Lustig and McLeod 1997)—suggest a negative correlation between higher minimum wages and poverty. On the other hand, the analysis of the Brazilian case by Neumark, Cunningham, and Siga (2006) finds no evidence of positive effects of the minimum wage on poverty and income inequality, and Gindling and Terrell (2007) find that minimum wage increases led to only modest poverty reduction in Honduras.

Mandated Benefits

There are two types of mandated benefits: those that vary with hours, such as additional wages or taxes (variable costs), and those that impose a fixed cost of employment per worker. The former can encompass mandated bonuses, vacation pay, maternity leave, or disability programs that are funded by an employer.

In a standard static model of the labor market, such mandated benefit contributions will shift the labor demand curve downward by the amount of the contribution, resulting in a lower direct wage and lower employment in equilibrium. Moving from point L, W to point L', W' in figure 18.2, panel a, shows the effect of a mandated benefit on the market in the case where the employee values the benefit at less than its cost to the employer. The predictable effect in this situation is a decrease in both employment and wages. On the supply side, if workers value benefits at less than the cost of the employer's contributions, they will have an incentive to seek out noncomplying work contracts. If the expected penalty for offering such work contracts is sufficiently low, profit-maximizing firms may prefer to employ such workers and capture some of the resultant rents. Thus, the formal sector might experience very different effects from mandated benefits than the informal sector, and analysis of official employment data may miss the employment, wage, or efficiency effects of such policies.

If a worker values a benefit at or above its cost, the effects of a mandated benefit on the labor market are less clearly negative. The direct wage is still

Figure 18.2   Cost of Mandated Benefits

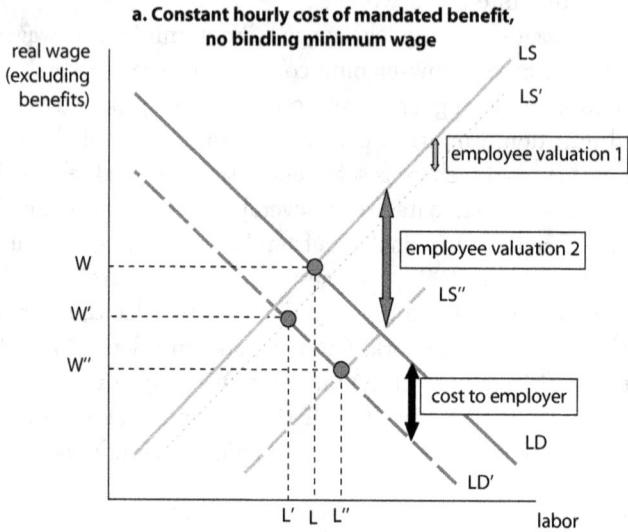

a. Constant hourly cost of mandated benefit, no binding minimum wage

real wage (excluding benefits)

LS
LS'
employee valuation 1
employee valuation 2
W
LS''
W'
W''
cost to employer
LD
LD'
L' L L''   labor

b. Cost of mandated benefit in proportion to hours worked, with minimum wage

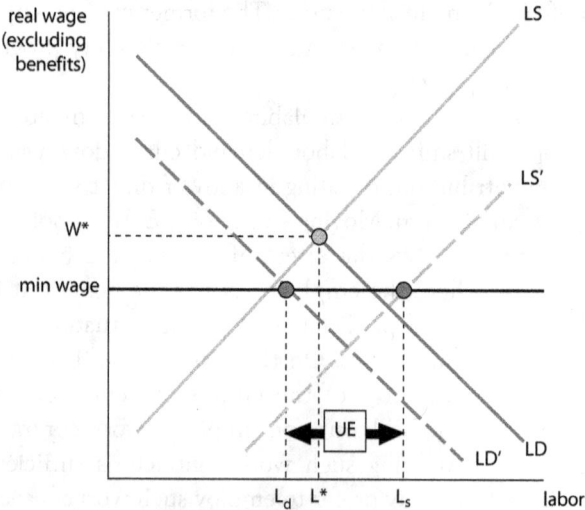

real wage (excluding benefits)

LS
LS'
W*
min wage
UE
LD' LD
L_d L^* L_s labor

Source: Boeri, Helppie, and Macis 2008, 22–23.
Note: LD = labor demand; LS = labor supply; W* = equilibrium wage; UE = unemployment. Employee valuation 1 indicates labor-supply effects with low valuation of the benefit. Employee valuation 2 represents the valuation of benefits above the cost to the employer. Point *L, w* represents equilibrium employment before a benefit is mandated. Point *L', W'* indicates a possible equilibrium under low employee valuation, and point *L'', W''* shows a possible outcome if a mandated benefit is highly valued by workers. In illustration b, the imposition of a mandated benefit may cause a minimum wage to bind (or exacerbate the effects thereof in cases where it already binds), causing unemployment even if a benefit is highly valued.

expected to fall, but the employment effect can be zero or positive (see point L'', w'' in figure 18.2, panel a) because of increased labor supply. The relative size of the wage effect compared to the employment effect clearly depends on the relative elasticities of the curves. It is important to note that an empirical finding of wage shifting and zero employment effects could be due to high employee valuation *or* to a highly or perfectly inelastic labor supply curve. In the former case, there would be no deadweight loss; in the latter, employees would bear the full deadweight loss.

Under this standard model, a binding minimum wage will exacerbate unemployment in the covered sector, since law-abiding employers will reduce employment if a wage reduction drops wages below the legal minimum. See figure 18.2, panel b, for an illustration of a mandated benefit that, while highly valued, creates or contributes to significant unemployment. This case of a binding minimum wage is particularly salient in developing countries where legal minimum wages apply to a large portion of the workforce. A mandated benefit may lead employers to shed workers or avoid hiring, causing unemployment even if the benefit is highly valued.

Regulation and the Private Sector

Market failures generally justify regulations. A common such failure involves externalities—cases where activities have spillover effects on others that the original sector does not consider. A second type of market failure is information asymmetry, where the producer may have more information about the safety or reliability of its products than the consumer. A third is monopoly power—market power that can be used to raise prices and lower output to maximize a firm's rent at the expense of the consumer. These market failures drive a wedge between the private interests of firms and those of society. They can also inhibit productive investments and growth. Thus, regulations can play a critical role in protecting society and consumers and promoting greater equity in private sector development.

Governments, however, must be careful to avoid overreaching in correcting these failures. While underregulation may fail to address social interests or externalities, overregulation can stifle the ability to pursue opportunities and curtail growth. In extreme cases, governments can set up regulations to extract rents or bribes. Such cases of "tollbooth" policies in "grabbing hand" states reinforce the benefits of simple, transparent, and enforceable regulations.

The share of firms that perceive a major or severe constraint to their business growth is much lower in high-income countries than in developing countries, according to the World Bank's cost-of-doing-business surveys. The share in high-income countries is often half that of lower-income ones, with the exception of licenses and permits and labor regulations, where the share is only marginally lower than for middle-income countries. Because the conditions in higher-income countries are generally better—for example, electrical outages are less common—their financial systems are more developed, and the procedures to comply with regulations are often more streamlined.

Access to electricity and finance are two top-priority issues in low-income countries, but their importance decreases dramatically as a country's income rises. This is true for other infrastructure variables, although telecommunications overall is not reported as too constraining in any area.

A number of areas related to regulations and governance are reported as most significant in middle-income countries. These are taxes, tax administration, informality, and corruption. It is often the low-income countries that have the most regulatory procedures and time delays associated with compliance. As income rises, these procedures and delays tend to decrease. On the other hand, enforcement of regulations often strengthens as income rises. Therefore, while the formal requirements may decrease, greater enforcement could explain why entrepreneurs in middle-income countries report more regulatory constraints. The results also suggest that corruption and regulatory constraints may go together.

Many studies show that the regulatory and institutional environment, access to finance, and infrastructure services are closely associated with firm performance (Dollar, Hallward-Driemeier, and Mengistae 2005). In particular, weaknesses in the business environment have been shown to shift the size distribution of firms downward (Aterido, Hallward-Driemeier, and Pages 2007). Interruptions in access to power are particularly significant in reducing the growth of large firms while encouraging the spread of small, more labor-intensive firms. A lack of access to finance lowers growth across the size distribution. Because the benefits of finance are particularly strong for small firms, a lack of access hurts them disproportionately (Beck and others 2004).

Busse and Groizard (2006) and others (see Hermes and Lensink 2003; Alfaro and others 2004; and Durham 2004) examine regulations to attract or deter foreign investors. They find that countries with better financial systems and financial market regulations can exploit foreign direct investment (FDI) more efficiently and achieve higher growth rates than countries that lack such systems and regulations. Some studies argue that countries need both a sound banking system and a functioning financial market to encourage entrepreneurship. Excessive regulations that prevent the reallocation of human and capital resources are likely to restrict the potential economic growth stemming from FDI. Further, costly regulations involving bureaucratic procedures that require entrepreneurs' time and resources can restrict the reallocation of capital flows to the most productive sectors.

Busse and Groizard (2006) use the Ease of Doing Business database (World Bank 2004) on government regulations to confirm that countries with restrictive regulations cannot exploit FDI inflows efficiently. They also find that FDI does not stimulate growth in economies with excessive business and labor regulations. Governments must first improve regulatory quality to reap the benefits of increased openness to foreign capital. Figure 18.3 shows one indicator of the relationship between "ease of doing business" and average per capita growth of gross domestic product (GDP) for 2000–05.

Numerous studies have established that regulatory quality is an important determinant of overall income levels, and regulation is strongly (negatively) correlated with income per capita levels. Similarly, the regulation indicator is also negatively associated with GDP per capita growth rates and FDI.

Figure 18.3   Average Per Capita GDP Growth and Ease of Doing Business

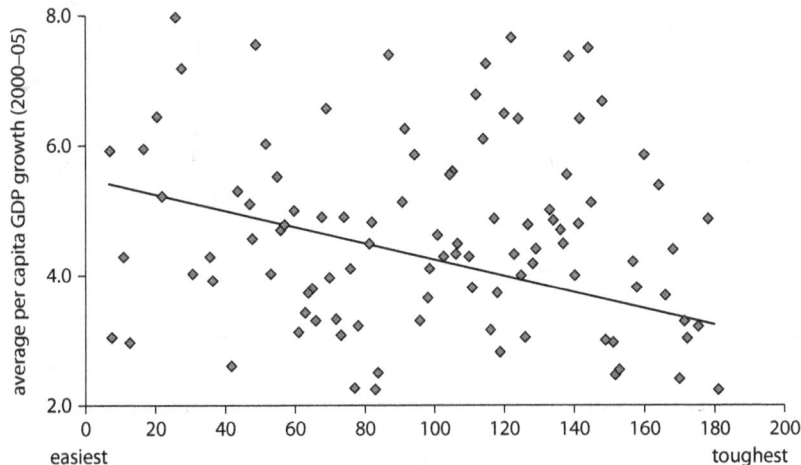

Source: Authors' computation from World Bank data on growth and the Doing Business database (World Bank 2009).

Financial Regulation

Barth, Caprio, and Levine (2001a) use two broad and competing theories to evaluate the merits of bank regulation by the government: (a) the *helping-hand* approach, in which governments regulate to correct market failures, and (b) the *grabbing-hand* approach, in which governments regulate to support political constituencies. More important, they assess the impact of regulatory and supervisory practices on banking sector development and fragility.[2] The helping-hand approach grants an important, powerful role to official regulators and supervisors, who believe that they can ameliorate market failures through proper supervision.

Banks are costly and difficult to monitor. Informational asymmetries can make banks prone to contagious and socially costly bank runs. Many countries also adopt deposit insurance schemes, which (a) create incentives for banks to take excessive risks and (b) reduce the incentives for depositors to monitor banks. Strong government supervision can ameliorate these market failures, improving bank performance and stability.

On the other hand, there are several theoretical reasons for enforcing fewer regulatory restrictions on banks (the grabbing-hand approach). First, doing so would permit the exploitation of economies of scale and scope in gathering and processing information about firms. Second, it would permit banks to better manage different types of customer risk, advertise and distribute financial services, enforce contracts, and build reputation capital among customers (see Barth, Brumbaugh, and Wilcox 2000; Claessens and Klingebiel 2000). Third, fewer regulatory restrictions may increase the franchise value of banks and thereby augment incentives for banks to behave prudently. Fourth, broader activities may diversify income streams and thereby create more stable banks. Finally, the grabbing-hand view holds that governments do not restrict bank activities to ease market failures. Instead, regulatory restrictions promote government power, create a bigger role for corruption through the granting of exceptions to the rules, and thereby hinder bank performance and stability.

Specific regulations affect country performance in different ways:

- Excessively generous official deposit insurance regimes inhibit bank development and increase bank fragility.
- Fewer restrictions allow banks to perform better, subject to a lower probability of crisis.
- Fewer limits on foreign bank entry enhance banking sector stability.

- Policies that promote the private monitoring of banks improve bank performance and reduce corruption. This supports the view that legal and regulatory reforms that promote and facilitate private monitoring of financial institutions constitute a useful financial reform strategy.

Finally, these findings raise a cautionary flag over reform strategies that rely on countries to adhere to an extensive checklist of regulatory and supervisory practices (such as direct government oversight of and restrictions on banks). Instead, the findings suggest that regulatory and supervisory practices that (a) force accurate information disclosure, (b) empower private sector oversight of banks, and (c) foster incentives for private agents to exert corporate control best promote bank performance and stability.

Policy Lessons from the Recent Crisis

The securitization meltdown of 2007 directly affected only a few developing countries. The rise in risk premiums—spreading recessionary pressures across most high-income countries—provided the main source of problems for these developing countries. In most crises, the periphery of financial-center countries suffers the most. The lessons for regulation and supervision afforded by crises are as relevant for regulators in developing countries as for anywhere else, and the breakdown of official supervision in several of the world's most developed countries shows the difficulty of aligning incentives. But transparent policy making can always remedy institutional weaknesses that undermine government accountability (Caprio, Demirgüç-Kunt, and Kane 2008). Other important considerations are as follows:

- Identifiable shocks that end booms or bubbles often reveal crises, although the underlying distortions accumulated over time.
- Over time, regulation-induced innovation leads to progressively more complex and less transparent risk shifting.
- Because institutions can count on the mismanagement of crisis resolution, safety-net subsidies flow to institutions willing to risk insolvency.
- The resolution of a crisis affects the frequency and depth of future crises.
- Past crises provide important lessons that are often ignored.

Financial crises expose weaknesses in the underlying incentive frameworks and the regulation and supervision systems that are supposed to reinforce them. Given the risky nature of the financial sector, it is not prudent to assume that regulation and supervision can eliminate the risk of crises. Yet reforms may improve the incentive structure of regulators and thus improve effectiveness.

Neither monetary policy nor capital controls can take the place of prudent regulation. While most observers agree that lax monetary policy in the United States in the early 2000s helped fuel the housing bubble, identifying such bubbles in a timely manner is very difficult.

More broadly, monetary authorities in most countries face two objectives: price stability and financial stability. Attempting to achieve two objectives with one instrument is not a promising strategy. A second instrument is needed for financial stability, and this is primarily a task for financial regulation. Capital requirements that can automatically be adjusted over the business cycle are an important pillar of regulation, providing incentives for financial intermediaries to hold more liquid assets in good times. Provisions, leverage ratios, and additional capital buffers can all be countercyclical. By switching the basis of capital adequacy requirements from levels of risk-weighted assets to their rates of growth, these measures require additional capital and liquidity when bank lending and asset prices are rising fast—and the relaxing of such requirements during downturns.

Despite their inherent fragility, financial systems underpin economic development. The challenge of financial sector policies is to align private incentives with public interest without unduly taxing or subsidizing private risk taking. Public ownership or overly aggressive regulation would simply hamper financial development and growth. Striking this balance has become increasingly complex in an ever more integrated and globalized financial system (Demirgüç-Kunt and Servén 2009).

Regulation and Reform of the Infrastructure Sector[3]

Basic infrastructure services—such as electricity, water, telecommunications, and transport—play a crucial role in supporting economic growth in developing countries. But such services are often highly politicized and susceptible to corruption, leading to poor performance that is a drag on economic growth and development.

Infrastructure services have suffered from poor management. Typically, technical performance is compromised because of widespread equipment outages, large amounts of excess labor, and low productivity. Often, prices are set too low to recover the costs of providing services, and sector enterprises have poor cash flows and encounter difficulties in mobilizing the financial resources needed to maintain equipment and construct additional capacity. Demand for infrastructure services is also compromised; many people are unable to secure these services because of high prices or are otherwise not connected without resorting to informal mechanisms such as bribery, theft, and political influence.

Historically, many of these services have been state-owned, vertically integrated "natural" monopolies, assigned with supply responsibilities, as was the case in the developed economies. But their services are potentially competitive, even though many require access to monopoly network facilities. Infrastructure sector reform may include privatization, restructuring to promote competition, or regulatory reform. The choice of reform program will depend on basic market institutions, income distribution and social concerns, legal and political institutions, and the economic attributes of different infrastructure sectors. Lessons drawn from the reform experiences of industrial countries should not be applied mechanically to developing countries.

Reasons for Poor Performance

Investments in infrastructure tend to be capital intensive and characterized by economies of scale and scope. A developing economy may not be in a budgetary position to finance and support extensive investments in infrastructure. Furthermore, political considerations may have led infrastructure prices to be set too low to meet operating costs and recover investments.

To attract new capital, regulatory and legal institutions need to provide credible commitments so that potential investors are certain of recovering their investment costs. Investors need to be aware of the prevailing legal restrictions on FDI as some infrastructure sectors may be prohibited from securing foreign capital. Furthermore, it is difficult to attract investors when corruption is rampant, when property rights and contracting institutions are poorly developed, and when infrastructure sectors are used to pursue social and political goals that siphon off revenues and increase costs.

Reforming Regulated Natural Monopolies

Joskow (1999) suggests specific ways of improving the performance of regulated natural monopolies:

- Prioritize regulatory reforms for the infrastructure sector.
- Address efficiency and rent distribution issues in the design of regulatory institutions.

- Provide credible, legal commitments to potential investors for respecting and enforcing private property rights and contracts.
- Set prices high enough to cover the costs of supplying and maintaining services at an appropriate level so as not to exploit consumers.

In sum, regulatory authorities must provide credible assurance that investors will not be exploited, that consumers will be protected from excessive prices and poor service, and that other goals for the sector will be achieved.

Reform Models

Joskow (1999) suggests a list of standard reform measures, arguing that a mix of several is more effective than pursuing a single strategy of privatization or deregulation. As a first step, he recommends developing effective regulatory institutions and competition policies to define the public policy goals for each infrastructure sector. Such goals might include

- improving the sector's ability to mobilize adequate financial resources and thus support the investments required to balance supply and demand efficiently;
- increasing sector productivity by reducing operating costs and investing in efficient plant and equipment; and
- aligning prices with costs to provide consumers with good price signals.

Good Organization and Procedures for Regulatory Agencies

The standard prescription for designing good regulatory institutions typically includes terms such as independence, transparency, accountability, expertise, and credibility. These terms convey important principles, the implementation of which relies on the legal and political institutions of different countries. But in reality, independent regulatory agencies are found in few countries. In most of these, including Canada and the United States, the independent regulatory commission has had nearly a century to evolve. Moreover, institutions using this conceptual procedure are obligated to make decisions based on a logical evaluation of the facts in light of their statutory responsibilities and subject to judicial review. This is alien to countries where policy decisions are made behind the closed doors of government ministries and departments and with limited due process.

Joskow (1999) advocates strongly that regulatory institutions should be an integral component of infrastructure sector reform, not an afterthought.

These institutions must be part of a framework that protects consumers from abuses of market power. They must promote efficient supply behavior by firms that provide residual monopoly services subject to public regulation. They must facilitate competition by implementing appropriate terms and conditions for access to bottleneck network facilities. Moreover, they must guard against cross-subsidization and unreasonable discrimination among competitors. Investors should perceive regulatory rules and procedures as credible commitments on which they can rely.

Creating effective regulatory institutions takes time. Perhaps the best way to begin is with simple regulatory rules and procedures, to be refined as information and experience accumulate. This would allow regulatory procedures to evolve in response to sector developments and regulator abilities. There is a trade-off between regulatory rigidity and flexibility. Going too far toward either extreme is not likely to yield regulatory institutions that perform well over long periods.

Impact of Regulation on Growth and Informality

Loayza, Oviedo, and Servén (2005) use seven indexes across a large sample of industrial and developing countries[4] to examine whether regulation hinders economic growth. Their data are based on surveys conducted in the late 1990s. They construct a product-market index by averaging the scores of five components, while an overall index consists of all seven. Figure 18.4 depicts scatter plots as to how the log of GDP per capita is affected by the (a) overall regulation (–0.41), (b) product-market regulation (correlation: –0.42), (c) labor regulation (not significant: –0.14), and (d) fiscal regulation (0.17).

The results of their analysis clearly suggest that high levels of regulation in product and labor markets are associated with lower growth. First, there is the distortionary effect of regulation on firm dynamics. Second, the disincentive because of regulation may create an opportunity for firms to work outside the legal framework, yielding to an informal sector.[5] Thus, increased regulation in the product or labor market could lead to its expansion whereas an increased *quality* of governance has the potential to mitigate informality. Similarly, if governance is not too low, an increase in fiscal regulation decreases informality, as does the provision of better public services and the enforcement of tax compliance.

The overall regulation plot suggests that heavily regulated economies tend to grow less and be more informal—a scenario found most commonly in developing countries—while developed economies tend to occupy the other end of the distribution. Product-market regulation and, to a lesser extent, labor regulation seem to slow growth the most. Conversely, greater fiscal regulation seems to drive better economic growth and foster a smaller informal sector.

Interestingly, the analysis of Loayza, Oviedo, and Servén (2005) suggests some predictions. If a typical developing country decreases its product-market regulation to the median level of industrialized countries while maintaining its level of governance (equal to the median of developing countries), then its annual growth rate would rise by about 1.7 percentage points. Similarly, if a country's index of labor regulation increased by one standard deviation in the cross-country sample and its level of governance was equal to the world median, then its annual rate of per capita GDP growth would decrease by 0.3 percentage points. These findings imply that streamlining regulation and strengthening governance in highly regulated countries could have a significant payoff in economic growth.

Informal companies evade fiscal and regulatory obligations, including value added taxes (VAT), income taxes, labor-market obligations (such as social security taxes and minimum wage requirements), and product-market regulations (including quality standards, copyrights, and intellectual property laws). Evasion varies by sector and by the nature of business. Informal retailers tend to avoid paying VAT, informal food processors ignore product-quality and health regulations, and informal construction firms underreport the number of employees and hours worked. Conventional wisdom has it that informality stems from corruption and lack of government resources. Farrell (2006) claims that governments are insufficiently aware of the huge positive economic and social gains that stem from reducing informality. Moreover, governments do not devote enough resources to the adequate enforcement of tax laws and other regulations (figure 18.5).

Three factors contribute to informality: (a) limited law enforcement of legal obligations—a result of poorly staffed and inefficiently organized government enforcement agencies; (b) the costs of operating formally (red tape, high taxes, and costly product-quality and worker-safety regulations); and (c) social norms—in some developing countries there is little social pressure to comply with the law. Many people see evading taxes and regulations as a legitimate way for small businesses to counteract the advantages of large, modern players.

Informality stifles economic growth and productivity in two ways: (a) the powerful incentives and dynamics that tie companies to the "gray"

Figure 18.4   Regulation and GDP per Capita

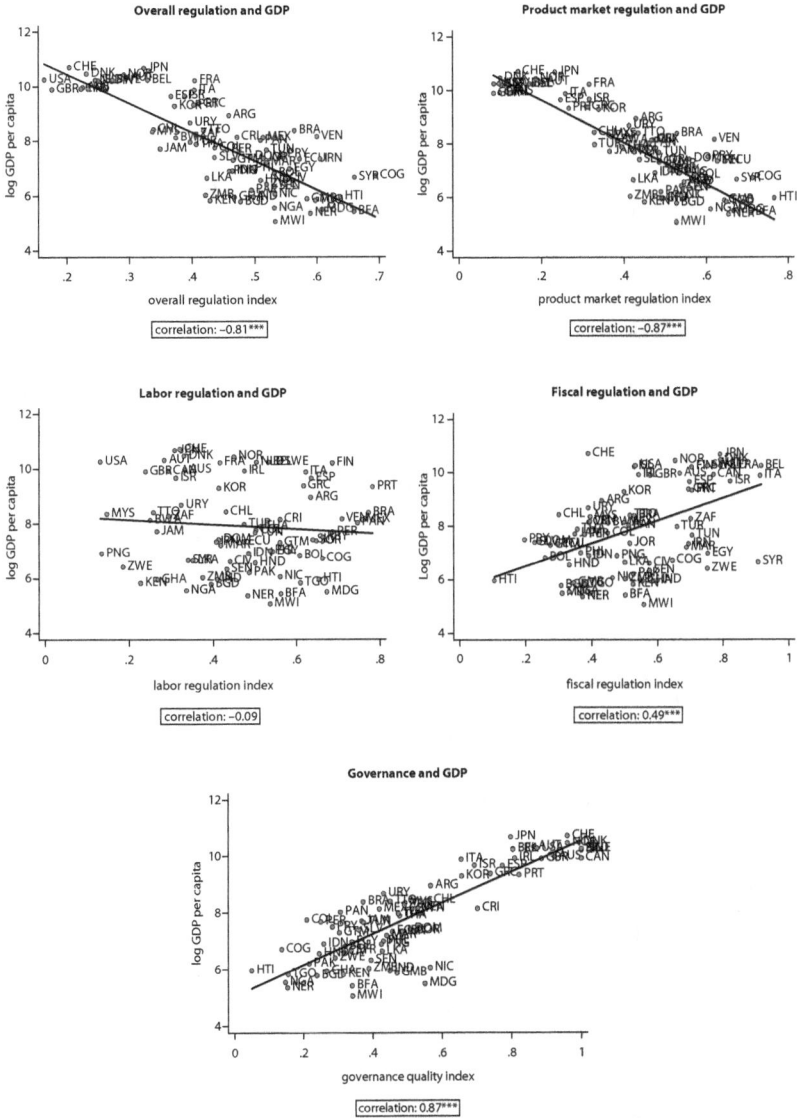

Source: Loayza, Oviedo, and Servén 2005, 18.
*** denotes significance at the 1% level.

Figure 18.5   Informal Economy across Several Countries and Sectors

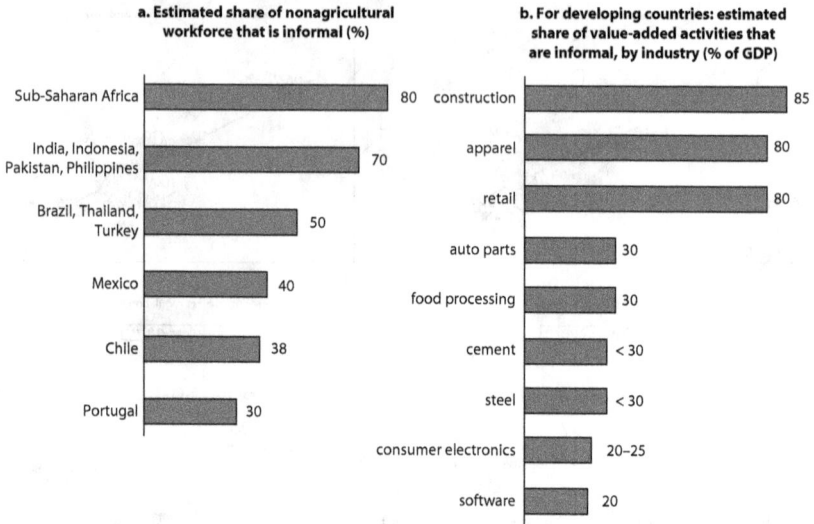

a. Estimated share of nonagricultural workforce that is informal (%)

Sub-Saharan Africa	80
India, Indonesia, Pakistan, Philippines	70
Brazil, Thailand, Turkey	50
Mexico	40
Chile	38
Portugal	30

b. For developing countries: estimated share of value-added activities that are informal, by industry (% of GDP)

construction	85
apparel	80
retail	80
auto parts	30
food processing	30
cement	< 30
steel	< 30
consumer electronics	20–25
software	20

Source: Farrell 2006, 144.

economy constrain their productivity, and (b) the cost advantages of avoiding taxes and regulations help informal companies steal market share from bigger, more productive formal competitors. Consequently, the adverse effects of informality are both economic and social (workers' income and health regulations are compromised, for example). Informal players persistently drag down a country's overall productivity and standard of living. In Portugal and Turkey, for instance, informality accounts for nearly 50 percent of the overall productivity gap with the United States.

Conclusion

Regulation should encourage competition while mitigating the adverse impact of market failures. Poor regulations limit productivity, growth, and service delivery in most countries. As such, regulations should be enacted with care, should be explicit and transparent, and should be enforced evenly. They should be adjusted on the basis of what works and does not work. The role of an effective regulatory regime is crucial in promoting productivity, investment, industrial expansion, economic growth, and development. The building of effective regulatory structures in developing countries involves both the technical design of appropriate regulatory instruments and the presence of good-quality supporting regulatory institutions. The ability of the state to provide effective regulatory institutions can strongly affect economic performance.

Notes

1. By which we mean reforms to product markets that stimulate competition, innovation, and economic growth.

2. These include regulations of (a) bank activities, (b) banking and commerce, (c) domestic and foreign bank entry, (d) capital adequacy, and (e) information disclosure. They also include deposit insurance system design features; supervisory power, independence, resources, loan classification stringency, provisioning standards, diversification guidelines, and prompt corrective action powers; the fostering of private sector monitoring of banks; and government ownership of banks.

3. In a comprehensive analysis titled "Regulatory Priorities for Infrastructure Sector Reform in Developing Countries" that was contributed to the "Annual World Bank Conference on Development Economics," Paul L. Joskow (1999), Elizabeth and James Kilhan Professor of Economics and Management, Massachusetts Institute of Technology discusses some important aspects of the topic summarized here. Interested readers are referred to the original article.

4. They are firm entry, labor markets, fiscal burden, trade barriers, financial markets, contract enforcement, and bankruptcy regulation. They are derived from the Ease of Doing Business database (World Bank), Index of Economic Freedom (Heritage Foundation), Economic Freedom of the World (Fraser Institute), the Labor Market Indicators Database (Rama and Artecona 2000), the Corporate Tax Rates Survey (KPMG), and the International Country Risk Guide (PRS Group) to study 75 countries.

5. The "informal" sector comprises (noncriminal) economic activities that go undeclared specifically to avoid compliance with costly regulations (such as employment-protection laws), tax payments, and social security contributions.

Bibliography

Aghion, P., and P. Howitt. 1992. "A Model of Growth Through Creative Destruction." *Econometrica* 60 (2): 323–51.

Alfaro, Laura, Areendam Chanda, Sebnem Kalemli-Ozcan, and Selin Sayek. 2004. "FDI and Economic Growth: The Role of Local Financial Markets." *Journal of International Economics* 64 (1): 89–112.

Andalon, M., and C. Pages. 2008. "Minimum Wages in Kenya." IZA Discussion Paper 3390, Institute for the Study of Labor, Bonn, Germany.

Aterido, R., M. Hallward-Driemeier, and C. Pages. 2007. "Investment Climate and Employment Growth: The Impact of Access to Finance, Corruption and Regulations Across Firms." IDB Working Paper 626, InterAmerican Development Bank, Washington, DC.

Azam, J. P. 1997. "Efficiency Wage and the Family: An Explanation for the Impact of the Agricultural Minimum Wage in Morocco." *Kyklos* 50 (3): 369–82.

Bartelsman, E. J., J. C. Haltiwanger, and S. Scarpetta. 2004. "Microeconomic Evidence of Creative Destruction in Industrial and Developing Countries." IZA Discussion Paper 1374, Institute for the Study of Labor, Bonn, Germany.

Barth, James R., R. D. Brumbaugh, and J. A. Wilcox. 2000. "The Repeal of Glass-Steagall and the Advent of Broad Banking." *Journal of Economic Perspectives* 14 (2): 191–204.

Barth, James R., Gerard Caprio Jr., and Ross Levine. 2001a. "Bank Regulation and Supervision: What Works Best." Working Paper 2725, World Bank, Development Research Group, and Financial Sector Strategy and Policy Department, Washington, DC.

———. 2001b. "Banking Systems Around the Globe: Do Regulations and Ownership Affect Performance and Stability?" In *Prudential Supervision: What Works and What Doesn't*, ed. Frederic S. Mishkin, 31–96. Chicago: University of Chicago Press.

Beck, T., A. Demirgüç-Kunt, L. Laeven, and R. Levine. 2004. "Finance, Firm Size, and Growth." NBER Working Paper 10983, National Bureau of Economic Research, Cambridge, MA.

Bell, L. 1997. "The Impact of Minimum Wages in Mexico and Colombia." *Journal of Labor Economics* 15 (3): S102–S134.

Bernard, A. B., J. Eaton, J. B. Jensen, and S. Kortum. 2003. "Plants and Productivity in International Trade." *American Economic Review* 93 (4): 1268–90.

Boeri, Tito, Brooke Helppie, and Mario Macis. 2008. "Labor Regulations in Developing Countries: A Review of the Evidence and Directions for Future Research." World Bank Discussion Paper 0833, World Bank, Washington, DC.

Borensztein, Eduardo, José De Gregorio, and Jong-wha Lee. 1998. "How Does Foreign Direct Investment Affect Economic Growth?" *Journal of International Economics* 45 (1): 115–35.

Busse, Matthias, and José Luis Groizard. 2006. "FDI, Regulations and Growth." World Bank Discussion Paper 3882, World Bank, Washington, DC.

Caballero, R., and M. Hammour. 1994. "The Cleansing Effects of Recessions." *American Economic Review* 84 (5): 1356–68.

———. 1996. "On the Timing and Efficiency of Creative Destruction." *Quarterly Journal of Economics* 111 (3): 805–52.

———. 1998. "The Macroeconomics of Specificity." *Journal of Political Economy* 106: 724–67.

———. 2000. "Creative Destruction and Development: Institutions, Crises, and Restructuring." NBER Working Paper W7849, National Bureau of Economic Research, Cambridge, MA.

Calomiris, Charles. 1995. "Financial Fragility: Issues and Policy Implications." In *Coping with Financial Fragility: A Global Perspective*, ed. Harald Benink, 47–64. Norwell, MA: Kluwer Academic Publishers.

Caprio, Gerard Jr., Asli Demirgüç-Kunt, and Edward J. Kane. 2008. "The 2007 Meltdown in Structured Securitization: Searching for Lessons, Not Scapegoats." Policy Research Working Paper 4756, World Bank, Washington, DC.

Claessens, S., and D. Klingebiel. 2000. "Competition and Scope of Activities in Financial Services." World Bank, Washington, DC.

Crampes, Claude, and Antonio Estache. 1996. "Regulating Water Concessions— Lessons from the Buenos Aires Concession." Public Policy for the Private Sector, World Bank, Washington, DC.

Demirgüç-Kunt, Asli, and Enrica Detragiache. 2002. "Does Deposit Insurance Increase Banking System Stability? An Empirical Investigation." *Journal of Monetary Economics* 49 (7): 1373–406.

———. 2005 "Cross-Country Empirical Studies of Systemic Bank Distress: A Survey." IMF Working Paper 05/96, International Monetary Fund, Washington, DC.

Demirgüç-Kunt, Asli, and Luis Servén. 2009. "Are All the Sacred Cows Dead? Implications of the Financial Crisis for Macro and Financial Policies." Policy Research Working Paper 4807, World Bank, Washington, DC.

Dollar, D., M. Hallward-Driemeier, and T. Mengistae. 2005. "Investment Climate and Firm Performance in Developing Economies." *Economic Development and Cultural Change* 54 (1): 1–31.

Durham, Benson. 2004. "Absorptive Capacity and the Effects of Foreign Direct Investment and Equity Foreign Portfolio Investment on Economic Growth." *European Economic Review* 48 (2): 285–306.

Farrell, D. 2006. *Driving Growth—Breaking Down Barriers to Global Prosperity.* Boston, MA.: Harvard Business School; London: McGraw-Hill.

Feliciano, Z. M. 1998. "Does the Minimum Wage Affect Employment in Mexico." *Eastern Economic Journal* 24 (2): 165–80.

Freeman, R. B. 2005. "Labor Market Institutions Without Blinders: The Debate about Flexibility and Labor Market Performance." NBER Working Paper 11286, National Bureau of Economic Research, Cambridge, MA.

Gallego, F., and N. Loayza. 2002. "The Golden Period of Growth in Chile. Explanations and Forecasts." In *Economic Growth: Sources, Trends and Cycles*, ed. Norman Loayza and Raimundo Soto, 309–42. Santiago: Central Bank of Chile.

Gindling, T. H., and K. Terrell. 2007. "Minimum Wages and the Welfare of Workers in Honduras." IZA Discussion Paper 2892, Institute for the Study of Labor, Bonn, Germany.

Goldberg, P., and N. Pavcnik. 2007. "Distributional Effects of Globalization in Developing Countries." *Journal of Economic Literature* 45 (1): 39–82.

Griffith, R., and R. Harrison. 2004. "The Link between Product Market Reform and Macro-Economic Performance." Directorate-General for Economic and Financial Affairs, Economic Papers 209, European Commission, Brussels.

Grossman, G. M., and E. Helpman. 1991. "Quality Ladders in the Theory of Growth." *Review of Economic Studies* 58 (1): 43–61.

Hermes, Niels, and Robert Lensink. 2003. "Foreign Direct Investment, Financial Development and Economic Growth." *Journal of Development Studies* 40 (1): 142–63.

Hossein, J., C. Kirkpatrick, and D. Parker. 2006. "The Impact of Regulation on Economic Growth in Developing Countries: A Cross-Country Analysis." *World Development* 35 (1): 103.

Joskow, Paul L. 1999. "Regulatory Priorities for Infrastructure Sector Reform in Developing Countries." In *Annual Bank Conference on Development Economics 1998*, ed. Boris Pleskovic and Joseph E. Stiglitz, 191–223. Washington, DC: World Bank.

Kane, Edward J. 1977. "Good Intentions and Unintended Evil: The Case Against Selective Credit Allocation." *Journal of Money, Credit and Banking* 9 (February): 55–69.

Krizan, C. J., J. C. Haltiwanger, and L. Foster. 2002. "The Link between Aggregate and Micro Productivity Growth: Evidence from Retail Trade." Working Papers 02–18, Center for Economic Studies, U.S. Census Bureau, Washington, DC.

Laffont, Jean-Jacques. 2006. *Regulation and Development*. Cambridge, U.K.: Cambridge University Press.

Loayza, Norman V., Ana María Oviedo, and Luis Servén. 2005. "The Impact of Regulation on Growth and Informality: Cross-Country Evidence." Policy Research Working Paper Series WPS 3623, World Bank, Washington, DC.

Lustig, N. C., and D. McLeod. 1997. "Minimum Wages and Poverty in Developing Countries: Some Empirical Evidence." In *Labor Markets in Latin America*, ed. S. Edwards and N. C. Lustig, 62–103. Washington, DC: Brookings Institution Press.

Melitz, M. 2003. "The Impact of Trade on Intra-Industry Reallocations and Aggregate Industry Productivity." *Econometrica* 71 (6): 1695–725.

Morley, S. 1995. "Structural Adjustment and the Determinants of Poverty in Latin America." In *Coping with Austerity: Poverty and Inequality in Latin America*, ed. N. C. Lustig, 42–70. Washington, DC: Brookings Institution.

Mortensen, D., and C. Pissarides. 1994. "Job Creation and Job Destruction in the Theory of Unemployment." *Review of Economic Studies* 61(3): 397–415.

Neumark, D., W. Cunningham, and S. Siga. 2006. "The Effects of the Minimum Wage in Brazil on the Distribution of Family Incomes: 1996–2001." *Journal of Development Economics* 80 (1): 136–59.

Nickell, S., D. Nicolitsas, and N. Dryden. 1997. "What Makes Firms Perform Well?" *European Economic Review* 41 (35): 725–96.

Rajan, R., and L. Zingales. 1998. "Financial Dependence and Growth." *American Economic Review* 88 (3): 559–86.

Rama, M., and R. Artecona. 2000. "A Database of Labor Market Indicators across Countries." Unpublished manuscript. Washington, DC: World Bank.

Ruster, J. 1997. "A Retrospective on the Mexican Toll Road Program (1989–94)." In *The Private Sector in Infrastructure: Strategy, Regulation, and Risk*, ed. World Bank Group, Finance, Private Sector, and Infrastructure Network, 117–25. Washington, DC: World Bank.

Schiantarelli, Fabio. 2005. "Product Market Regulation and Macroeconomic Performance: A Review of Cross-Country Evidence." Working Paper 3770, World Bank, Washington, DC.

Schumpeter, J. A. 1942. *Capitalism, Socialism and Democracy*. New York: Harper and Brothers.

Van de Berg, Caroline. 1997. "Water Privatization and Regulation in England and Wales." In *The Private Sector in Infrastructure: Strategy, Regulation, and Risk*, ed. World Bank Group, Finance, Private Sector, and Infrastructure Network, 9–12. Washington, DC: World Bank.

World Bank. 2004. *Ease of Doing Business Survey*. Washington, DC: World Bank.

———. 2009. *Ease of Doing Business Survey*. Washington, DC: World Bank.

CHAPTER 19

Shocks, Volatility, and Growth

Throughout business cycles, economies face both negative and positive shocks. In 2007–08, three major negative crises hit the global economy: food, fuel, and financial. Oil prices doubled in a few months in 2008, while rice, wheat, and corn prices jumped by 40 to 50 percent during the same period. The bursting of the housing bubble in the United States and Europe led to the failure of commercial and investment banks, exacerbated the credit crunch, and resulted in global financial turmoil by September 2008. Standard policies could have handled any of these three shocks independently. Their interplay, however, made policy decisions much more difficult.

This chapter investigates both crises (negative shocks) and booms (positive shocks). The focus will be on common elements of fast-growing countries.

Avoiding Economic Downturns

Studies indicate that sustainable long-term growth requires macroeconomic policies that absorb commodity price shocks, asset shocks, and banking crises, and reduce the risk and frequency of financial crises. "Successful" countries—defined, for this purpose, as those reducing their per capita gross domestic product (GDP) gap with industrial economies—more effectively responded to macroeconomic shocks than others. Table 19.1 shows that, on average, developing countries experience a year of negative per capita growth once every three years, East Asian "miracle" economies once every six years, and Organisation for Economic Co-operation and Development (OECD) countries once every nine years. The success of East Asia's economies was partly a result of the macroeconomic policies that steered them away from downturns and periods of low growth.

But African countries are different. African exports are mostly primary commodities: oil in Angola, Nigeria, and Sudan; cotton in several West

Table 19.1   Importance of Avoiding Downturns in Growth

	Year in which growth rate from 1960–2002 was			
	Negative	*Below 1 percent*	*Below 2 percent*	*Above 2 percent*
All developing countries	14	19	24	18
Sub-Saharan Africa (28)	18	22	27	15
Botswana	2	3	4	38
Lesotho	10	15	16	26
South Asia (5)	8	11	17	25
Bangladesh	11	15	21	21
India	8	10	14	28
Nepal	10	18	22	20
Sri Lanka	4	6	14	28
Middle East and North Africa (6)	15	18	22	21
Egypt, Arab Rep.	4	10	15	27
Latin America and the Caribbean (21)	12	19	25	17
Chile	7	11	18	24
East Asia and Pacific (7)	7	8	10	32
China	5	6	7	35
Indonesia	7	8	10	32
Malaysia	5	5	7	35
Thailand	2	2	6	36
High-income OECD (22)	5	8	16	27
Korea, Rep.	3	3	4	38

Source: World Bank 2003.

Note: The table shows evidence for the 89 countries for which growth data were available for the four decades 1960–2002. Regional aggregates are medians. The Republic of Korea "graduated" into a high-income category in the early 1990s and is thus classified here in the high-income OECD group rather than in the East Asia and Pacific group.

Figure 19.1   Commodity Price Growth and Real GDP Growth in Sub-Saharan Africa, Three-Year Moving Average

Source: Deaton 1999.

African countries; tobacco in Malawi; tea and cut flowers in Kenya; copper in Zambia; diamonds in Botswana and South Africa, and so on. World prices for most of these commodities are unpredictable and volatile, and the upward and downward fluctuations in prices are not symmetrical. This creates economic fluctuations in export revenues, local-currency-exchange-rate appreciation, and the so-called Dutch disease that affects wages in the booming sectors.

Short-term agricultural price effects are different from the oil and other nonagricultural price changes. Figure 19.1 shows a strong correlation between growth of commodity prices and real economic growth, both in the short and long term: the former leads to the latter. Import-substituting industrialization, financed by the commodity booms of 1970s and 1980s, did not work in Africa. Commodity booms and busts are frequent in natural-resource-dependent economies. African countries need more human capital to capitalize on surpluses and diversify their economies.

Interdependence of North and South

As the world's developed countries (the "north") and developing countries (the "south") become increasingly interdependent, the impact of the economic policies of the north on the south increases. Developing countries commonly complain that the global financial system is run by creditors and, as such, that advanced countries place more importance on maintaining the stability of the financial system than on mitigating financial crises.

Globalization—defined as the increasingly free flow of ideas, people, goods, services, and capital that leads to the integration of economies and societies—has become a major driver of world change; however, the Washington Consensus was silent on how countries should cope with globalization, especially with the reversal of capital flows, which destabilized 10 middle-income countries during 1994–99, pressured their exchange rate and financial systems, bankrupted their firms and banks, decreased per capita incomes, and unleashed severe political turmoil in countries such as Mexico and Indonesia. In several emerging market crises, such as that experienced by Asian countries in 1997–98, imbalances in the private sector savings and investment were not large enough to explain the virulence of the crises that followed. Refinancing public and private debt—and considerations of the debt's magnitude, maturity, and currency composition—were important in several crises.[1] These factors suggest that financial crises in emerging markets could result not only from their domestic policies but also from those of the advanced economies, such as excessive capital flows to the emerging markets.

The Synchronized Movement of Developed and Developing Countries

How much do the economic cycles of the United States affect Europe and Japan? During 1974–90, output gaps (defined as actual output minus potential output) in all advanced countries were large, with an estimated correlation coefficient of about 0.60. Between 1991 and 2000, however, this correlation dropped to 0.12. Asymmetric shocks explain how and why the transmission to output of the international business cycle differs over time and across countries. For example, the German reunification affected other European countries (such as France) but not the United States or Japan. Similarly, the bursting of the asset-price bubble in Japan affected the East Asia region starting in 1993—but not other advanced countries.

These differences in correlations do not support the idea of a single business cycle in the developed world. Yet, in light of the 2008 financial crisis's impact both on major European countries and on the United States—as well as its impact on most middle-income countries—there is strong evidence to the contrary. Instead, it seems that the strength of advanced countries' business-cycle correlations depends on the magnitude and origin of disturbances as well as relevant trade and financial links. Empirically, one finds that the U.S.-Canada-U.K. correlation is strong, in particular because of financial linkages. Across advanced countries in the 1990s, the synchronized movement of national stock markets increased dramatically; meanwhile, the pattern of the business cycle across these same countries remained mostly unchanged.

How do advanced economies affect developing ones? In contrast to advanced countries, the amplitude of output fluctuations in developing countries increased during the 1990s, in part because of the emerging market crises. Globalization increases the links between advanced and developing economies, primarily through trade and capital flows. As such, transmission of shocks across borders is now faster, which could cause national economies to permanently move in step, reducing their ability to steer domestic markets out of crisis.

Evidence of the comovement of financial markets is clearer than that for the real (nonfinancial) economy across countries. As in most advanced economies, the stock markets of emerging-market economies became increasingly synchronized in the 1990s, while real comovement remained stable.

The effect of financial integration on real comovement is ambiguous. On the real side, economies tend to comove with important trading partners, particularly regional leaders, as recessions and expansions are exported across borders. Financial integration, however, makes it possible for countries to diversify consumption without having to diversify production; this leads to economic specialization, which tends to reduce real comovement. On the other hand, if investors exhibit herd behavior, capital will flow in similar patterns across countries, thereby increasing real comovement. Trade openness allows economies to specialize in industries and services in which they have a comparative advantage. As such, trade and financial integration can indirectly lower real comovement by influencing the extent of specialization, even if the direct effects of financial and trade integration increase real comovement. The degree of comovement in real and financial indicators depends on the following:

- *The integration of the country's trade and financial systems with the global economy*, especially for countries and regions that interact with industrial countries.
- *The size of the developing country.* Larger countries such as China, India, and the Russian Federation, have higher comovements with rich countries after controlling for trade and financial openness than smaller ones (Head 1995). Comovement is stronger between high-income countries and advanced countries, as well as between small, tourism-dependent economies (Caribbean and the Pacific islands) and advanced countries.
- *The size and volatility of capital flows.* Volatile capital flows contribute to credit booms and busts, thereby reducing the correlation between developing economies and mature ones.

The Complexity of North–South Links

As summarized in table 19.1, industrial countries' growth rates, real interest rates, and exchange rates, among other policies, have major short-term effects on developing countries. The policy impacts are detailed below.

Business-cycle transmission. Transmission primarily takes place through the two channels of trade and finance. The trade channel comprises foreign demand shocks, productivity shocks, and terms-of-trade changes. The finance channel comprises private capital flows, aid flows, and global financial market conditions.

Foreign demand shocks. The size of the U.S. economy means that its business cycle affects the rest of the world, especially Canada and the East Asian and Latin American countries. This is true of most advanced countries: when GDP growth rates are strong, developing countries benefit, largely through trade. Likewise, a recession in the north causes a fall in imports from the south: demand falls, driving down prices on the world markets (especially for primary commodities), and the north raises import barriers (for example, on steel and pharmaceuticals in the United States). These conditions lower the export earnings of developing countries, depressing their external-debt-servicing ability (such as during the debt crises of the 1980s).

Despite globalization, the economic prospects of each region still depend on its largest economy. For example, the economic performance of East Asian countries closely tracks the economic performance of Japan and, more recently, China. Similarly, the performance of the U.S. economy affects the Latin American countries, and the performance of the European and South African economies affects other African countries. Every 1 percent increase in the advanced economies' growth rates is likely to raise growth rates in emerging markets by 0.78 percent (but only by 0.4 percent for all developing countries).

Productivity shocks. Much of the south depends on advanced countries for technology transfers. Developing countries with strong trade ties with advanced economies suffer during slowdowns in technology imports—productivity shocks account for 5 to 20 percent of the variation in output of some developing countries (Kouparitsas 1996).

Terms-of-trade changes. Economic cycles in advanced countries normally influence variations in commodity prices, which are deeply felt in African countries (see, for example, Deaton and Miller 1995). When trade slows down for any reason, economic growth and trade credits also decline, increasing the likelihood that the number of nonperforming loans in developing countries will increase. Such an increase throws commercial banks' balance sheets out of alignment, putting the banking system under stress.

Protectionist policies, especially during recessions. The United States' decision in 2001 to put tariffs on imported steel was met with approval or, at worst, indifference at home, but in Western Europe, it generated more opposition than any of President Bush's policies, including his widely criticized Middle East policy. By at least three to one, people in France, Germany, Italy, and the United Kingdom disapproved of the tariffs. Across the globe, people expressed broad opposition to the American and Western economic policies.[2]

In high-income countries, subsidies account for nearly one-third of agricultural revenue. Most of the subsidies artificially boost production and undercut the market for farmers in developing countries. For example, U.S. subsidies to cotton growers totaled $3.9 billion in 2001–02 (Devereaux, Lawerence, and Watkins 2006, 275), three times the U.S. foreign aid to Africa. This depressed world cotton prices, cutting poor farmers' incomes in West Africa, Central and South Asia, and other poor regions. European Union sugar subsidies had the same effect.

Advanced countries benefit at the expense of developing countries when they enforce quotas and provide agricultural subsidies to domestic producers. Lack of trade liberalization by the industrial countries means tying of aid (estimated to cost 30 percent). Aid to developing countries is only about $75 billion per year, compared with agricultural subsidies of $350 billion. Protection in industrial countries costs poor farmers in the developing world $150 billion each year, while implementing the World Trade Organization agreements has cost the developing world $130 million. Since the failure of the Cancún follow-up meeting in September 2003, the Group of 22 has pressed countries in the north to end agricultural subsidies.[3]

The recent backlash in the United States against business-process outsourcing (as represented, for example, by offshore customer-service call centers) is another example of protectionist pressure during an economic downturn. The general public focuses on downsides of free trade—job losses, increased competition, and dislocation—and ignores its benefits, including lower prices (they can now buy items that are made in China for a third of the price of similar items made in the United States). Likewise, the United States' pressure on China to move the exchange rate to solve the U.S.-China bilateral trade deficit is misplaced. Pending legislation would place a 27.5 percent penalty tariff on Chinese-manufactured goods imported into the United States.

Labor immigration. During recessions, advanced countries often tighten their borders. For example, the recent increase in worker remittances from the United States to the developing countries could be a result of uncertainties surrounding the September 11, 2001, attacks and ensuing job losses in these countries, resulting in a repatriation of workers as well as workers transferring assets to their home countries. In a truly integrated world economy, barriers to labor integration would be rare.

Aid flows. According to Bulir and Hamann (2001) and other studies, aid flows are both volatile and uncertain (normally more so than tax revenues, except in Africa) because many advanced economies link their aid policies not only to geopolitics but also to GDP levels and domestic politics. Such volatility complicates fiscal, monetary, and exchange-rate policies of the aid-recipient countries, and uncertainty is detrimental to their economic growth.

Private capital inflows. Many developing countries rely heavily on external financing to fund their domestic policies and cover their current account deficits. Recessions in the United States are not necessarily bad for emerging markets because the volume of capital flows to emerging markets increases during these periods. But an analysis of the composition of these capital flows indicates that foreign direct investment (FDI, the more stable component) does contract during U.S. downturns, potentially forcing emerging markets to depend for a time on short-term flows to substitute for FDI and portfolio flows. A slowdown in the north usually coincides with higher capital flows (especially in bank lending to the emerging markets) but at a time when the demand for loans in the domestic economies of the south is already declining because of a slowdown there as well.

Therefore, a slowdown in mature economies is normally associated with a reduction in export volumes, deterioration of the terms of trade, and a slowdown in aid flows to most developing countries. An economic downturn in the north coincides with weaker trade and current account balances for the south (see table 19.2). Advanced countries can deliver on their pledges to open markets that benefit poor people in developing countries by reducing distortionary agricultural subsidies.

Table 19.2   North–South Links

Type of policy/shock	Transmission channel	Outcomes in north
Growth cycle: Recessions in G-3 (United States, Japan, and the 12 European Union countries)		
Income effects	Lower exports to G-3	Lower growth
Relative price effects	Decline in terms of trade for the south	Lower growth
Import barriers (for example, on steel, textiles)	Lower exports from the south	Lower growth
Restrict outsourcing	Lower overseas outsourcing	Lower growth
Agriculture subsidies	Lower agriculture exports from the south	Lower exports
Aid flows	Lower aid to the south (because aid is % of GDP)	Lower growth
International capital flows	Higher bank lending to emerging markets	Higher growth
Restrict labor	Tightened immigration in the north	Lower remittances
Interest-rate cycle		
Easy monetary policy—lower interest rates in G-3		
International capital flows	Higher portfolio flows to emerging markets	Higher growth
Debt servicing	Lower cost	Higher growth
Interest earnings	Declining interest income	Ambiguous
High volatility in G-3		
Interest rates	Complication of debt management in emerging markets	Ambiguous
	Reduced investment because of uncertainty	Lower growth
Bilateral exchange rate	Trade reduction between north and south	Lower growth

Source: Based on Reinhart and Reinhart 2001.

Monetary Policies and Capital Flows

The following paragraphs discuss the effects of monetary policies on capital flows.

Interest rates. Peaks in the London Interbank Offered Rate and high interest rates in the north led to the international debt crises of the 1980s, while low interest rates in the United States and other industrialized countries in the 1990s moved capital from the north to emerging markets. This ran counter to the prevailing wisdom that the domestic policy reforms of emerging markets would attract capital inflows. For example, the seven separate increases in the U.S. Federal Reserve's interest rates over the course of 1994 were a proximate cause of the Mexican financial crisis of 1995 (the political disturbances of 1994 also contributed).

High global interest rates depress real economic activity and may lower prices of basic commodities produced by developing countries. They also raise debt-service costs, particularly if they are floating interest rates linked to the London Interbank Offered Rate. High interest rates in the north make investments in the south less attractive to investors, leading to a gradual loss in foreign exchange reserves for the southern countries. In a period of speculative attack, developing countries may be forced to raise domestic interest rates, which can lead to a loss of confidence if the increase is severe. A 1 percent increase in the real interest rate leads to an estimated drop of 17 percent in the composite index of equities of the emerging countries.

An easy monetary policy, which coincides with a slowdown in the north, leads to lower real interest rates. Lower global interest rates make investments in developing countries more attractive, enabling economic expansion, creating attractive primary commodities prices, and lowering debt-servicing costs. In the early 1990s and again during the past few years, capital left the north and moved toward the south because of the low rate of return in the north (12 countries received the bulk of these capital flows, however). On the other hand, a reversal of conditions in the north can lead to financial crises in the south, as in Mexico in 1995 and the East Asian countries in 1997–98.

Historically, developing countries grow fastest when fast U.S. growth puts pressure on labor and investment (a later stage of the U.S. business cycle); consequently, the U.S. Federal Reserve tightens monetary policy. Because a tighter monetary policy and rising interest rates in the United States lead to lower capital flows to emerging markets, a recession in the north may dampen FDI flows to the south, as these are linked to trade.

Therefore, the window of opportunity for expansion is quite narrow for developing countries.

Exchange rates. When capital inflows turn to outflows, pegged exchange regimes cannot cling to a peg and lose international reserves to delay devaluations. This strategy is usually costly (for example, Brazil, Mexico, the Republic of Korea, and Thailand in the 1990s). Many emerging market currencies are implicitly or explicitly tied to the U.S. dollar, euro, or yen; therefore, any movement in the value of major currencies affects the competitiveness of many emerging markets.

Some considered the volatility of industrial countries' exchange rates a factor in the financial crises that plagued emerging markets in the late 1990s. In particular, the prolonged appreciation of the dollar against the yen and the deutsche mark before the Asian crisis worsened the competitive positions of many emerging market economies.[4] Reducing the variability of the exchange rates among the Group of Three (G-3) currencies—those of the United States, Japan, and the 12 members of the European Union—by establishing target zones could reduce destabilizing shocks emanating from abroad. Some have contended that a target zone for G-3 currencies would benefit emerging market countries. But empirical findings by Reinhart and Reinhart (2001) suggest that policy makers use caution before implementing such a zone.[5]

The interest rate–exchange rate trade-off. The G-3 central banks (the U.S. Federal Reserve system, the Bank of Japan, and the European Central Bank) could maintain the relevant exchange rates within the specified zone by either of two means: (a) a sterilized intervention[6] in the foreign exchange market to restrict the movement of bilateral exchange rates or impose restrictions or capital controls (such as a transactions tax or prudent reserve requirements for the banking system) or (b) a change in domestic market conditions to keep the exchange rates of their currencies within a desired range. Because sterilized intervention has proved to be ineffective and the international community generally supports the free mobility of capital, the only viable option for developing countries is to manage domestic conditions to keep their exchange rates within a desired range. For example, if the exchange value of the dollar against the yen was rising toward the upper limit of the agreed-upon target zone (that is, if the dollar was appreciating against the yen), then the Federal Reserve could reduce it by buying yen with dollars. This, in turn, would increase the reserves in the U.S. banking system and lead to lower U.S. short-term interest rates. There would be a trade-off: the G-3 domestic short-term interest rates would have to become more variable to make the G-3 exchange rates less variable. Thus, a target zone could reduce the exchange-rate volatility while increasing interest-rate volatility.

Though more stable G-3 exchange rates (and higher interest-rate volatility) would mean more stable terms of trade for emerging markets, they would also increase the volatility of the costs of servicing foreign debt. Large increases in borrowing costs induce balance sheet strains and lead to credit rationing, which hurts a country's income prospects.

Policy makers in the United States have long spoken of the need for China to adopt a more flexible exchange-rate policy. Greater exchange-rate flexibility, they say, would give China more room to pursue an independent monetary policy, help cushion its economy against adverse shocks, and facilitate adjustment to its major structural reforms.

On the other hand, the United States cannot blame its bilateral deficit with China on the Chinese exchange-rate policy. In fact, exports from other Asian countries that used to go directly to the United States now go to China for finishing. Accordingly, a deficit between China and the other Asian countries now counterbalances the United States' huge deficit with China. Therefore, revaluing the renminbi would not change China's comparative advantage.

North–South Capital Flows

According to conventional economic theory, capital moves from low-interest-rate northern countries to high-interest-rate emerging markets, benefiting both. While emerging markets generally run larger current-account deficits, which are financed by net capital inflows, the inflows cease during crises. Calvo, Leiderman, and Reinhart (1993) were the first to warn about the reversal of external factors leading to capital outflows, two years before the Mexican crisis. Asian countries switched from current-account deficits to surpluses during 1997–99, and during the 1990s, the U.S. economic boom led to large U.S. current-account deficits—deficits far larger than those of all developing countries combined, thereby making less capital available for developing countries.

To stimulate capital inflows, emerging markets rely not only on domestic policies, such as stock market liberalization and privatization of state-owned enterprises, but also increasingly on depositary receipts and cross listings and institutional investors. For example, foreign-owner restrictions decreased more than 60 percent in Asia and more than 70 percent in Latin America during the 1990s. Mergers and acquisitions resulting from privatization and the easing of restrictions on foreign participation in banks in emerging markets were also important factors in FDI flows. Institutional investors in the advanced countries (such as mutual funds, pension funds, hedge funds, and insurance companies) have also become an important conduit for capital flows.

Not surprisingly, net flows to emerging markets from 1970 to 1999 were considerably larger in real terms during times of U.S. expansion compared to recession. For example, FDI flows went up nearly threefold from recession to expansion, and portfolio investment flows rose almost fivefold. Other net inflows—mainly bank lending—tended to dry up when the United States expanded. Apparently, banks sought lending opportunities abroad more avidly when the domestic demand for loans weakened and interest rates fell, as often happens during recessions. Demand for loans from industrial countries presumably picks up when the FDI dries up. Two examples of the cyclicality of these other net inflows include the U.S. bank-lending boom to Latin America in the late 1970s and early 1980s and the surge in Japanese bank lending to emerging Asian markets in the mid-1990s. Although a U.S. recession may not be all bad news for capital flows to emerging markets, those flows consist principally of less stable, short-term financing rather than more stable FDI.

In the years when the United States eased its monetary policy, emerging markets in all regions (with the exception of Africa, which was almost entirely shut out of international capital markets) received a markedly higher volume of capital inflows. Although FDI and portfolio investment flows do not change much during the interest-rate cycle, other (short-term) flows fluctuate considerably.

Reinhart and Reinhart (2001) report that between 1970 and 1999, real capital flowed according to whether the G-3 real exchange rates were more (or less) volatile than the median experience and whether U.S. real short-term interest rates were more (or less) volatile than the median. Volatile G-3 exchange rates generated average annual capital flows roughly equal to those generated by stable rates. On the other hand, exchange-rate volatility was associated with a move away from portfolio investment and toward direct investment. In contrast, greater-than-average U.S. short-term interest-rate fluctuations significantly affected various capital flows. Between 1970 and 1999, capital flows were higher when interest rates changed more because of a larger net portfolio and other capital flows, predominantly bank flows. On the other hand, private direct investment suffered from interest-rate volatility.

Globalization, Volatility, and Growth

Recent work on this topic by Kose, Prasad, and Terrones (2004) indicates that volatility in growth has increased with growing interdependence between the north and south. Economic theory suggests that globalization should have a positive impact on growth, but it does not specify how volatile that growth will be. Until the mid-1980s, volatility had only a minor influence on economic growth. Since then, however, a growing number of developing countries have integrated the global economy through trade and financial liberalization, and this greater openness has coincided with greater volatility, as evidenced by the financial crises of the 1980s and 1990s, primarily in the emerging markets. For example, work by Ramey and Ramey (1995) indicates that macroeconomic volatility due to shocks and policies may actually reduce long-term growth. But while output volatility has increased, relatively open economies also recorded higher than average growth rates. Does this mean that in a period of rising globalization, the negative relationship between growth and volatility has changed?

From 1960 to 2000, growth and volatility, as measured by the standard deviation of per capita output growth, were negatively related. But the relationship in fact appears positive for industrial economies and emerging markets, indicating that a country's level of development affects the relationship: volatility is not necessarily associated with lower growth. Instead, the negative relationship holds for developing countries that have not participated significantly in globalization.

The level of trade and financial integration also affects the relationship between volatility and growth. For the emerging markets, the two are negatively related before trade liberalization and positive afterward. In other words, trade integration changes the sign of this relationship in these countries.

Other factors affecting the relationship between growth and volatility include a country's initial income level, the national investment rate, population growth, and the percentage of the population that has at least a primary-level education. When these potential determinants of growth are included, volatility is still, on average, negatively associated with growth. Trade integration clearly has a positive effect on growth, but the effect of financial integration is less obvious.

The interaction of trade and financial integration tends to have a positive relationship with growth, however, attenuating the negative effects of volatility. In other words, because of their trade openness, emerging markets can withstand higher levels of volatility than other developing countries, or post higher growth rates when experiencing a similar level of volatility.

The Financial Crisis of 2008 and Global Growth

Against a backdrop of the large U.S. current-account and fiscal deficits during 2001–07, the bursting of the housing bubble in 2007 and 2008 resulted in a surge in home mortgage defaults and foreclosures. This in turn led to a plunge in the prices of mortgage-backed securities, which were underpinned by assets whose value ultimately came from mortgage payments. These financial losses left many financial institutions with too little capital or too few assets compared to debt. The excessive debt assumed by the government, households, and financial firms during the bubble years compounded the effects of the mortgage market's collapse. Financial institutions with too many large, bad loans tied to housing and too little capital were unwilling and unable to provide the credit demanded by the entire economy.

The crisis began in the United States and spread to the United Kingdom and other European countries before enveloping the emerging markets. In late 2008, the effects snowballed: a worldwide recession (especially in Europe, Japan, and the United States), a slowdown in the major emerging economies (including Brazil, China, India, Russia, and South Africa), rapid stock market declines and volatility (in Brazil, China, India, Indonesia, Russia, and South Africa), evidence of currency and money-market runs requiring policy intervention (in Brazil; Hong Kong SAR, China; India; Korea, and Taiwan, China), large outflows from funds dedicated to emerging markets (around $30 billion in 2008), and a credit squeeze on corporations and banks.

Growth Booms

The first part of this discussion draws heavily from the Commission on Growth and Development's *Growth Report* (2008, widely known as the Spence Report) to underscore the common elements among 13 economies identified in the report that have managed to maintain growth rates of 7 percent or more for at least 25 successive years (table 19.3). In addition, we examine findings from academics' country-specific case studies on successful growth policies. We also address the topic of microefficiency as it relates to aggregate growth.

Table 19.3   Thirteen Successful Economies
constant 2000 US$

		Per capita income	
Economy	Period of high growth	At start of growth period	2005
Botswana	1960–2005	210	3,800
Brazil	1950–1980	960	4,000
China	1961–2005	105	1,400
Hong Kong SAR, China	1960–1997	3,100	29,900
Indonesia	1966–1997	200	900
Japan	1950–1983	3,500	39,600
Korea, Rep.	1960–2001	1,100	13,200
Malaysia	1967–1997	790	4,400
Malta	1963–1994	1,100	9,600
Oman	1960–1999	950	9,000
Singapore	1967–2002	2,200	25,400
Taiwan, China	1965–2002	1,500	16,400
Thailand	1960–1997	330	2,400

Source: Ramirez-Djumena and Rodriguez 2008, 32.
Note: A 7 percent cutoff was chosen because growth at these rates produces very substantial changes in incomes and wealth: income doubles every decade at 7 percent.

At first glance, these 13 economies appear to have been chosen solely on the basis of the objective analysis of growth data. But one soon realizes that there was a subjective element to this decision. For example, India has been growing for 25 consecutive years. Similarly, Chile, Mauritius, and, more recently, the Lao People's Democratic Republic, Poland, Vietnam, and others have sustained growth for long periods. Moreover, the sample of 13 economies comprises a large number of city-states and small economies such as Botswana; Malta; Oman; Singapore; and Taiwan, China; most are also politically restrictive economies. What can we learn from these characteristics?

Easterly (2009) criticizes the choice of these 13 economies on the grounds that much of their performance is temporary, with a permanent component of only 5 percent. In addition, he highlights the researchers' heuristic biases: drawing conclusions from too small a number of successes; exhibiting a "hot-hand bias," in which good luck (such as favorable terms of trade) is mistakenly attributed to skill; and the "halo effect," which makes a successful economy appear faultless, even though its trajectory toward success may have been fraught with error. Moreover, it is not clear that the successes of any of the above economies can be replicated by other economies under similar circumstances.

The common characteristics of countries with sustained high growth include: (a) macroeconomic stability (relatively low inflation, fiscal deficits, and a manageable debt level); (b) high savings and investment rates; (c) engagement with the global economy (relying on markets, keeping labor and capital mobile, and adopting new technologies); and (d) a strong political commitment to economic reforms, growth, and poverty reduction (figure 19.2). The Spence Report's findings are supported by the extensive analysis presented in the earlier chapters of this volume.

A sound growth and poverty reduction strategy includes the following ingredients:

Strong political commitment to improving economic welfare. Effective governance and leadership build consensus behind policies designed to improve citizens' lives. These policies, however, must be based on the right models and strategies for growth. Competitive markets are fragile and can be hurt both by weak governments (lack of regulation) and by

Figure 19.2   Common Characteristics of the 13 Successful Economies

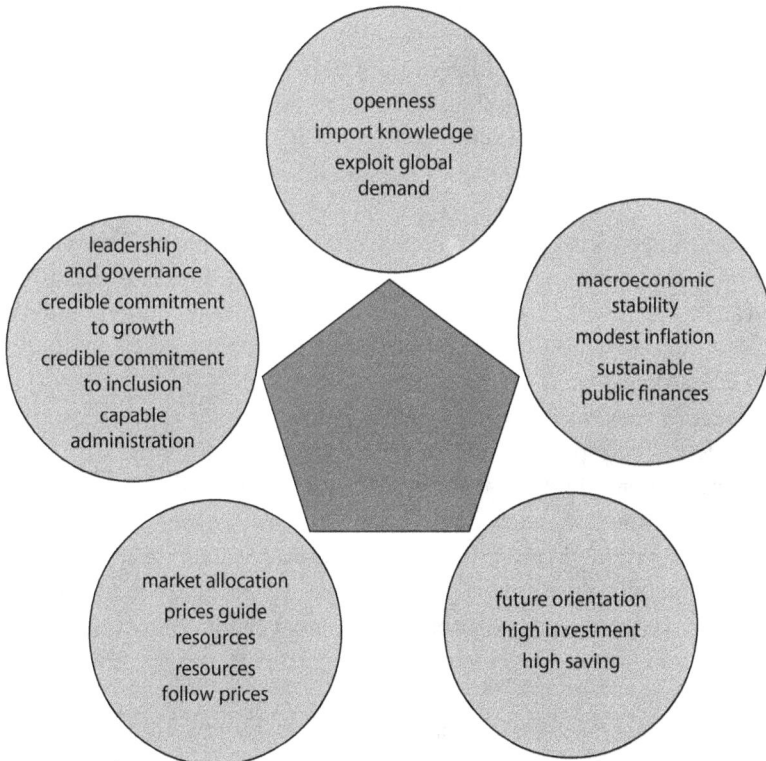

Source: Commission on Growth and Development 2008, 22.

too-intrusive governments (stifling regulation). The government and private sector need to work together.

Reliance on market pricing, incentives, and property rights for resource allocation. Maintaining macroeconomic stability keeps inflation low, which protects the income of the poor, allows some flexibility in spending, and ensures manageable deficits and debt levels. Policies that lead to damaging periods of very high inflation and policies that bring inflation down through slow growth should both be avoided. Reliance on market mechanisms requires fully developed market institutions. In many cases, however, market institutions and related government regulatory processes mature, deepen, and evolve as part of the development process. This is clearly evident in China, where the reform process grew out of a centrally planned economy.

Promotion of high savings and investment rates. High levels of saving characterized the 13 successful economies. For example, Southeast Asia and Latin America had similar savings rates in the mid-1970s—20 years later, savings rates in Southeast Asia were 20 percentage points higher (Commission on Growth and Development 2008). Going back 25 years, China has saved more than a third of its national income annually. This has been accompanied by high rates of domestic investment. High rates of investment, especially public and private sector investment (for example, in physical and social infrastructure, education, and health) are critical for growth and poverty reduction. Infrastructure investment and investment in human capital go hand in hand, contributing to total factor productivity growth. Creating an adequate investment climate, particularly one that eases the entry and exit of firms, will stimulate and sustain private investment. Improvements in the investment climate will also reduce the transaction costs for business and enhance growth at the firm and industry level.

Resource mobility. Resource mobility, particularly labor mobility, combined with the rapid creation of new productive employment and the rapid movement of people from rural to urban areas, reduces poverty and stimulates growth, though poor regions may experience the effect less than entire nations. Economic activity tends to concentrate around urban centers. Specific government programs may be necessary to ensure that the poor are connected to urban areas and benefit from their growth through new jobs or key social services critical to the accumulation of human capital.

Leveraging of the global economy to accelerate growth. The most important shared behavior of the 13 economies has two components: (a) the inbound transfer of knowledge and technology and (b) the drawing on global demand to complement domestic components. The former rapidly increases the potential output of the economy, while the latter further accelerates growth, with exports as the driving force.

Real economic growth may occur even if it involves the depletion of a country's natural resource base. Sustainability should thus be an important criterion for assessing the quality of a country's economic growth and the poverty reduction process.

Responsibility of the international community to avoid global disruptions. This requires fostering a global macroeconomic framework that supports widespread economic growth as a means of resolving the food, fuel, financial, and other crises that threaten the global economy. It also involves (a) opening up markets to allow the flow of goods and services, labor, finance, and technology, and (b) using these to promote the provision of global public goods, to provide increased financial assistance to the poorest countries, and to attack the sources of climate change.

Rodrik (2004) points out that successful growth strategies vary by country and include a mix of the orthodox Washington Consensus policies and other country-specific approaches. For example, the governments of the East Asian "miracle" economies (Indonesia, Korea, and Malaysia, among others) deployed an extensive set of industrial policies such as directed credit, trade protection, export subsidization, and tax incentives implemented through the ministries of industry and trade. Growth policies in Korea and Taiwan, China, exhibited significant departures from the Washington Consensus: neither economy undertook significant deregulation or liberalization of trade and financial systems until the 1980s. Both China and India have shown deviations from market-oriented policies as well, while still experiencing significant growth since the late 1970s (China) and the early 1980s (India). India deregulated its policy regime slowly and undertook very little privatization, and its trade regime remained heavily restricted late into the 1990s. China did not even adopt a private-property-rights regime; instead, it implemented the household responsibility system under which land was "leased" to individual households according to their size. Mauritius, on the other hand, supported export processing zones to ensure export-led growth.

Rodrik (2004) also emphasizes the importance of customization of development policies by countries, sustained and continuous political commitment, and strong leadership in sustaining growth. He postulates a two-pronged effort: (a) a short-run strategy aimed at stimulating growth by increasing investment (through removing barriers to private entrepreneurs, complemented by public investment in regulation and essential infrastructure) and (b) a medium- to long-run strategy aimed at sustaining growth by building and strengthening institutions such as the following:

- market-*creating* institutions, through property rights and contract enforcement;
- market-*regulating* institutions, through regulatory bodies and other mechanisms for correcting market failures;
- market-*stabilizing* institutions, through monetary and fiscal institutions and institutions of prudential regulation and supervision; and
- market-*legitimizing* institutions, through democracy, social protection, and social insurance.

In light of the diverse growth experiences of the post–World War II period, Pritchett (2006) makes a strong case for countries with different levels of per capita income that require unique growth equations. He groups these countries into five categories: (a) advanced countries, (b) countries growing and rapidly converging toward advanced countries, (c) countries growing but not converging, (d) growth-collapse countries, and (e) low-income, no-growth countries.

Washington Consensus policies emerged in the early 1980s, while the collapse of the Soviet Union in 1989–90 led to the introduction of the "big bang" or wholesale reform packages in a number of Eastern European countries. Technical and political problems emerged in the implementation of such reforms that limited strategies to what was possible, rather than what was desirable. Under these approaches, most countries had little growth to show for their reforms. Current growth analytics as proposed by Rodrik, Hausmann, and Velasco (2005) seek to find binding constraints on economic growth and target only major distortions. The process of reviewing and analyzing the most binding constraints on growth is called "growth diagnostics."

According to growth diagnostics, investments and entrepreneurial activities are determined by the connection of private returns, economic activities, and financial costs. An approach that the World Bank has piloted in a select number of country reports seeks to capture the main constraints on growth due to low productivity (technology, institutions, risks, and other factors) or low levels of production inputs (land, labor, and capital) and locate the main bottleneck to growth (figure 19.3). The binding constraints on pro-poor growth (also called integrated economic analysis) take the above analysis further, integrating the macroeconomic

Figure 19.3   Obstacles to Growth

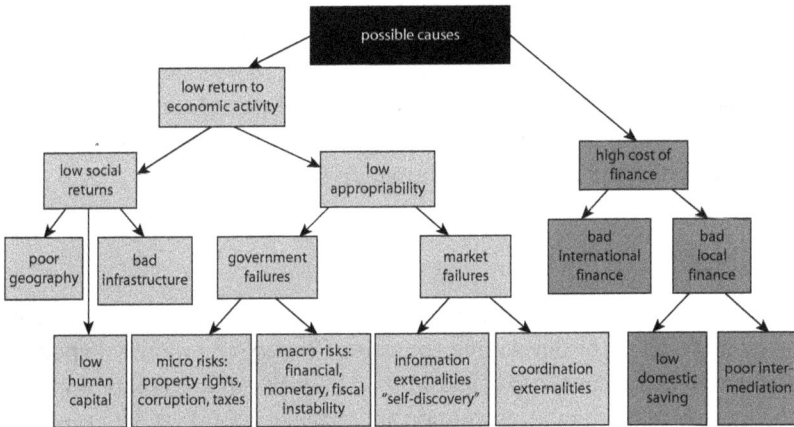

Source: Rodrik, Hausmann, and Velasco 2005.

analysis with the investment climate and employment analysis to identify a bundle of binding constraints and propose a sequence of reforms
to address them.

The Microeconomic Foundations of Growth

Researchers are increasingly looking at the microlevel evidence for factors
affecting firm performance and links to overall economic growth. The
microlevel evidence is primarily the microsurvey data available in a number of countries (investment climate assessments, cost-of-doing-business
surveys, and informal sector surveys).

Recent microstudies in India and China, for example, show that the
quality of the investment climate varies significantly by the state, province,
or city, and that improvements in business climate tend to be correlated
with increased income levels and reduced poverty. The poor and small and
informal firms tend to benefit most from improvements to the investment
climate, as these improvements generate jobs (larger corporations have
special connections to overcome inadequate legal and regulatory regimes).
Informal sectors have grown in almost all developing countries primarily
as a result of corruption and bureaucratic harassment; in these countries,
the government has little or no accountability in the provision of public
services. Removing unjustified entry barriers for firms (particularly small
and medium-sized enterprises), strengthening the competition policy,

removing burdensome regulations, and ensuring property and contracting rights are key contributors to microefficiency, as reflected in the survey data from a large number of countries. For example, firms exposed to greater competition tend to be more productive, more innovative in terms of launching new products, and more beneficial to consumers. Firms also need access to financing, which necessitates modernized regulations relating to the collateral and credit information systems.

Conclusion

Managing growth when buffeted by shocks is important for the long-term economic success of developing countries. Primary commodity exporters such as the African countries and Middle East oil producers face a special challenge in smoothing consumption and managing short- and longer-term growth. In addition to natural disasters, policies in the developed countries (such as commodity prices, interest rates, and exchange rates) can generate a shock in the developing countries. The world trade and financial system today is not well prepared to handle the large-scale, highly contagious financial crashes of the 1990s and 2008; policy responses to future crises will likely be improvised and the institutional arrangements to deal with them will essentially be ad hoc. This last point will be especially true as the ongoing financial crisis unfolds not in an emerging market but in a large industrial country deeply integrated into the global economy. Attempts to control such turmoil with longer-term capital controls and restrictions are misguided. Even powerful industrial countries and large financial firms are subject to the harsh judgment of the markets. The adoption of sound economic policies even during periods of crisis makes much more sense and provides greater opportunities for growth.

Notes

1. These crashes created confusion around the world. People questioned trade and financial liberalization, doubted whether currencies should float freely, and debated whether countries were better off with a currency board or pegged rate. The International Monetary Fund program bailouts were argued to be a source of moral hazard and global instability. Debates centered on the fix or float of exchange-rate regimes, capital-account liberalization, the question of inflation versus deflation, and the global financial architecture.

2. A Pew Foundation–funded Gallup survey of Muslim nations showed that a relatively small minority (no more than a quarter in any nation) believed that the

United States and other Western nations generally care about the poorer nations. Yet the vast majority of Americans (78 percent) think that the United States and other Western nations are concerned about impoverished countries.

3. It is estimated that India, by cutting its own tariffs (especially in textiles, clothing, and footwear) and pressing other countries to do the same (while also reducing restrictions on trade in agriculture and services to fully implement the multilateral trade liberalization agenda outlined in the Doha Round and Uruguay Round), got a net welfare gain of $7 billion or 1.7 percent of the country's projected 2005 GDP.

4. Calvo and Reinhart (2002) suggest a "fear of floating" as many currencies track the dollar or euro closely even when these countries officially maintain free and flexible exchange-rate regimes.

5. Limiting currency fluctuations by establishing a target zone essentially swaps exchange-rate uncertainty for interest-rate uncertainty. While maintaining G-3 exchange rates in target zones may lead to more stable prices in emerging markets, the effect on the interest rates may be to make debt-servicing costs more unpredictable while producing income volatility in developed countries that could decrease demand for emerging market exports (Davis 2002).

6. A sterilized intervention takes place when the monetary authorities (a central bank, for example) offset the monetary impact of reserve buildup through an offsetting sale of government paper (or other instruments) to the public (usually banks).

Bibliography

Bulir, Ales, and Javier Hamann. 2001. "How Volatile and Predictable Are Aid Flows, and What Are the Policy Implications?" IMF Working Paper WP/01/167, International Monetary Fund, Washington, DC.

Calvo, G., and C. Reinhart. 2002. "Fear of Floating." *Quarterly Journal of Economics* 117 (2): 379–408.

Calvo, G., Leonardo Leiderman, and Carmen Reinhart. 1993. "Capital Inflows and Real Exchange Rate Appreciation in Latin America: The Role of External Factors." *IMF Staff Papers* 40 (March): 108–50.

Commission on Growth and Development. 2008. *The Growth Report: Strategies for Sustained Growth and Inclusive Development.* Washington, DC: World Bank.

Davis, M. 2002. "No Gain from Reducing G-3 Currency Volatility." NBER Digest, National Bureau of Economic Research, Washington, DC. http://www.nber.org/digest/jan02/w8535.html.

Deaton, Angus. 1999. "Commodity Prices and Growth in Africa." *Journal of Economic Perspectives* 13 (3): 23–40.

Deaton, A., and R. I. Miller. 1995. *International Commodity Prices, Macroeconomic Performance, and Politics in Sub-Saharan Africa.* Princeton, NJ: Princeton University.

Devereaux, C., R. Z. Lawerence, and M. Watkins. 2006. *Case Studies in U.S. Trade Negotiation, vol. 2: Resolving Disputes.* Washington, DC: Institute for International Economics.

Easterly, William Russell. 2009. "How the Millennium Development Goals Are Unfair to Africa." *World Development* 37 (1): 26–35.

Frankel, J., and Nouriel Roubini. 2001. "The Role of Industrial Country Policies in Emerging Market Crises." NBER Working Paper 8634, National Bureau of Economic Research, Cambridge, MA.

Head, A. C. 1995. "Country Size, Aggregate Fluctuations, and International Risk Sharing." *Canadian Journal of Economics* 28 (4b): 1096–119.

Kose, A., E. S. Prasad, and M. E. Terrones. 2004. "Volatility and Comovement in a Globalized World Economy: An Empirical Exploration." In *Macroeconomic Policies in the World Economy,* ed. Horst Siebert, 89–122. Berlin and New York: Springer.

Kouparitsas, Michael. 1996. "North–South Business Cycle." Working Paper 96–9, Federal Reserve Bank of Chicago, Chicago.

Pritchett, Lant. 2006. "The Quest Continues." *Finance and Development* 43 (1): 18–22.

Ramey, Gary, and Valerie Ramey. 1995. "Cross-Country Evidence on the Link between Volatility and Growth." *American Economic Review* 85 (December): 1138–51.

Ramirez-Djumena, N., and J. Rodriguez. 2008. "Picture This: The Ingredients of Sustained Growth." *Finance and Development.* 45 (4): 32–33.

Reinhart, Carmen, and Vincent Reinhart. 2001. "What Hurts Most? G-3 Exchange Rate or Interest Rate Volatility." NBER Working Paper 8535, National Bureau of Economic Research, Cambridge, MA.

Rodrik, Dani. 2004. "Growth Strategies." John F. Kennedy School of Government, Harvard University. http://ksghome.harvard.edu/~drodrik/growthstrat10.

Rodrik, Dani, Ricardo Hausmann, and Andrés Velasco. 2005. "Growth Diagnostics." John F. Kennedy School of Government, Harvard University. http://ksghome.harvard.edu/fs/rhausma/new/growthdiag.pdf.

World Bank. 2003. *World Development Indicators 2003.* Washington, DC: World Bank.

CHAPTER 20

The Politics of Growth and Poverty

In the days of Adam Smith, David Ricardo, and Alfred Marshall, the study of economic behavior was called political economy. Although this term fell out of vogue for a while, the interaction between politics and economics regained momentum with the work of Huntington (1968) and Hibbs (1973). In the 1970s and 1980s, several schools of thought emerged that focused on the difference between economic equilibrium and political equilibrium and how the intersection of these two subjects explains the real world of economic policy making. Rent-seeking theory, the public choice school, new political economy, patron-client relationships, and other approaches tried to account for the success and failure of reform policies and aid allocation in a number of developing countries. This chapter focuses on the politics of economic policy making and its implications for growth and poverty reduction.

Two questions are essential to examining the relationship between economic development and democratic institutions. Do countries become democratic only at high levels of per capita income? And does democracy enhance economic development—and if so, when? Scholars are divided on both questions. Most observers would agree with Lipset (1959) and Barro (1999), who assert that since richer countries are democracies, economic development favors transition toward political freedom. But

Acemoglu, Johnson, and Robinson (2005) suggest that this cross-sectional evidence is not robust enough to control for factors that simultaneously affect income and political institutions. When these researchers add country-fixed effects in repeated cross-country regressions, they find that income level has no effect on democracy. Huntington (1991) argues that progress toward democratization is not linear but rather moves in back-and-forth waves.

Evidence on the second question is mixed.[1] Perhaps democratic institutions increase redistributive pressures[2] that may harm growth (especially in middle-income countries); for this reason, Barro (1996) argues that countries should not become democracies before their per capita income reaches a certain level. But Mulligan, Sala-i-Martin, and Gil (2003) do not find much of a difference among the public policies of democracies and nondemocracies, casting doubts on whether the form of government and economic performance are linked.[3] Glaeser and others (2004) also question the causal effects of political institutions on economic growth.

Very few studies address both questions jointly. Two exceptions are Przewroski and others (2000) and De Mesquita and others (2003). Persson and Tabellini (2006) examine the transition from democracy to dictatorship and the concept of the accumulated stock of democratic capital, concluding that the latter is conducive to simultaneous growth and consolidation of democratic institutions.[4] Giavazzi and Tabellini (2005) analyze the timing of economic and political liberalization.

In this chapter, we will focus on the second question: does democracy enhance economic growth and if so, when? Most existing papers on the subject employ aggregate data on income levels and economic growth. By contrast, this chapter uses disaggregated data to shed new light on the debate. Unlike most other work, it also develops the idea that political institutions, and democracy in particular, may have different effects on different sectors of the economy. Democratic institutions and political rights enhance growth of the more advanced sectors, namely sectors close to the technological frontier because political accountability reduces the protection of vested interests and entry, in turn, is known to be generally more growth enhancing in sectors that are closer to the technological frontier (Acemoglu, Aghion, and Zilibotti, 2006). We can summarize our results in two points:

- Political rights are associated with the freedom of entry, which is especially important for sectors close to the technological frontier.

In fact, the entry of new firms and competition spur innovation at high levels of technological development, whereas it may discourage innovation in less-developed sectors, as argued by Aghion and others (2005b).

- More advanced economies benefit more from democratic institutions than less-developed ones; therefore, the demand for democracy should increase with the level of per capita income in a country. This calls into question, indirectly at least, Acemoglu, Johnson, and Robinson's (2005) suggestion that development does not bring about democratic institutions.

Acemoglu (2009), among others, has already explored democracy's positive and negative effects on growth. A higher level of democracy tends to be good for growth by reducing the extent to which oligarchies can prevent market entry. On the other hand, democracy leads to higher tax rates in equilibrium, which tend to discourage innovation. Unlike in our analysis below, however, in Acemoglu (2009), the comparison between the costs and benefits of democracy does not interact with the economy's proximity to the world technological frontier.

Our focus is different from our predecessors' in that we employ disaggregated data on industrial sector growth rates to shed light on the connections among democracy, a country's development level, and economic growth. We argue (on the basis of empirical evidence) that democratic institutions favor growth in the sectors of the economy that are particularly advanced in terms of value added per worker, or, in our terminology, that are close to the world technological frontier. We believe that democracy is more beneficial in these sectors because they rely heavily on freedom of entry into the market, competition, and innovation. Thus, our analysis introduces a technological motive for political freedom, a dimension that has not received much attention in the wide empirical literature on democratization. We also suggest that the demand for democracy should be higher in the richer countries, where more sectors are close to the technological frontier.

We examine the politico-economic literature, focusing on the differential effects of the political institutions on economic outcomes. The same institutional features affect components of the economy in different ways. The next steps in this research program would be to (a) explore more deeply the various channels whereby democracy fosters growth in the more advanced sectors and (b) analyze the process by which economic demand for democracy translates into a real transition to democracy.

Political Power and Economic Institutions

How are economic and political institutions created, and under what conditions do institutions foster growth? Good institutions that create incentives to save, invest in physical and human capital, take risks to start new businesses, and create and adopt new technologies must also ensure protection of property rights, provide equality of opportunity, and enforce equality before the law. Equal distribution of political power, political rights, political influence, and access to political systems are prerequisites for the emergence of good institutions. For example, countries that have relatively high Gini coefficients (corresponding to greater economic inequality) also tend to have greater political inequality.

More egalitarian distribution of political power naturally leads to a more egalitarian distribution of economic resources. For example, countries with more secure property rights and better institutions have higher average incomes than other countries (World Bank 2005). Political inequality can lead to economic and social institutions and arrangements that favor the elites and the politically connected at the expense of the poor. These inequalities in economic, social, and political access tend to persist over time and across generations.

Economic Origins of Political Regimes

Acemoglu and Robinson (2006) focus on a unified theory of democracy and nondemocracy. Democracy is defined as a situation of political equality and the implementation of pro-majority or pro-poor policies. In contrast, nondemocracy is less majoritarian than democracy, with a few elites involved in most policy making. What factors influence the ebb and flow of democracies and dictatorships? The dynamics of regime change depend on the interaction of the elite (or rich) and the poor. The unified framework consists of two main components: (a) economics, where all individuals have well-defined preferences over outcomes or circumstances (such as people preferring more income to less or preferring peace to war) and behave strategically to achieve these goals, and (b) politics, which is assumed to involve an inherent conflict between elites and others over which policies and programs society should adopt.

Acemoglu and Robinson (2006) focus on three paths to development: (a) the creation of democracy from nondemocracy and the gradual consolidation of democracy over time (as in the United Kingdom), (b) the creation of a democracy that can quickly collapse (as in Argentina in the twentieth century), and (c) the delayed transition from nondemocracy to democracy (as in Singapore and the East Asian countries). The last path is subdivided into two. In the first, democracy is never created, because the society is relatively egalitarian and prosperous—which ensures social and political stability and maintains the status quo—and because the people are materially satisfied and never challenge the system. This is contrary to Sen's argument for freedom as development (Sen 1999) and Maslow's pyramid, where individuals move from satisfying material needs to higher and higher nonmaterial aspirations of political and spiritual freedom (Maslow 1943). In the second subpath, an unequal, exploitative society (as in apartheid South Africa) is controlled by elites through violence and other means of repression to avoid democracy or any discussion of it (which could lead to riots and revolution).

Basic Theory of Democratization

The basic theory of democratization holds that elites prefer nondemocracy, while other citizens prefer democracy. Both elites and citizens want policies that will benefit them—not only today but also tomorrow. Political institutions, because of their longstanding nature, can act as a negotiating mechanism and regulate policies over time.

In a nondemocracy, the elites have de jure political power, and if unconstrained, generally choose policies that are most beneficial to them (for example, low taxes and tariffs and no redistribution of wealth to the poor or middle classes). Sometimes, the majority of nonelite citizens will challenge the status quo; for example, through revolution the poor can gain temporary de facto political power. While this power is often transitory, the majority group can use it to change the system to its benefit. Elites want to prevent such revolutionary situations and therefore make promises—often not credible—of pro-majority policies within the existing political system. To make such promises believable, some power is transferred to the majority, initiating democratization, which then proceeds in fits and starts over time.

Elites controlling the political system generally do not want to extend voting rights to citizens or transfer political and economic power to them (as in Argentina, for example). Therefore, democratic transition will not occur without the threat of revolution. The strength and nature of civil society organizations are important for the creation and consolidation of democracy.

Role of the Middle Class in the Consolidation of Democracy

The middle class—materially more comfortable and educated than the poor—is an important driver of change during the transition of power from the elites to the majority. The middle class acts as a buffer between the two extremes, ensuring consolidation of democracy by limiting redistribution (as in Colombia and Costa Rica). The lack of a middle class is said to be a problem in El Salvador and Guatemala, where democracy is not being consolidated.

Do Democratic Countries Grow Faster than Dictatorships?

When democracy is defined as the process of regular, free, and competitive multiparty elections, then democracy should, in theory, be negatively related to growth. Why? Because in a politically open country, interest groups can pressure government into implementing expansive fiscal and redistributive economic policies. In developing countries, increasing the size of government in response to these interest groups is the policy of least resistance; alternatively, capital spending is drastically cut to pay for the redistributive policies of transfers, subsidies, and increased social spending. Democracies also face the difficulty of building a consensus of policy, which takes time. As such, democratic institutions often respond to exogenous shocks slowly. In addition, incumbent politicians in democracies have a short time horizon (because of the frequency of elections) and formulate suboptimal economic policies when pressured (for example, by labor unions, private business associations, farmers' associations, and so on).

But Ames (1987) and others point out that even dictatorships must please special constituencies to remain in power and to avoid coups and revolutions. Redistribution is therefore a problem in dictatorships as well as in democracies. Moreover, benevolent dictators in China, Indonesia, the Republic of Korea, Malaysia, and Singapore (until the mid-1990s) all generated high growth rates. On the other hand, kleptocratic regimes in Africa and Latin America have done terrible damage.

Another definition of democracy takes into consideration economic liberties and constraints (for example, capital mobility, trade and exchange rate restrictions, size of government) and civil rights (for example, the Gastil Index and, more recently, the Heritage Foundation Index). While economic liberties foster entrepreneurship, private-sector-led activities, and higher growth, civil liberties are likely to lead to redistributive pressures. On the other hand, Barro (1991) and Ozler and Rodrik (1992) find a correlation between civil liberties and growth and investment. Still, it is not clear whether democracy with civil liberties promotes economic liberties and economic development.

Figure 20.1   Economic Freedom and Political Rights Are Positively Associated

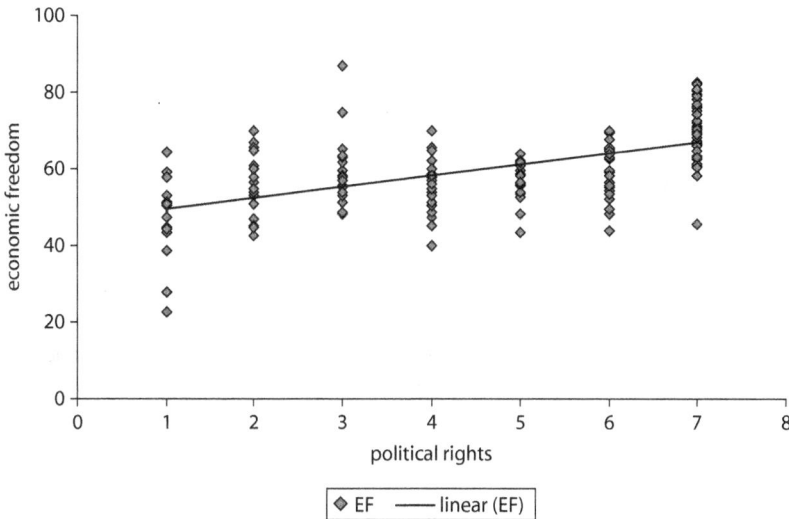

Source: Heritage Foundation 2009; Freedom House 2009.
Note: Economic freedom (EF)—highest = 100; political rights—highest = 7.

Does political stability foster growth or vice versa? And conversely, does political instability—which is usually a composite index of several political variables, such as coups, riots, demonstrations against the incumbent government, and political assassinations (Taylor and Jodice 1983)—lead to economic instability and lower growth?

We explored the relationship of economic freedom and political freedom using the Heritage Foundation's *Index of Economic Freedom* (2009) and the Freedom House's *Freedom in the World* (2009) and found that these two freedoms are positively associated (that is, greater political rights foster higher economic freedom, as shown in figure 20.1).

The Interplay of Politics and Economics

In general, poor countries exhibit limited private investment, low revenue collection, slow growth in per capita income, high informal employment and output, and an inequitable growth pattern and provision of public services. Are these tendencies due to weak administrative and implementation capacity or to politicians' inability to stand up to powerful groups and implement comprehensive economic reforms? A long tradition of political-economy analysis of the economic performance of developing countries explores this question.

When asked about state capacity for better economic management, a majority of the respondents in 18 African countries in 2005 said they believed that their governments had the capacity to solve major developmental challenges in the short to medium term (Bratton 2006). Ordinary African citizens who were surveyed did not view the lack of state capacity as a problem, pointing to their recent satisfaction in the delivery of education and health services. This is in contrast to the state-decline argument presented by political scientists such as Rothenberg (1994).

According to Fosu and O'Connell (2005), "syndrome-free"[5] economies can account for the growth of some African countries. In fact, each of the 12 countries sampled survived the adverse effects of one or more of the four syndromes and are now syndrome free.[6] But what explains the disparities in public spending and uneven growth performance among the 12 countries? Fosu and O'Connell (2005, 18) suggest that part of the explanation may lie in the "ethno-regional polarization inherited from the colonial period," in which a few large, regionally based groups dominated the economic and political arena.

Van de Walle (2001) argues that the political elites in Africa, in response to donor-driven economic reforms, have simply changed their methods of rent seeking, enacting a series of partial or incomplete reforms (barely enough to satisfy donors) without altering private sector development—hence the likelihood of a "permanent crisis" in the African countries. This argument is similar to that of Eifert, Gelb, and Ramachandran (2006). Tangri (1999) argues that the minority Asian community in East Africa (and possibly the Arab private sector in West Africa) coexists with the small, wealthy, black private sector, often closely aligned with the top political leadership, whose success is defined more by political networking and rent-sharing arrangements than by business expertise. Emery (2003) goes further and asserts that the bureaucracy and state apparatus are used to dispense patronage.

In line with the above arguments, numerous political observers have pointed out that benefits are not shared equitably, because countries in the tropics have tended to produce exploitative regimes that protect the interests of a small elite. For example, Olson (1965) argues that the interests of the elites are narrowly defined, as they prefer local and regional public goods to national public goods that benefit all segments of the population. In our sample countries, the elites appear to capture government spending on social sectors, subsidies, and transfers intended to benefit the poor and vulnerable groups. In addition, the poorest 20 percent have problems accessing essential services, and the quality of services (when provided) is often questionable. Even when government funds are allocated for schools and health clinics, teachers receive their salaries despite frequently missing class, and nurses and doctors are frequently absent from the clinics. Data from 250 schools and 100 health facilities in Uganda, for example, indicate that only 13 percent of the intended per-student grant actually reached the schools during 1991–95, while the other 87 percent "leaked out" en route from the central to local governments. Similarly, in Tanzania in 1998, 57 percent of nonwage funds to primary education did not reach their target.

More recently, a growing body of work has examined the influence of politics on economic inputs and outcomes. North (1992), for example, argued that politically determined structures (of property rights, government spending allocations, and so on) do not necessarily maximize the efficiency or growth potential of the economy. Rather, the elites—political leaders, rulers, or strong groups—use these structures to maximize their own returns. If we follow this logic, then both developed and developing countries distort the allocation of resources and retard growth and development.

Others have argued that the patron-client relationship strongly influences policy making in both developing and developed countries. Bates (1981) argues that collusion between the urban-based interest groups and political elites has resulted in the punitive taxation of agriculture. Adam and Connell (2004) note that small groups who exchange growth for redistribution are likely to capture governments of countries lacking restraining institutions. More recent work by Acemoglu, Ticchi, and Vindigni (2006), Easterly and Levine (1997, 2003), and Alesina and LaFerrara (2005) also describes state capture by the elites, whether along the urban-rural divide or motivated by economic sector interests (agriculture versus manufacturing), ethnic diversity, or ethnolinguistic fractionalization. We define state capture as the effort of affluent individuals or groups, private firms, or oligarchs to shape the laws, public policies, rules, and regulations of the state to their own advantage. This shaping may be done not only by private firms or richer elites (the top 20 percent on the income distribution scale) but, in some countries, by ethnic groups or powerful economic groups. To fully account for the dynamics of state capture, we must analyze how it benefits or harms various income groups, powerful groups, and vested interests, including the bureaucracy. In other words, state capture and redistributive conflicts are part of the same spectrum of good-to-bad governance.

In a sample study of 12 African countries[7] by Nallari (2008), the argument that state capture is achieved by a small group of elites appears to hold. Nallari finds that African business elites, particularly indigenous firms, have been colluding with politicians and, with the help of the bureaucracy, extracting rents rather than investing in productive activities.[8] Because the transition to democracy in these African countries is so slow, even stagnant, African citizens are unlikely to kick the political elites out of power through elections.

On the other hand, we now know from 60 years of development experience that Southeast Asian countries (authoritarian regimes with few constraints on executive power) have generated successful economic outcomes, in contrast to African countries (most with strong rulers). To explain this contrast, political scientists and economists cite the term "weak and strong economic states." Weak economic states have limited capacity, if any, to tax, regulate, and play a developmental role; these include states that cannot extract revenues from society to invest in public goods. In addition, in the 12 African countries under study, trust between indigenous African businesses—including those operated by Asians and Arabs—and the political elites exists to generate and sustain economic rents. Self-interested elites prefer to capture rents now because they are uncertain about a weak state's capacity to favor them in the future.

As shown in figure 20.2, the enterprise survey evidence indicates that while the prevalence of illegal political funding (and the extent to which it influences policy) differs from region to region, there is, overall, a major governance issue. Other problem areas include the reported ineffectiveness of parliaments; the illicit purchase (capture) by elite enterprises of regulations, policies, or laws; and the way public procurement contracts are often awarded to influential interests rather than those with merit.

This, in turn, suggests that misgovernance and corruption cannot always be viewed as symptoms of more fundamental political forces; in some settings, misgovernance and corruption actually shape political forces and outcomes, as in the case of state capture and illicit political funding. Under these circumstances, any analysis must go beyond a mechanistic assessment of whether the political leadership is committed to change; it must take into account the complex web of conditions in which political will exists. Political leaders are often strongly influenced by powerful outside interests. Accordingly, further operational research on influential institutions, state capture, and the nature of political funding and its links with governance is warranted. The work initiated more

**Figure 20.2   Politics and Inequality of Influence Can Be Measured:
A Major Governance Challenge**

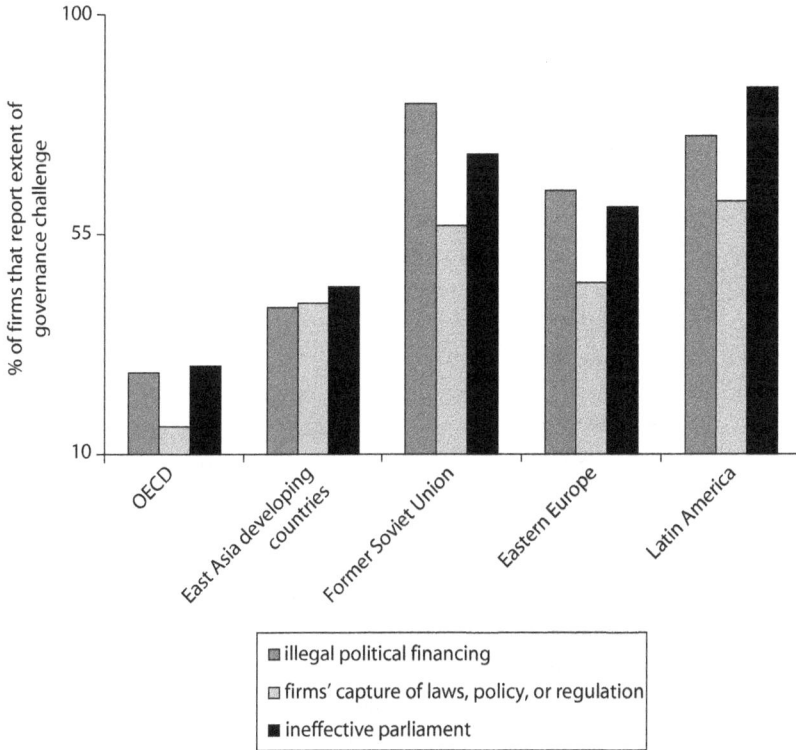

Source: Kaufmann 2005.
Note: OECD = Organisation for Economic Co-operation and Development.

than 30 years ago by Scott (1970) on the typologies of the interface between politics and corruption (extended by Johnston and Van de Walle 1996) must also be considered.

There is a strong correlation among low growth, high inequality, a large informal economy, and the capture of subsidies by top quintiles. For example, the higher the income inequality in the sample, the lower the gross domestic product (GDP) growth. Similarly, effective governments and countries with higher "voice and accountability" ratings (Kaufmann 2005) appear to be correlated with lower income disparities between the top and bottom quintiles and lower capture of social sector spending, including subsidies by affluent groups. In contrast, despite the rhetoric of "limited government" and "constrained executive power," stronger states such as the Organisation for Economic Co-operation and Development

(OECD) countries and the developing countries in East Asia tend to have higher revenue-to-GDP ratios and invest more in public goods than do weaker states. This is not only because elites in these countries are confident that rents can accrue to them now and in the future, but also because they know that citizens can replace their leaders if their policies are not in the people's interests. Private investment and growth is higher in the stronger states than in weaker states, and garnering of subsidies by the elites is generally lower.

High rates of elite capture may extend to all or most of a country's institutions (such as the parliament and political parties) and key individuals, including public administrators, judges, and bureaucrats. The capture may take place jointly or separately, depending on the economic interests of the powerful groups or elites. For example, Eifert, Gelb, and Ramachandran (2006) point out that indigenous private firms, including businesses run by Asians and Arabs in African countries, are closely tied to African political elites. Moreover, a majority of the Afrobarometer survey (Nallari 2008) respondents in 11 of the 12 African countries (all except Tanzania) said that the members of parliaments and local councilors "never" or "only sometimes" listen to their constituents. The findings of the same surveys indicate that ministers and parliamentarians do not frequently visit their constituencies once elected. Almost 50 percent of the respondents in the Afrobarometer surveys conducted in 8 of the 12 fast-growing countries in the sample said that the leaders and powerful members of society are above the law and are not held accountable for their actions. For example, the gap between the anticipated enforcement of laws and regulations for ordinary citizens and that for top government officials is 65 percent in Benin and Kenya, 50 percent in Mali, 42 percent in Uganda, and somewhat lower in the remaining countries.

A highly captured country, therefore, in the absence of effective institutions, is likely to suffer from low tax revenues, low private and public investment, high redistribution, and, consequently, slow output expansion and inadequate provision of public services to the poor. Not only are tax revenues low in the 12 fast-growing countries, but so is total investment (the range is 15 to 20 percent of GDP), and most of that investment is funded by public borrowing and high levels of aid (for example, 12 percent of GDP per year in Tanzania and Uganda).

Firms and groups that cannot compete with favored firms or accommodated groups will go under unless they resort to the informal sector. The rapid increase in the size of the informal sector—in terms of both output and employment—in the 12 fast-growing African countries could reflect the cheap labor working informally to service the elites and may be fallout from these "redistributive conflicts" or the result of burdensome regulations combined with inadequate public provision of infrastructure services. Investment climate assessments in Kenya and other countries point to a growing frustration with inadequate public provision of services (electricity, water, and roads) among small and medium-size firms. By choosing to stay in the shadows, informal enterprises can circumvent government regulations relating to property rights, minimum wages, workers' safety, the environment, price controls, and licensing, as well as avoid taxes and fees. To avoid detection and punishment for operating informally (and usually illegally), enterprises operate on the basis of trust and reputation, conducting transactions among closed networks of customers and suppliers.

In a number of sample countries, affluent groups benefited disproportionately from education, health, infrastructure, and subsidies. For example, the top quintiles benefited more from the secondary school subsidy than the bottom quintile. This gap was much lower for primary school and much higher for tertiary education. There is even evidence that kerosene subsidies, which are primarily intended to benefit the poorer segments of the population, have disproportionately accrued to the top quintile. The incidence of education and health spending becomes more pro-poor as governance indicators improve (Kaufmann, Kraay, and Mastruzzi 2005). In recent years, a large body of literature has emerged on how poor governance cuts into governments' revenues and distorts the allocation of resources, thereby diminishing the quality of public-provided services and creating adverse distributional outcomes. Governance indicators in African countries rank quite low in comparison with other developing countries. Across the 12 African countries, better governance indicators (greater accountability, rule of law, effective government, quality of regulations, political stability, and lower corruption) are associated with pro-poor benefit incidence.

Conclusion

Growth in various segments of the population and geographical areas has been uneven in both the developed and developing countries and shows the disparities between the rich and poor in income and services delivery. Collusion among big-business groups, politicians, and bureaucracy perpetuates (and often exacerbates) traditional power structures and facilitates capture of economic rents and public service provision by a small group of elites to the detriment of the poor and the middle class. Incomplete political transition toward democracy in several developing countries limits citizens' ability to throw political elites out of office for providing inadequate jobs or access to public services. The above discussion provides a brief overview of state capture and how it relates to governance and economic performance in 12 African countries. Surveys over the past few years show that ordinary citizens in these countries have not had their needs met, particularly in the areas of political representation, job creation, and public services related to water, electricity, roads, and telephones. A majority of the respondents raise concerns about the preferential enforcement of laws and policies in favor of political leaders and powerful groups. Only sustained pressure from domestic advocacy groups and the international community can persuade the elites in these developing countries to implement reforms and move from rent sharing to higher shared growth.

Notes

1. See, for instance, Helliwell (1994), Barro (1996), and Papaioannou and Siourounis (2004) and the references cited therein.
2. For some results consistent with this observation, see Aghion, Alesina, and Trebbi (2004) and Adserà and Boix (2003).
3. They consider education spending, spending on pensions and welfare, and trade openness, among other variables.
4. On a related topic, see also Rodrik and Wacziarg (2005).
5. Syndrome free refers to economies that combine political stability with reasonably market-friendly policies (Fosu and O'Connell 2005, 18).
6. The four syndromes examined were regulatory (degree of state intervention), adverse redistribution, intertemporally unsustainable spending, and state breakdown syndrome.
7. Those countries were Benin, Burkina Faso, Ethiopia, Ghana, Kenya, Madagascar, Malawi, Mali, Mozambique, Senegal, Tanzania, and Uganda.
8. Eifert, Gelb, and Ramachandran (2006) call this "low-level political equilibrium."

Bibliography

Acemoglu, Daron. 2009. *Introduction to Modern Economic Growth*. Princeton, NJ: Princeton University Press.

Acemoglu, D., P. Aghion, and F. Zilibotti. 2006. "Distance to Frontier, Selection, and Economic Growth." *Journal of the European Economic Association* 4 (1): 37–74.

Acemoglu, D., S. Johnson, and J. A. Robinson. 2005. "Institutions as the Fundamental Cause of Long-Run Growth." In *Handbook of Economic Growth,* ed. Philippe Aghion and Stephen Durlauf, chapter 6. North-Holland: Elsevier.

Acemoglu, D., S. Johnson, J. A. Robinson, and P. Yared. 2005. "From Education to Democracy?" *American Economic Association, Papers and Proceedings* 95 (2): 44–49.

Acemoglu, D., and J. A. Robinson. 2006. "Persistence of Power, Elites and Institutions." NBER Working Paper 12108, National Bureau of Economic Research, Cambridge, MA.

Acemoglu, D., D. Ticchi, and A. Vindigni. 2006. "Emergence and Persistence of Inefficient States." NBER Working Paper 12748, National Bureau of Economic Research, Cambridge, MA.

Adam, C., and S. Connell. 2004. "Aid Versus Trade Revisited: Donor and Recipient Policies in the Presence of 'Learning By Doing.'" *Economic Journal* 114 (1): 150–73.

Adserà, A., and C. Boix. 2003. "The Political Economy of Trade and Economic Integration: A Review Essay." In *Bridges for Development: Policies and Institutions for Trade and Integration,* ed. Robert Devlin and Antoni Estevadeordal, 75–93. Washington, DC: Inter-American Development Bank; distributed by the Johns Hopkins University Press.

Aghion, P., A. Alesina, and F. Trebbi. 2004. "Endogenous Political Institutions." *Quarterly Journal of Economics* 119 (2): 565–611.

Aghion, P., R. Burgess, S. Redding, and F. Zilibotti. 2005a. "Entry Liberalization and Inequality in Industrial Performance." *Journal of the European Economic Association* 3 (2–3): 291–302.

———. 2005b. "On the Unequal Effects of Liberalization: Theory and Evidence from Indian Delicensing Data." London School of Economics and Harvard Institute for International Economic Studies.

Alesina, A. F., and E. LaFerrara. 2005. "Ethnic Diversity and Economic Perform-ance." *Journal of Economic Literature* 63 (September): 762–800.

Alesina, Alberto, Reza Baqir, and William Easterly. 1999. "Public Goods and Ethnic Divisions." *Quarterly Journal of Economics* 114 (November): 1243–84.

Ames, B. 1987. *Political Survival: Politicians and Public Policy in Latin America.* Berkeley, CA: University of California Press.

Aryeetey, Ernest, and Andrew McKay. 2007. "Ghana: The Challenge of Translating Sustained Growth into Poverty Reduction." In *Delivering on the Promise of*

Pro-Poor Growth, ed. Timothy Besley and Louise Cord, 147–68. Washington, DC: World Bank and Palgrave Macmillan.

Barro, R. J. 1991. "Economic Growth in a Cross-Section of Countries." *Quarterly Journal of Economics* 106 (2): 407–43.

———. 1996. "Determinants of Economic Growth: A Cross-Country Empirical Study." NBER Working Paper 5698, National Bureau of Economic Research, Cambridge, MA.

———. 1999. "Determinants of Democracy." *Journal of Political Economy* 107 (6): S158–83.

Bates, Robert. 1981. *Markets and States in Tropical Africa*. Berkeley, CA: University of California Press.

Belsey, T., and L. Cord, eds. 2007. *Delivering on the Promise of Pro-Poor Growth*. Washington, DC: World Bank and Palgrave Macmillan.

Bourguignon, F., and B. Pleskovic, eds. 2006. "Growth and Integration." Annual Bank Conference on Development Economics, World Bank, Dakar, Senegal, January 27, 2005.

Bratton, Michael. 2006. "Are You Being Served?" Afrobarometer, Working Paper 65. http://www.afrobarometer.org/abseries.html#.

Byerlee, D., and C. Jackson. 2005. "Agriculture, Rural Development and Pro-Poor Growth." Paper prepared for Operationalizing Pro-Poor Growth Research Program, World Bank, Washington, DC.

Coulombe, Harold, and Quentin Wodon. 2007. "Poverty, Livelihood, and Access to Basic Services in Ghana: An Overview." Washington, DC: World Bank. http://siteresources.worldbank.org/INTGHANA/Resources/CEM_poverty.pdf

De Mesquita, B. B., A. Smith, R. M. Siverson, and J. D. Morrow. 2003. *The Logic of Political Survival*. Cambridge, MA: Massachusetts Institute of Technology Press.

Easterly, William, and Ross Levine. 1997. "Africa's Growth Tragedy: Policies and Ethnic Divisions." *Quarterly Journal of Economics* 112 (4): 1203–50.

———. 2003. "Tropics, Germs, and Crops: How Endowments Influence Economic Development." *Journal of Monetary Economics* 50 (1): 3–47.

Eifert, Benn, Alan Gelb, and Vijaya Ramachandran. 2006. "Business Environment and Comparative Advantage in Africa: Evidence from the Investment Climate Data." Working Paper 56, Center for Global Development, Washington, DC.

Emery, James. 2003. "Governance and Private Investment in Africa." In *Beyond Structural Adjustment: The Institutional Context of African Development*, ed. N. van de Walle, N. Ball, and V. Ramachandran, 241–62. New York: Palgrave Macmillan.

Fosu, A. K., and S. O'Connell. 2005. "Explaining African Economic Growth: The Role of Anti-Growth Syndromes." Mimeo. Swarthmore College, Swarthmore, PA.

Freedom House. 2009. *Freedom in the World*. Washington, DC: World Resources Institute.

Giavazzi, F., and G. Tabellini. 2005. "Economic and Political Liberalizations." *Journal of Monetary Economics* 52 (7): 1297–330.

Glaeser, E., R. La Porta, F. Lopez-de-Silanes, and A. Shleifer. 2004. "Do Institutions Cause Growth?" *Journal of Economic Growth* 9 (3): 271–303.

Helliwell, J. F. 1992. "International Growth Linkages: Evidence from Asia and the OECD." NBER Working Paper 4245, National Bureau of Economic Research, Cambridge, MA.

———. 1994. "Empirical Linkages between Democracy and Economic Growth." *British Journal of Political Science* 24 (2): 225–48.

Heritage Foundation. 2009. *Index of Economic Freedom*. New York: Heritage Foundation.

Hibbs, Douglas A. 1973. *Mass Political Violence*. New York: Wiley.

Huntington, S. P. 1968. *Political Order in Changing Societies*. New Haven: Yale University Press.

———. 1991. *The Third Wave: Democratization in the Late Twentieth Century*. Norman, OK: University of Oklahoma Press.

Johnston, T. A., and N. Van de Walle. 1996. *Improving Aid to Africa*. Washington, DC: Overseas Development Council; Baltimore, MD; distributed by Johns Hopkins University Press.

Kaufmann, D. 2005. "Click Refresh Button: Investment Climate Reconsidered." *Development Outreach*. March.

Kaufmann, D., A. Kraay, and M. Mastruzzi. 2005. "Governance Matters IV: Governance Indicators for 1996–2004." Growth and Investment Team Policy Research Working Paper 3630, Global Programs Division and Development Research Group, World Bank Institute, World Bank, Washington, DC.

———. 2006. "Governance Matters V: Aggregate and Individual Governance Indicators for 1996–2005." Growth and Investment Team Policy Research Working Paper 4012, Global Programs Division and Development Research Group, World Bank Institute, World Bank, Washington, DC.

Kaufmann, Daniel, Gil Mehrez, and Tugrul Gurgur. 2002. "Voice or Public Sector Management—An Empirical Investigation of Determinants of Public Sector Performance." World Bank Research Working Paper, World Bank, Washington, DC.

Lipset, Seymour Martin. 1959. "Some Social Requisites of Democracy: Economic Development and Political Legitimacy." *American Political Science Review* 53 (1): 69–105.

Maslow, A. H. 1943. "A Theory of Human Motivation." *Psychological Review* 50 (4): 370–96.

Mulligan, C. B., X. Sala-i-Martin, and R. Gil. 2003. "Do Democracies Have Different Public Policies than Nondemocracies?" NBER Working Paper 10040, National Bureau of Economic Research, Cambridge, MA.

Nallari, Raj. 2008. "Twelve Fast-Growing African Countries." Referenced in "The Quality of Growth," Ramon Lopez, Vinod Thomas, and Yan Wang, IEG Working Paper 2008/6, Independent Evaluation Group, World Bank, Washington, DC.

Ndulu, B., L. Chakraborti, L. Lijane, V. Ramachandran, and J. Wolgin. 2006. *The Challenges of African Growth*. Washington, DC: World Bank.

North, D. C. 1992. "Transaction Costs, Institutions, and Economic Performance." Occasional papers, International Center for Economic Growth 30, ICS Press, San Francisco, CA.

Olson, Mancur. 1965. *The Logic of Collective Action: Public Goods and the Theory of Groups*. Cambridge, MA: Harvard University Press.

Ozler, S. and D. Rodrik. 1992. "External Shocks, Politics and Private Investment: Some Theory and Empirical Evidence." *Journal of Development Economics.* 39 (1): 141–62.

Papaioannou, Elias, and Gregorios Siourounis. 2004. "Democratization and Growth." Working Paper, London Business School. http://www.cepr.org/meets/wkcn/1/1623/Papers/Papaioannou.pdf.

Patillo, Catherine, Sanjeev Gupta, and Kevin Carey. 2006. *Sustaining and Accelerating Pro-Poor Growth in Africa*. Washington, DC: International Monetary Fund.

Persson, T., and G. Tabellini. 2006. "Democratic Capital: The Nexus of Political and Economic Change." NBER Working Paper 12175, National Bureau of Economic Research, Cambridge, MA.

Przewroski, A., M. E. Alvarez, J. A. Cheibub, and F. Limongi. 2000. *Democracy and Development: Political Institutions and Well-Being in the World, 1950–1990*. Cambridge, U.K.: Cambridge University Press.

Reinikka, Ritva, and Jakob Svensson. 2004. "Local Capture: Evidence from a Central Government Transfer Program in Uganda." *Quarterly Journal of Economics* 119 (2): 679–705.

Rodrik, D., and R. Wacziarg. 2005. "Do Democratic Transitions Produce Bad Economic Outcomes?" *American Economic Review, Papers and Proceedings* 95 (2): 50–55.

Rothenberg, L. S. 1994. *Regulation Organizations and Politics: Motor Freight Policy at the Interstate Commerce Commission*. Ann Arbor, MI: University of Michigan Press.

Schneider, Friedrich. 2006. "Shadow Economies and Corruption All Over the World: What Do We Really Know?" IZA Discussion Paper 2315, Institute for the Study of Labor, Bonn, Germany.

Scott, J. C. 1970. "Corruption, Machine Politics, and Political Change." In *Political Corruption: Readings in Comparative Analysis*, ed. A. Heidenheimer, 549–63. New Brunswick, NJ: Transaction Books.

Sen, A. K. 1999. *Development as Freedom*. New York: Knopf.

Tangri, Roger. 1999. *The Politics of Patronage in Africa*. Trenton, NJ: Africa World Press.

Taylor, C. L., and D. A. Jodice. 1983. *World Handbook of Political and Social Indicators*. New Haven: Yale University Press.

Van de Walle, Nicolas. 2001. *African Economies and the Politics of Permanent Crisis, 1979–1999*. Cambridge, U.K.: Cambridge University Press.

World Bank. 2000. *Can Africa Claim the 21st Century?*. Washington, DC: World Bank.

———. 2005. *World Development Report*. Washington, DC: World Bank.

———. (various years). *African Development Indicators*. Washington, DC: World Bank.

CHAPTER 21

Climate Change and the Wealth of Nations

In this chapter, we examine how resource-rich countries develop and how they are responding to the threat of global climate change. Natural resources are special economic goods because they are not produced and require proper management to provide sustained growth. They yield economic rents that can be used for development; on the other hand, wide fluctuations in prices of mineral wealth (for example, copper, oil, and natural gas) lead to booms and busts. In low-income countries, natural resources make up a significant share of the total wealth—often more than that of produced physical capital (figure 21.1).

The economic performance of oil-producing countries since 1980 has been worse than that of non-oil-producing developing countries; they have had lower growth, lower savings, higher unemployment, and less equitable distribution of wealth. What explains this poor performance? So far, most researchers have focused on oil-revenue management during booms and busts.

But could the mere presence of oil be the problem? In other words, could a country fail to grow despite ample natural resources? Robust empirical evidence supports the "resource course" phenomenon, showing a strong negative relationship between natural resource wealth and economic growth. Resource-poor countries engage earlier than resource-rich

Figure 21.1   Composition of Natural Wealth in Low-Income Countries, 2005

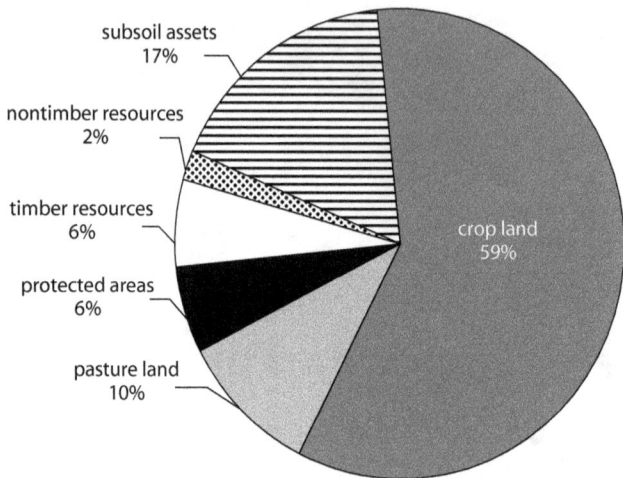

subsoil assets
17%

nontimber resources
2%

timber resources
6%

protected areas
6%

pasture land
10%

crop land
59%

Source: World Bank 2006.
Note: Oil-producing countries are excluded.

countries in labor-intensive and competitive manufacturing, which supports faster diversification, higher saving rates, and faster accumulation of physical, human, and social capital (Auty and Gelb 2001). Resource-rich countries may also engage in competitive industrialization, but their reliance on the primary sector tends to dampen its beneficial effects. Moreover, natural resource rents favor the creation of factional states in which those managing the rents wield economic and political power. Rents are deployed through indirect means such as trade protection, unproductive job creation, and overextended public expenditure. These conditions, in turn, lead to lower investment efficiency and ultimately slower economic growth.

National Wealth and Genuine Saving

The wealth of nations data compiled by the World Bank (2005b) consist of the sum of (a) natural capital, (b) produced capital, and (c) intangible capital. In practice, a nation's wealth is calculated in a series of additions and subtractions made over time to an initial stock—the sum of the value of gross investments minus the depreciation of produced capital in constant 1995 U.S. dollars, converted at nominal exchange rates. This is known as the perpetual inventory method (as opposed to net present value). Adjusted net, or genuine, savings represent the true level of savings in a country after accounting for the depreciation of the produced capital; investments in human capital (as measured by education expenditures); depletion of minerals, energy, and forests; and damage from pollutants.

While wealth composition to some extent determines the development options available to a particular country, the quality of development depends on the change in wealth over time. Natural capital can be transformed into other forms of capital, given the efficient investment of resource rents. While the data limit estimates of natural wealth—fish stocks and over-extraction of subsoil water are not measured, nor are the environmental services that underpin human societies and economies—the "total wealth," in line with economic theory, is estimated as the present value of future consumption. Produced capital stocks are derived from historical investment data using a perpetual inventory model. Natural resource stock values are derived from country-level data on physical stocks and from estimates of natural resource rents based on world prices and local costs. Intangible capital is the difference between total wealth and the other produced and natural stocks.

Available data suggest that most of the mineral-rich countries have exhibited low or even negative genuine savings over many years (World Bank 1997). The sheer concentration of rent streams in mineral-dependent economies also make corruption and rent seeking likely. In addition, the boom-and-bust nature of natural-resource markets creates significant problems for governments that are highly dependent on revenues from such resources. The tendency to boost subsidies and consumption expenditure during boom times is difficult to reverse when the bust arrives, resulting in soaring government deficits and, ultimately, in inflation and macroeconomic instability. Managing resource income requires the ability to buffer revenues, policies to match investment programs to the economy's absorptive capacity for productive investments, and mechanisms for restraining expenditures when resource prices fall. In this case, a "genuine saving" or resource conservation is least likely (see figure 21.2).

Consumption, Saving, and a Counterfactual to the Hartwick Rule

Some have referred to development as a process of portfolio management. Evidence suggests that to some extent, other forms of capital can substitute for natural resources. The Hartwick rule[1] for sustainability

Figure 21.2   Resource Abundance and Capital Accumulation

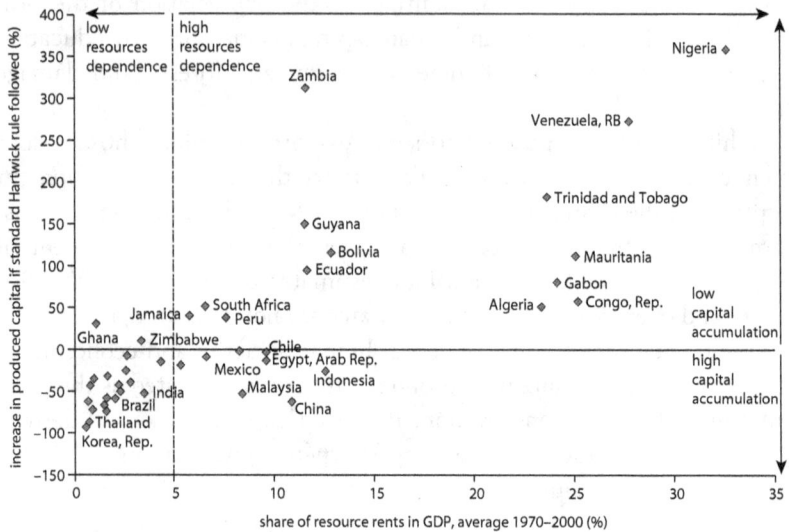

Source: World Bank 2006, 55.

maintains that countries should invest their rents from natural resources to achieve sustainable consumption. Drawing on 30 years (1970–2000) of resource-rent data underlying the adjusted net savings (World Bank 2005a), the analysis constructs a Hartwick rule counterfactual: How rich would countries have been in 2000 if they had followed the Hartwick rule since 1970?

Figure 21.2 shows resource dependence, expressed as the average share of exhaustible resource rents in the gross domestic product (GDP) against the percentage difference between actual capital accumulation and counterfactual capital accumulation (that is, constant 5 percent investment of the 1987 GDP). It compares the level of actual capital in a given country with the counterfactual level of capital in the same country had it followed a sustainability rule, such as the Hartwick rule (see note 1), aimed at making the relative investment efficiency across countries less salient. Countries with high natural-resource dependence and counterfactual capital stock higher than the actual (baseline) capital stock occupy the top-right quadrant. Countries with low natural-resource dependence and low baseline capital stock occupy the bottom-left quadrant. Together, these country clusters indicate a high negative correlation between resource abundance and the difference between baseline and counterfactual capital accumulation. The countries in the top-right quadrant—Nigeria (oil), República Bolivariana de Venezuela (oil), Trinidad and Tobago (oil and gas), and Zambia (copper)—defy the Hartwick rule, showing low levels of capital accumulation despite high rents. With the exception of Trinidad and Tobago, all of these countries experienced declines in real per capita income from 1970 to 2000. In the bottom-left quadrant are countries with low exhaustible-resource rent shares but high levels of capital accumulation; these include Brazil, India, the Republic of Korea, and Thailand. A number of high-income countries are also in this group. Figure 21.2 shows that no country with resource rents higher than 15 percent of the GDP has followed the Hartwick rule.

World Bank (2005a) calculations show how even a moderate effort at saving—equivalent to the average saving effort of the poorest countries in the world—could have substantially increased the wealth of resource-dependent economies. In 2000, Nigeria, a major oil exporter, could have had a stock of produced capital five times higher than it did. Moreover, if these investments had taken place, oil would play a much smaller role in the Nigerian economy than it does today, likely benefiting policies affecting other sectors. Similarly, República Bolivariana de Venezuela could have accumulated four times as much produced capital. In per capita terms, the economies of Gabon, República Bolivariana de Venezuela, and Trinidad and Tobago, all rich in petroleum, could today have a stock of produced capital of roughly $30,000 per person, comparable to that of the Republic of Korea.

How Does Natural Capital Affect Well-Being?

Intangible capital (assets that are unaccounted for in the estimates of produced and natural capital—for example, labor force expertise, social capital, or governance elements that boost the productivity of labor) account for most of a country's wealth. This suggests that an economy with an efficient judicial system, clear property rights, and an effective government would have higher total wealth and, thus, a higher intangible capital residual. The World Bank (2005a) regression analysis found that human capital and the rule of law account for the majority of the variation in the residual. Investments in education, the functioning of the justice system, and policies aimed at attracting remittances are the most important means of increasing the intangible components of total wealth.

The World Bank analysis also found that as countries become richer, produced and intangible assets become more important than natural assets. Thus, the development process primarily entails growth in the modern sectors of manufacturing and services, which depend heavily on the more intangible forms of wealth. Yet the value of natural resources per person does not decline as income rises, particularly for agricultural land.

In fact, some believe that land and other natural resources are necessary to sustaining income generation. The results do not suggest that the elasticity of substitution between the natural resource (land) and other inputs is low. Wherever land is a significant input, it has an elasticity of substitution approximately equal to or greater than one. This finding not only confirms that countries' opportunities are not necessarily dictated by their endowments of natural resources, but also validates the importance of the Hartwick rule dictating that saving the rents from the exploitation of natural resources encourages sustained income generation.

High Carbon, High Growth

Climate change epitomizes the complexity of the development challenge in a globalizing but still unequal world. It magnifies growing concerns about food security, water scarcity, and energy security; threatens to reverse hard-earned development gains; and raises difficult questions about economic disparity, political power, and social justice. The poorest countries and communities will suffer the earliest and the most. Yet the poorest countries depend on the ethical considerations and actions of other nations. While climate change adds costs and risks to development, a well-designed and well-implemented global climate policy can open new economic opportunities to the developing countries. Greenhouse gas (GHG) stabilization depends on fostering their economic growth sustainably.

One of the most difficult features of climate change is the major asymmetry in the distribution of the causes and impacts across countries. Moreover, industrial and developing countries both face the difficult challenge of adapting to the inevitable climate change of the coming decades. Fiscal policy will play an important role in facilitating the sustainable use of natural resources and in safeguarding the environment. For example, harmful subsidies and inappropriate tax policies that lead to excessive exploitation of natural resources will need to be phased out; energy prices must reflect their social costs, and government expenditure programs that more directly benefit small farmers must replace subsidies for pesticides and fertilizers, which contribute to the over-farming of land.

Industrial countries have contributed most to the existing stock of emissions both in absolute terms and on a per capita basis; accordingly, they bear the burden of implementing policies to prevent the overexploitation of the world's environmental resources.

The threat is particularly alarming for the world's poor, as inadequate responses to climate change would threaten progress on all the dimensions of the Millennium Development Goals. Climate change demands unprecedented global cooperation, involving concerted action at different development stages supported by a measurable, reportable, and verifiable transfer of finance and technology from developed to developing countries. Developing countries must trust in the equity and fairness of a global climate policy, and supporting institutions must remain neutral for such cooperation to succeed.

The problem of pollution and climate change involves a failure of markets: those who cause damage by emitting GHGs generally do not pay for the damage. This global problem requires cooperation and collaboration among countries. In particular, developed countries must lead the developing world in dramatically reducing their emissions, promoting the use of new technologies that can mitigate the effects of climate change, supporting programs to combat deforestation, encouraging effective market mechanisms (such as cap and trade), and honoring their aid and trade commitments to the developing countries. All of these measures are part of the Bali Action Plan of December 2007 (see box 21.1).

Mitigation of and Adaptation to Climate Change

An effective response to climate change must combine both mitigation and adaptation. Most of the warming trends observed since the mid-twentieth century are very likely due to an increase in anthropogenic GHG concentrations, particularly carbon dioxide (CO_2), caused by activities such as fossil fuel use and land use changes. Already, the earth has warmed up by 2 degrees centigrade; we must now curtail global GHG emissions to manage the now unavoidable consequences of our actions without catastrophic costs. A delay in reducing GHG emissions would significantly constrain opportunities to achieve lower GHG atmospheric concentration stabilization levels and would likely increase the risk of severe (and perhaps irreversible) impacts and the cost of adapting to them.

Carbon dioxide emissions from fossil fuel combustion and manufacturing activity were estimated to be in excess of 27 billion metric tons in 2003 for the entire global economy, an increase of 19 percent over 1990 levels. In 2003, the United States contributed 22 percent of the total emissions, Europe 9 percent, and Japan 5 percent, while Sub-Saharan

Box 21.1

Climate Policy in the International Arena

Global climate policy in the international arena

The United Nations Framework Convention on Climate Change (UNFCCC) guides global climate policy. It was adopted in 1992 to set goals for preventing "dangerous human interference with the climate system" and has now been ratified by 192 member states. Guided by the principle of common but differentiated responsibilities and respective capabilities, the convention seeks not only to commit industrial countries to reduce their emissions but also to help developing countries adapt to increased climate risks and slow their emission-growth trajectories in a way that will support their economic development. The 1997 Kyoto Protocol was the first binding international instrument under the UNFCCC to codify GHG emission reduction targets for 37 industrial countries, economies in transition, and the European Commission. The targets amount to an average of 5.2 percent against the 1990 levels over the five-year period 2008–12. As of May 2008, 181 nations and the European Commission had ratified the treaty.

Bali Action Plan highlights

At a meeting in Bali in December 2007, the UNFCCC parties committed themselves to a framework for comprehensive, long-term cooperative action on climate change. They agreed on enhanced action(s) in the following areas:

- Mitigation of climate change
- Adaptation to climate change
- Development and transfer of technology to support mitigation and adaptation
- Provision of financial resources and investment to support mitigation and adaptation.

Source: World Bank 2008.

Africa had the least emissions (in part because of the limited access to modern energy sources and a heavy reliance on biomass fuel). Between 1990 and 2003, per capita emissions from China and India grew more than 50 percent, but the 2003 levels were still a fraction of those in high-income countries. Even though their share of the world's population is only about 20 percent, industrial countries are responsible for 75 percent of the world's cumulative-energy-related CO_2 emissions since 1850.

Table 21.1   Savings, Fuel Use, and CO_2 Emissions by Region and Income Group

Group	Adjusted net saving — Percent of GNI — 2005	of which, global damages caused by CO_2 emissions 2005	Annual change (percentage points, 1990–2005)	Carbon dioxide emissions — Metric tons per capita — 2003	Percent increase 1990–2003	Annual deforestation — Forest cover lost 1990–2005 — Annual area lost (sq km)	Annual percent lost	Use of traditional fuels — Combustible renewables and waste (% of total energy) — 2004	Annual change (percentage points, 1990–2004)
World	7.4	0.4	−0.19	4.0	−0.2	83,484	0.14	10.3	−0.03
Low income	6.2	1.0	0.24	0.9	1.6	71,694	0.59	44.9	−0.53
Fragile states	−25.1	0.8	−0.57	0.5	−2.0	31,799	0.56	78.1	0.07
Non-fragile states	11.0	1.0	0.31	1.0	2.5	39,891	0.62	39.1	−0.76
Middle income	9.5	0.9	−0.12	3.9	−0.4	18,288	0.03	9.0	−0.08
Low & middle income	8.0	1.0	−0.01	2.4	−0.6	90,621	0.21	17.5	−0.07
East Asia & Pacific	25.3	1.2	0.45	2.7	1.3	4,939	−0.22	16.1	−0.61
Europe & Central Asia	−2.0	1.2	−0.89[a]	6.9	−3.1	−1,789	−0.02	2.4	0.04[c]
Latin America & Caribbean	3.7	0.4	−0.11	2.4	0.4	45,753	0.44	14.8	−0.25
Middle East & North Africa	−13.0	1.2	−0.92[b]	3.4	2.4	−747	−0.49	1.2	−0.04
South Asia	16.4	1.1	0.64	1.0	3.0	−831	−0.18	38.0	−0.79
Sub-Saharan Africa	−7.3	0.7	−0.20	0.8	−0.8	43,296	0.58	55.7	−0.01
High income	7.7	0.3	−0.21	12.8	0.7	−7,137	−0.09	3.1	0.01
High income: OECD	8.2	0.3	−0.19	12.8	0.6	−7,041	−0.09	3.3	0.01

Source: World Development Indicators.
Note: Carbon dioxide figures refer to emissions from combustion of fossil fuels and cement manufacture.
a. Annual change refers to the period 1995–2005.
b. Annual change refers to the period 1993–2005.
c. Annual change refers to the period 1992–2004.

No one knows for certain how climate change will affect the planet and economic performance. Table 21.1 presents some data on savings, fuel use, and carbon emissions by region and income group over the period 1995 to 2004. Most scientists agree that the human-made emissions of GHGs have contributed to a rise in global temperature. The temperature change may lead to a rise in sea levels; increased frequency of heat waves, droughts, hurricanes, and floods; and loss of biodiversity. Therefore, countries worldwide must design policies to mitigate climate change. For example, a fast-growing economy is likely to generate higher emissions and have increasing abatement costs, weakening the country's incentives to achieve the quantity-based emissions targets (cap and trade scheme). If a price-based carbon tax is in place, the abatement costs will likely be smaller.

The complex web of climate-economic outcomes involves several causes and effects, including agricultural output, fisheries, freshwater access, storm frequency, and tourism, among others. In addition, there appears to be links between global warming and labor productivity (as a result of climate change over decades), child and adult mortality, incidence of crime, drought conditions, and related conflict occurrences, all of which have direct and indirect effects on economic activity.

To account for the numerous transmission channels mentioned above, researchers have estimated the overall economic impact of climate change using an integrated assessment model, which estimates each mechanism's effect separately and then adds them up to assess the full economic impact of climate change (see, for example, Nordhaus and Boyer 2000; Mendelsohn, Dinar, and Williams 2006). But the integrated assessment model requires a large number of assumptions and combines direct and indirect effects.

Dell, Jones, and Olken (2008) took a more direct approach and constructed a database that includes fluctuations in countries' temperature and precipitation as well as data on economic growth for the period 1950–2003. Making relatively few assumptions, they show that (a) in poorer countries, a one-degree centigrade rise in temperature in a given year is likely to reduce growth by about 1.1 percentage point; (b) in richer countries, changes in the temperature have little or no effect on growth; (c) temperature influences growth by affecting agricultural yields and hence output, as well as labor productivity; and (d) in poorer countries, rising temperatures persistently affected economic output (the temporary and permanent effects were assessed by varying the lags of temperature). Further, by using estimates of the overall change in climate from 1970 to 2000 rather than yearly changes, Dell, Jones, and Olken (2008) found that there were larger negative effects on output estimated in poorer countries, suggesting that adaptation may undo these effects in the medium term.

Other things remaining equal, it is possible that continuous climate change may significantly widen income gaps between rich and poor countries. Horowitz (2001) independently predicts that a two-degree Fahrenheit increase in all temperatures will reduce world income by roughly 4 percent. Horowitz claims that this estimate is remarkably robust across samples, functional forms, and two methods for separating historical from contemporaneous effects, but admits that the figure is higher than most other predictions. More recently, Dell, Jones, and Olken (2008) examine the effect that rising temperatures will have on per capita income and suggest a negative relationship (figure 21.3).

Conclusion

A number of developing countries have experienced high growth while degrading their environmental assets and generating high carbon emissions. Managing the wealth of nations is critical for sustaining high-quality

Figure 21.3   Rise in Temperature Will Lower Per Capita Income

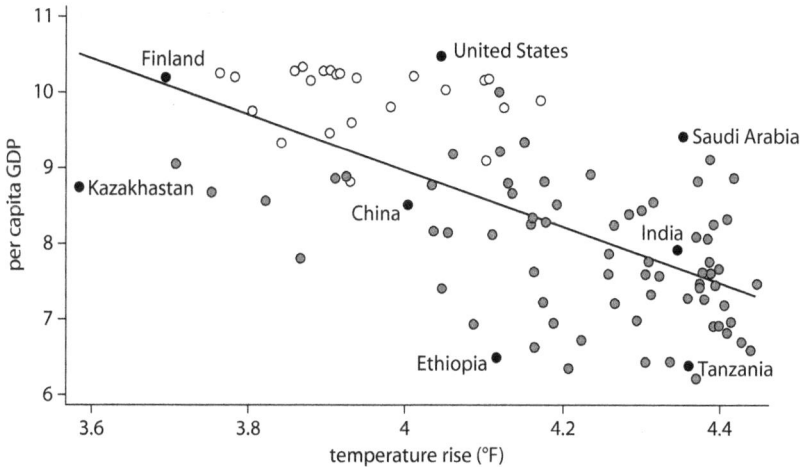

Source: Dell, Jones, and Olken 2008.
Note: This figure shows a log-log regression with no other covariates. White dots represent Organisation for Economic Co-operation and Development (OECD) countries. Gray dots represent non-OECD countries. Black dots show a selected set of representative countries.

growth. The problem of high carbon emissions and climate change involves a failure of markets; namely, that those who cause damage by emitting GHGs generally do not pay for the damage. The global problem requires a global solution, with the advanced and developing countries taking action to dramatically reduce carbon emissions, supporting programs to combat deforestation, and encouraging effective market mechanisms, such as cap and trade.

Annex Empirical Evidence of the Causes of Growth

We explore the real-world data to broadly examine what factors of production are associated with "output" as measured by gross domestic product (GDP) (in constant U.S. dollars) for a large sample of countries. We begin by following Easterly and Levine (2001), who state that the empirical literature on national policies and economic growth is "huge" while disagreement over which policies are most strongly linked with growth is "considerable." Some would argue that international trade (Frankel and Romer 1999) or financial development (Beck, Levine, and Loayza 1999) is the key, while others would argue for macroeconomic polices (Fischer

1993). All agree that some indicator of national policy is strongly linked with economic growth, confirming the argument made by Levine and Renelt (1992, 942). Those authors point out that "most investigators consider only a small number of explanatory variables" in their search. Moreover, empirical assessments are plagued by shortcomings such as (a) the failure to confront endogeneity, (b) omitted variable bias in traditional cross-country regressions, and (c) inclusion of lagged real per capital GDP as a regressor.

With these caveats, we assemble the data from the Levine and Renelt (1992) country sample of 119 countries and add another 13 including China, the Russian Federation, and several countries previously in the Eastern bloc. We use a general regression model of the following form, as specified by Levine and Renelt (1992):

$$Y = \beta_i\, I + \beta_m\, M + \beta_z\, Z + u \qquad\qquad (21A.1)$$

where Y is GDP in "constant dollars," I is a set of variables always included in the regression, M is a variable of interest, and Z is a subset of variables used in their study.

We gather data from 1990 to 2007 for 132 countries. We use the log of "population" and the log of "gross capital formation," which have highly significant coefficients for the I variables. M variables consist of "secondary school enrollment (% gross)" and "life expectancy at birth"— in total years, where both are significant at the 95 percent level. As Z variables, we use "aid (% of gross national income [GNI])," "foreign direct investment," "gross saving," "lending interest rate," and "percent of (exports + imports) over GDP as an indicator of openness," which are also significant. The 2007 data are complete in all respects, but most years have data gaps, so we use World Development Indicators (WDI) in a time series cross-section (TSCS) set using a random effect generalized least squares (GLS) procedure considered a recent econometric technique. The technique produces a matrix-weighted average of the "between" (country) and "within" (country) growth results.

These new techniques ameliorate potential biases. The goal here is not to identify the most important policies influencing economic growth but to identify key stylized facts associated with long-run growth. In fact, the results of the TSCS regression with "country" as the dependent variable are consistent with policies having significant long-run effects on national growth rates on a steady-state level of national output (that is, GDP in constant value).

Some Preliminary Results

The results of the above procedure were applied to the model in four regressions, namely to estimate the three groups I, M, and Z and a restricted set of variables in the fourth. The results are shown in table 21A.1. The I variable regression clearly establishes the "general notion of the production function," where the output as measured by the GDP (measured in constant dollars) is a function of the labor (substituted as population between ages 15 to 64) and "gross capital formation" (in constant dollars), with high and significant coefficients. These are further supported by a

Table 21A.1   Procedure: Random Effects GLS Regression (Dependent Variable: Log GDP)

Dependent variable: Log GDP (constant US$)	I variables	M variables	Z variables	Overall
	Coefficient (standard error)			
Log of (population ages 15–64, total)	0.666 (0.020)**	0.585** (0.025)	0.676** (0.027)	0.587** (0.037)
Log of (gross capital formation—constant 2000 US$)	0.382 (0.009)**	0.309** (0.014)	0.302** (0.016)	0.313** (0.026)
School enrollment, secondary (% gross)		0.002** (0.0)		0.002** (0.0)
Life expectancy at birth, total (years)		0.019** (0.002)		0.01** (0.002)
Aid (as % of GNP)			−0.002* (0.001)	−0.002 (0.002)
Foreign direct investment, net inflows (% of GDP)			−0.011 (0.002)	−0.004 (0.002)
Gross savings (current US$)			0.0** (0.0)	0.0** (0.0)
Lending interest rate			0.000* (0.0)	0.0* (0.0)
Openness—ratio of [(imports + exports)/GDP]			0.0158** (0.03)	0.076 (0.051)
Market capitalization (listed companies)			0.0** (0.0)	0.0** (0.0)
Constant	4.91** (0.25)	4.81** (0.35)	6.24** (0.41)	6.65** (0.539)
Observations	1,842	925	638	295
Wald-Chi	6,987.1**	4,474.3**	2,363**	1,222**
Hausman Test (Chi sq.)	721.5	106.0	254.1	49.3
R^2—within	0.77	0.76	0.80	0.75
R^2—between	0.83	0.90	0.84	0.89
R^2—overall	0.83	0.90	0.86	0.91

Source: Staff computations with WDI data.
Note: Number of countries in the sample: 132; period: 1990–2007.
** significance at the 95 percent level or higher.

very high Wald-Chi statistic and the R-squares of "within," "between," and "overall," as per the procedure.

In the second regression (M variables), we added two variables to represent "human capital" and its development, namely "school enrollment, secondary (% gross)" and "life expectancy at birth, total (years)," where both are significant but smaller coefficients. Notice also that the number of observations dropped to 925 from the initial 1,842.

Similarly, as Z variables, we added the following: gross savings (current US$), lending interest rate, "openness of the economy" as measured by the ratio of [(imports + exports)/GDP], and market capitalization (of listed companies as a percent of GDP). Finally, the Z variables were combined with I and M variables to assess their overall effect on GDP in a final regression.

The results indicate that "within country R-squares" improve as explanatory variables are added. Similarly, a lower Hausman test statistic suggests that a random effect procedure is the correct specification for the regression. We also noticed that "market capitalization of listed companies" also adds to the "within country R-squares," suggesting that wealth effects matter for GDP output, in the sense of increased production capacity.

We repeated the exercise with "GDP per capita growth" (table 21A.2). We substituted "gross capital formation, annual growth" in lieu of "gross capital formation (in constant dollars)." Notice that the "within R-squares" have risen as we add explanatory variables, along with "between" and "overall" R-squares. The Hausman test statistic indicates that the "random effect" specification is the appropriate model, while a low value of the "rho" suggests an absence of serial correlation. As discussed by Levine and Renelt (1992), the significance of the Z variables varies depending on other accompanying variables, perhaps due to multicollinearity; thus, our interpretations are limited.

Does the Wealth Effect Matter?

We also tested the importance of the wealth effect, especially in terms of wealth as an exhaustible resource. Instead of the TSCS data, we use single period data for the year 2000 for which the World Bank has computed the total wealth of nations.[2] The total wealth measures were incorporated with the economic data for the year 2000, and we applied the standard ordinary least squares procedure to measure the wealth effect on GDP.

The three coefficients are both considerable and significant at the 95 percent level with high R-squares. Notice also that the total wealth

Table 21A.2   Procedure: Random Effects GLS Regression (Dependent Variable: GDP Per Capita Growth)

Dependent variable: GDP per capita growth as annual percent	I variables	M variables	Z variables	Overall
	Coefficient (standard error)			
Population ages 15–64, total	0.0** (0)	0.0** (0.0)	0.0** (0)	0.0** (0)
Gross capital formation, annual growth	0.109** (0.005)	0.148** (0.007)	0.123** (0.044)	0.138** (0.010)
School enrollment, secondary (% gross)		0.013* (0.007)		0.044** (0.010)
Life expectancy at birth, total (years)		0.031 (0.227)		0.0 (0.027)
Aid (as % of GNP)			−0.099** (0.033)	−0.061 (0.137)
Foreign direct investment, net inflows (% of GDP)			0.077* (0.044)	0.008 (0.059)
Gross savings (current US$)			0.0 (0)	0.0 (0)
Lending interest rate			−0.028** (0.004)	−0.030** (0.005)
Openness—ratio of [(imports + exports)/GDP]			0.298 (0.512)	1.65** (0.552)
Market capitalization (listed companies)			0.002 (0.003)	−0.008* (0.004)
Constant	0.962** (0.16)	−2.108 (0.14)	1.928** (0.432)	−1.428 (1.762)
Observations	1,898	944	638	296
Wald-Chi	529.6	388.7	431.7**	.045
Hausman test (Chi sq.)	2.3	2.5	19.8**	24.7
R^2—within	0.21	0.28	0.41	0.51
R^2—between	0.22	0.43	0.39	0.63
R^2—overall	0.22	0.29	0.43	0.54
Rho	0.172	0.176	0.172	0.082

Source: Staff computations with WDI data.
Note: Number of countries in the sample: 132; period: 1990–2007.
** significance at the 95 percent level or higher.

is entered multiplicatively (in logs). In a second regression, we also included variables such as "school enrollment, secondary (% gross)," "external debt, total (% of GNI)," "openness—ratio of (exports + imports)/GDP," "household final consumption expenditure (constant 2000 US$)," and "aid (% of GNI)." The sign of the coefficients of "openness of the economy" and "aid" turn negative but remain significant at

Table 21A.3   Wealth Effect on GDP per Capita

Dependent variable: Log (GDP per capita)	Coefficient (standard error)	
Log of (population ages 15–64, total)	0.444** (0.044)	−0.553** (0.056)
Log of (gross capital formation—constant 2000 US$)	0.558** (0.042)	0.577** (0.056)
Log of (total wealth)	0.425** (0.043)	0.487** (0.064)
School enrollment, secondary (% gross)		0.001 (0.001)
External debt, total (% of GNI)		0.001** (0.001)
Openness—ratio of [(imports + exports)/ GDP]		−0.176** (0.067)
Household final consumption expenditure (constant 2000 US$)		0.0 (0.0)
Aid (% of GNI)		−0.011* (0.006)
Constant	−0.058 (0.262)	−1.640** (0.637)
Observations	98	62
$F \sim (8, 53)$	6,516.9	341.7
R^2	0.99	0.98
Adj. R^2	0.99	0.98

Source: WDI indicators, Wealth of Nations data, and staff computations.
* significance at 90 percent; ** significance at 95 percent.

the 95 percent and 90 percent level, respectively. The results are shown in table 21A.3.

Conclusion

We find that in addition to the effect of stylized explanatory variables, which influence growth, "wealth" (defined as market capitalization and natural wealth of a nation) plays a significant role in an economy's output and growth. Therefore, the depletion of natural resources is strategic and prudent in order to maintain sustainable economic growth.

Notes

1. The Hartwick rule (Hartwick 1977; Solow 1986) offers a rule of thumb for sustainability in exhaustible-resource economies: a constant level of consumption can be sustained if the value of investment always equals the value of rents on extracted resources.

2. See appendix 2 in World Bank (2005a).

Bibliography

Auty, R. M., and A. Gelb. 2001. "Political Economy of Resource-Abundant States." In *Resource Abundance and Economic Development*, ed. R. M. Auty, 126–44. New York: Oxford University Press.

Bacon, Robert W., Soma Bhattacharya, Richard Damania, Masami Kojima, and Kseniya Lvovsky. 2007. *Growth and CO$_2$ Emissions: How Do Different Countries Fare?* Washington, DC: World Bank.

Beck, Thorsten, Ross Levine, and Norman Loayza. 1999. "Finance and Sources of Growth." World Bank Policy Research Working Paper 2057, World Bank, Washington, DC.

Dell, M., B. Jones, and B. Olken. 2008. "Climate Change and Economic Growth Over the Last Half Century." NBER Working Paper 14132, National Bureau of Economic Research, Cambridge, MA.

Easterly, William, and Ross Levine. 2001. "It's Not Factor Accumulation: Stylized Facts and Growth Models." *World Economic Review* 15 (2): 177–219.

Fischer, Stanley. 1993. "The Role of Macroeconomic Factors in Growth." *Journal of Monetary Economics* 32 (3): 485–512.

Frankel, J. A., and David Romer. 1999. "Does Trade Cause Growth?" *American Economic Review* 89 (3): 379–99.

Hartwick, John M. 1977. "Intergenerational Equity and the Investing of Rents from Exhaustible Resources." *American Economic Review* 67 (5): 972–74.

Horowitz, John. 2001. "The Income-Temperature Relationship in a Cross-Section of Countries and its Implications for Global Warming." Unpublished paper, Department of Agricultural and Resource Economics, University of Maryland.

Levine, Ross, and David Renelt. 1992. "A Sensitivity Analysis of Cross-Country Growth Regressions." *American Economic Review* 82 (4): 942–63.

Mendelsohn, Robert, Ariel Dinar, and Larry Williams. 2006. "The Distributional Impact of Climate Change on Rich and Poor Countries." *Environment and Development Economics* 11 (2): 159–78.

Nordhaus, William, and Joseph Boyer. 2000. *Warming the World.* Cambridge, MA: Massachusetts Institute of Technology Press.

Solow, Robert M. 1986. "On the Intergenerational Allocation of Natural Resources." *Scandinavian Journal of Economics* 88 (1): 141–49.

World Bank. 1996. *Monitoring Environmental Progress: A Report on Work in Progress.* Washington, DC: World Bank.

———. 1997. "Expanding the Measure of Wealth: Indicators of Environmentally Sustainable Development." *Environmentally Sustainable Development Studies and Monographs Series* 17. World Bank, Washington, DC.

————. 2004–08. "Environment Matters." Various issues from 2004 to 2008. World Bank, Washington, DC.

————. 2005a. *Where Is the Wealth of Nations? Measuring Capital for the 21st Century*. Washington, DC: World Bank.

————. 2005b. *World Development Indicators 2005*. Washington, DC: World Bank.

————. 2008. *Development and Climate Change: A Strategic Framework for the World Bank Group*. Washington, DC: World Bank.

What We Know and What We Do Not Know

The challenge in the 1960s was to lift low-income countries from the low-growth and high-poverty trap. What have we learned from 50 years of growth experimentation? The world now has many fast-growing emerging economies, but the vast majority of countries in the world remain low income. We face the same challenge that we faced in the 1960s. High and sustained growth is necessary for accelerated poverty reduction. In turn, poverty reduction and lower inequality in economic opportunities and asset ownership are required for high-quality growth. But growth does not persist over time, while poverty does.

A high incidence of poverty and inequality in income and assets, seen in different regions of the world, is partly due to historical circumstances, inherited economic structures, and resource endowments. Targeting policies and programs toward the poor can help reduce social inequities while improving the chances of a high and sustained growth rate. A move toward a virtuous circle of growth and poverty reduction requires policies in several areas. For instance, the poor face substandard schools and a lack of essential services; expected returns on their investment in education and training is also lower. Similarly, poor regions do not attract infrastructure investments and financing. In such cases, social safety nets that increase jobs in poorer regions could also increase returns on education for the poor.

Ample evidence suggests that historical factors, such as inherited institutions, affect longer-term steady growth; meanwhile, short-term fluctuations in output growth are primarily driven by shocks, especially commodity booms and busts.

Investment in physical infrastructure and human capital also drives growth. High levels of investment spending must be complemented by strong market institutions (such as decent financial systems, property rights, and the enforced rule of law) to support efficient resource allocation and lower transaction costs. Human capital complements the physical infrastructure and is required for innovation and improvements in total factor productivity, though what factors drive technological innovation and adoption is unclear. Manufacturing sector growth interplays with technology adoption and urbanization.

Openness to trade and capital flows ensures global competitiveness and the adoption of cutting-edge technology and global standards. A stable political system is absolutely necessary for economic markets.

In the judging of the policies necessary to achieve real economic growth and poverty reduction, it is vital that pro-poor sectors, such as agriculture, construction, and manufacturing, also grow. Policies that specifically target income-creation opportunities for the poor have included microcredit schemes, public works for the unemployed, agricultural land titling, and the provision of training and agricultural extension. Optimal redistributive policies require targeted cash transfers—with some work requirement—without excessively high marginal tax rates. Redistributional efforts also take the form of government subsidies for the provision of basic social services—in education and health—which contribute not only to the current welfare of the poor but also to the accumulation of human capital in younger generations of the poor so that they can escape poverty. And, of course, education and health programs seek to build up the human capital of poor children to enhance their capacity for productive employment in the future.

In most countries with high growth rates, inequality has also risen—but the growth has been fast enough to reduce poverty in the official statistics. Either the official statistics are flawed and do not reflect the reality on the ground, or economic policy changes and globalization create winners and losers—in assets, between genders, and among ethnicities and other salient groups.

Growth in the context of high-income inequality is not likely to have a large impact on poverty reduction. Further, public support for sustaining policy reforms is most likely when the distribution of income and opportunities to attain economic advancement are seen as relatively fair. Thus, redistributive policies (particularly expenditure policies) are widely recognized and supported as a way to improve the income distribution in countries. Even if income poverty is reduced, lack of education, health care, clean water, and sanitation facilities should be a cause for concern. Growth will not automatically lead to improvements in social indicators, such as infant and child mortality and life expectancy.

Accelerated and slowed growth are due to shocks (commodity prices, housing and stock prices, domestic and global banking shocks, and so on). The developing countries are better able to manage oil shocks because of a lower energy intensity of production (developed after earlier oil shocks). Knowledge of economic policy has also enabled countries to absorb food and other commodity shocks. It is becoming increasingly clear that shocks that appear to have short-term impacts on growth may have longer-term impacts on human capital efficacy and poverty reduction.

If one looks ahead, growth and poverty will be determined by the use of knowledge and technology in economic processes and urbanization, energy use and its likely shortages, and global warming and its impact on economic activities. Above all, the distribution of political and economic power within and across countries will determine the direction and dynamics of growth and development. *As in the 1960s, the challenge remains: how to lift countries out of the low-growth and high-poverty trap. We have traveled the world only to return home.*

Glossary

Absolute advantage. The ability of an economic actor (an individual, household, or firm) to produce some particular good or service with a smaller total input of economic resources (labor, capital, land, and so on) per unit of output than other economic actors. In international trade theory, a country with an absolute advantage in producing a good is able to produce that good more efficiently (more output per unit of input) than any other country. In trade, it is important to distinguish *absolute* from *comparative* advantage, since it is comparative advantage that determines the potential welfare gains from specialization and trade.

Accelerator principle. In macroeconomic models the accelerator principle relates changes in the rate of real output growth to the level of desired investment spending (investment demand) in the economy. A decline in the rate of real gross domestic product (GDP) growth, for example, would cause the amount of investment demand to decrease (the investment demand curve would shift to the left).

Aggregate demand. In macroeconomic theory, aggregate demand is the total demand for final goods and services in an economy at a given time and price level, which is the demand for the GDP of a country when inventory levels are static.

Aggregate expenditure. The aggregate demand identity states that $Y = C + I + G + (X - M)$, which simply means that a single country's aggregate demand for national product (Y) is always equal to the total demands of its households for consumer goods and services (C), plus the total demands of its firms for investment goods (I), plus the total demands of its various government agencies for goods and services (G), plus the net demands of foreign consumers, firms, and governments for the country's goods and services (exports minus imports).

Aggregate supply curve. In macroeconomic theory, the short-run aggregate supply curve relates the total quantity of goods and services supplied and the price level (as measured by the GDP deflator) ceteris paribus. The long-run aggregate supply curve is a vertical line at the full employment (capacity output) level of GDP.

Amortization. Paying off debt through installments of principal and earned interest over a definite time.

Automatic stabilizer. A government-spending program that responds to changes in the level of national income in such a way as to offset those changes. For example, unemployment insurance benefits typically rise when the economy enters a recession and decline when prosperity returns.

Balance of payments. An accounting statement of the money value of international transactions between one nation and the rest of the world over a specific time period. The accounting of a country's international position in terms of exports and imports of goods, services, and income (the current account), and financial inflows and outflows (the capital account). In theory, the current account must balance the capital account; that is, money coming in must equal money going out.

Balance of trade. A record of a country's exports and imports of goods and services. If exports of goods exceed imports, the trade balance is said to be favorable; if imports exceed exports, the trade balance is said to be unfavorable.

Base year. In calculating price indexes, values in the current year are compared to values in some arbitrarily chosen earlier, or base, year.

Bilateral aid. The transfer of funds, goods, or services from one government to another.

Budget. A statement of a government's planned or expected financial position for a specified period of time (usually one year), based on estimates of the expenditures to be made by government's main subdivisions (including wages and salaries of government employees; consultants' fees; purchases of equipment, supplies, real estate, and so on; and money transferred to beneficiaries of various programs) during the specified period, along with estimates of the revenues. The budget of a government may be seen as a comprehensive plan of what government will spend for its various programs during the next fiscal year and how it expects to raise the money to pay for them.

Budget deficit. The excess of government spending over government income during a specified period; the amount of money that government has to raise by borrowing or currency emission to make up for the shortfall in tax revenues.

Budget surplus. The amount by which government revenues exceed government spending during a specified period.

Business cycle. The wavelike pattern of movements of national output, through expansions and recessions.

Capital. Usually refers to machinery and equipment, structures, and inventories; produced goods for use in further production.

Capital account. That part of the balance of payments that records a country's lending and borrowing transactions.

Capital consumption. The use of real capital without maintenance or replacement as it wears out.

Capital goods. Unlike goods intended for consumption, capital goods are used to produce other goods, such as factory machinery.

Central bank. The principal monetary authority of a nation, which performs several key functions, including issuing currency and regulating the supply of credit in the economy.

Central bank intervention. The buying or selling of currency (foreign or domestic) by central banks to influence market conditions or exchange-rate movements.

Change in demand. An increase or decrease in the quantity demanded over a range of prices shown by a shift of the demand curve.

Comparative advantage. The ability to produce a tradable good or service at a lower opportunity cost than possible in another country. This concept underlies the justification for free trade.

Competition. In the general sense, a contest among sellers or buyers for control over the use of productive resources. Sometimes used as a shorthand way of referring to perfect competition—a market condition in which no individual buyer or seller has any significant influence over price.

Competitive devaluation. A situation in which countries devalue their currencies in sequence in a bid to wrest economic advantage through increased exports.

Consumer price index. A weighted index of prices of the commodities commonly purchased by households. The consumer price index is typically used in the calculation of the inflation rate.

Consumer surplus. The net benefit realized by consumers when they buy a good at the prevailing market price. It is equivalent to the difference between the maximum amount consumers would be willing to pay and the amount they actually do pay for the units of the good purchased. Graphically, it is the triangle above the market price and below the demand curve.

Consumption function. Generally, the relationship between consumer expenditures and all the factors that determine them. More specifically, the relationship between consumers' disposable incomes (personal income minus taxes) and the amount they wish to spend on consumer goods and services.

Consumption spending. Spending on consumer goods and services.

Coordinates. Intersections of vertical and horizontal values plotted on a graph.

Cross-elasticity of demand. The (percentage) change in the quantity demanded of a good consequent upon a (1 percent) change in the price of an associated good.

Crowding out. The possible tendency for government spending on goods and services to put upward pressure on interest rates, thereby discouraging private investment spending.

Currency appreciation. An increase in the value of one currency relative to another currency. Appreciation occurs when—because of a change in exchange rates—a unit of one currency buys more units of another currency.

Currency depreciation. A decline in the value of one currency relative to another currency. Depreciation occurs when—because of a change in exchange rates—a unit of one currency buys fewer units of another currency.

Currency devaluation. A deliberate downward adjustment in the official exchange rate established, or pegged, by a government against a specified standard, such as another currency or gold.

Currency revaluation. A deliberate upward adjustment in the official exchange rate established, or pegged, by a government against a specified standard, such as another currency or gold.

Current account. That part of a country's balance of payments that records the value of goods and services exported minus the value of goods and services imported. Current account balance calculations exclude transactions in financial assets and liabilities.

Cyclical unemployment. Unemployment caused by the low level of aggregate demand associated with recession in the business cycle.

Debt restructuring. A technique whereby debt-service payments are deferred and the payback period of the original loan is stretched over a longer period.

Debt service. The interest that must be paid on accumulated debt.

Debt, national. The total sum of the outstanding debt obligations of a country's central government. The national debt represents the accumulated total of all government budget deficits of the past years, less the accumulated total of all government budget surpluses of the past years.

Default. The failure to make debt-service payments.

Deficit. The shortfall in any one year between a government's revenues from taxation and its expenditures. Government must then borrow money to meet its expenditures.

Deflation. A fall in the general level of all prices; the opposite of inflation.

Demand. The willingness and ability of the people within a market area to purchase particular amounts of a good or service at a variety of alternative prices during a specified time period.

Demand, law of. Other things being held constant, the lower the price of a good (or service), the greater the demand for it by purchasers at any given time.

Depreciation. The using up or wearing out of capital goods.

Devaluation. A reduction in the official rate at which one country's currency is traded for another. A devaluation makes a country's exports cheaper abroad and makes imports more expensive.

Discount rate. The interest rate that banks pay on loans to them from a central bank. An increase in the discount rate tends to cause a decrease in the money stock and higher short-term interest rates. In contrast, lowering the discount rate is expansionary. As the cost of borrowing from the central bank to meet a temporary emergency falls, bankers are more likely to reduce their excess reserves to a minimum, extending more loans and thus increasing the money stock, which tends to lower interest rates in the short term.

Disposable income. The income a person or household has left to dispose of after income tax has been deducted from personal income. Disposable income may either be spent on consumption or saved.

Economic growth. An increase in the quantity of goods and services produced in a nation, as traditionally measured by the GDP.

Economics. The branch of social sciences concerned primarily with analyzing and explaining human behavior in making decisions about the allocation of scarce resources.

Economies of scale. A decrease in per unit cost of production as a result of producing large numbers of a good.

Efficiency. A concept referring to making the most productive use of available resources.

Elasticity. When used without a modifier (such as "cross-," or "income-"), elasticity usually refers to price elasticity, which is the percentage change in the quantity demanded of a good or service divided by the percentage change in its own price.

Elasticity of supply. The price elasticity of supply is the percentage change in the quantity supplied of a good or service divided by the percentage change in its own price.

Employment rate. The percentage of the labor force that is employed. The employment rate is one of the economic indicators that economists examine to help understand the state of the economy. See also *unemployment rate*.

Equilibrium price. A price at which the quantity supplied equals the quantity demanded. At this price, there is no excess of quantity demanded or supplied—nor is there any deficiency of either—and, consequently, the price will remain at this level.

Equilibrium quantity. The quantity of a good demanded and supplied at the equilibrium price.

Equity. In the context of the income distribution theory, it refers to an objective, goal, or principle implying "fairness." In a financial context it may refer to a share or portion of ownership.

Exchange rate. The price of a country's currency in terms of another country's currency.

Externality. A benefit or cost associated with an economic transaction that is not taken into account by those directly involved in making it. A beneficial or adverse side effect of production or consumption.

Fiscal policy. Use of government's powers of taxation and spending to influence economic activity and employment.

Fixed exchange-rate system. A system in which exchange rates between currencies are set at predetermined levels and do not move in response to changes in supply and demand.

Floating exchange-rate system. A flexible system in which the exchange rate is determined by the market forces of supply and demand, without intervention.

Foreign direct investment (FDI). Investment in a country by foreign-owned firms. FDI is a measure of foreign ownership of productive assets such as factories, mines, and land. There are two types of FDI—inward FDI and outward FDI that results in a net FDI inflow (positive or negative) and a stock of foreign direct investment.

Free trade. Trade arrangements in which tariffs or other barriers to the free flow of goods and services are eliminated.

Frictional unemployment. Unemployment caused by the loss of jobs because of technological change, the entry of new participants into the labor market, or other normal labor market adjustments.

GDP deflator. Nominal GDP divided by real (constant dollar) GDP, multiplied by 100. Nominal GDP is the value of output measured in terms of the prices prevailing in the accounting period in question. Real GDP is that output measured in terms of the prices prevailing in some base period. The value of the deflator in the base period is always 100.

Gini coefficient. A measure of income inequality, which ranges from 0 (complete inequality) to 1 (complete equality). The ratio of the area between the 45-degree line depicting complete equality and a Lorenz curve to the entire area of the triangle below the 45-degree line.

Government spending. The total outlays by government on goods and services during some accounting period, usually a year. Government outlays, such as welfare benefits to households, are normally excluded from this amount on the grounds that they are merely transfers of income from taxpayers to the beneficiaries of such programs.

Gross domestic product (GDP). A statistical measure of the value of final goods and services produced by a nation's economy in a given period, normally a year.

Gross investment. Total investment during the accounting period. It includes both additions to the capital stock (net investment) and investment to replace worn-out capital (to make up for depreciation).

Gross national expenditure. The sum of all spending on consumption and investment, plus government spending on goods and services and net exports (total exports minus imports). It is equivalent in value to GDP.

Growth theory. The part of economic theory that seeks to explain (and hopes to predict) the rate at which a country's economy will grow over time.

Human capital. The stock of knowledge and acquired skills embodied in individuals.

Income effect. The effect of a change in income on the quantity of a good or service consumed.

Indirect taxes. Taxes levied on a producer, which the producer then passes on to the consumer as part of the price of a good. Distinguished from direct taxes (such as sales taxes), which are visible to the person who pays them.

Infant mortality rate. The number of deaths per 1,000 live births before the first birthday.

Inferior good. A good for which the demand decreases when income increases. When a household's income goes up, it will buy a smaller quantity of such a good.

Inflation. A general rise in the average level of *all* prices.

Interest group. A group of people who share common traits, attitudes, beliefs, or objectives and who have formed a formal organization to serve specific common interests of the membership.

Interest rate. The market rate for borrowing or lending money.

International financial institutions. The World Bank, the International Monetary Fund (IMF), and regional development banks.

International Monetary Fund (IMF). An international organization with 146 members, including the United States. The main functions of the IMF are to lend funds to member nations to finance temporary balance of payment problems, to facilitate the expansion and balanced growth of international trade, and to promote international monetary cooperation among nations. The IMF also creates special drawing rights, which provide member nations with a source of additional reserves. Member nations are required to subscribe to a fund quota paid mainly in their own currency. The IMF grew out of the Bretton Woods Conference of 1944.

Investment spending. The total amount of spending during some period of time on capital goods.

Labor force. The total number of people employed, plus those actively looking for work.

Laissez faire. Literally "let do," a philosophy that advocates minimal government interference in the economy.

Land. All natural resources. The "gifts of nature" that are economically useful.

Law of demand. The inverse relationship between the price and quantity of a good or service demanded.

Lender of last resort. A nation's central bank has the authority and financial resources to act as the "lender of last resort" by extending credit to depository institutions or to other entities in unusual circumstances involving a national or regional emergency in which failure to obtain credit would have a severe adverse impact on the economy.

Lorenz curve. A curve showing the cumulative percentage of income plotted against the cumulative percentage of population.

Macroeconomics. The branch of economic theory concerned with the economy as a whole. It deals with large aggregates such as total output, rather than with the behavior of individual consumers and firms.

Marginal benefit. The increase in total benefit consequent upon a one-unit increase in the production of a good.

Marginal cost. The increase in total cost consequent upon a one-unit increase in the production of a good.

Marginal propensity to consume. The part of the last dollar of disposable income that would be spent on additional consumption.

Marginal propensity to save. The part of the last dollar of disposable income that would be saved.

Market failure. When a free market is unable to achieve an optimum allocation of resources.

Millennium Development Goals. Eight targets—to be met by the year 2015—set down by the United Nations in an effort to reduce global poverty and disease: (a) eradicate extreme poverty and hunger; (b) achieve universal primary education; (c) promote gender equality and empower women; (d) reduce child mortality; (e) improve maternal health; (f) combat HIV/AIDS, malaria, and other diseases; (g) ensure environmental sustainability; and (h) develop a global partnership for development.

Minority goods. Goods that have a very low elasticity of supply. That is, even large increases in their price call forth little, if any, additional supply—which means that only the very wealthy can afford them. Large, secluded waterfront properties might be an example.

Monetarism. School of economic thought, led by Milton Friedman, that believes that inflation is caused by excessive growth in monetary supply.

Monetary base. "High-powered money": cash in commercial banks, cash in circulation, and deposits of commercial banks at the central bank.

Monetary policy. A central bank's actions to influence the availability and cost of money and credit as a means of promoting national economic goals. The use of the central bank's power to control the domestic money supply to influence the supply of credit, interest rates, and ultimately the level of real economic activity. The policy that tries to control the size of the total stock of money (and other highly liquid financial assets that are close substitutes for money) available in the national economy to achieve policy objectives that are often contradictory: controlling the rate of increase in the general price level (inflation), speeding up or slowing the overall rate of economic growth (mainly by affecting the interest rates that constitute such a large share of suppliers' costs for new investment, but partly by influencing consumer demand through the availability of consumer credit and mortgage money), managing the level of unemployment (stimulating or retarding total demand for goods and services by manipulating the amount of money in the hands of consumers and investors), or influencing the exchange rates at which the national currency trades for other foreign currencies.

Money. Anything that serves as a generally accepted medium of exchange, a standard of value, or a means of saving or storing purchasing power.

Money supply. Total quantity of money available for transactions and investment (also referred to as the *money stock* or simply *money*).

Monopoly. Strictly defined as a market situation in which there is a single supplier of a good or service, but often used to suggest any situation in which a firm has considerable power over market price.

Moral hazard. The risk that a party to a transaction has not entered into a contract in good faith; has provided misleading information about its assets, liabilities, or credit capacity; or has an incentive to take unusual risks in a desperate attempt to earn a profit before the contract settles.

Multiplier effect. The tendency for a change in aggregate spending to cause a more-than-proportionate change in the level of real national income.

National income. The general term used to refer to the total value of a country's output of goods and services in some accounting period without specifying a formal accounting concept, such as the GDP.

National income (GDP) deflator. A general way of referring to the price index that measures the average level of the prices of all the goods and services comprising the national income or GDP.

Net exports. The total value of goods and services exported during the accounting period minus the total value of goods and services imported.

Net immigration. The total number of people leaving the country to take up permanent residence abroad minus the number of people entering the country for the purpose of taking up permanent residence.

Net investment. Total investment during some accounting period minus the amount of depreciation during the same period.

Nominal interest rates. Current stated rates of interest paid or earned.

Nonaccelerating inflationary rate of unemployment. Also called the *natural rate of unemployment*. The theory behind the nonaccelerating inflationary rate of unemployment is that if the unemployment rate falls too low, inflation will be triggered.

Normal good. Any good for which the demand increases as income increases.

Open-market operations. Purchases and sales of government securities (and certain other securities) in the open market by the central bank. Purchases inject reserves into the banking system and stimulate growth of money and credit; sales do the opposite.

Opportunity cost. The best alternative sacrificed to have or to do something else.

Per capita income. Total income divided by the size of the population.

Perfect competition. A market situation in which there are so many sellers (and buyers) that no one seller (or buyer) can exert any influence on the price. All participants in such markets are "price takers."

Political economy. A branch of the social sciences that takes as its principal subject of study the interrelationships between political and economic institutions and processes. That is, political economists are interested in analyzing and explaining the ways in which various sorts of government affect the allocation of scarce resources in society through their laws and policies, as well as the ways in which the nature of the economic system and the behavior of people acting on their economic interests affects the form of government and the kinds of laws and policies that get made.

Price. What must be paid to acquire the right to possess and use a good or receive a service.

Price discrimination. The selling of a good or service at different prices to different buyers or classes of buyers in the absence of any differences in the cost of supplying it.

Price elasticity of demand. The percentage change in the quantity of a good demanded by the percentage change in its own price.

Principle of diminishing marginal utility. The proposition that the satisfaction derived from consuming an additional unit of a good or service declines as additional units are acquired.

Principle of diminishing returns. The proposition that the marginal product of the last unit of labor employed declines as additional units of labor are employed.

Private goods. Goods that cannot be consumed without payment and whose supply is reduced when consumed.

Privatization. The selling off of publicly owned enterprises to private owners.

Production possibilities. Levels of output that are within the range of possibilities for a particular economy.

Production possibility curve. A graphical representation of the boundary between possible and unattainable levels of production in a particular economy.

Productivity. The amount of physical output for each unit of productive input.

Public goods. Goods that can be enjoyed by an unlimited number of people (nonrival) and from which others cannot be excluded (nonexcludable).

Purchasing power parity. The adjustment in the exchange rate between any two currencies that reflects changes in price levels across their two countries.

Quantity theory of money. The idea that there is a direct link between the quantity of money in the economy and the price level.

Quota. A limitation on the amount of a good that can be produced or offered for sale domestically or internationally.

Rational behavior. Behavior that is consistent with the attainment of an individual's perception of his or her own best interest.

Real balance effect. The influence a change in the quantity of real money has on the quantity of real national income demanded.

Real GDP. GDP adjusted for inflation. Real GDP provides the value of GDP in constant dollars, which is used as an indicator of the volume of the nation's output.

Real interest rates. Interest rates adjusted for the expected erosion of purchasing power resulting from inflation. Technically defined as nominal interest rates minus the expected rate of inflation.

Real national income. National income adjusted for inflation.

Recession. A significant decline in general economic activity extending over a period of time.

Redistribution policy. Measures taken by government to transfer income from some individuals to others.

Relative prices. The relationship between the prices of different goods and services; may be thought of in terms of the amount of one good that can be had for a certain expenditure, compared with the amount of another good that can be had for the same expenditure.

Rent seeking. Action taken by individuals or firms to obtain special privileges, such as monopoly power, that will enable them to increase their incomes. Also, using up resources to win such privileges from governments or their agencies.

Reserve requirements. The amounts that certain financial institutions must set aside in the form of reserves, as required by the central bank. Reserve requirements act as a control on the expansion of money and credit and may be raised or lowered within limits specified by law (lowering reserve requirements allows more bank lending and money growth; raising requirements, less lending and money growth).

Reserves. A depository institution's vault cash (up to the level of its required reserves), plus balances in its reserve account (not including funds applied to its required clearing balance).

Risk. Those undertaking investments or the production of goods and services for sale cannot know with certainty whether they will recover the outlays needed to conduct these activities. Although some risks can be insured against (the risk of fire losses, for example), there is no way of insuring against the possibility of business losses because of the uncertainty of the marketplace.

Saving. The act of abstaining from consumption. In terms of the national accounts, the difference between personal income less taxes and total consumption spending.

Scarcity. The fact that human wants exceed the means of satisfying them.

Seignorage. The profit that results from the difference between the cost of making coins and currency and the exchange value of coins and currency in the market.

Social cost. The real cost to society of having a good or service produced, which may be greater than the private costs incorporated by the producer in its market price.

Substitute goods. Goods that may be used in place of other goods.

Substitution effect. The change in the quantity of a good demanded resulting from a change in its relative price, leaving aside any change in quantity demanded that can be attributable to an associated change in the consumer's real income. It may also be thought of as a change in the quantity demanded as a result of a movement along a single indifference curve.

Tariff. A tax imposed on an imported good.

Terms of trade. The ratio of the price of exports to that of imports. Deteriorating terms of trade mean the price of exports has decreased relative to the price of imports.

Total factor productivity. The growth of real output beyond what can be attributed to increases in the quantities of labor and capital employed.

Transfer payments. Social benefits paid to individuals or households by government.

Unemployment. The nonutilization of labor resources; the condition in which members of the labor force are without jobs. Sometimes used more broadly to refer to the waste of resources when an economy is operating at less than its full potential.

Unemployment rate. The percentage of the labor force that is unemployed and actively seeking a job.

Utility. An economic concept referring to the precise degree of personal satisfaction, pleasure, or sense of want-fulfillment an individual derives from consuming some quantity of a good or service at a particular time.

Velocity. The rate at which money balances turn over in a period for expenditure on goods and services (often measured as the ratio of GNP to the money stock). Higher velocity means that a given quantity of money is associated with a greater dollar volume of transactions.

Voluntary export restraint. A restriction placed by an exporting country on the volume of exports it sends to a particular country.

Wages. The general term applied to the earnings of the factor of production, labor.

Wants. People's apparently limitless desires or wishes for particular goods or services.

World Bank. Originally known as the International Bank for Reconstruction and Development, the World Bank was set up after World War II to facilitate the reconstruction of economies in Europe devastated by the war. In later years, it took on the role of providing loans to countries for economic development purposes. It is a sister organization to the IMF. Both organizations are based in Washington, DC.

World Trade Organization. A Geneva-based free trade association with 128 member nations. Formed in 1995 to administer the General Agreement on Tariffs and Trade as well as the trade in services and intellectual property. World Trade Organization panels rule on trade disputes among member nations.

Yield. The return on a loan or investment, stated as a percentage of the price.

Index

Boxes, figures, notes, and tables are indicated by *b*, *f*, *n*, and *t* following the page numbers.

International Development Association
(IDA), 145, 176, 177
International Finance Corporation (IFC), 2
international financial institutions, 180n4,
471. *See also specific institution by
name*
International Labour Organization (ILO),
271, 272, 281, 286, 292n2, 345
International Monetary and Financial
Committee (IMFC), 137, 164n9
International Monetary Fund (IMF).
See also Heavily Indebted Poor
Countries (HIPC) Initiative;
Poverty Reduction Growth Facility
(PRGF); Structural Adjustment
Facility (SAF)
bailouts, 418n1
described, 471
Enhanced Structural Adjustment Facility
(ESAF), 174, 176, 261n2
on HIPC Initiative, 179
on money laundering, 357
ODA guidance, 137
World Economic Outlook, 211, 214
investment climate's effect on economic
development, 179, 280, 414,
417, 433
investment income, 44
Ireland
entrepreneurial activity, 328
outsourcing business to, 324
irrigation, 308

J

Jack, W., 249, 253, 261n8
Jacoby, H., 304, 305
Jahjah, Samir, 126
Jalilian, Hossein, 114, 119
Jamison, D., 250, 251, 261n7
Japan
entrepreneurial activity, 328
openness to foreign technology, 216
technology and, 322
Johnson, S., 61, 249, 422, 423
Joint United Nations Programme on
HIV/AIDS (UNAIDS), 259
Jones, B., 450
Jorgenson, Dale, 320b
Joskow, Paul, 385, 386, 391n3
Jovanovic, B., 119
Jubilee 2000 debt relief campaign, 3

K

Karlsson, Charlie, 326, 330, 331
Kaufmann, Daniel, 215, 356, 357, 365
Kenya
economic performance, comparison of
full income and GDP per capita,
251, 251f
investment climate, 433
land tenure, 305
primary school completion in, 229
TFP growth, effect of, 320
wages, 286
women workers and export crops,
313n1
Khan, H. M., 300, 313n2
Khanna, T., 341
Kimko, D. D., 222
Kireyev, Alexei, 127
Kirkpatrick, Colin, 114, 119
Kirzner, I. M., 325
knowledge for development, 57
Koo, Jun, 348
Korea, Republic of
capital accumulation vs. resource
rents, 445
dictatorship, 426
growth policies in, 415
Kose, A., 410
Kraay, A., 64, 65, 66, 70–71, 189, 192,
357, 365
Krueger, Anne, 188, 192
Krugman, Paul, 348

L

labor force, 8, 269–91. *See also*
employment elasticity
defined, 471
in developing countries, 280–91
labor supply and unemployment,
282–86, 283t
skills, 287–89
wages, 286–87, 287f
women and children in labor force,
289–91, 290t, 291f
economic growth and, 270–80
employment rate, 468
immigration, 404
mobility, 414
regulation, 374–79
LaFerrara, E., 429
Laffer debt curve, 171, 173

U

Udry, C., 297
Uganda
  development assistance in, 153
  educational funding, ineffectiveness
    of, 429
  land assets, 296
  poverty reduction, 64, 64f, 67–68
  spend-but-do-not-absorb approach,
    155–56
U.K. Commission on Africa, 236
underemployment, 344
unemployment, 270, 344, 477
unemployment insurance, 280–81
unemployment rate, 281, 344–45, 477
UNESCO, 236
UN-HABITAT statistics on slums, 347
United Arab Emirates, primary school
    completion in, 229
United Kingdom
  Commission on Africa, 236
  democracy, creation of, 424
  industrial age, 61
United Nations
  development assistance for health, 256
  effectiveness of aid, 156
  on maternal health, 262n20
  on urban slums, 345
United Nations Development Programme
    (UNDP), 286
United Nations Framework Convention
    on Climate Change (UNFCCC),
    448b
United Nations Population Fund
    (UNFPA), 345
United States
  agricultural subsidies, 74, 195
  development assistance for health, 256
  economic downturns
    capital flows and, 404–5
    global shocks from, 402, 405t, 411
  entrepreneurial activity, 328
  governance and economic growth,
    213b, 215
  health improvements and economic
    growth, 261n13
  industrial age, 61
  monetary policy leading to financial
    crisis, 384
  outsourcing, 404
  property rights, 209

technology and, 322
urban agglomeration, 348
universal primary education (UPE), 221,
    222, 228, 230–31, 231t, 234
UN Millennium +5 Summit in
    New York (2005), 135
UN Millennium Project Task Force on
    Gender Equality and Education, 236
unreported economy, 49
UPE. See universal primary education
urbanization, 9, 337–52
  economic growth and, 340–42, 341f
  income and employment, 344–45
  key issues in, 342–51
  land management and housing, 350–51
  megacities and urban agglomeration,
    348–49, 349f
  the poor and, 342, 343t
  slums, 345–47, 346f, 347t
  trends in, 337–40, 338f, 339t, 340f
  urban slums, 345–47, 346f
U.S. Millennium Challenge Account, 147
utility, 477

V

value added tax (VAT), 90, 91, 388
value of a statistical life (VSL), 250–51
Van de Walle, Nicolas, 428
Van Rijckeghem, Caroline, 359
Velasco, A., 416
velocity, 477
Vietnam
  development assistance to, 156
  economic growth, 412
  food-energy intake (FEI) method, 22
  poverty reduction, 64, 64f
Vindigni, A., 429
Viscusi, W. K., 250
Vishny, R. W., 362
voice and accountability, 204–5, 205f
volatility, 42–43
Vollrath, D., 301, 302, 303, 313n3
voluntary export restraint, 188, 478
Vosloo, W. B., 325
vulnerability and poverty, 16, 25
vulnerable employment, 270–72, 271t, 283

W

Wade, Paul, 364
wages, 286, 478
  minimum wages, 375–77, 376f

ECO-AUDIT
Environmental Benefits Statement

The World Bank is committed to preserving endangered forests and natural resources. The Office of the Publisher has chosen to print **Understanding Growth and Poverty: Theory, Policy, and Empirics** on recycled paper with 50 percent post-consumer waste, in accordance with the recommended standards for paper usage set by the Green Press Initiative, a nonprofit program supporting publishers in using fiber that is not sourced from endangered forests. For more information, visit www.greenpressinitiative.org.

Saved:
- 7 trees
- 2 million British thermal units of total energy
- 664 pounds of net greenhouse gases (CO_2 equivalent)
- 3,196 gallons of waste water
- 194 pounds of solid waste